Facing Racism in Education

—■—■—■—

THIRD EDITION

Edited by
Sonya L. Anderson
Polly F. Attwood
and
Lionel C. Howard

Reprint Series No. 39
Harvard Educational Review

Copyright © 2004 by the President and Fellows of Harvard College

All rights reserved. No part of this publication may be reproduced or transmitted in any form or by any means, electronic or mechanical, including photocopy, recording, or any information storage and retrieval systems, without permission in writing from the publisher.

Library of Congress Catalog Card Number   2004106624
ISBN   0-916690-42-3

Harvard Education Publishing Group
8 Story Street
Cambridge, MA 02138

Typesetting: Sheila Walsh
Cover Design: Anne Carter
Cover Photo: Corbis

The typefaces used in this book are New Baskerville for text and ITC Fenice for display.

Contents

v	Preface
1	**Part One: Experiences of Racism**
5	Building 860 *Christian Neira*
13	Navajo Youth and Anglo Racism: Cultural Integrity and Resistance *Donna Deyhle*
57	Reading the World of School Literacy: Contextualizing the Experience of a Young African American Male *Arlette Ingram Willis*
77	Why the "Monkeys Passage" Bombed: Tests, Genres, and Teaching *Bonny Norton and Pippa Stein*
95	More than "Model Minorities" or "Delinquents": A Look at Hmong American High School Students *Stacey J. Lee*
119	**Part Two: (De)Constructing Racism**
123	The Silenced Dialogue: Power and Pedagogy in Educating Other People's Children *Lisa D. Delpit*
145	The Politics of Culture: Understanding Local Political Resistance to Detracking in Racially Mixed Schools *Amy Stuart Wells and Irene Serna*

171 Bilingual Education for Puerto Ricans in New York City:
     From Hope to Compromise
     Sandra Del Valle

195 **Part Three: The Practice of Anti-Racism**

199 Talking about Race, Learning about Racism:
     The Application of Racial Identity Development Theory
     in the Classroom
     Beverly Daniel Tatum

227 Beyond the Methods Fetish: Toward a Humanizing Pedagogy
     Lilia I. Bartolomé

249 Violence, Nonviolence, and the Lessons of History:
     Project HIP-HOP Journeys South
     Nancy Uhlar Murray and Marco Garrido

277 Blind Vision: Unlearning Racism in Teacher Education
     Marilyn Cochran-Smith

311 About the Contributors

315 About the Editors

Preface

Our present silence on the subject of racism is evidence that we are now living through a downswing of national conscience. . . .

Four recent Supreme Court decisions have dealt severe blows to programs that traditionally have protected the rights of Asian Americans, Blacks, Latinos, and Native Americans. . . .

Our hope is that this collection will renew reflective conversation and generate collective educational response to the problem of racism in an increasingly hostile and indifferent national climate.

Facing Racism in Education (First Edition, 1990)

In the last five years the nation has moved from a "silence" on the reality of racism to the outright denial of its existence, as a privileged few claim that racism is a problem of the past that has been conquered. It is apparent to many of us in education, however, that the "downswing of national conscience" is approaching a moral nadir.

Facing Racism in Education (Second Edition, 1996)

These quotes from the previous two editions of *Facing Racism in Education* name the "silence" that has undercut meaningful discussion about racism and disavowed its impact on schools and classrooms, teachers, and students. As we present this third edition, we are struck by the paradoxical relationship between "talk" and "silence," between "facing racism" and denying its continued existence in 2004. While conversations about the importance of and need for "diversity" are occurring in some schools and public discourse, many politicians and educators fail to recognize the equally prevalent social and educational inequities that continue to plague our communities. Moreover, they resist challenging the structures of privilege and power that perpetuate the daily impact of racism on the lives and learning of students of color in contemporary American society.

The *Harvard Educational Review* has a long history of addressing the challenges of racism. In 1988, the Editorial Board published a special issue entitled *Race, Racism, and American Education: Perspectives of Asian Americans, Blacks, Latinos, and Native Americans*. In 1990, following the positive response to this issue, the Board published the first edition of *Facing Racism in Education*. A second edition, published in 1996, retained many of the original articles and also included more recent pieces that highlighted additional dimensions of the ongoing struggle against racism in education. In light of the continuing demand for this publication, and given our continued publication of articles examining this topic, the Board decided to publish a third edition. This third edition retains five articles (and six authors) from earlier editions, and offers seven new pieces that have been published since 1996. We hope this edition will give readers new insights and ideas for change, thus challenging the assumption that we can ever be done with this work.

Although some politicians and educators express concern about the "achievement gap" and about "at-risk" students, such framings often blame students, families, and/or communities while denying the social and economic conditions that systematically place students of color at risk and undermine their achievement in schools. Moreover, current national education policies call for "no child left behind," while the government's simultaneous support for educational privatization robs public schools of the resources they desperately require to meet the learning needs of their most vulnerable students.

As the country marks the 50th anniversary of the U.S. Supreme Court's landmark *Brown v. Board of Education* decision, we are aware that many people want to declare that racism no longer exists, that an earlier generation took care of those ills, and that it is time to move on. We ask of those who push us toward this national amnesia, Who benefits and who is disserved by the current educational system? Whose voices are heard and whose are silenced? Which questions are being asked and which remain unspoken? How do educators and politicians explain that many schools today are as segregated and as unequally funded as they were in 1954? Lastly, how can we as a nation "move on" from the continued presence of racism in schools and public discourse about education when the "problem of the color line" has not only persisted since DuBois' initial observation in 1903, but has in fact expanded to include the full spectrum of racial and ethnic groupings that we find in American society today?

The contributors to this volume address the many forms of racism still present in today's schools and classrooms, yet they also bear witness to the courage and conviction of communities, students, and teachers who work to deconstruct the logic of racism in education and dismantle its structures. They remind us that, as we question how far we have come since *Brown*, we must also recommit ourselves to the daily work of undoing racism through antiracist practice. While some might ask, "Aren't we done with this yet?" we maintain that, like democracy, diversity and commitment to educational equity represent more than an "outcome"; they are part of a *process* that each generation must take up, reinvent, and reinvigorate to ensure its continuation for generations to come. We hope these essays will support this process and challenge educators to continue to do this important and essential work.

PREFACE

While the voices in this volume all speak to the challenges and possibilities for facing racism in education, it is also important to recognize the many voices that are not present. In editing such a text it is a challenge to represent fully the many forms of racism experienced by all ethnic and racial groups. To this end, we advise readers to exercise caution in relating the experiences of one group to those of another, as all groups and individuals are unique in the ways that they experience, respond to, and understand racism. At best readers can recognize the impact of racism across groups — both historically and contemporarily — and (re)commit themselves to the process of educational equity and excellence.

Sonya L. Anderson
Polly F. Attwood
Lionel C. Howard
Editors

PART ONE

Experiences of Racism

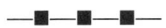

> If I didn't define myself for myself, I would be crunched into other people's fantasies for me and eaten alive.
> — *Audre Lorde*[1]

For many students of color, the historical and contemporary landscapes of compulsory education are best characterized as racist. Historically, overt forms of racism have dominated this landscape, as evidenced by the landmark *Brown v. Board of Education* ruling that challenged the inequities inherent in "separate but equal" education for minority students. Today, racism has reinvented itself in a more subtle and covert manner that goes unnoticed, and potentially unchallenged, upon a cursory glance. However, a closer examination of the multiple dimensions of schools and classrooms (e.g., pedagogy, curriculum, and educational policies) reveals the racism that underlies these dimensions, which are often designed with the best of intentions and characterized as "best practices" in education. Within these historical and contemporary landscapes, minority students have experienced a host of challenges to their educational endeavors, which have led to the questioning of their cognitive capacity, motivation, culture and cultural identity, and interest in all things deemed academic. The authors presented in Part One bring these experiences of racism, and its subsequent implications, to life as they bear witness to the experiences of their students, their children, and themselves.

In "Building 860," Christian Neira shares his experiences of racism as a student caught between two worlds — the housing project and community in which he resides and the elite preparatory school he attends. These two worlds, stark in contrast, differ in the morals, behaviors, thinking, and perspectives that govern their existence. Acutely aware of the different cultures, Neira and his classmates, who are considered foreigners in both worlds and whose allegiance is challenged, are placed in the position of having to change their "character every morning and afternoon to adapt to two different worlds," which is likely to endanger their identity.

Donna Deyhle, in "Navajo Youth and Anglo Racism: Cultural Integrity and Resistance," also highlights the incongruence between two cultures, namely, Anglo and Navajo. In her decade-long ethnography of Navajo youth in a border reservation community, Deyhle used a lens of cultural difference and structural theories to examine the racial and cultural struggles between Anglos and Navajos, and she describes the ways these struggles manifest in schools and the workplace. Within the school context, for example, the vocationally centered assimilationist curriculum offered to Navajo youth is a clear reflection of power relations existing within the larger community. Understanding the interconnectedness of differences and power relations, Deyhle puts at center the existing racial conflict and cultural dissonance in her effort to understand the lack of school success and the underachievement of Navajo youth.

Recognizing the importance of cultural and linguistic background, Arlette Ingram Willis presents a riveting and richly textured account of the literacy schooling experiences of her elementary school–aged son, Jake, in "Reading the World of School Literacy: Contextualizing the Experience of a Young African American Male." Struggling to affirm himself as a literacy learner and an African American, Jake moves from being an engaged, active writer and learner to a young man silenced by the lack of awareness and appreciation of the historical roots and cultural context from which he writes. After framing her son's struggles within the historical and cultural context of racism — typically experienced by individuals from diverse cultural and linguistic backgrounds — Willis argues that it is necessary to expand teachers' understanding of the children they serve. In her own work in preservice teacher education, Willis raises the awareness of her students with respect to their own racial heritage and the assumptions they bring to the classroom about others.

Assumptions about race and ethnicity are not limited to negative representations and stereotypes. For some minorities, quite the opposite occurs when they are cast as "model minorities" and high-achievers. Even more complex is the polarized identity — model minority or delinquent — ascribed to many young Hmong Americans, an identity that is often mediated by generation status. In an attempt to move beyond this dichotomized representation, Stacey Lee presents a more complex picture of the schooling experiences of Hmong American students in her article, "More than 'Model Minorities' or 'Delinquents': A Look at Hmong American High School Students." Lee explores the way economic forces, relationships with the dominant society, perceptions of opportunities, family relationships, culture, and educational experiences affect the attitudes and contribute to the variation of schooling experiences of 1.5- and second-generation Hmong youth. Most notable in Lee's research is the finding in Hmong culture that addresses the issues of acculturation and assimilation practices, and the differing generational responses to racism.

INTRODUCTION TO PART ONE

Closing out Part One is an article by Bonny Norton and Pippa Stein, "Why the 'Monkey Passage' Bombed: Test, Genres, and Teaching." These authors explore issues of textual meaning, testing, and pedagogy based on their work as two White educators in post-apartheid South Africa piloting a reading test to be used for college entrance examination for Black students. Surprised by the two contrasting readings of the passage, the authors explore the ways that the politics of different social locations contribute to the production of multiple meanings. Moreover, they highlight the assumptions held about objective test development and the influence of power in the production of multiple meanings. Although Norton and Stein recognize the important need for educators to be cognizant of others' historical and cultural contexts, they suggest that it is also important to understand these contexts within their relationship to the current social location of the individuals with whom they are interacting.

Note

1. In Janet Cheatham Bell, ed., *Famous Black Quotations* (New York: Warner Books, 1995), p. 21.

Building 860

CHRISTIAN NEIRA

When trying to live in two different worlds, one is in peril of not belonging to either of them. One is left in a state of confusion. The morals, behavior, thinking, and perspective of the world of a New York City housing project are radically different from those of an elite preparatory school in the same city. Being put in the position of changing one's character every morning and afternoon to adapt to two different worlds endangers one's identity.

I remember one incident during high school that demonstrates the tightrope that I walked. I was coming out of my home when I saw one of my neighbors also leaving for school. While waiting for the elevator, we began to talk. I was dressed in compliance with the dress code of my school: tie and jacket. She told me she went to Joan of Arc, the public junior high school across the street from my school. I told her I was dressed like this because I went to the Trinity School. Her expression was one of deep shock and pity. She asked, "How do you survive?" I first thought she meant how did I survive living in the projects, but later that day in school I came to the realization that she meant to ask how I survived at the preparatory school.

Each of the two cultures considered me a foreigner, one who did not belong. Where my allegiance resided was their question. Neither world fully understood me because these two cultures almost never meet, and when they meet on the street, violence and suspicion are their common language.

The Week

Monday morning. It begins with a distant rumbling sound that intensifies as it approaches. The walls begin to vibrate. The sound reaches a crescendo of steel against steel as the New York City subway rolls by my window. I look at the graffiti-covered train as it passes, and I remember the kid at school whose parents are art collectors and collect graffiti paintings. The worst vibrations occur when two subways pass simultaneously. The only benefit of having an elevated train so close by is that it is a most effective alarm clock on a Monday morning.

There are three locks and a chain on my apartment door. As I open the door, the wind rushes in from the hallway, and with it comes the odor of rotten food. Outside, the hall is barely five feet wide, not enough space for two people to walk along side by side. The ceiling always leaks and pieces of paint and plaster sometimes fall on you as you walk along. The hall was recently painted, painted by someone with a spray paint can, that is. He left his street name painted on the floor.

As I walk toward the elevators I can only pray that they will be working this morning. One has been out since Saturday. I look through the hole in the elevator door to see if any cables are moving, the indicator that the elevator is working. After a few minutes of waiting for any signs, I resign myself to taking the stairs. Waiting any longer is futile.

The door to the stairs scrapes the floor as I try to push it open; it is held in place by only one hinge. Something is blocking the door from swinging open. As I squeeze through the opening, the odor of discarded food, plastic wrappers, and cans strikes me in the face. I quickly turn away in disgust and run down the stairs.

The best way to get down the stairs is to run, but it is not the safest way. Taking the stairs is like plunging into the darkness of a cave hoping to emerge at the other end. There are no lights; the bulbs have either burned out or the sockets simply do not work. As you run down you have to be careful not to lose your balance on the crack vials that litter the floor.

On the first floor I see a mother with a stroller waiting for the elevator. As I push the front door open and emerge onto the street, I yell to her that the elevators aren't working. My friend Mike is already waiting for me at the train station.

Monday lunch. The usual bunch of us sit together. The only thing we all have in common is that we eat lunch together. Some of us have shared experiences; others in the group have experiences and backgrounds that are foreign.

The discussions on Mondays start with Jonathan Swaine III telling the rest of us about his weekend. It is all very predictable, something about a country house somewhere. I never pay much attention to his stories because they do not seem real and tangible to me. They are very much a part of his life, but the stories of weekend country houses are not meaningful to me. I don't think he tells us his weekend stories to impress us; he must have gotten the impression long before that his stories had no effect on the rest of us in either a positive or negative ways. He sits with us because he wants to learn from our experiences, which are different from his own. We are a "good experience" that somehow reveals to him a different world. He takes advantage of the "diversity" of the school to have an "interesting experience."

Ragavendra is supposed to give Jonathan that unique experience. The name Ragavendra was Americanized into Rags by the teachers. Since reading the *Autobiography of Malcolm X*, Rags had become a fervent Indian nationalist. He tells us that he did not do anything exciting over the weekend. "The usual," he said. Translated this means that he spent the weekend working as a stock boy at the small bodega (grocery store) only three blocks from where I live.

Rags lives just north of me. I once visited his home. It is in a five-story tenement building next to a vacant lot. There were kids having a snowball fight in the lot; they would hide behind piles of discarded ties and abandoned cars. Another group of kids climbed a dumpster and jumped onto an old box spring that they used as a trampoline to fly into the sky.

To enter Rags's home you had to walk through the kitchen. There were four large pots of boiling water giving off heat, and the oven was turned to broil. The landlord refused to give any steam, saying that the boiler was broken. The tenants had retaliated with a rent strike, but were being served with eviction notices. A white sheet hung outside the window of the apartment, emblazoned with the words, "SUPPORT OUR RENT STRIKE."

The next person down the table is my friend Mike, who waits for me every morning at the train station. He spends his weekends and some week nights patrolling the buildings of the Frederick Douglass Housing Projects. A group of tenants wear jackets that read on the back, "Tenant Patrol." They set up a desk in the front lobby of a building which has no lock on the front door and try to ensure that only tenants enter the building. There are more than two dozen buildings in the Douglass Projects, and their efforts are, to a large degree, futile. No amount of time or effort could ensure any degree of safety to the people who enter these buildings.

No lunch group like ours would be complete without a person who desperately needs to be around people very different yet similar to himself. his real name is Eduardo Fernandez, but he wants people to call him Edward. I compromise and call him Ed. His mother is on the school's Board of Trustees and his father is a bank executive. They grew up in El Barrio (Spanish Harlem), but now live in a penthouse on Fifth Avenue. In many ways, Ed's parents' success is what Mike, Rags, and I hope to duplicate. Yet we fear Edward; he has what Rags once called the "Oreo disease." Trying to hide his real name is only a small part of the confusion he has about his cultural background. He would never call himself Latino, but he knows he cannot call himself a WASP. His parents shelter him so much from the environment that they grew up in that he is reduced to hearing about El Barrio over the lunch table. Ed gropes to understand his Latino background but at the same time denies it, trivializing it in order to move within the WASP culture of the school.

By the time the conversation reaches me, lunch is almost over, so I simply tell them I gardened. There is a neighborhood community garden on what was once the site of a dope house that the city tore down. So, in the minds of city officials the problem was resolved, but the rubble of the building was left in the lot. The community finally cleared the lot and established a garden on the site. It was planted with flowers and assorted plants. Still, the garden is not a pretty sight. Cardboard, pieces of plywood, and a chain-linked fence serves as a fence around the lot. The bricks that once littered the lot are used for pathways through the garden. Tires are used to hold up some plants.

One section is devoted to vegetables. Urban kids who have never seen the plants that vegetables come from always try to guess what each plant produces. Once, one boy pointed to a plant and said with a great deal of authority, "That's a pickle plant!" An older girl snapped back, "No, no, dummy, there's no such thing as a pickle plant. It's a tomato plant."

One section of the garden is devoted to food and medicinal herbs. Señora Rosa works in the herb section; she is the "country doctor" of the community. After people have tried countless doctors and their ailments persist, they consult Señora Rosa. The patient makes an offering (usually money) to Señora Rosa's statue of the Virgin Mary, and she prescribes the necessary herbs. The herb section also serves as the community bulletin board; people gather there to pick the herbs Señora Rosa recommends and to exchange neighborhood gossip.

Monday afternoon. There is a large crowd in front of my building as I approach. No one can get into the building because the front door is locked. Management decided to put a lock on the door because residents had complained that people could just walk in off the street. The problem was that management had forgotten to give anyone the key to the lock. In every group, someone has a bright idea. One kid reaches for the fire hose and uses the metal part to break the glass part of the door, reaches in, and opens the door.

Now a second wait begins, the wait for the elevator. One of them is rumored to be working so everyone waits in anticipation. Everyone tries to listen for the sound of chains rattling that indicates the elevator is moving. The waiting crowd grows, as more people enter, using the new doorknob. After what seems like an interminable wait, one elevator reaches the first floor. Before anyone can get off, the crowd presses forward. Three boys file out. One man in the waiting crowd accuses them of holding up the elevator. They snap back, telling the old man to mind his own business.

Close to fifteen people file into the completely dark elevator. The light bulb is missing. We all take a breath of air before the door swings shut. Our bodies are pressed so close together that no one can move. At every stop, everyone must file out to let someone off and then file back in. By counting the glimpses of light that reflect off other people's faces, I count the number of floors passed.

Tuesday night. Outside on the street are voices yelling at each other over the noise of their boom-box radio. Someone from the building yells at them to go away; it is two in the morning. The yelling and music continue, only louder. After a few minutes, I see a bottle sailing through the air. It came from above me and I live on the eleventh floor. The bottle crashes on one of the yelling men, and I say to myself, "Good hit!"

A couple of hours later while I am writing an English paper, I hear the fire alarm go off. I run toward the living room and see smoke coming through the racks in the front door. Outside, the hallway is filled with people and smoke. I run to call the fire department. After I give the operator my address, the first questions she asks is whether I'm calling form the projects. "Yes, yes," I scream into the receiver, "just hurry — there's a fire in the building!"

By the time the fire department arrives, we have extinguished the fire in the garbage chute. People passed buckets of water and poured them down the chute. The garbage had been backed up to the fifth floor and had caught on fire. The entire scene reminded me of a nineteenth-century bucket brigade.

Wednesday English class. I recount last night to my English teacher because I do not have my creative writing assignment. He simply stares at me, neither in surprise not disbelief. He is clueless; he does not know how to judge my story. No amount of training in preparatory schools has equipped him with the tools to evaluate this excuse. The rest of the class files into the room, and they begin to read out loud the stories they had written the night before. One story keeps ringing in my mind:

> This was one of the scariest experiences of my life. I was walking along 72nd and Park Avenue heading downtown. I stopped at the curb to wait for the light to change. On my left there appeared three guys about my age. I continued to walk along and crossed towards Fifth. I looked back and realized that those same three guys were following me. I started to walk a little faster, then run, but they were still following me. On 66th and Fifth one of the guys grabbed me from behind. I turned around and looked at this greasy, hairy, slimy Rican right in the eyes.

My chest tightens. The entire class is looking straight into Mike's eyes — the Puerto Rican in the class. There is a long, tense pause and only Mike can break the silence. He say, "Oh, was that you we got? Sorry."

There is a laughter of relief.

Thursday afternoon. By the end of the day the incident in English class has spread throughout the school. The story and reaction are slightly different in every version I hear. One version had Mike picking up his desk and throwing it across the room.

Rags and I walk home together. We retell the story over and over again, laughing at the incident in the beginning but becoming more and more angry with each retelling. "That's what they think of Blacks and Latinos. They have no other image," he says. "The only contact they have with any Black or Latino is as their doorman or their housecleaner. Then you have people like Edward that, instead of being a positive image of a Chicano, is wrapped up in trying to be a WASP. A double-stuffed Oreo is what he is! The rest of us are there to legitimize their White institution. You know the building they are building across the street from the school? Ten years ago the school sued the city not to build a low-income building on the lot. Now the school has gotten its way; they are building a luxury building on the lot. So, to 'improve relations with the neighborhood' they let the kids in the community center use the pool, and they let in a handful of Blacks and Latinos to add color to the place."

As we approach home, Rags and I start to laugh again at the story; there is not much of anything else we can do. We stop in front of the garden to see if anything has grown. From behind me I hear an echoing noise and then some screams. Before I can figure out that the noises I hear are gun shots, I am pushed to the ground. All I can do is hold my bookbag tightly over my head. My face is buried in Rags's back as we both crouch behind a car not knowing where the noises are coming from. One man kneeling beside me yells in my ear that there is a pusher shooting madly into the air in front of 860.

"I will never get home," I think to myself, "860 is my building." After a few noiseless minutes, people start to run toward their buildings and up the stairs.

A couple of hours later when I am trying to get some schoolwork done, I look at my social studies paper topic: "In light of our discussion on the rights and protections afforded to citizens by the Constitution, discuss the question of the 'right' of the government to make certain drugs illegal and whether these drugs should be legalized." I tear up the paper in disgust.

Friday night. I get off the crosstown bus on 96th and start to walk down Fifth. As I approach the building on 88th, the door swings open and the doorman asks if I am here for Edward's party.

"Right, for Eduardo's party," I reply.

He directs me to the elevator on the left. The elevator is already waiting for me. On the way up I begin to talk to the elevator man; his name is Señor Manuel. I know him from other visits I have made and because he is the husband of Señora Rosa. We talk about how the garden is growing this year and how it needs a fence. The lights on the elevator panel finally reach PH. The elevator door opens onto another door. There is no hallway to walk, just another door. Inside, the entire school is having a party.

In need of some air, I walk onto the terrace. Mike is leaning against the wall looking out toward the lighted skyline and over Central Park. We do not say much for a while. Then he asks, "What you think of the story yesterday? I mean, you think I said the right thing?"

I look across the park uptown toward the group of buildings where we live. They are easily differentiated from the other buildings if you know what to look for.

"What else was I suppose to say? If I hit the guy like I wanted, out I go. One less Puerto Rican in the school is not going to bother them. These people have no sense that we exist in that school. No matter what they do or say we are simply nameless bodies that walk the halls. No name. No character. It is beyond the stage where they don't want us there; now they simply are oblivious to our presence. We only figure in their minds when we are called upon to agree that their notions of us are the right ones."

On the way home, we walk across Central Park in silence. The scenery changes very quickly when you walk uptown. We reach my building. I push the door open; the lock has been taken off, and pieces of glass are still on the floor. Ms. Johnson is waiting in front of the elevators. She is in a wheelchair.

"I've been waiting for the elevators for more than an hour and I can't get home," she says.

Mike gets into the elevator and presses all the buttons. It does not move. "Maybe if we call the cops they can do something," I say. "A woman that was here earlier called but they haven't come. Housing cops never come," she says. "Well, it's close to midnight and we can't leave her here," Mike says to me. Mike needs to prove something to himself tonight.

Before I know what I have gotten myself into we are carrying Ms. Johnson up the stairs, all twenty flights. It takes us over three hours to carry Ms. Johnson in her wheelchair. She never stops talking during those three hours. She tells us that she is going to City College and studying to become a social worker. Mike and I can barely talk as we concentrate on moving up the stairs.

A Closing Thought

Poised between two different worlds, I have learned that the emotional power of some experiences can never be conveyed to another. Outsiders can only begin to appreciate that which is foreign to them when they realize that they will never fully understand.

Navajo Youth and Anglo Racism: Cultural Integrity and Resistance

DONNA DEYHLE

Graduation day was near at Navajo High School.[1] Young Navajo men wearing blue jeans, T-shirts, and Nikes stood in the hall talking to the shop teacher. "You learned lots of skills in my class. Try the job services office in town. They can help you find jobs," he told them. One student disagreed. "I haven't really seen any Navajo people working, like in convenience stores or grocery stores. So, the job outlook is pretty slim. Unless you figure out something else to do. Like shoveling snow or something. But the job outlook isn't really great. For Indians, you know."

Several of the students nodded in agreement. The teacher continued, "There are lots of jobs out there. You just have to look for them." As I passed them, I remembered a Navajo parent's comment: "It's the way it has always been. The Anglos keep the jobs for themselves, they don't hire real Navajo. That's the way it is."[2]

I continued down the hall to the library to interview one of the graduating seniors. She was in the top 10 percent of her class and had turned down two college scholarships to stay home with her family on the reservation. "I've always wanted to do things but it's like I couldn't because of school. That's what has held me back. I feel that." Going to college away from the reservation would cause her to miss opportunities to participate in, for example, traditional Navajo ceremonies. She explained her decision: "If I go to college, I will get a job in the city and then I won't come back very often. When am I going to have time to spend with my grandmother learning about my culture? I feel that kind of resentment towards school. I feel cheated out of my own culture."

This article is about the lives, in and out of school, of young Navajo men and women in a border reservation community.[3] Here, school success and failure are best understood as one part of the larger process of racial conflict, which I have seen fought out in the workplace and in schools in this polarized community. This article will illustrate how Anglos maneuver to acquire the best jobs (some of which are teaching jobs) and how they systematically prepare Navajos for the lowest level jobs. These Navajo people are subject to racial discrimination in the workplace and at school. Young Navajos may respond to the vocational, assimilationist curriculum in their schools by withdrawing or resisting "education." For Navajo students, one of the most life-affirming strategies is to embrace reservation life and traditional Navajo culture. Indeed, the students in my study who were able to maintain Navajo/reservation connections gained a solid place in Navajo society and were also more successful in the Anglo world of school and workplace.

As an anthropologist interested in issues related to American Indian education, I discovered an absence of ethnographic research on American Indian adolescents' lives in and out of school since Murray Wax, Rosalie Wax, and Robert Dumont published *Formal Education in an American Indian Community* in 1964.[4] No such studies existed on the Navajo. In the early 1980s, a doctoral student, who at the time was an elementary school principal in the local school district, invited me to conduct a similar study in his community. District administrators and Navajo parents were concerned with the high dropout rate of Navajo youth, and requested a study that would examine the reasons for the school success and failure of these students. In the fall of 1984, I moved to the community as an ethnographer to start this study. Over the next ten years, I listened to Navajo youth talk about their lives and watched them grow up and have families of their own. I attended their high schools, joining them in over three hundred classes, watching their struggles, successes, and failures. With field notes of observations and casual conversations, audiotapes of meetings and interviews, and ethnohistorical archival data, I documented their lives over the past decade.

Border High School (BHS) is located in a small town of 3,500 people about twenty miles from the Navajo reservation. Almost half of the student population is Navajo. Navajo High School (NHS) is located on the Navajo reservation, and almost 99 percent of the student population is Navajo. Both high schools, as part of one large public school district in one county, are administered from a central district office. They use both state and local standardized curricula.

For this study, I developed a main database that tracked by name all Navajo students who attended BHS and NHS during the school years from 1980–1981 to 1988–1989. This master list contained attendance data, grade point averages, standardized test scores, dropout and graduation rates, community locations, current employment situations, post–high school training, and General Education Diploma (GED) or regular high school graduation diploma received for 1,489 youth. Formal interviews took place with 168 youth who had left school and another one hundred who were either still in school or had successfully graduated. Teachers, administrators, political leaders, parents, and community members also answered my endless questions within the context of formal and casual conversations over the past ten years. During this time, I became involved in extracurricular school activities, including athletic

14

games, plays, dances, and carnivals, and "hanging out" on Main Street and at local fast food restaurants. I attended school and community meetings with Navajo parents. After several years, I was invited to participate in discussions with Navajo parents and to help develop strategies to intervene in school district decisions, such as disciplinary codes, attendance regulations, busing schedules, equal band equipment, and bilingual education. I watched and participated as parents fought for local political control over their children's education and struggled through racist treatment by the Anglo community. These parents were clearly aware of racist practices that occurred, and which I observed, on a daily basis.

I lived for two summers with a Navajo family on the reservation, herding sheep and cooking with children and adolescents. Over the years, as I continually returned to their community, they decided it was worth their time and energy to "educate" me about their cultural norms and values. The oldest daughter, Jan, was a student I had come to know from my initial observations at BHS. She explained her family's decision: "That first year, my Dad said you wouldn't come back. Most people come and study Navajos and leave. He was surprised you came back the next year. And every year you came back. So he said we could trust you." This family introduced me to others, who in turn introduced me to still other families. My hosts graciously explained their perceptions of life, school, and education. I was invited to attend traditional ceremonies as "part of the family." From the ceremony I describe in this article, I have chosen to reveal only dialogue that is relevant to education in order to avoid disclosing any confidential religious beliefs. I have shared drafts of this article over the years with Navajos in the community who have confirmed my observations and who have helped me represent their experiences and concerns more accurately. They have agreed that this article should be published, in order to share with others both the concerns Navajos have for their children's education and the importance of having their children remain faithful to their Navajo traditions.

Anglos living in the community on the border of the reservation also patiently answered my endless questions in over one hundred informal interviews. Approximately 85 percent of the Anglos are members of the Church of Latter Day Saints (LDS), commonly called Mormons. I attended religious meetings at the Indian Ward (a local unit of the LDS Church), seminary classes (religious training) at the two high schools, and interviewed several religion teachers who were bishops in the LDS Church. My research with Navajo youth was a frequent topic of conversations at picnics, dinners, and socials, where Anglos carefully explained their personal understanding, as well as the LDS Church's views, of American Indians. The Anglo voices in this community do not represent a definitive Mormon perspective, but they do illustrate a cultural view that is influenced, in part, by religious beliefs. In the context of this community, Mormon and non-Mormon Anglo voices are consistent in opposition to their Navajo neighbors.[5] As an outsider to both the Navajo and Anglo communities, I was supported, tolerated, and educated by many local people in my efforts to understand the contemporary lives of Navajo people.[6]

Theoretical Framework

Educational anthropologists and sociologists who attempt to explain minority youths' responses to school primarily present either a cultural difference theory or a sociostructural theory.[7] Cultural difference theorists such as Cummins argue that cultural conflicts and other problems develop in minority classrooms because of the differences between students' home and school cultures.[8] Sociostructural theorists such as Ogbu argue that the explanations for minority school failure lie outside of the school itself, specifically in the racial stratification of U.S. society and the economy.[9] Both of these positions provide a useful perspective and have contributed to our understanding of cultural conflict. In particular, I find Ogbu's[10] structural analysis of castelike or involuntary minorities and the job ceiling they face and Cummins's analysis of cultural differences and cultural integrity useful in understanding the situation faced by these Navajo youth.[11]

My research represents a more traditional anthropological approach. I am not attempting to create a general theory of castelike minorities, but rather to represent the specific Navajo experience. In so doing, I take a different position than Ogbu. This ethnographic study speaks to some general claims made by Ogbu, but it does not replace his theory. Specifically, I speak about "racial warfare" to capture two points on which my interpretation and Ogbu's theory diverge: First, Navajos and Anglos conflict economically, politically, and culturally in both the schools and workplace. While Ogbu views the schools as a relatively neutral terrain, I portray the ways in which teachers and students play out this racial conflict. Second, Navajos have substantive ethical disagreements with the Anglo values manifested in the schools and the greater economy. The concept of racial warfare is intended to represent the integrity of Navajo culture and to avoid reducing this culture to a reinterpretation of traditional values in reaction to denial of opportunity in the Anglo-dominated schools and businesses, as I believe Ogbu does.

Young Navajo men and women face a racially polarized landscape, in which historically defined racial conflicts between Navajos and Anglos continue to engulf their lives. As a result, political and economic power remains in the hands of local Anglos who maintain a limited "place" for Navajos. This discrimination is basic to Navajos' attitudes towards schools. As Ogbu has pointed out, any comprehensive understanding of minority students' responses to school must include the power and status relations between minority and majority groups, as well as the variability among different minority groups.

According to Ogbu, the main factor differentiating the more successful from the less successful minorities appears to be the nature of the history of subordination and exploitation of the minorities, and the nature of the minorities' own instrumental and expressive responses to their treatment. In Ogbu's analysis, immigrant groups who came to this country more or less voluntarily arrived with an intact culture developed *before* contact with the dominant group. They viewed schooling as a means for increased opportunity and economic mobility, not as a threat to their cultural identity. In contrast, castelike minorities, which include African Americans, Mexican Americans, and American Indians, have been historically positioned as involuntary subordinates through slavery, conquest, or colonization. Ogbu argues that castelike minorities face schooling with a set of secondary cultural characteristics — a reinterpretation of traditional culture that is developed *after* contact with the dominant White group — to help them cope with the social, economic, political, and psychological history of rejection by the dominant group and its institutions. Schools, as sites of conflict with the dominant group, are seen as a threat to their cultural identity. These castelike minorities have developed oppositional cultural responses to schooling as they reject a system that has rejected them. Ogbu sees this resistance, which takes the form of truancy, lack of serious effort in and negative attitudes toward school, refusal to do classwork or assignments, and delinquency, as an adaptation to their lower social and occupational positions, which do not require high educational qualifications. This, in turn, has been counterproductive to school success. Specifically, pressure from the minority community not to "act White," coupled with feelings that they will not get jobs anyway, further decreases students' school efforts because they struggle with the fear of being estranged from their community if they are successful. The dominant group maintains this "adaptation" by providing inferior education and by channeling the students to inferior jobs after they finish high school.

Although Ogbu's general framework, which combines structural barriers and culturally based reactions, generally "fits" the Navajo situation, there are also striking differences between Navajos and other "castelike" minorities. Navajos have not played the same role in the national economy as other castelike minorities. African Americans, for example, have historically played a central role in the White-dominated economy. Navajos, in contrast, have never been an essential part of the White-dominated economy, except in regard to land procurement. Navajos accurately perceive that they are shut out of the job market, and that their school success is not linked to their economic prosperity.

Whereas Ogbu views the cultures of castelike minorities as a reaction to the dominant White group, I believe that Navajo practices and culture represent a distinct and independent tradition. Navajos do occupy a castelike, subordinate position in the larger social context. However, only a small part of Navajo cultural characteristics can appropriately be called "secondary" or "oppositional." Navajos face and resist the domination of their Anglo neighbors from an intact cultural base that was not developed in reaction to Anglo subordination. An oppositional description of Navajo culture ignores the integrity of Navajo culture and neglects the substantive value disagreements between Navajos and Anglos.

Navajo success is closely tied to family and reservation economic and cultural networks. It is these traditional values that parents seek to pass on to their children. For example, traditional Anglo notions of "success" — school credentials, individual careers, and individual economic prosperity — do not reflect those of the Navajo. The successful Navajo is judged on intact extended familial relations, where individual jobs and educational success are used to enhance the family and the community and aggressive individualism is suppressed for the cooperation of the group. These Navajo values — the communal nature of success and the primacy of the family — exist in well-developed institutional structures on the reservation independent of Anglo culture, and during social and economic crises, help secure the Navajos' identity as a people.

These cultural characteristics in themselves do not necessarily result in school failure, although they contribute to the tension and misunderstanding between Navajos and Anglos. Youth who have little identity as Navajos and who are not accepted by Anglos because they are not White face the greatest risk of school failure and unemployment. To understand this position more fully, it is necessary to turn to Cummins, who argues that the strength of one's cultural identity is a vital factor in the expressive responses to the schooling experience. Cummins states that "widespread school failure does not occur in minority groups that are positively oriented towards both their own and the dominant culture, that do not perceive themselves as inferior to the dominant group, and that are not alienated from their own cultural values."[12] This position suggests that Navajo youth who are better integrated into their home culture will be more successful students, regardless of the structural barriers they face. In other words, the more Navajo students resist assimilation while simultaneously maintaining their culture, the more successful they are in school.

In this article, I draw upon three events — a racial fight, a meeting of the Native American Church, and a high school career day — to portray the race struggle between Navajos and Anglos and the way that struggle manifests itself in schools. My position captures, but also moves beyond, central insights from both cultural difference theory and structural theory. Like cultural difference theorists, I believe that differences in culture play a role in the divisions between Anglo teachers and Navajo students. Anglos do not understand Navajo values, and thus manufacture deficit explanations to account for behavior they assume is unguided by specific beliefs. When Navajo students act on their beliefs, they act in contrast to existing institutional values.

Furthermore, like Ogbu, I believe that these cultural differences become barriers because of the power relations involved. However, Ogbu implies that castelike minority students withdraw from academic effort not only because of the power relations in schools, but also because of the job ceiling and their own communities' social realities or folk theories that undermine the importance of school success. As a result, he takes the accommodationist position that castelike minorities would do better to adopt the strategies of immigrant groups, accept the school's regime, and succeed by its standards. Ogbu does not see culture as a terrain of conflict, nor does he perceive the significance of race as contributing to racial warfare, as I do; rather, he believes it is possible for the culture of the student to be left "safely" at home so that his or her cultural identity can be disconnected from what occurs in school.

This is not possible for Navajo youth. My data supports Navajo students' perception that Anglos discriminate against them and that they have no reason to believe that their cooperation with the educational regime would bring advantages in either schools or in the workplace. The issue for Navajo students is not that doing well in school is to "act White," but that playing by the rules of the classroom represents a "stacked deck." Educational compliance, or succeeding in the *kind* of schooling available to them, does not result in economic and social equality in the Anglo-dominated community. I argue, in this article, that the Navajos' experiences of racial and cultural warfare must be placed at the center of an explanatory model of their education and work experiences.

The Fight: Racial Conflict

Racial polarization is a fact of life in this border community. In 1989, a fight broke out between a Navajo and an Anglo student at BHS. Claiming his younger cousin had been verbally and physically assaulted, a Navajo junior struck an Anglo student across the face in the school hallway during lunch. Navajo and Anglo students quickly gathered at the scene as the principal and the football coach pulled the boys apart. Police were called to the school; the Anglo student was released to his parents, while the Navajo student was taken to jail. The Navajo community demanded a meeting with school officials to discuss the incident, which more than seventy-five Navajo parents attended. The superintendent, the two high school principals, and several teachers also attended, along with the school district lawyer, the DNA lawyer, the local sheriff, and myself.[13] The tension felt in the meeting was a reflection of the larger battles lived out between Navajos and Anglos in the community each day.

The president of the parent association, who served as the meeting translator, spoke first in Navajo and then in English. His son-in-law was the Navajo youth involved in the incident:

> It kinda hurts to hear this information. The parents hurt over this. The parents have come to me with the problem. It hurts the parents and the students. We have to get over this problem. When kids come home and say they have been thrown around, they can't concentrate on their work. It hurts. Word gets around that the Indians are having an uprising. No. It is not true. We want our kids to go to school and do well. They are far behind. We want them to do well in academics. I hope we can talk about this. It gets worse every time we talk. I hear the police came into school and took him away. This is not fair, to knock around youth. If this is happening in school, I want to know about it.

As he sat down, the principal from the high school where the fight occurred stood up. He glanced at notes on a yellow pad, cleared his throat, and spoke:

> Let me express very strongly that there are a lot of things that cannot occur in a school for students to succeed. One thing is that they must feel safe. One of our goals is that it be a safe place. A week ago, following a school dance, a group of Anglos and Navajos got into a fight. They have a history of not getting along. The following week there was a fight in school, only one blow. I didn't talk to the Anglo boy because the police did.

The Navajo student accused of starting the fight interrupted the principal. "You have a problem. The Anglo started it. He was picking on a little kid and I told him to stop. Then he fought me."

The vice principal shook his head in disagreement. Several Navajo students shouted that Anglo students were always picking on and making fun of Navajos.

The principal, still standing, responded, "This is the first time I have heard this. I didn't know the Indian students were being picked on."

Sharon, a Navajo senior who witnessed the fight, stood and faced the principal. "We are never asked. I was not asked. I never get anything from Anglos." Her mother asked, "Why is it so hard for the kids to go to you with their problems?" Sharon persisted in questioning the principal. "I don't like the way Whites treat Indians. Why do you believe what the Anglo students say only? It's one side in this case. Can you guarantee that they won't continue?" The Navajo crowd clapped.

The principal responded, "We can talk about it. No, I can't guarantee. That's what you have to do as an individual. You have to take it." Murmurs of discontent echoed throughout the room. The principal continued, "Rumors of a fight were all around the school on Thursday, so I called in the police. There was no fight that day. Because of the tension we invited the police in to investigate. On Friday morning there was a fight. Both the students were taken in and charged."

The DNA lawyer stood and asked the principal, "Is it true that the Anglo student was not charged and the Navajo student was?" The principal uttered softly, "Yes." Again the crowd muttered their disapproval.

"That cop tried to get me to fight him," shouted the Navajo youth involved in the fight. "He said, 'Come and fight me.' They told me not to step a foot in the school. Not to ever come back."

After a pause for a translation into Navajo, the principal urged parents to come to him with their problems. "If you feel your kids have been made fun of, you should come up to the school. You must come up to the school. We will do everything we can to help. If I can't help, you can go to the superintendent and say, 'That crazy principal can't help us.' That is the avenue we have in the district. We will do everything to help." At this point the superintendent stood and moved to the front of the room to stand by the principal:

I want to say two things. We expect a lot of our principals, but not to be policemen. We don't expect them to do that. We have a good relationship with the police, so we turn problems over to the police. And then the school gives up jurisdiction. The world is a great place. I hope that the students we turn out have great opportunities. Our schools are good schools, but not perfect.

An elderly Navajo woman brought the discussion back to the issue of discrimination. "Why is it so hard for us to understand that we have this problem? It has been this way for years. I think the problem is that we have the police treating people differently. So you see, the policeman is the problem." A mother added, "I used to go to that high school. I bear the tragedy with the students now. The higher I went, the greater pressure I got. So I left and went to another high school to graduate." An elderly medicine man spoke last:

We are just telling stories about each other now. Who was in the incident should be up front talking. When my kids were in school it was the same. And we are still trying to solve this problem. These kids who were talking tonight were in elementary school when my kids had this problem in high school. And I think the kids who are in elementary school now will also have this problem. We need to talk about it. Each time we talk about it the problem continues.

The meeting ended shortly before midnight. The school officials quickly left the building. Many of the Navajo parents and children continued to talk in small groups. Although charges against the youth had been dropped, he was not allowed to return to school. "They told me I was eighteen so I could not go to high school any more. I was told to go to adult education to finish."

As I sat with his family, his mother-in-law bitterly complained she should have said the following to the vice-principal, with whom she had gone to school twenty years before: "You know what it is like for the high school kids. You used to do the same things the kids are doing now against Indians. You remember when you put the pins in my seat? All the things that you used to do to Indians, it is still going on here and now. You did it, and now your kids are doing it."

I left with Sharon, the senior who spoke during the meeting, and her mother. We went to my house and continued talking about the incident. Sharon spoke of her own experiences in the racially mixed school. "They always give us trouble. Like there is this one group of guys. I told one, 'Shut up you pale face, or you red neck!' When they are rude to me I call them everything I know. They think Indians stink. I tell them, if you don't like Indians, why did you move here!"

Important public officials, like those who attended the meeting, are Anglos, and their ability to ignore Navajo concerns speaks to the security of their power base. All public institutions in the county are controlled by Anglos and by members of the Mormon Church.[14] The school superintendent, all four high school principals, four out of five elementary school principals, and the administration of the local community college are all LDS members. Over half of the county's population is Navajo, but Navajos account for only 15 percent of the teaching staff, and more than half of those have converted to Mormonism. The few Navajos in power have been sponsored for upward mobility since they joined the LDS church.[15] Locally, these converted Navajos are described by Anglos as "responsible," "good," and the "right kind" of Navajo. Anglo-controlled political and economic networks open slightly for these few individuals. Even for Navajos who hold middle-class jobs, racial stratification limits their place in the community. Navajos and Anglos do not socialize, and they pass each other without acknowledgment in stores, banks, and restaurants. As the meeting revealed, even when Navajos speak they are seldom heard, contributing to a strong sense of disempowerment.

Over the last one hundred years, the Anglo population has expanded and prospered.[16] The Navajo population has also expanded, now comprising 54 percent of the county's population, but they have not prospered. Their life conditions speak loudly of discrimination. A colonized form of government exists in the county where the Anglo population benefits disproportionately from Navajo resources: 60 percent of the county's economic resources comes from the reservation, but only 40 percent is returned in goods and services. Almost 50 percent of the Navajo in the county live without running water or utilities. Their per capita income is $3,572, compared to $11,029 for Anglos. Almost 60 percent of Navajo families have incomes below the poverty level, compared to less than 10 percent of Anglo families. Nearly 90 percent of those in the county on public assistance are American Indian — Navajos or Utes. The unemployment rate of Indians is over 40 percent, four times the unemployment rate for Anglos. Navajo youth and their families are well aware of this economic marginalization. Shoveling snow, envisioned as a job possibility by a young Navajo student at the beginning of this article, speaks powerfully of the job ceiling in this arid, high desert community.

Racial Conflict in the Schools

Racism and cultural beliefs, particularly the issues of assimilation and resistance, are at the heart of the interactions between Navajos and Anglos. The Anglo perspective is informed by a century-old model of assimilation that views Navajo culture and language as a problem to be eradicated. During this period, the Navajo have resisted assimilation and successfully struggled to maintain a Navajo way of life. Faced with continued colonization and discrimination, few Navajos remain silent.

The antagonisms apparent at the meeting also produce tensions in schools. Discrimination takes different forms between teachers and students in classes and in the hallways. Some racism is overt: Anglo students and teachers speak openly about disliking Navajos. Other interactions are more subtle, disguising racism in ostensibly well-intentioned actions, such as teachers lowering their academic expectations to "accommodate" the culture of their Navajo students. Some paternalistic racism exists, such as when teachers assume Navajos are "childlike" and that educators know what is best for "their Navajos." Still other racism is based on superficial stereotypes of Navajo culture, which assume that because Navajo families do not share middle-class Anglo values they hinder their children's success in schools. This section depicts the cultural and racial warfare that comes as a result of dismissing Navajos as being culturally inferior.

Daily encounters with Anglo peers and teachers demonstrate the power of the racial and cultural struggle occurring in schools. Shortly after the meeting, Sharon spoke of her embarrassment and the anger she had towards the science teacher:

> He is prejudiced. He talks about Navajos and welfare. "You all listen, you aren't going to be on welfare like all the other Navajos." He shouldn't talk like that! And then the White students say things like that to us. Like all Navajo are on welfare. I'm not like that. We work for what we have. He shouldn't say things like that. It makes us feel bad.

Some youth use subtle counterattacks when put down by their non-Indian peers. One day in class, two Anglo students teased a young Navajo studying to be a medicine man about his hair bun, lice, and the length of his hair: "Hey, how long did it take you to grow that?" The Navajo boy replied with a soft smile, "Ten minutes." Other confrontations are not so subtle. One young woman, whose last name was Cantsee, explained why she was no longer in math class: "When I came into class late, that teacher said, 'Oh, here is another Indian who can't see how to get to class.' I told him to go to hell and left class."

Teachers' lack of experience in the Navajo community and stereotyping of Navajos results in both the distortion and the dismissal of Navajo culture. During an English class I attended, a teacher was discussing the romantic and realist periods in literature:

> Have you ever dreamed about something that you can't get? That is romanticism, when you dreamed that everything would work out. But then there is the realism period. Some people during this time in your literature text, they lived together six to a room with fleas and lice and everything. They had dreams but they weren't coming true. I hope all of you have bigger dreams than that.

A Navajo student whispered to a friend, "It sounds like he is describing a *hogan* [the traditional Navajo one-room round home]!" In a reading class I observed, the teacher said, "We are studying tall tales. This is something that cannot be true. Like Pecos Bill. They said he lived with the coyotes. You see, it can't be true." Two Navajo students looked at each other and in unison said, "But us Navajo, we live on the reservation with the coyotes." The teacher replied, "Well, I don't know anything about that. Let's talk about parables now."

Although some teachers' actions may be seen as "innocent" or "ignorant," others clearly reveal a hostile edge. Some teachers do know that coyotes are a fact of life on the reservation and still dismiss and mock students' lives. For example, during Sharon's senior year, her career education teacher lectured the class on the importance of filling out job applications. "You must put your address. When you are born, you are born into a community. You are not isolated. You are part of a community at birth. So you have an address." To which a student replied, "But I was born waaaaaaay out on the reservation! Not in a community." "I don't care if you were born out there with the coyotes. You have an address," argued the teacher. Students hooted, groaned, and laughed as several shouted, "Yessss, lady!" to which the teacher shouted back, "You sound like you are all on peyote. Let's go to the occupations quiz in your books."

Just as all Navajo youth are not dropouts, all Anglo teachers are not racist. Some teachers care deeply about their Navajo students. However, continued resistance to their educational efforts frustrates even the best teachers. I shared the frustration of Sharon's English teacher, who urged her Navajo students to perform in class: "You guys all speak two languages. Research shows that bilinguals are twice as smart. Language is not your problem. It's your attitude. You have given up because Whites intimidate you. Don't you want to be a top student?" "No!" the class responded loudly, "we don't care." This teacher, who had expressed a great deal of concern and empathy for her Navajo students three years earlier, recently told me, "You are not going to like what I say about Indians now. I am a racist! I'm not kidding. Working with these Indian kids makes you a racist. They just sit here and do nothing." Throughout the district, at both elementary and high school levels, administrators and teachers believe Navajo students have difficulties in school because of their language and culture.

Equally damaging to Navajo students' school experiences are teachers who refuse to acknowledge the racial discrimination in the community. By reducing racial conflict to "others' problems" or a thing of the past, the local power struggle is kept out of the classroom. During the last week of studying *To Kill a Mockingbird* in a twelfth-grade English class, the teacher focused on racial conflict between Whites and Blacks, and summarized the discussion of the book by saying:

> It used to be that Whites treated Blacks badly. Remember, this is racial discrimination, when one group treats another badly just because of the color of their skin, and it is against the law. It was a sad part of history and I'm glad it doesn't happen any more.

A Navajo student turned to me and said, "But it happens to us! Why didn't he say that? What about what happens to us?"

Navajo students' attempts to make racial discrimination visible within the school have been silenced by the Anglo students and school administrators. Shortly after the fight and community meeting, Sharon's journalism class called a "press conference" to discuss Navajo education and racial prejudice for an article in the school paper. The journalism teacher, who was also the faculty advisor for the school paper, suggested the conflict between Navajo and Anglo students was an important topic to be covered by the newspaper. The students, fourteen Anglos and two Navajos, voted to invite Navajo parents, the high school principal, the Indian advisor, and myself to be interviewed. We had all attended the community meeting following the fight. At the press conference, an Anglo student who was new to the district spoke first:

> When I came I didn't know about Indians. The kids here tried to scare me, told me about Indian witches and evil spirits. It made me afraid of Indians, that they were weird or gross and they were out to scalp Whites!

The principal suggested that when students hear discriminatory comments they should correct them. Another Anglo student replied, "What do we do when teachers say bad things about Indians? Like the AP [advanced placement] history teacher. We don't have any Indians in there, and he says really awful things about Indians." The principal shook his head, "I'm sure most teachers don't do that. If they do you kids can tell us." He continued, "All students, Anglo and Navajo, are just the same. I don't see the difference. Kids are just kids. The fight between the Anglo and Navajo boy was an isolated incident. We have taken care of the problem." A Navajo parent, who had been silent, then stood and said:

> I hear that there was this Anglo kid who was caught stealing a little radio. But then the teacher found out the boy was from an important family here, so the teacher did nothing to the boy. So, you see, we still have this problem.

The bell rang. The press conference was concluded. The students, concerned that discussions of racial prejudice would both demoralize Navajo students and embarrass Anglo students, decided not to print the story.

Racial attitudes are also evident in teachers' and administrators' expectations of Navajo students. These attitudes include assumptions about the "academic place" for Navajos. The sixth-graders from an elementary school feeding into Border High School all scored above the national norm in mathematics on the Stanford Achievement Test. Yet upon entering high school, Navajo children were systematically placed in the lowest level mathematics class. When asked about the placement the principal explained, "I didn't look at the scores, and elementary grades are always inflated. Our Navajo students always do better in the basic classes." These attitudes about race and culture place a ceiling on learners; in a school-administered survey, 85 percent of the teachers in one school indicated that Navajo students had learned "almost all they can learn." Standardized test scores showed an average seventh percentile for the school, the lowest in the state, which the principal explained, saying, "Our district level scores are low and dropout rate high because we have Navajo students."

Racism surfaces not only in ill-intentioned treatment of Navajo students, but also when well-intentioned educators make demeaning assumptions about them, representing a cultural mismatch. Anglos frequently distort Navajo values and view them as inadequate compared to their own cultural values. For example, Navajos are viewed as present oriented and practical minded. "I've never met a Navajo that planned far in the future, to like go to college. It's more [about] what to do tomorrow and the day after," said an Anglo school counselor. Another explained, "The Navajo are very practical minded. They think, 'What value is it to me in my everyday life?' A lot of abstract ideas in education just don't mean anything." Anglo stereotypes of Navajos also include the perception that they work well with their hands. A career education teacher said, "Well, I mean, they are good in spatial things. Working hands-on. They don't learn theoretically. You can talk until you are blue in the face. It's much better if there is practical hands-on application." Anglos intertwine such "descriptions" of Navajo culture with the belief that the Navajo family does not teach children school-appropriate values. A counselor explained:

> We [Anglos] were brought up every day with the question, "What are you going to be when you grow up?" And that is something that the Navajo parents never ask. And then I bring them in the counseling office and I ask, "What are you going to be when you finish high school?" That is the first time they have even heard the question. It's just not done at home. And it's my values. The importance of an education and a job. They don't think to the future.

Embedded in this cultural distortion of Navajo values is the assumption that the closeness of Navajo family ties (i.e., "cultural pressure") is problematic for "progress" and that it "causes" school failure. One of the teachers explained it graphically with a story about lobsters:

> You know what they say about lobsters? You can put them in water this high [indicating a depth of a few inches] and they won't get out. As soon as one tries to climb out the others pull him back in. [Laughter] That's what it is like with the Indians. As soon as one of their kind tries to better himself, the others pull him back in.

The owner of a local pottery factory, who employs work-study students from the high school, also saw the problem not as a lack of individual skills, but as one of the demands of family responsibilities:

> Many of them have been through all sorts of training programs. Take Tom. He is a graduate from technical school. A welder. But he came back here and is working here painting pottery. . . . They come back here to live with their families. There is a good and a bad side to that. Over there on the reservation they are getting strangled. It really strangles them over there with families. They can't make it on their own and their families strangle them with responsibilities.

It is within this racially divided community that Navajo youth must navigate the school system. Over the past ten years, in a district with 48 percent Navajos, one out of every three Navajo students left school before graduation; almost 80 percent of the district's dropouts are Navajos.[17] During a district-wide meeting, administrators identified the following as the causes of these youths' school failure: lack of self-esteem; inadequate homes; inadequate preparation for school; lack of parenting skills; poor communication between home and school; poor student attendance; limited vocabulary and language development; limited cultural enrichment opportunities; too academic a curriculum; poor attitude and motivation; and fetal alcohol syndrome. All of these place the blame on deficits of the students and their families. In contrast, only three causes listed found fault with the schools: questionable teacher support, lack of counseling, and non-relevant curriculum.

Navajo students paint a different picture. Acknowledging racism (i.e., citing it as one of the central reasons they leave school), over half of the 168 students I interviewed who had left school said simply, "I was not wanted in school." Over 40 percent of those who left school saw the curriculum as having little relevance for their lives. Although they acknowledge home difficulties, over half of the Navajo youth who left school complained of problems with administrators and uncaring teachers who would not help them with their work.

Assimilation: "Navajoness" as the Problem

Navajos became wards of the federal government in 1868. In accordance with treaty provisions signed at that time, the federal government was to provide schooling for all Navajos. Ever since, schooling has been used by policymakers and educators at the district and federal levels as a vehicle for cultural assimilation. Because public officials considered Navajo culture and language problematic and superfluous, education became a way to eliminate the "Indian problem."

In 1976, the district lost a suit filed by Navajo parents. As a result of the court's decision, the district was required to build two high schools on the reservation and to develop a bilingual and bicultural program for all grades. Construction of the high schools took eight years. The bilingual and bicultural program sat unused, gathering dust in the district's materials center for fifteen years. In 1991, after an investigation by the Office for Civil Rights in the Department of Education, the district was again found out of compliance with federal requirements concerning English as a Second Language (ESL).[18]

The district then created a new bilingual plan, which the newly appointed director of bilingual education presented at a parent meeting at the beginning of the 1993 school year. The district's latest plan calls for a total immersion of Navajo students in the English language to eradicate the Navajo language "problem." It requires that all Navajo students be tested for English-language proficiency, after which, the proposal states, "All Limited English Proficient (LEP) (ESL) [the two terms are used interchangeably] students are placed in the regular classroom with fluent English proficient students to insure optimal modeling of language." This plan will operate even in schools with a 99 percent Navajo population. No special ESL classes will be provided for students who are Navajo-language dominant.

Navajo parents expressed disbelief that the new program would be implemented, and questioned whether Navajo would actually be used for instruction in their children's classrooms. The parents had reason to be concerned. The district had agreed to such a program seventeen years earlier and it still did not exist. The bilingual project director responded, "Trust us. We are now sincere."

The Office for Civil Rights rejected the most recent plan, issuing a citation of non-compliance to the district and turning the investigation over to the Education Litigation Division of the Justice Department. During the summer of 1994, U.S. Attorney General Janet Reno authorized the Justice Department to intervene in this case as "party-plaintiff." Based on a preliminary investigation, the Justice Department believes the school district has discriminated against American Indian students, violating federal law and the Fourteenth Amendment, by failing to adopt and implement an alternative language program for Limited English Proficient students. The district is accused of denying American Indian students the same educational opportunities and services, such as equal access to certain academic programs, provided to Anglo students, and of denying qualified American Indians employment opportunities equal to those provided to Anglos.

Throughout the district (at both Navajo and Border High Schools), administrators and teachers believe Navajo students have difficulties in school because of their language and culture. This explains, in part, why the district refuses to implement a bilingual program that uses Navajo as a language of instruction. "These kids we get are learning disabled with their reading. Because they speak Navajo, you know," the ESL teacher explained. "The Indian students need to learn English and basic skills to survive in the Anglo world. That bilingual and bicultural stuff is not important for them. The jobs are off the reservation, so they need to learn how to work in the Anglo world." Another teacher, in a letter to the editor of the local newspaper, argued, "Bilingual education will become the greatest obstacle a Navajo student has to overcome and an impediment to the education of all other students."

English language difficulties are acknowledged by Navajo parents; over a two-year period, the topic was brought up at eighteen parent meetings. "Our kids speak Navajo, they need more of those ESL classes to help them learn." But at the same time, they speak of the importance of Navajo culture. "Our kids learn White history. When are you going to have Navajo language and culture, too?" At each meeting, school administrators and teachers assured the parents that their children were getting the help they need to learn English, and that Navajo language and culture were part of the school's curriculum. Over the past ten years of my fieldwork, only four semester-long classes were offered in Navajo language, history, or culture. All ESL classes have been eliminated in the high schools and replaced with general reading classes, even though few teachers in the district are certified in reading education.

This model of assimilation, which views native culture and language as a barrier to be overcome, has always framed educational policy in schools for American Indians.[19] Various programs have attempted to eliminate native cultures, measuring success in part by how many students do not return to their homes and families on the reservation. In the late 1890s, the superintendent of the Carlisle Indian School, the first boarding school for American Indian students, informed a congressional committee that between 25 percent and 30 percent of their students found a job and earned a livelihood away from their home; the remainder returned to the reservation. Even a year or two at school, he said, gave the youth a new life, and only a small percentage go "back to the blanket" and "do nothing."[20]

While the structure has changed somewhat, this educational practice has changed very little in the past one hundred years. In 1990, Sharon's counselor explained, "Most of the kids want to stay right here. On the reservation. It's kinda like, we say, they have 'gone back to the blanket.' They will sit in their *hogan* and do nothing." Counselors cannot comprehend that a youth does not want to leave the reservation. Their typical comments include: "He said he wanted to be a medicine man![21] He can't really mean it. His card [counselor's student aspiration list] says the military," and "It's real progress when they want to get off the reservation. There is nothing for them to do out there." Today, as throughout history, American Indians who resist assimilation by maintaining their culture and remaining on the reservation are described as failures. Such was the case with Sharon. Upon her return to the reservation after college in 1992, I was told by her counselor, "It's too bad. She didn't make it away from here. And I had so much hope for her succeeding." The college graduate is viewed positively, but those who "come home" are labeled "failures" by the Anglo community.

Racial beliefs about Navajos, embedded in a model of assimilation, guide Anglos' "understandings" of how to teach or interact with Navajos. For Anglos, these assimilationist beliefs are generally used to frame either the need to "change" Navajos to fit into the outside world or to adjust educational and economic opportunities downward to be "appropriate" for Navajo culture. Either way, Navajo culture is seen as undesirable. Teachers and administrators believe students fail because of their impoverished homes, culture, and language. Counselors assume Navajo students are not bound for college, and that they therefore should receive practical, vocation-oriented instruction; additionally, they should be encouraged to leave their families for jobs off the reservation. The educational assimilation policies described in this section are part of the larger race war in the community. Within this context, the school curriculum is not "neutral." Navajo youth who resist school are in fact resisting the district's educational goal of taking the "Navajoness" out of their Navajo students.

As Cummins points out, virtually all the evidence indicates that, at the very least, incorporating minority students' culture and language into the school curriculum does not impede academic progress. He argues that Anglos' resistance to recognize and incorporate the minority group's language and culture into school programs represents a resistance to confer status and power (with jobs, for example) on the minority group.[22]

From this angle, Navajo culture is considered *the* reason for academic failure. To accept Navajo culture and language would be to confer equal status, which is unacceptable to the Anglo community. Navajo culture and students' lives are effectively silenced by the surrounding Anglo community. Navajo language and traditions are absent from the school curriculum. Teachers' ignorance of Navajo student's lives results in the dismissal of the credibility of Navajo life. Racial conflict is silenced, either on the premise that it does not exist or that to acknowledge racism is to "cause problems." This "silencing" is a clear denial of the value of the Navajo people's way of life.

Navajoness and School Success

The Anglo community views assimilation as a necessary path to school success. In this view, the less "Indian" one is, the more academically "successful" one will become. Anglos perceive living in town, off the reservation, to be a socially progressive, economically advantageous move for Navajos. In fact, the opposite is true. The more academically successful Navajo students are more likely to be those who are firmly rooted in their Navajo community. This is consistent with Cummins's position that school failure is *less* likely for minority youth who are not alienated from their own cultural values and who do not perceive themselves as inferior to the dominant group. Failure rates are *more* likely for youth who feel disenfranchised from their culture and at the same time experience racial conflict. Rather than viewing the Navajo culture as a barrier, as does an assimilation model, "culturally intact" youth are, in fact, more successful students.

Located on the Navajo reservation, Navajo High School (NHS) is more "successful" than Border High School in retaining and graduating Navajo students. The dropout rate from this school, 28 percent, is slightly less than the national average.[23] These students come from some of the most traditional parts of the reservation. Navajo is the dominant language in most of the homes, and 90 percent of them qualify for subsidized school meals. NHS has four certified Navajo teachers, a group of Anglo teachers with an average of five years' experience, and a school curriculum that is identical to other schools in the district. The differences in Navajo students' performance between BHS and NHS indicate the importance not only of the student's cultural identity, but also of the sympathetic connection between the community and its school. Where there are fewer Anglo students and more Navajo teachers, racial conflict is minimal and youth move through their school careers in a more secure and supportive community context. Nevertheless, even NHS students experience "well-intentioned" racism from some teachers and a vocationalized curriculum.

This pattern — reservation youth succeeding academically more than Navajo town youth — is also repeated *within* the Navajo student population at Border High School (BHS). Almost half the Navajos who attended BHS are bused to school from the reservation. Among Navajos living in town, only 55 percent graduate from BHS, whereas almost 70 percent of the Navajo students living on the reservation graduate from Border High School.[24] In other words, Navajo students who live in town and attend BHS are less successful than those who live on the reservation and attend NHS. Also, within the BHS Navajo population, the Navajos that are bused from the reservation do better than those who live in town. The most successful students, like Sharon, are from one of the most traditional areas of the reservation. In contrast, those who are not academically successful are both estranged from the reservation community and bitterly resent the racially polarized school context they face daily.

Many of the Navajo BHS students who live in town take a confrontational stance toward school: many of their teachers express fear and discomfort with them in their classrooms. Over three-fourths of the school's disciplinary actions involve these Navajo youth. These students' resistance is clear: the schools don't want them and they don't want the schools. The racial conflict in this school is highly charged, with each side blaming the other for the problem.

Faced with a school and community that refuse to acknowledge their "Navajoness" positively, and coming from homes that transmit little of "traditional" Navajo life, these youth clearly are living on a sociocultural border, with little hope of succeeding in either cultural context. Only 15 percent are employed, and fewer than 10 percent of those who leave school attempt educational training later on.

Navajo youth respond in a variety of ways to the racial treatment they experience. Many leave school, while others simply fade into the background of their classrooms. Most report suffering racial discrimination. Sharon's experiences mirror those of many high school graduates. Although Sharon felt unwanted in school, she persisted, and graduated in 1991. Of her six elementary school girlfriends, Sharon was the only one to finish school. Her persistence was framed by her experience growing up on the reservation. Sharon's ability to speak at the meeting and her school success reflect her own sense of confidence — a confidence supported by traditional influences. Her early years were spent with her grandparents in a *hogan* on the reservation. As she explains:

> After I was born my mom was working. My grandma and grandpa, they were the ones that raised me until I started going to school. He was a traditional, a medicine man, so he was strict with us. And he made us go to school all the time. I am thankful to him. His influence is all around me now. . . . I'm modern. I guess I'm kind of old-fashioned, too. I keep all those traditions. I really

respect them. I really respect those old people. Like they tell me not to do something. I listen to them. I go to all kinds of ceremonies. I'm proud to be a Navajo.

Sharon places her traditional beliefs alongside those of the dominant culture and honors both. Her grandfather's advice supports her decision. "He told me that it was okay for me to go to both. He said, 'take what was good from both and just make it your life.' So that's what I did. If some old medicine man or somebody told me I needed some kind of ceremony, I'd do it. I'd do it both ways. I'd go for the blessing, too."

Sharon was an academically successful high school and college student. She completed her freshman year at the state university with a 2.8 grade point average, and then decided to return home. This choice securely embedded Sharon within her family and the Navajo community. She reflects on her decision:

I used to think those people that go to college never come back. They always promise to come back to the reservation, but they never do. And now I understand why, because all the jobs are up there [in the city] and I mean, if I major in physical therapy, there is nothing I can do with that down here at home. I thought I could do it without Indians. I thought I could do it by myself, but it does make a difference. It makes me feel more at home. It is good to see some Indian people once in awhile. It really motivates me.

Sharon now lives with her mother on the reservation. She took community college classes for one year to certify as a Licensed Practical Nurse, but left after deciding the classes were boring. "You see, they make the classes easy because most of the students were Navajo. It was too easy and I got tired of it." She occasionally works as a medic on the county's ambulance. With a characteristically broad smile, she said:

Maybe I'll go back [to the university] someday. I sometimes feel sucked in here. Like I'm stuck here. It's so hard to get out. But it feels good to be at my home with Navajo people, even though those Whites sometimes give us trouble. [Reflecting back on the racial fight and community meeting, she said little had changed.] . . . My brother, he is still at that school. And he is fighting back. You just have to keep doing it. Otherwise they just treat you like a dumb Indian. I will always fight. And someday my children will also go to school and fight and get jobs and be Indian.

Despite their treatment by a racist Anglo community that continues to dismiss the values and viability of Navajo life, the Navajo remain a culturally distinct and unified group of people. The continuity of Navajo culture provides a supportive framework or network of family and community for young Navajos, which increases their chances of academic success. This insistence on cultural integrity is visible in life on and near the reservation — where 70 percent of the Navajo youth will choose to live their lives.

The Native American Church: Cultural Integrity

The Native American Church (NAC) and traditional Navajo ceremonies have a central place in the lives of almost of all these Navajo youth. Embedded in Navajo ceremonies are beliefs about the communal nature of success and the primacy of the family. Jobs and educational success are means to enhance the group, not just the individual. Jobs are seen as a means of earning necessary money, not as "good" in and of themselves. This contrasts sharply with Anglo values of hard work for individual mobility, agency, and economic success. To understand the Navajo perspective, it is necessary to experience Navajo life on the reservation, to see the goals and vitality of the Navajo community.

One ceremony I was invited to attend reveals a glimpse into this life. I had been invited by Joe, the father of the family with whom I had lived on the reservation:

> We are going to have a Peyote meeting for the girls.[25] For Jan's birthday, too. To help pray for them to finish school. Jan is trying to graduate this year. If you could come it would help to have an educated person like yourself, a professor.

I was asked to "go in," joining the family and friends for the all-night ceremony in a *tipi* [a traditional Plains Indian structure used for most Native American Church meetings]. Of the twenty-eight participants, I was the only *bilagaana* [Navajo for White person]. We sat around a central fire and a half-moon shaped altar that represented the path of life — from birth to death. The fire and altar were attended to by the Fire Chief. Songs and prayers started with the passing of prayer sticks and a drum, and continued over the next four hours until holy water was brought into the *tipi* at midnight. I spoke and offered prayers during the meeting when I was invited to do so by the Fire Chief, who spoke to Jan and her sister first in Navajo, and then for my benefit in English:

> You are young still. You do not know what will happen to you in ten years. It is important that you take this path, and finish school. Your parents love you very much. You must get your education. I pray for you, it is so important.

He spoke passionately for twenty minutes. Tears were rolling down his face as he pleaded with his kin to succeed in school. As the singing resumed, more participants spoke of their own problems and offered prayers for the hosts' daughters. An uncle spoke:

> I want you to have the good in life. It is hard. It is like a job. You are in school and you must work hard, like a job. We want you to get a good education, and then someday you might have a job like a secretary or something like that, in an office. I can see that. Your parents try hard, but it is up to you to get an education. We know it is hard, but it is important.

The meeting ended at dawn, with a second pail of holy water and ceremonial food. Afterwards, the men remained in the *tipi,* stretched out comfortably as they smoked and told stories. They allowed me to remain and took the opportunity to educate me. The Fire Chief spoke seriously about the general concerns Navajo parents had for their children:

> The things our grandparents knew, we do not know now, and our children will never know. There is a new life, forward, to live in this here dominant culture. This is what I think. Our children need to go out and get the best they can. Go to school and college and get everything they want, and then come back here, to their homes, here between the four sacred mountains. In the past Navajo parents told their children to go out and get an education. Go to college. And they did and they stayed in Albuquerque, in the towns, and then the parents were sad because they said they never saw their children again. But Navajo parents now have to tell their children to go out and get their education. To college. And graduate school. And then to come back home, where they belong. Here on this land. This is where they belong. They need to bring their education back here to the reservation, their home. Then we can be a whole people. This is what I think.

The Native American Church meeting captures the solidarity of the Navajo community and the cultural vitality of its people. Although often invisible to their Anglo neighbors, who view Navajo youths' lives as a "cultural vacuum," ceremonies and family gatherings cloak and support these Navajo youth.[26] The Enemy Way, a five-day ceremony for the purpose of curing illness caused by a ghost, an alien, or an enemy, occurs frequently during the summer months. Additional ceremonial dances occur in the area at least monthly, and a strong Native American Church is active weekly on the reservation. All but one of the young women in the study had their *Kinaalda,* a Navajo puberty ceremony that marks the beginning of Navajo womanhood.[27] Ceremonies are frequently used to bless and support youths' life paths, including their progress in schools and at jobs. In all ceremonies and events, the group serves to support and bond the individual to the Navajo community. Individual economic success becomes a part of the Navajo community's larger economic network.

As was expressed in the NAC meeting, Navajo parents want their children to succeed in both the Anglo and Navajo worlds. However, it is clear that the family and community are of paramount importance, and that educational success brings community and family responsibility. There is a dual side to this message. Navajos are not trying to "get away" from Anglo culture, just from assimilation. Thus, they do want certain material goods and school success, but not at the expense of their cultural identity. As Jan said shortly after her NAC ceremony, "They [parents] tell us to do good in school, but that we will always be Navajo."

Cultural Integrity and Resistance

Traditional Navajo cultural values still frame, shape, and guide appropriate behavior in the Navajo community. Navajo youths' choice to remain a part of the community assures them economic support through local kinship networks unavailable off the reservation. This choice also puts these youth in opposition to the goals set for them by school officials. Specifically, the choice to remain on the reservation and the insistence on maintaining culturally different values are central to the power struggle in the larger community, because these choices are defined as impoverished by Anglos. However, if one understands the viability of the Navajo community, resistance to assimilation is seen as a rational and appropriate choice.

The Navajos are a conquered and colonized people who have successfully resisted assimilation. They have survived over four hundred years of Anglo subjugation and exploitation with a culture that, although changed, has remained distinct in its values, beliefs, and practices. These Navajos have remained on their ancestral land; Anglos are the immigrants. The Navajo Nation, the largest American Indian reservation in the United States, comprises 26,897 square miles, an area approximately the size of West Virginia. Treaty rights recognize sovereignty status, a separate "nation within the nation," for the 210,000-strong Navajo Nation. John David reports that the total personal income in 1991, including wages and salaries, transfer payments, livestock, and crops, was $900,032,754, with a per capita income of $4,106.[28] Accurate portraits of reservation poverty, however, leave non-reservation residents unprepared to understand that there are viable economic and social institutions on the reservation. The Navajo Nation's budget supports an infrastructure of education, law enforcement, and health and human social services with revenues from oil, gas, mining, timber, taxes, and federal and state funds.

Unique to this governmental structure is the infusion of Navajo culture. Traditional home sites that are determined by sheep and cattle grazing rights are maintained by a Land Permit Office; a tribal court system relies on a Navajo legal code, as well as a federal legal code; the Navajo Medicine Men's Association is housed in the complex of the tribal headquarters, with an office at the local hospital; all significant tribal meetings are prefaced with a traditional prayer from a Medicine Man; and the Navajo Nation publishes its own newspaper to provide a Navajo perspective on local and national matters. In 1986, 286 retail businesses, ninety-four of them Navajo owned, operated on the reservation. The Navajo Communication Company provides cable television and telephones to homes with electricity, and the Native American Public Broadcasting Consortium provides local news to radio listeners. The Navajo Community College, a multi-campus institution with seven branches, serves over two thousand students.[29] In 1992, a total of three thousand students were awarded tribal scholarships totaling $3,320,377. This insistence on tribal autonomy and resistance to "blending in" has assured their youth their continuity as Navajos. Specifically, Navajo choices cannot be compared, as in Ogbu's theories, to other minorities, because Navajos only stand to lose by integration into the larger society. The U.S. Commission on Civil Rights explains this unique position:

> Politically, other minorities started with nothing and attempted to obtain a voice in the existing economic and political structure. Indians started with everything and have gradually lost much of what they had to an advancing alien civilization. . . . Indian tribes have always been separate political entities interested in maintaining their own institutions and beliefs. . . . So while other minorities have sought integration into the larger society, much of Indian society is motivated to retain its political and cultural separateness.[30]

It is important to realize that Navajo individuals do not monolithically represent "the" Navajo culture. There are hundreds of different ways of "being" Navajo. However, within this cultural constellation, specific values are maintained. These Navajo beliefs and values surround the young as they learn how and what it means to be Navajo. Although the autonomy of the individual regarding possessions and actions is strongly maintained, consensus and cooperation for the good of the group is emphasized over aggressive individualism.[31]

The insistence on recognizing Navajo cultural allegiance begins at an early age and continues throughout life. Children learn to support and be supported by families. "Like there are all these things we do differently," explained Jan, "but I don't know them all. You learn them when you do something wrong. Then they show you what to do right." These lessons are learned and challenged against a backdrop of an Anglo world. Sometimes these worlds successfully co-exist. Matt, Jan's youngest brother, explained how a Navajo ceremony made things "right." Lightning, which is a powerfully negative force in Navajo beliefs, hit the transformer at the trading post. He continued, "We were afraid we could never drink a coke or get candy from there again! But then they had a medicine man do something and it was okay to eat there again."

Other situations provide challenges to the adherence of Navajo values. Navajos feel it is arrogant to try to control nature by planning every detail in the future. After a counseling session during her senior year, Jan explained, "It's dangerous. You can't change things that happen. That's the way it is. But my counselor said I could change everything by planning on a career. I don't think that would work." Navajos have a more humble view of "individual choice," which acknowledges both the dependence of the individual on the group and the importance of the extended family. When receiving sharply negative comments from an Anglo friend about the crowded living conditions at her home, Jan "turned the lens" and expressed disapproval of the Anglo nuclear family: "The way Whites live seems to be lonely. To live alone is kind of like poverty."

The Navajo depend upon extended family networks of economic and social support, critical factors in their lifestyle. On the reservation, the extended family relies on multiple (often minimum wage) incomes to provide support for the group. Joe's 1990 tax forms claimed twelve dependents supported on a $26,000 salary from a uranium plant. Their new pink, double-wide, three-bedroom trailer houses four daughters, two sons, five grandchildren, and the husbands of two of their daughters. Over the past several years, family members supplemented Joe's income with work in the uranium plant and on road construction crews, and as clerks, waitresses, cooks, motel maids, pottery painters, and temporary tribal employees. Sons and daughters move off the reservation in search of employment, and return when temporary employment ends. The family makes "kneel-down bread" with corn from the garden and sells it at fairs and in town.[32] All who can, work at jobs or at home. Pooled resources buy food, clothing, and necessities, and pay for car and insurance bills.

Along with the economic stability the extended family supplies, there is pressure to place the family ahead of individual prosperity and careers. As an elderly Navajo man said, "You can't get rich if you look after your relatives right. You can't get rich without cheating some people."[33] And as Jan said, "In the traditional way and now, the family is the most important thing you can do. Life is too short to worry about jobs. The family is needed for all those ceremonies." Jobs are seen as a way of earning necessary money, not as a way of life in and of itself.

Navajo families struggle with racial and economic discrimination imposed by their Anglo neighbors at the same time they speak with pride of their "freedom" on the reservation. As Jan's father explained, "We don't have electricity, and we don't have electric bills. We haul water, and we don't have water bills. And out here we don't have to pay for a [trailer] space." Nightly television watching, lights, and the vacuum cleaner only require an adapter and a car battery. Jan's aunt added,

> A medicine man warned us about what happens when you leave. He said, "They educate us to be pawns. We are educated to do a thing, and then we become pawns. Must work for money to pay for the water bills, the electricity. We become pawns." So you see, we have our water, even though we haul it from sixteen miles away, we have our warm house, and our meat, and food from the land. In town we have to pay for these things, and then we become dependent.

A move to the city does not necessarily mean an increase in standard of living or "success." For example, in 1992, Jan and her husband moved to a large city to stay with his relatives and seek employment. After three months with only sporadic employment, they returned to her family. "It was lonely in the city," Jan said. "My mother needed us, her daughters, so we moved back. The family is real important. That is the main thing. You depend on the family to teach each other, and to be brought up right. If it is not the whole family being involved in it, then it is like lack of communication." Jan reminded me of a Navajo insult: "She acts as if she doesn't have any relatives." The individual without family is an isolated and unsatisfied person. This echoes the Fire Chief's plea at the Native American Church meeting: ". . . and then come back home. Then we can be a whole people." Jan has successfully followed this life path. She has settled into rearing her own children in the home of her mother on the Navajo reservation.

Submerged in an Anglo-controlled social landscape that restricts employment opportunities for Navajos, over half of the youth who remain on the reservation try, like Jan, to continue their schooling to enhance their chances for employment. After graduating from high school, almost all of them attend the local community college, their last chance to learn job skills to qualify for local employment. This path, starting with the traditional "Career Day" experienced by most U.S. high school seniors, appears egalitarian in that a multitude of opportunities and choices are "open" to youth after high school. For these Navajo youth, however, the Anglo belief of "equal educational opportunity for all" leading to "equal employment opportunities" is racially restricted. Anglos construct educational "choices" or paths for Navajo youth that lead through a vocationalized curriculum in both high school and college. This path dead ends, however, in the secondary labor market.

Post–high school options offered Navajo youth include a combination of local job ceilings, impersonal universities, and the local community college. Navajo students face a world segmented by unattractive choices with which schools and career counselors never come to grips. Although Navajo youth enter high school with high aspirations about their future opportunities, their future aspirations are thwarted by the racism they experience in school. After high school, Navajo youth face a choice between a university-city route that works against their cultural beliefs, and a local job and school market that is totally subject to the racial struggle in the community.

High School Career Day: Racially Defined Choices

On one of my days of observation, I pulled into the small paved parking lot in front of Navajo High School five minutes before school began. The green athletic field stood in sharp contrast to the red dirt and sandstone bluffs. Sheep grazed on the lush lawn, rubbing against the chain-link fence that separated the school from the surrounding Navajo reservation. As I entered the windowless, one-story, red brick school for another day of fieldwork, I was joined by Vangie, a Navajo friend. "It's career day, so you can come with me, Professor, while I learn about schools!" she exclaimed. The juniors and seniors were excused from classes to attend presentations from seven regional colleges and universities, two vocational or technical schools, and the Job Corps. The Navajo Nation's Education Office had a representative to explain tribal scholarships. Students were to attend four information sessions located throughout the school.

Vangie and I attended two regional college presentations. "Some classes are outside and are so much fun. Then there is the choir. You should take that your first year, it is really fun. And you meet all sorts of nice people," a recruiter said. A professionally developed video accompanied the presentation. The second recruiter also showed a polished, upbeat video with smiling faces, a brief glimpse of a professor lecturing in a large amphitheater, shots of athletic events, tennis courts, and leisurely images of students reading books on rolling campus greens. The recruiter said:

> If you want to be a policeman don't come here. But if you want to go into the computer field, or nursing, or in-flight training, come here. It is beautiful and the campus is lots of fun. You can do all sorts of things while you are in school.

Students talked excitedly about which college would be more fun.

The representative from a local vocational training school slowly went through a slide presentation as he explained the school's program:

> And that girl there, she is working at a real good job in a TV station. And that one, she is underemployed. She could get a real good job if she would leave here! See, in all these pictures we have the old and the totally up-to-date equipment. You never know when you will be working in a small place that has old equipment. So we teach with the old and the new.

Looking at a student audience of only seven Navajo females, he backed up to a previous slide:

> See that computer on that slide. If you are going to work in a big office, you have to learn about computers. And then we have a heavy equipment program. We could use more girls. Because of the Equal Opportunity Program, we could place forty girls a year if they completed the program.

The students were quiet and attentive.

We stopped in the library to look at the literature brought by the local community college. District school staff were discussing with the dean of the college their success in sending many of the Navajo youth away to school after graduation. One of the counselors said, "Over 60 percent of the graduating class got accepted to college. Some went to the Job Corps. One year later they are all back. Every one of them!" The Dean of the local community college explained:

> We don't recruit our students. They come to us. Many of the Indian students go to large universities and they fail. Then they come to us. After they have been with us, they all — 100 percent who go to larger colleges — will succeed. If we recruited them to start with us, they might think they have missed something. They can get what they need here.

The booth was full of pictures of Navajo students sitting at computers, building houses, working in hospitals, and sitting in lectures. The recruiter was the only Navajo on the professional staff at the college. Raised by a Mormon family, he had recently returned to work at the college.[34] He spoke softly to several Navajo students. "You can get a good education here. And your Pell Grant will pay for everything. It's close to home so your parents can watch you girls!" They laughed and moved on to examine the pamphlets in the Job Corps booth.

The last presentation was by the state's largest university, my employer. Two student recruiters stood in front of the small group and emphasized the importance of filling out the applications correctly and getting financial aid forms into the university on time. "It is very important that you do things on time and correctly. It is a huge university. But we also have support for minority students and we want you to seriously consider coming to the university." The presentation continued with a list of the academic fields offered by the university and the statement, "The classes may be hard, but they are real interesting. And you can get a good education at our university." The presentation was dry, the "fun" of college life was presented as "getting an education," and the recruiters did not smile.

After these presentations, students moved into the auditorium for two films by the College Board on financial aid. Students filled the room, talking about the sessions they had attended, graduation plans, their personal relationships, and after-school activities. The first film pictured an African American man, one of several individuals interviewed who had "made it." He urged others to attend college. "Anyone can go to college. It is worth it. A small sacrifice now to have the money to go to college. But it is worth it. I am glad I went." The second film, a cartoon on how to correctly fill out financial aid forms, covered topics from estimating summer earnings to who in the household was the legal "provider." Students were bored and restless with the films and cheered when the lights came on, and then left for lunch. A counselor spoke to me as we were leaving the auditorium:

> We are the ones that fill out the forms. The students don't do it. About half will go on to some kind of school and almost all of them will be on financial aid grants. And the other half will sit out on the reservation and do nothing.

We left school early. As I was driving Vangie, her brother Sam, and several of their friends home, the conversation turned to what they were going to do after graduation. "I'm thinking about going to Dartmouth. They have a special Indian program. But I don't know if I want to be so far away from home. I might go into the Army. They will pay for my college." Another said, "I'll probably end up with a baby and be stuck here." She laughed, "I really want a baby of my own. I would be really happy, then, at home with my baby. That's what us Navajo do." Vangie jumped into the conversation. "There are a lot of girls that get pregnant. I'm just not going to do it. It will ruin your life if you have a baby. I want to go to college and get away from here so I can get a good job!" One said, "My parents tell me to do what I feel I want to do. I want to go to college. I hear college is a lot of fun. I want to have a business or something and come back to the reservation to live and help my people. I go crazy about thinking about taking care of my parents in the future." Another, who had been silent, softly spoke, "I want to be a race car driver. But my mom thinks it's too dangerous. So I guess I can be a secretary or nurse. She wants me to have a good job like a secretary or something and live at home." Vangie and Sam's home was the last stop. As they climbed out of my car, Sam teased his sister, "I'm not going to have a baby either! At least till I get married and have a job."

Educational and Economic Marginalization

The images shown during Career Day of youth lounging on green fields, smiling faces in a choir, a class, using computers, and laboratories, filled the picture window of opportunities facing youth beyond high school. Few Navajo youth will realize the life depicted in these tableaux. Their dreams of a wide range of occupational choices and jobs in distant big cities dim with the reality of their limited academic skills, which relegate them to semi-skilled jobs. High school career days present hollow images for Sam and most of his peers, who do not face "unlimited" opportunities dependent only on individual achievement, but rather a set of political, economic, and social constraints that intertwine in schools and communities to limit their possibilities. Economic disparity is maintained by the continued role of vocational education in local schools and colleges as one aspect of an ongoing racist strategy to limit the opportunities of Navajo and secure opportunities for Anglos. Navajo youth are trained to remain below the job ceiling.

Sam's experiences, which follow in this section, mirror that of many Navajo youth. Sam and Vangie have ten brothers and sisters. They live on the reservation ten miles from the bus stop in a complex that includes eighteen relatives, a new government home, an older stone home, traditional *hogans*, and a satellite dish. They haul their water from a well six miles away, but have electricity from a nearby oil rig. Shortly before graduation in 1989, while flying kites near their home, Sam talked about what he wanted to do with his life: "I want to go into business or finance. Or maybe electronic engineering. Or maybe the military. I would like to go to Berkeley, in California, but I will need a tribal scholarship. I am working on getting my grades up." He had a 2.1 grade point average. Navajo tribal scholarships require a 3.5, a goal he did not reach. The rhythmic whishing of the oil pump was the only sound on the mesa. Sam proudly pointed out the canyon where their livestock grazed and to the far mountains where his father was born. "I have relatives up there that I don't even know. I would like to come back here to live on the reservation. It would be all right. But they say that it is better to get off the reservation to get jobs." His brother was an example. "My brother, he travels all over the world with his job. He works with computers." But there remains the pull of home. "There are not many jobs here. But I like it here. It is home for us Navajo."

Students' experiences in and out of school modify their expectations about future job possibilities. For the Anglo students, future possibilities increase as students approach graduation. Navajo youths' aspirations, on the other hand, are greater than the future envisioned for them by the schools. After four years in high school, their aspirations often match the vocational orientation constructed by their schools. Even though Sam intended to go to college, with the help of a counselor, he filled his senior year schedule with basic and vocational level classes. The counselor explained:

> We are not supposed to track kids, it is against the law. But by the time these kids are in high school they know what they are going to do. So we have most of our Indian students in vocational classes. After all, most won't go to college anyway.

The assumption that Navajo youth knew they wanted a future in vocational jobs early in high school was not supported by my data. During the 1987–1988 school year, 132 Anglo and Navajo students in grades nine through twelve completed the JOBO, a career inventory test that translated student "interest" into job fields. Although 20 percent of the Navajo ninth-graders indicated interest in professional careers requiring college, twice as many Anglo ninth-graders saw their future jobs as being in professional fields. The reverse was true regarding vocational, semiskilled jobs. Almost half, 47 percent, of the Navajo ninth-graders were interested in such jobs, whereas only 30 percent of the Anglo students saw vocational jobs as part of their desired future. This pattern changed by the twelfth grade. The Anglo students desiring vocational jobs dropped by half, from 30 percent to 15 percent, and over 60 percent now desired professional careers. Just the opposite occurred with the Navajo seniors: 62 percent of these students had readjusted their goals downward, towards vocational jobs, and only 15 percent remained determined to achieve professional careers. These figures must be viewed against the backdrop of the dropout rate: by their senior year, close to 40 percent of Navajo youth had already left school — leaving behind the most academically successful Navajo youth.

Navajo culture and local employment opportunities are used by the Anglo educators as a rationale to limit Navajo students' educational opportunities, while, in reality, a vocational curriculum assures the continuity of the local job ceiling for Navajos. The principal at Sam's high school explained the school's vocational orientation:

> I'm interested in equal educational opportunity. I have been here for ten years. We used to be 75 percent academic and 25 percent vocational. Now we have 75 percent vocational and 25 percent academic. We need to recognize the needs of the people in this local area. I'm not saying we should ignore the academic classes. But the vocational training is where the jobs are for the local Navajo people.

His vice principal added:

> Academics are very important in this world, but we've got to realize that half the kids or more out of this high school are not going into academic jobs. They are going to go into vocational. In fact, the majority of jobs in the future are still going to be vocational. They're not going to be in the white-collar type job. But how do you tell them that?

In 1990, the district received a $3.5 million grant to construct a vocational career center. In an open letter to the community, an administrator explained the new thrust of the school district into technology and job preparation. Citing a state statistic that 40 percent of youth finish college or university training when only 20 percent of the available jobs require a four-year degree, he told of the shock facing graduates who have to be retrained in vocational and technical areas. "Since only 20 percent of the jobs in Utah will require a college degree, the secondary schools must take a more active role in preparing students for employment." He explained the necessity for the curriculum to be responsive to employers' needs:

> This concept does not mean a lowering of academic standards; to the contrary, most technical jobs now require a strong background in math, physics, and language. Nor does this concept infer that all students should know a specific vocational skill prior to leaving high school. The jobs in our society are changing so rapidly that students will be much better served if they develop certain basic skills and attitudes toward work. Most employers now prefer to train their own employees in specific skill areas. What they want from high schools are students with basic understandings of technology, good basic academic skills, and the flexibility to be retrained as often as the job market requires.

This emphasis in high schools sets the stage for focusing the educational careers of Navajo youth onto vocational paths. The district's "state of the art" vocational school is Navajo High School; the predominantly Anglo high school in the northern part of the district remains college preparatory. This assures college-educated Anglo youth a brighter job future in the community.[35] The administrator's state statistic that 40 percent of youth finish college or university reflects the 97 percent Anglo population of the state, not the local Navajo population served by the district. Almost half of the Navajo youth from the local school district attempt some kind of post–high school education. Out of one thousand youth, one-third eventually attend the local community college, 6 percent attend universities, and 7 percent attend vocational institutions. Regardless of these efforts, less than one-half of 1 percent complete a four-year degree, only 2 percent complete two-year degrees, and 5 percent receive a vocational certificate. None of the youth who attend the community college go on to finish a four-year degree. Over 90 percent of the Navajo youth do not receive a degree higher than their high school diploma. Sam and his friends are in this group.

Sam graduated in 1989 from Navajo High School. During his senior year, he fluctuated among wanting to study business or finance, joining the military, or wanting to go to technical school to learn electronics. He decided to go to the city to hunt for a job. Off the reservation, Navajo family networks are utilized for economic support — both for the family left behind and the person moving to the city. Youth who leave for the city do so only if there is a relative who can assist with housing and the location of a job. The housing tends to be low-income and jobs are usually minimum-wage labor in fast food restaurants, motels, and factories. During the two years following high school, Sam worked at an airplane parts factory in Salt Lake City and did construction work in Phoenix. He lived with relatives in both cities. Back on the reservation to visit his family, he stopped by my house:

> It has been two years since I graduated and I haven't gotten it together to go to college. And now my younger brother is already up at the university ahead of me! I would like to come back here to live on the reservation. It would be all right. But they say that it is better to get off the reservation to get jobs. That's what I did. There are not many jobs here. But I like it here. It is my home. And the air is clear.

Sam stayed on the reservation. He enrolled in the community college in a program that promised good local employment. "It's for electronics. Job Services and the college are running it. I will be able to get a good job with the certificate."

The two-year community college Sam attended is where most Navajos finish their time in higher education. The creation of this community college ten years ago has been an economic boom for the local Anglo community, whose members occupy all of the teaching positions and 99 percent of the administrative and support staff. The college is supported, due to its two-thirds Navajo student population, by federal tuition grants targeted for "disadvantaged" youth and from the Navajos' own oil royalties money.[36]

One Navajo high school counselor explained, "The college comes with scholarship money and says they [youth] can come to the college free. Many don't know about other places. And they need the money to go. And the college needs them to survive." Last year the community college established a scholarship fund for all county residents, using $500,000 from Navajo royalty money to establish matching funds from the state.[37] Prior to this, Navajo students could use their scholarships to attend the college of their choice. Now, under the guidelines of the new scholarship fund, all scholarships are limited to attendance at the local college. By putting these stipulations on the funding, the community college has insured middle-class jobs for the Anglos and vocational training for jobs that do not exist for Navajos.

As in high school, Navajo youth at the community college are encouraged to seek terminal degrees in vocational areas. As the academic dean explained, "We have looked into the economic development of the next decade and it is in the service industry. Our students want to stay in this community and these are where the jobs will be." I argued for encouraging more students to go for four-year professional degrees, reminding him that the better jobs in the county required a college degree. He argued, "Most of the jobs here are in the service industry. We are happy if we can keep a Navajo student for a one-year program. That is success." The mission statement of the college supported his emphasis. Only its concluding goal mentioned preparing students to go on to four-year institutions.[38]

The college has a large vocational program. During the 1992 winter quarter, out of almost one hundred courses offered, two-thirds were in vocational or technical areas. Certificates of Completion, requiring one year of study, are offered in accounting, auto mechanics, general clerical, secretarial occupations, office systems, practical nursing (LPN), stenography, and welding. In addition to these specialties available to all its students, the college offers special vocational programs for Navajo students that are cosponsored by the Navajo tribe. Designed to fill immediate job needs, these latter certificates are offered in marina hospitality training, needle trades (sewing), building trades, sales personnel training for supermarket employment, security officers, building maintenance training, pottery trades, modern office occupations, restaurant management, and truck driving. These latter "Navajo only" certificates are designed to prepare students for local employment. An instructor explained, "These programs are designed to prepare the student for good jobs that are out there. They are extensive, lasting for three quarters. One quarter they are prepared with communication skills. And then how to get along with their bosses. It is the general social skills, work skills, and the particular skills for the job."[39] These programs are not without criticism. Another instructor explained:

> We trained forty or fifty people at a time to run cash registers. That's good. But how many stores around here are going to hire all those people? They're training for limited jobs. Why send everybody to carpenter's school? In this small area we have tons of carpenters. Why teach them all welding? You can do it at home, but how many welders are there in this area? Probably every other person is a welder.

During the last decade at this community college, 95 percent of the vocational certificates were earned by Navajo youth and adults. Even this training, however, did not necessarily result in a job. The Dean of the college explained: "Our marina hospitality program was a good one. And it was going to get a lot of Navajo jobs. The tribe had built a new marina and the tourist dollars were going to be good. But then they had the flood. It wiped out the marina. It hasn't been built again. So all those people, almost one hundred, were trained for jobs that never happened." And then there was the needle trades program. "We trained twenty-four women, but there weren't many jobs. The one sewing factory closed down. The other only hired a few." The employment results from the truck driver program were minimal. "We trained over thirty for that program. The uranium tailings over on the reservation were supposed to be hauled away, so we trained truck drivers. It's still in the courts and so no one was hired. We could have gotten them good jobs in other states, like Oklahoma, but they didn't want to leave the reservation." And the largest program, sales personnel, a joint effort of business, the tribe, and the college, placed students in local supermarkets for "on-the-job training" with the understanding that they would receive employment after completing the program. The supermarkets supervised the student trainees for three months while they learned job-required skills, such as boxing, shelf stocking, and check-out packing:

> We had a real good success with this one. A lot of our students were working in the supermarkets in towns. But then there were problems with the supermarkets not hiring them after the training. Cutbacks, you know. But some people thought they were just using the Navajo students for cheap labor. And then they didn't hire them.

Some vocational training programs lead to jobs. Most do not.

After completing the one-year certificate in electronics, Sam found a job — at a factory in the city. Again, he left the reservation. After eighteen months, he was laid off. In 1993, he returned to his home, this time with a wife and child. Sam said, "I'll find something around here, or we will try the city again. Right now I have things to do at home. My parents need help, after my sister died in the car accident, so I need to be here. I have things to do, you know. My younger sister is going to have her *Kinaalda* and the wood has to be gathered. I can get a job around here." After six months without a job, he enrolled at the community college again. He is studying building trades in a community that saw a 9 percent reduction in the construction industry in 1992.

The only successful job networks Navajo youth have are through their parents or relatives, which are for low-level jobs. Mothers grew up working in the local restaurants and school cafeterias, or as maids in the three local motels. Fathers worked at temporary construction jobs, and in the local oil and uranium fields. Sons and daughters have access into the same lines of employment, especially when the training paths available to them in high school and at the community college limit them to these kinds of jobs.[40] If they remain in their home community (as most do), even Navajo youth with a high school diploma face a future of semi-skilled jobs, training programs, and seasonal work, mirroring the lives of their parents.

High school graduates are twice as likely to have jobs as those who do not finish school.[41] On the surface, this seems like an incentive for youth to finish high school. However, there is little difference in the *kinds* of jobs held by graduates and non-graduates. With rare exceptions, both groups of employed youth work at the same kinds of service industry jobs characterized by low pay with few or no benefits, seasonal employment, and a highly transitional work force: cooks, motel maids, school aides, bus drivers, tour guides, making or painting pottery, clerical workers, electrical assistants, janitors, waitresses, seamstresses, the military, uranium and oil workers, and construction. Working at the same job alongside peers who dropped out of school, many Navajo youths question the relevance of their high school and college diplomas. At the very least, Navajo youth see a successful academic effort paying off less for them than for their Anglo peers. On the one hand, leaving school is not the route most youth choose, as it affects their chances for employment, and completing school is a goal encouraged by their families and the community. On the other hand, they are acutely aware that completing school does not guarantee employment at other than menial jobs. The Navajo youths mentioned at the beginning of this article who disagreed with their shop teacher about the limited job opportunities facing them after high school clearly understood this dilemma.

Regardless of school success or failure, after high school, all of these youth face the same structural barriers in the community because they are Navajo. Here, Ogbu's model partly explains this situation. He argues that the existence of a "job ceiling," intertwined with a "rejection" of the Anglo world, mediates against school success for some castelike minorities. Ogbu states:

> Members of a castelike minority group generally have limited access to the social goods of society by virtue of their group membership and not because they lack training and ability or education. In particular, they face a job ceiling — that is highly consistent pressures and obstacles that selectively assign blacks and similar minority groups to jobs at the lowest level of status, power, dignity, and income while allowing members of the dominant white group to compete more easily for more desirable jobs above that ceiling.[42]

Ogbu implies that the job ceiling affects student attitudes towards school and that vocational tracking is the school's adaptation to the job market. A picture of the economic landscape of the community illustrates the racial stratification that frames the employment possibilities of Navajo youth like Sharon, Jan, and Sam. Although American Indians comprise over half of the local population, they are marginalized to either low-paying jobs or no jobs.[43] The unemployment rate for Indians, 41 percent, is over four times the unemployment rate for Anglos. A breakdown of the jobs in the county by occupation illustrates the different opportunity structures faced by Anglo and American Indian workers. Over 90 percent of official and management jobs are held by Anglos. Only 8 percent of these top-level jobs are held by American Indians. In other professional positions, Anglos hold over two-thirds of the jobs. Twenty-five percent of all jobs in the county are classified in these two management and professional categories, but few American Indians make it into these powerful positions. In other areas, Anglos occupy almost 90 percent of the jobs as technicians, 91 percent of the sales workers, 80 percent of office and clerical workers, and 63 percent of the skilled craft workers. American Indians are employed in the service-maintenance and the construction trades, and as laborers and paraprofessionals. All of the assemblers and hand-working jobs, 75 percent of non-precision machine operators, 50 percent of construction, 61 percent of cleaning and building services, 50 percent of laborers, and 47 percent of food preparation and service jobs are held by American Indians. This job ceiling is faced by all Navajo youth — dropouts, graduates, and community college students.

The Navajo in this community experience a racially defined job ceiling, but student attitudes toward the job ceiling do not result in the rejection of schooling or of the Anglo world. Rather, Navajo reject assimilation as a path they must follow in order to be defined as "successful." Navajo students on the reservation, where there are fewer jobs than in town, are more successful in school, even though they are acutely aware of their limited economic opportunities in the community. Historical experiences and the job ceiling alone do not explain how Navajo youth respond to school; rather, their response to school is mediated by culture, especially the cultural integrity of the group.

Regardless of students' "cultural stance" (degree of acculturation or assimilation), a key factor in the relationship between schools and students seems to be what schools *do* to students — successful students are still limited by the *quality* of their schooling experience. In viewing schools as sites of conflict, vocational tracking is one part of the racial struggle in this community.

Navajo students are counseled into vocational classes in high school, limiting their access to college preparatory classes. By the time these youth leave high school, their "academic fate" is assured. Almost half of them try schools away from the area, but with minimal academic skills and limited economic resources, they drop out and return home. They then move into the "arms" of the community college to complete the education they will "need" to live, training locally for semi-skilled jobs.[44] Ironically, Navajo youths' failure to succeed educationally "outside" actually enhances the local Anglo economic power base by assuring the continuity of the community college.

Navajo youth are encouraged to leave the area for "good" jobs, which in turn also fits with the Anglos' interest in maintaining good local jobs for their group. Many Navajos work in factories in cities for a while, but, separated from their families, they remain detached, isolated, and poor. Most return home and seek whatever paying job they can find. Unlike middle-class youth, who attach their self-image to the kinds of job they strive for, these Navajo youth view a job as a means of making money, which is necessary for survival. The kind of job they work at does not define their "goodness." That is defined by their family relationships. As Paul Willis argues, the concept of "job choice," from semiskilled to professional jobs, is a middle-class construct.[45] Some people get "jobs," others have "careers." Structural and economic determinants restrict individual alternatives, but choices are made among the remaining possible choices. Navajo youth seek whatever jobs are available to them in their community. In doing so, they support their families with an income and secure the continuity of Navajo culture.

Regardless of the dismal job ceiling, Navajos are persistent in their schooling efforts to enhance their employability. Navajo men and women who do hold the credentials necessary for better jobs are increasingly competitive for these positions. Almost without exception, these educational credentials are earned at schools outside of the county. These few hold positions as teachers, social workers, health care providers, and administrators for tribal and county programs. Without these credentials, however, Navajo people are guaranteed to lack qualifications for positions of leadership and power in the community — a community that has always been their "home" and where most of them will live their lives.

Navajo Lives: Cultural Integrity

Navajos are treated differently from Anglos in this community's educational and economic institutions. However, as John Ogbu, Margaret Eisenhart and M. Elizabeth Grauer, and Margaret Gibson have pointed out, there is intragroup variability in responses to schooling within each minority group.[46] The Navajos are no exception. Clearly, Navajo youth are not homogeneous in their responses to schooling. Some, like Sharon, Jan, and Sam, follow paths that Gibson calls "accommodation without assimilation" and that Ogbu calls an "alternative strategy or the immigrant strategy," even though they are from a "castelike" group. They are successful in the educational system, even though this does not necessarily translate into economic stability. At the same time, they insist on maintaining their place as Navajos within the community. By refusing to accept either assimilation or rejection, these youth force us to look at new ways of viewing success. The school success of these Navajo students, with strong traditions intact, is explained, in part, by a model of "cultural integrity." Supported by a solid cultural foundation, they resist by moving through high school as a short "interruption" in their progression to lives as adult Navajo men and women. For them, high school is something one tolerates and sometimes enjoys; school success does not pose a serious threat to their cultural identity. What is clear from the lives of these Navajo youth, however, is that rather than attempting to erase Native culture and language, schools should do everything in their power to use, affirm, and maintain these if they truly want to achieve equity and promote Navajo students' academic success.

Even though Navajo youth develop a variety of responses to their schooling experiences, what is significant is that the school system issues a homogeneous institutional response to the Navajo youth, regardless of their "good" or "bad" student status. Focusing on student behaviors and their values towards school must be coupled with what schools *do* to these students, such as subjecting them to racial humiliation and vocational tracking. As I have illustrated in this article, the school context and curriculum are not neutral. Racism frames the stage and remains a barrier for all Navajo youth, regardless of their academic success or social compliance. Ironically, academic achievement under these conditions is questionable because of the watered-down curriculum and the persistent discrimination in the job market. This suggests that school reform and changes in the job market must be connected in order to talk about educational success in a meaningful way.

In looking at the variability of Navajo youths' responses to education and the homogeneity of Anglo responses, "cultural identity" is used by both to establish cultural boundaries and borders.[47] Cultural boundaries can be thought of as behavioral evidence of different cultural standards of appropriateness. These can be manifested in different speech patterns, child-rearing practices, and learning styles. The presence of these cultural differences, by themselves, is a politically neutral phenomenon. Navajo youth, securely rooted in their culture, move back and forth between their community and the surrounding

Anglo community. The cultural framework surrounding Navajo youth, unlike secondary cultural differences, did not initially arise to maintain boundaries and to provide the ability to cope with Anglo subordination. Cultural boundaries, however, are often turned into cultural borders or barriers during intergroup conflict. In this situation, cultural differences become politically charged when rights and obligations are allocated differently. The Anglo community uses Navajo culture as a border, a reason to deny equality by claiming the privilege of one kind of knowledge over another. Navajo families are judged by what they don't have — money, middle-class Anglo values, higher education, and professional jobs — rather than by what they do have — extended families, permanent homes, strong Navajo values and religious beliefs.

Remaining Navajo is a desired goal, not one settled on by default. Life in homes on the reservation, surrounded by family, friends, and similar "others," is a sound choice for youth, with or without school credentials. The choice to remain on the reservation represents failed attempts to find security and happiness in towns and cities amid racial isolation and under- or unemployment. This choice also represents an ethical commitment and valuing of families and Navajo traditions. The Navajo community provides a place of social acceptance and economic survival unavailable in Anglo-dominated communities off the reservation. This choice, however, situates Navajo youth within a local Anglo community structure that dismisses their lives and limits their educational and economic opportunities.

Cultural and racial differences serve both as reasons used by the Anglo community to deny equal educational or economic opportunity to Navajos and as a means Navajos use to resist cultural homogeneity. Jan, Sharon, and Sam chose a "boundary" strategy, resisting assimilation by maintaining pride in their culture and language, which led them successfully through school. They followed the "rules of the game," even though they knew they faced a "stacked deck." This path, fraught with conflict, uncertainty, and pain, was not easy. For some Navajo youth, however, boundaries become borders. A few cross over and leave their families and lives on the reservation. Most, however, choose their families and Navajo traditions over the illusory promises of wealth in the larger society. As Jan said earlier in this article, "They [parents] tell us to do good in school, but that we will always be Navajo." This choice assures the continuity of the Navajo people, and answers the plea expressed in the NAC meeting: "They need to bring their education back here to the reservation, their home. Then we can be a whole people."

Notes

1. In this article, I use pseudonyms for the schools and the individuals who participated in my research.
2. Although somewhat contested as a term that attempts to represent all majority people, I use the term "Anglo" as it is used by the Navajos in this community, as a political category that unifies all White people.

3. "Border" refers to the economic, social, and political marginalization of the Navajo. It also describes the literal "border" of the reservation community, which is divided geographically by a river. Most of the Anglos live in the North and almost all Navajo live in the South.
4. Murray Wax, Rosalie Wax, and Robert Dumont, *Formal Education in an American Indian Community* (Prospect Heights, IL: Waveland Press, 1989). The original study was published in 1964 by another publisher.
5. I shared my research with LDS and non-LDS Anglos. They also helped me correct my understandings of the Mormon Church.
6. For a more detailed analysis of my fieldwork relations, see D. Deyhle, G. A. Hess, and M. LeCompte, "Approaching Ethical Issues for Qualitative Researchers in Education," in *Handbook of Qualitative Research,* ed. M. LeCompte, W. Millroy, and J. Preissle (San Diego: Academic Press, 1992); Donna Deyhle, "The Role of the Applied Anthropologist: Between Schools and the Navajo Nation," in Kathleen Bennett deMarrais, *Inside Stories: Qualitative Research Reflections* (Mahwah, NJ: Lawrence Erlbaum Associates, 1998).
7. See Frederick Erickson, "Transformation and School Success: The Politics and Culture of Educational Achievement," *Anthropology & Education Quarterly, 18* (1987), 335–356; John Ogbu, "Variability in Minority School Performance: A Problem in Search of an Explanation," *Anthropology & Education Quarterly, 18* (1987), 312–334; and Henry T. Trueba, "Culturally Based Explanations of Minority Students' Academic Achievement," *Anthropology & Education Quarterly, 19* (1988), 270–287, for debates on these positions.
8. Jim Cummins, "Empowering Minority Students: A Framework for Intervention," *Harvard Educational Review, 56* (1986), 18–36.
9. John Ogbu, *Minority Education and Caste: The American System in Cross-Cultural Perspective* (New York: Academic Press, 1978).
10. Ogbu, *Minority Education and Caste.*
11. Cummins, "Empowering Minority Students," p. 22.
12. Cummins, "Empowering Minority Students," p. 22.
13. DNA is short for *Dinebeiina Nahiilna be Agadithe,* which translates to English as "people who talk fast to help people out." The DNA is a legal service that provides free legal counsel to low-income Navajos.
14. Racial issues in the county are made more complex by the relationship between the dominant religion, The Church of Latter Day Saints (LDS), or Mormons, and non-Mormons. A majority of the Anglos in the county are Mormons. A majority of the Navajos were either traditionalists or members of the Native American Church. The LDS church teaches that American Indians are "Lamanites," descendants of Laman, Lemuel, and others who, having emigrated to the Americas, rejected the gospel. Righteous groups are White, while those who had rejected the covenants they had made with God received a "sore cursing," even "a skin of blackness . . . that their seed might be distinguished from the seed of their brethren" (*Book of Mormon, 2,* Nephi. 5:21; Alma 3:14). Converting back to the gospel results in the "scales of darkness" falling from Lamanites' eyes and a return to a "white and delightsome" being.
15. For an analysis of the relationship between Mormons and American Indians, see Mark P. Leone, *Roots of Modern Mormonism* (Cambridge: Harvard University Press, 1979); Dan Vogel, *Indian Origins and the Book of Mormon* (Signature Books, 1986); and Wallace Stegner, *Mormon Country* (Lincoln: University of Nebraska Press, 1970).
16. The Anglo population in this county arrived in the 1800s as pioneers from the Church of Jesus Christ of Latter Day Saints (Mormons). Sent by Brigham Young, the 236 settlers were to start a colonizing mission among Navajos and to increase the land base and religious influence of the LDS church throughout the region. From the be-

ginning, cloaked within the assimilationist philosophy of the LDS church, the Mormons dismissed Indians' claims to political and cultural sovereignty.
17. I determined the graduation and dropout rates in this community by following "cohorts" of Navajo youth throughout their school careers. A total of 629 students forming six different cohorts from two schools, from the class of 1984 to the class of 1989, are represented with complete four-year high school records. Combining the data from both schools revealed that 59 percent graduated through either traditional or nontraditional means, 34 percent left school, and 7 percent remained "unknown." The graduation rate of 59 percent is lowered to 49 percent when reporting only students who graduated on time in the traditional high school program. Over half, 55 percent, of the youth that dropped out did so during the twelfth grade.
18. This was based on the *Lau v. Nichols* court decision, which mandated that school districts test and provide special English instruction to non-native English speakers. See, for example, Courtney B. Cazden and Ellen L. Leggett, "Culturally Responsive Education: Recommendations for Achieving Lau Remedies II," in *Culture and the Bilingual Classroom*, ed. Henry T. Trueba, Grace Pung Guthrie, and Kathryn Hu-Pei Au (Rowley, MA: Newbury House, 1981), pp. 69–86, for the educational implications of this court decision.
19. See, for example, Margaret C. Szasz, *Education and the American Indian: The Road to Self-Determination Since 1928* (Albuquerque: University of New Mexico Press, 1977); Gloria Emerson, "Navajo Education," in *Handbook of North American Indians, 10,* ed. Alfonso Ortiz (Washington, DC: Smithsonian Institution, 1983), pp. 659–671; and Estelle Fuch and Robert Havighurst, *To Live on This Earth: American Indian Education* (Albuquerque: University of New Mexico Press, 1972).
20. Robert A. Trennert Jr., *The Phoenix Indian School: Forced Assimilation in Arizona, 1891–1935* (Norman: University of Oklahoma Press, 1988).
21. Navajo medicine men and women are regarded as the most powerful people within Navajo culture. One studies to obtain the knowledge and practices throughout a lifetime, as all of Navajo beliefs about their origin, and reasons and ways to live one's life are intertwined with ceremonies to "balance" and guide themselves for a healthy life. The medicine men and women are the mediators between the beliefs of a tradition and personal health. In addition to conducting large-scale religious ceremonies, such as the Enemy Way, Navajo medicine men and women perform traditional weddings and *Kinaaldas,* as well as being called upon by families for curing illnesses that range from headaches and nightmares to cancer and diabetes. Most Navajo use the services of both traditional medicine men and women and Western trained medical doctors. See, for an example, Clyde Kluckhohn and Dorothea Leighton, *The Navajo* (Cambridge: Harvard University Press, 1974); Gladys Reichard, *Navaho Religion* (Tucson: University of Arizona Press, 1983); and Leland C. Wyman, "Navajo Ceremonial System," in *Handbook of North American Indians, 10,* ed. Alfonso Ortiz (Washington, DC: Smithsonian Institution, 1983), pp. 536–557.
22. Cummins, "Empowering Minority Students," p. 25.
23. U.S. Department of Education, *State Education Statistics* (Washington, DC: U.S. Department of Education, January 1984 and January 1986).
24. The situation has worsened. The dropout rate among Navajo students has increased over the past five years. Although the combined cohort rate at BHS shows only a dropout average of 41 percent, 75 percent of the 1991 class at Border High School did not graduate. In 1991, the district reported that the dropout rate for Navajo students was five times higher than for Anglo students; 80 percent of the dropouts were Navajos.
25. The Native American Church, commonly referred to as the Peyote religion, is a pan-Indian, semi-Christian, nativistic religious movement in the course of whose ritual believers eat the Peyote cactus, a substance containing more than 10 alkaloids, the best

known of which is mescaline. It is pan-Indian in the sense that its ideology emphasizes the unity of Indians and their distinctness from Whites. Its origins are traced to the Plains Indian nativistic religious movements at the turn of the century. It was introduced to the Navajo by the Ute, their neighbors to the north of the reservation. See David Aberle, *The Peyote Religion among the Navajo* (Chicago: University of Chicago Press, 1982). Peyote meetings are jointly conducted by a Fire Chief and a Roadman.

26. This ideology asserts that the Indian home and the mind of the Indian child is meager, empty, or lacking in pattern. See Wax, Wax, and Dumont, *Formal Education,* for an excellent examination of this ideology. This study of a Sioux community and its school was conducted over thirty years ago; many of these researchers' results were mirrored in this Navajo community.

27. With a Navajo girl's first menses, she becomes a young woman and has a "coming of age" ceremony to usher her into adult society. The chief aim of the four-day ceremony is to impart the physical, moral, and intellectual strength she will need to carry out the duties of a Navajo woman, following the example set by Changing Woman in the creation story. Details of the ceremony are reported by Shirley M. Begay, *Kinaalda: A Navajo Puberty Ceremony* (Rough Rock, AZ: Rough Rock Demonstration School, Navajo Curriculum Center, 1983), and Charlotte J. Frisbe, *Kinaalda: A Study of the Navaho Girl's Puberty Ceremony* (Middletown, CT: Wesleyan University Press, 1964).

28. David L. John, *Navajo Nation Overall Economic Development Plan 1992–93* (Window Rock, AZ: The Navajo Nation, 1992).

29. Both Anglos and Navajos teach at the College. The President and Board are Navajo — this is a strong, Navajo-controlled organization. Navajo philosophy, language, and culture are part of the curriculum. The school is currently working on developing a Navajo teacher-training program.

30. U.S. Commission on Civil Rights, *Indian Tribes: A Continuing Quest for Survival* (Washington, DC: U.S. Government Printing Office, 1981), pp. 32-33.

31. Louise Lamphere, *To Run after Them: Cultural and Social Bases of Cooperation in a Navajo Community* (Tucson: University of Arizona Press, 1977).

32. "Kneel-down" bread is a traditional food of the Navajo. A fist-sized ball of ground corn is wrapped in fresh corn leaves and buried in an underground pit oven. The name comes from the process of having to "kneel down" when putting the bread into the pit.

33. Kluckhohn and Leighton, *The Navajo,* p. 300.

34. In 1954, the LDS Church officially adopted, as part of their missionary activities, the Indian Student Placement Program, in which American Indian children were "adopted" by a Mormon family. American Indian youth lived with foster families during the year, went to public schools, and were educated into the LDS Church. Home visits occurred for a few weeks or months during the summer. By 1980, approximately 20,000 Indian students from various tribes had been placed in LDS foster homes. The program is no longer expanding, placing only 1,968 in 1980, and in the future will be focusing on high-school-age children. This program had touched almost all of the Navajo families in this area. In every family, close or distant clan members have experienced LDS foster homes. For some, the experience was positive; for others it was disastrous. See the following for a discussion of this program: J. Neil Birch, "Helen John: The Beginnings of Indian Placement," *Dialogue: A Journal of Mormon Thought, 18* (Winter 1985), 119–129; Lacee A. Harris, "To Be Native American — and Mormon," *Dialogue: A Journal of Mormon Thought, 18* (Winter 1985), 143–152; and M. D. Topper, "Mormon Placement: The Effects of Missionary Foster Families on Navajo Adolescents," *Ethos, 7,* No. 2 (1979), 142–160. There were many reasons for parents to put their children in this program, including the chance for better educational opportunities in the cities, more economic security in White families, and, in situations of extreme poverty, better food.

35. A local county report revealed that two-thirds of the jobs in the county were located in the northern portion of the county, where almost 75 percent of the Anglo population lived. The government ranked as the number one employer, the school district the second, and the county the third. These three provided a total of 750 jobs, or 23 percent of the county's employment. A majority of these jobs required either a college degree or some college education. Specifically, 20 percent of jobs in the state of Utah will require a college degree, 40 percent will require six months to four years post–high school training, and 40 percent will require less than six months of training.
36. In 1933, Congress passed a bill that added this area to the Navajo reservation located in Utah. The bill gave the Navajo people in these areas the right to 37.5 percent of any gas or oil royalties, to be used for tuition for Navajo children, for building or maintaining roads on the lands added to the reservation, and for other benefits for these residents. The state of Utah was the trustee of this trust. In 1956, great quantities of oil were discovered in this area. In lawsuits filed in 1961, 1963, 1977, 1984, and 1987, the Court found in favor of Navajos who claimed the Utah Division of Indian Affairs had failed to comply with the terms of the 1933 Act by using the money for the benefit of non-Navajos. In the most recent lawsuit, in 1992, the Navajos accused the state of breach of trust and breach of fiduciary duties, and are suing to recover millions of dollars lost through this mismanagement. Estimates of how much could be awarded in the case run to more than 50 million dollars.
37. After Navajo complaints of mismanagement, the state attorney general's office audited the trust fund. The audit found a questionable use of funds, including $146,000 to finance the administration building, science building, and dormitories; $35,000 for nursing faculty; and $43,500 for a counselor who administered the scholarship program. The audit questioned using Navajo monies to defray the costs of a state institution.
38. "... the curriculum includes associate degree programs, vocational-technical programs, developmental programs, adult and community education programs and courses which are transferable towards four year degrees."
39. During the 1992 Winter Quarter, this instructor taught twenty-four one- to six-credit cooperative education classes. Each class covered a different subject area, such as anthropology, auto mechanics, geology, drafting, and secretarial work, with a title that included, "Work Experience."
40. Out of two hundred employed graduates from my database, 25 percent of the males were in the military, the National Guard, or the Marines, and 75 percent were in trade types of occupations, particularly construction, welding, electrical, and oilfield work. Most of the women were in traditional low-paying pink collar jobs, such as LPN, office worker, seamstress, pottery painter, and clerk. One woman had a bachelor's degree and was teaching; one other was a supervisor at K-Mart.
41. All the Navajo youth, from the high school classes of 1982 to 1989 in two different schools, were tracked in my database over the past eight years to determine what happened to them after they had graduated or left school. Two-thirds of these youth were successfully located. The percentages given are based on these youth. Out of 732 youth, both graduates and non-graduates, 32 percent were employed, 39 percent were unemployed, and 29 percent were students. Higher employment, lower unemployment, and more student status were revealed by examining the high school graduates separately. Out of 499 graduates, 39 percent were employed, 26 percent unemployed, and 35 percent were students. The image is bleaker when looking at the youth who left school prior to graduation. Of these 233 youth, only 19 percent were employed, 66 percent were unemployed, and 15 percent were students. There were slight gender differences. More men were employed, 37 percent, compared to 27 percent of the women. Close to half, 47 percent, of the women were unemployed,

compared to 34 percent of the men. An equal number of men and women were students. The label "student" is one that needs to be viewed cautiously. Over 80 percent of these were enrolled in the local community college. Many of these youth attended school on a part-time basis, lived at home, and were otherwise unemployed.
42. John Ogbu, "Societal Forces as a Context of Ghetto Children's School Failure," in *The Language of Children Reared in Poverty*, ed. Lynne Feagans and Dale C. Farren (San Diego: Academic Press, 1982), p. 124.
43. In this rural county, existing jobs are limited. The services industry sector (lodging, personal, business, repair, health, and educational services) was the largest contributor of jobs in the county, accounting for 21 percent in 1986. The largest occupational group, representing 36 percent of all jobs in 1986 and 37 percent in 1991, was in production, operations, and maintenance — basically in the blue collar group of occupations. These jobs were concentrated primarily in the goods-producing industries of agriculture, mining, construction, and manufacturing. Second in the number of jobs hierarchy are the professional, paraprofessional, and technical groups, followed by service and clerical occupations. The Utah Department of Employment Security published a projected occupations outlook from 1986 to 1991 specific for this county. The occupations listed as being in demand included: blue collar workers, supervisors, cashiers, combined food preparation and service workers, continuous mining machine operators, conveyor operators and tenders, electricians, underground mining machinery mechanics, maintenance repairers (general utility), roof bolters, secretaries, sewing machine operators, and shuttle car operators. This local profile mirrors that of the state in general. The services and trade industry will account for half of all jobs in Utah by 1991 and will claim 58 percent of all new job growth over the same period. Brad M. McGarry, "Utah's Affirmative Action Information 1987: A Blueprint for Hiring," Utah Department of Employment Security Labor Market Information Services, May 1988; John T. Matthews and Michael B. Sylvester, "Utah Job Outlook: Statewide and Service Delivery Areas 1990-1995," Utah Department of Employment Security Labor Market Information Services, January 1990.
44. For a discussion of how community colleges function to "cool out" students, limiting rather than leading them to professional degrees, see Steven Brint and Jerome Karabel, *The Diverted Dream* (New York: Oxford University Press, 1989); Burton Clark, "The 'Cooling-Out' Function in Higher Education," *American Journal of Sociology, 45* (1960), 569–576; Kevin J. Dougherty, "The Community College at the Crossroads: The Need for Structural Reform," *Harvard Educational Review, 61* (August 1991), 311–336; and W. Norton Grubb, "The Decline of Community College Transfer Rates," *Journal of Higher Education, 62* (March/April 1991), 194–222.
45. Paul Willis, *Learning to Labour* (Westmead, Eng.: Saxon House, 1977).
46. Ogbu, *Minority Education and Caste;* John Ogbu, "Variability in Minority School Performance: A Problem in Search of an Explanation," *Anthropology & Education Quarterly, 18* (1987) 312–334; John Ogbu, "Understanding Cultural Diversity and Learning," *Educational Researcher, 21* (November 1992), 5–14; Margaret A. Eisenhart and M. Elizabeth Grauer, "Constructing Cultural Differences and Educational Achievement in Schools," in *Minority Education: Anthropological Perspectives,* ed. Evelyn Jacob and Cathie Jordan (Norwood, NJ: Ablex, 1993); and Margaret A. Gibson, *Accommodation Without Assimilation: Sikh Immigrants in an American High School* (Ithaca: Cornell University Press, 1988).
47. Erickson, "Transformation and School Success," p. 346.

Although they must remain unnamed, I wish to thank the hundreds of Navajo and Anglo women, men, children, and young adults who have patiently listened to my questions, tirelessly corrected my misconceptions, and honestly tried to teach me about their lives. Without their help this research would not have been possible. I would like to thank Frank Margonis, John Ogbu, Harvey Kanter, Laurence Parker, Beth King, Audrey Thompson, and the members of the Cultural, Critical, and Curriculum Group in the Department of Educational Studies at the University of Utah for their insightful critiques on numerous drafts of this article. I bear sole responsibility, however, for the interpretations presented. I would also like to acknowledge the financial support for this research from the Spencer Foundation and the University of Utah.

Reading the World of School Literacy: Contextualizing the Experience of a Young African American Male

—■-■-■—

ARLETTE INGRAM WILLIS

L et me share a conversation that I had with my nine-year-old son, and the context in which it occurred:

It's a cold, frosty winter morning, and everyone has left for work or school except my youngest son Jake and me. I am busy applying last-minute touches to my makeup and encouraging Jake, in the next room, to "step it up." I wonder why he is dragging around; school starts in ten minutes and we haven't yet left the house. Jake knows the routine; I wonder if something is troubling him. So, I peek around the corner and find him looking forlorn — you know, a scowl on his face, a look of growing despair and sadness. I forget about the clock and attend to him.

"Jake, what's wrong? Why are you so unhappy?" I ask.

"We have the Young Authors [writing] Contest today, and I don't have anything to write about."

"Sure you do. There are lots of things you can write about," I encourage him. (I believe people write best about those subjects they know and care about.) "Why don't you write about baseball or soccer?"

"No," he replies. "A kid at our school wrote about cancer last year, and the story went all the way to the next state [regionals]."

"Well," I answer, "maybe you should write about something funny — like when you go to the barbershop. You and your brothers are always talking about your trips there."[1]

"Oh no, Mom, they wouldn't understand. When I just get my haircut, they always ask me, 'Why do you have that line in your hair?' 'It's not a line, it's a part,' I try to tell them. I can't write about the barbershop. They won't understand."

"Well," I say, trying to clarify what I really mean, "I don't mean write about getting a haircut. I mean writing about all the funny people that come in and the things that happen while you are at the barbershop. You and your brothers always come home tellin' a funny story and laugh about it for the rest of the week. That's what I mean by writing about the barbershop."

"No, Mom. They won't understand," he insists.

"What do you mean, 'they won't understand?' Who is this 'they'?" I ask.

"The people in my class," he replies, somewhat frustrated.

Jake continues, "You should read this story that M. wrote. It is a mystery story and it's really good. I can't beat that story. I'll bring you a copy of it if I can. I know it will win." (Sadder now that he has had time to consider his competition, Jake turns and walks toward his room.)

Wanting him to participate in the contest, I ask, "How do you know M.'s story is good?"

"She read it in class. Everybody said it's really good," he responds.

"Well, I still think you should try. You are a really good writer. Look at all the 'good stuff' you wrote in Mrs. S.'s room. You could rewrite some of it and turn it in."

Finally he answers, "I'll think about it," and we go off to school.

As I remember the conversation, Jake's tone of voice hinted at both frustration and defensiveness. I interpreted his use of phrases like "they always ask" and "I try to tell them" to mean that since he gets his hair cut every two weeks, it gets pretty tiresome answering the same questions from his classmates so frequently.[2] Furthermore, I interpreted his intonation to mean that he has had to stand his ground with other children who either do not agree with his definition of a "part," or who try to define its meaning for him.

I believe that Jake cannot bring this aspect of his life and culture into the classroom because he doesn't feel that it will be understood by his classmates and teacher. When Jake says "They won't understand," I interpret his words to mean that if his classmates cannot understand the simplest action in getting a haircut — the barber taking less than ten seconds to place a part in his hair — how can he expect them to understand the context and culture that surround the entire event. Also, I see Jake's reluctance to share something as commonplace in his home and community life as a haircut as a way of distancing this portion of his life from the life he leads at school. It seems that he has come to understand that as an African American he must constantly make a mediating effort to help others understand events that appear to be commonplace on the surface, but are in fact culturally defined.

Several interwoven incidents have helped me to understand the conversation with Jake. I will briefly describe them to provide the context for my understanding of the subtle, yet ever-present and unquestioned role of cultural accommodation that occurs in the school literacy experiences of children from diverse backgrounds. I have been teaching courses in multicultural literature at my university for several years. After my fall 1993 course, I reflected, using journal writing, on my growing experience teaching multicultural literature courses.[3] Teaching these courses has led me to a more informed understanding of how, in the practice of school literacy, there are many culturally defined moments of conflict that call daily for cultural understanding, knowledge, and sensitivity from teachers. These "moments" also challenge non-mainstream students to choose between cultural assimilation and accommodation, or resistance. My journal entries centered on my readings, research, and, most importantly, my daily conversations about school life with my three sons, who range in age from nine to seventeen. In my classes, I have often shared my sons' school experiences and my reactions to them in an effort to help my students understand how teachers' daily subtle and seemingly inconsequential decisions can affect the learning of the children they teach.

A striking example of a teacher's unintentional disregard for the cultural history, understanding, experiences, and voice of a student occurred when my oldest son struggled to meet the requirements of a national essay contest entitled, "What it means to be an American." One of the contest's restrictions was that students should not mention the concept of race. My son thought this was an unfair and impossible task to complete, since his African American identity is synonymous with his being American. Yet, his efforts to articulate the difficulty of the task to his English teacher were frustrated by her response that, although she was empathic, she did not have the authority to change the rules. I intervened and spoke with the teacher at length about my son's values, beliefs, and his unwillingness to compromise himself in order to compete in an essay contest in which he had little or no interest other than a grade.

My second son also had a similar experience involving unintentional cultural insensitivity. He is a member of the school band, which was having its fall concert. While attending, I noticed that all the music the band played was composed by Europeans or European Americans. I spoke with one of the band directors, and asked rhetorically if there were any songs that the band members could perform that were composed by people of color. She responded that she had never considered the choices she made as nonrepresentative of all the students who had to learn them, while I could see little else than the absence of cultural diversity. I was pleased when the winter concert included some Hanukkah tunes. It was a start.

Reflections

Though my conversation with Jake is now months old, it has continued to haunt me. I have been deeply concerned about a noticeable shift in my son's attitude toward writing. Jake's early writing experiences in kindergarten and first grade revealed that he found writing to be a natural outlet for self-expression. He often wrote for pleasure and has kept all of his drafts. Jake learned the process approach to writing in first grade and treasures his portfolio, which he had originally developed in that class. I have found him in his room revisiting a piece he had written earlier. However, this past year I have noticed a change in his level of production. Jake no longer writes detailed accounts. Instead, he spends a great deal of time thinking about what to write and how to say it. While I believe these are laudatory traits of a good writer, his teachers often accuse him of being under-productive.

Reflecting on our conversation, I sense that Jake believes (understands?) that his perceived audience will neither value nor understand the cultural images and nuances he wishes to share in his writing. Jake is a child wrestling with an internal conflict that is framed by the sociohistorical and sociocultural inequities of U.S. society. He is trying to come to grips with how he can express himself in a manner that is true to his "real self," and yet please his teacher and audience of readers who are, in effect, evaluating his culture, thinking, language, and reality.

Jake's perception of an unaccepting audience is not unique. Several researchers have expressed similar concerns about the narrowly defined culture of acceptable school literacy and the growing literateness of culturally and linguistically diverse children (Delpit, 1986, 1991, 1993; Gutierrez, 1992; Heath, 1983; Labov, 1972; Ovando & Collier, 1985; Reyes & Molner, 1991; Sawyer & Rodriguez, 1992).[4] Why is it clearer to children than to adults that there are systematic, institutional inequalities in the decisions teachers make about the "appropriate" methods and materials used to enhance their students' literacy development?

Like millions of culturally and linguistically diverse people, Jake understands the unstated reality of schooling in U.S. society: It is built upon a narrow understanding of school knowledge and literacy, which are defined and defended as what one needs to know and how one needs to know it in order to be successful in school and society. As Barrera (1992) explains:

> The school culture can be seen to reflect the dominant class and, so too, the cultures of literacy and literature embedded within the school culture. For this reason, the teaching of literacy and literature are considered to be neither acultural nor neutral, but cultural and political. (p. 236)

The real question is, why do we as educators continue this "sin of omission" — that is, allowing the cultural knowledge of culturally and linguistically diverse children to be ignored, devalued, and unnurtured as valid sources of literacy acquisition? Excerpts from the writings of five noted African Americans help to illustrate my point.

The Past Revisited

The problem of defining one's literary self is not a new one. As noted scholar W. E. B. DuBois argued in 1903:

> After the Egyptian and Indian, the Greek and Roman, the Teuton and Mongolian, the Negro is a sort of seventh son, born with a veil, and gifted with second-sight in this American world, — a world which yields him no true self-

consciousness, but only lets him see himself through the revelation of the other world. It is a peculiar sensation this double-consciousness, this sense of always looking at one's self through the eyes of others. . . . One ever feels his twoness, an American, a Negro; two souls, two thoughts, two unreconciled strivings; two warring ideals in one dark body, whose dogged strength alone keeps it from being torn asunder. The history of the American Negro is the history of this strife, — this longing to attain self conscious manhood, to merge his double self into a better and truer self. (1903/1965, pp. 214–215)

Similarly, historian Carter G. Woodson (1933/1990) stated:

In this effort to imitate, however, those "educated people" are sincere. They hope to make the Negro conform quickly to the standard of the whites and thus remove the pretext for the barriers between the races. They do not realize, however, that if the Negroes do successfully imitate the whites, nothing new has thereby been accomplished. You simply have a larger number of persons doing what others have been doing. The unusual gifts of the race have not thereby been developed. (p. 4)

Poet Langston Hughes (1951) expressed a similar notion:

> I guess being colored doesn't make me not like
> the same things other folks like who are other races.
> So will my page be colored that I write?
> Being me, it will not be white.
> But it will be
> a part of you, instructor.
> You are white —
> yet a part of me, as I am a part of you.
> That's American.
> Sometimes perhaps you don't want to be a part of me.
> Nor do I often want to be a part of you.
> But we are, that's true!
> As I learn from you,
> I guess you learn from me —
> although you're older — and white —
> and somewhat more free. (pp. 39–40)

Novelist Ralph Ellison (1952) writes: *they see what they want to see*

I am invisible, understand, simply because people refuse to see me. Like the bodiless heads you see sometimes in circus sideshows, it is as though I have been surrounded by mirrors of hard, distorting glass. When they approach me they see only my surroundings, themselves, or figments of their imagination — indeed, everything and anything except me. (p. 3)

And, finally, Toni Morrison (1992) refers to the phenomenon of double consciousness as "writing for a white audience" (p. xii). She asks:

> What happens to the writerly imagination of a black author who is at some level *always* conscious of representing one's own race to, or in spite of, a race of readers that understands itself to be "universal" or race-free? In other words, how are "literary whiteness" and "literary blackness" made, and what is the consequence of these constructions? (p. xii)

Like other culturally and linguistically diverse people before him (including myself and every other person of color with whom I have shared this incident), Jake has encountered the struggle of literary personhood.

Questions and concerns flood my mind: Where, I wonder, has he gotten the idea of a "White" audience — that is, the sense that his classmates and others who read his writing will not appreciate what he has to share? When did his concept of a "White" audience arise? My questions persist: How long has Jake known, intuitively perhaps, that his school literacy experiences have been tempered through a mainstream lens? Will Jake continue to resist "writing for a white audience?" When do culturally and linguistically diverse children learn that they must choose between selfhood and accommodation?[5] When do they learn that "the best way, then, to succeed — that is, to receive rewards, recognition . . . is to learn and reproduce the ways of the dominant group?" (Scheurich, 1992, p. 7). Must there be only one acceptable culture reflected in current school literacy programs? What thoughts, words, and language is Jake replacing with those of the dominant culture in order to please his audience? Will he ever be able to recapture his true literate self after years of accommodation?

As a third grader, Jake is writing, but not for pleasure. Whereas once he wrote as a way of expressing himself or as a hobby, now he does not. He only writes to complete assignments. Much of the "joy" he experienced in writing for pleasure seems to have waned. I recently read some of his writings and noted that he concentrated on topics that do not reflect African American culture. For example, his most recent entries are about his spoon collection, running track, rocks, and football — pretty generic stuff.

My fears are like those of all parents who believe they have prepared their child, having done all that they have read and know a parent should do, yet see their child struggling with a history, a tradition, that is much larger than they can battle.[6] What can I do to help my son and children like him enjoy the freedom of writing and reading? How can I help them value the culturally relevant events in their lives? How can school literacy programs begin to acknowledge, respect, and encourage the diverse cultural knowledge and experiences that children bring to school?

In this article, I am speaking as a teacher educator and parent. This article is an attempt to begin conversations with my colleagues that will address cultural complexities so often ignored in literacy research and practice. For too long, the only perspective published was European Americans' understanding of literacy events. Over the past few years, other cultural perspectives have been published and, more recently, a few have questioned the connection between the theoretical notions of literacy and the historical, and daily, reality of institutionalized inequalities.

As a scholar, I can begin conversations with my colleagues about reexamining theories of literacy to include the role of culture and linguistic diversity. Moreover, teachers and teacher educators like myself can then extend these conversations to reinterpret literacy development, school literacy programs, and teacher education methods and materials to include the experiences of nonmainstream cultures. Finally, I can further extend these conversations into rethinking how we teach and practice school literacy.

Broadening the Scope

Several contemporary positions on literacy serve to enlighten our understanding of how literacy is defined in the field and how it is defined in practice. In this section, I will offer a brief look at several definitions. First, Cook-Gumperz (1986) describes two competing definitions of school literacy that are useful in framing this discussion. She states that "inherent in our contemporary attitude to literacy and schooling is a confusion between a prescriptive view of literacy, as a statement about the values and uses of knowledge, and a descriptive view of literacy, as cognitive abilities which are promoted and assessed through schooling" (p. 14). Second, a more expansive definition of how literacy is conceptualized is offered by Freire and Macedo (1987). They suggest that "literacy becomes a meaningful construct to the degree that it is viewed as a set of practices that functions to either empower or disempower people. In the larger sense, literacy is analyzed according to whether it serves a set of cultural practices that promotes democratic and emancipatory change" (p. 141). Further, they clarify their position on literacy by noting that "for the notion of literacy to become meaningful it has to be situated within a theory of cultural production and viewed as an integral part of the way in which people produce, transform, and reproduce meaning" (p. 142). Third, more general discussions of literacy define literacy as functional, cultural, or critical. Each of these concepts also refers to very different ways of thinking about literacy. *Functional literacy* refers to mastery of the skills needed to read and write as measured by standardized forms of assessment. This view of literacy is similar to Cook-Gumperz's (1986) notion of a descriptive view of literacy. The functional view promotes literacy as a cognitive set of skills that are universal, culturally neutral, and equally accessible through schooling, and is based on a positivistic ideology of learning. Further, this view is heavily dependent on the use of standardized testing measures as a proving ground for literacy acquisition. Most basal reading series and programmed reading approaches embrace the functional/descriptive view of literacy.

Cultural literacy is a term that is most often associated with E. D. Hirsch's 1987 book, *Cultural Literacy: What Every American Needs to Know*. Hirsch defines cultural literacy as "the network of information that all competent readers possess. It is the background information, stored in their minds, that enables them to take up a newspaper and read it with an adequate level of comprehension, getting the point, grasping the implications, relating what they read to the unstated context which alone gives meaning to what they read" (p. 2). Cook-Gumperz (1986) has labelled this form of literacy "prescriptive." In effect, this form of cultural literacy validates language forms, experiences, literature, and histories of some and marginalizes or ignores the language forms, experiences, literature, and histories of others. In the United States, the prescriptive view can be seen in the use of standard English, Eurocentric ways of knowing and learning, a Eurocentric literary canon, and a conventional unproblematic rendering of U.S. history. This form of the cultural/prescriptive view marginalizes the pluralistic composition of U.S. society by devaluing the language, contributions, and histories of some groups. Traditional or conventional approaches to school-based literacy take this form. McLaren (1988) argues that there is a second form of cultural literacy. He writes that this form of cultural literacy "advocates using the language standards and cultural information students bring into the classroom as legitimate and important constituents of learning" (p. 214). Cultural literacy, thus described, suggests that the language and experiences of each student who enters the classroom should be respected and nurtured. This form of cultural literacy recognizes that there are differences in language forms, experiences, literature, and histories of students that will affect literacy learning. Social constructivist theories fall into this prescriptive/cultural literacy category. These approaches to literacy emphasize the active engagement of learners in making meaning from print, the social context of literacy learning, and the importance of recognizing individual and cultural differences.

Critical literacy refers to the ideologies that underlie the relationship between power and knowledge in society. The work of Brazilian educator Paulo Freire has been influential to U.S. efforts to adopt a critical literacy position. Freire, among others, suggests that literacy is more than the construction of meaning from print: Literacy must also include the ability to understand oneself and one's relationship to the world. Giroux's (1987) discussion is worth quoting here at length:

> As Paulo Freire and others have pointed out, schools are not merely instructional sites designed to transmit knowledge; they are also cultural sites. As sites, they generate and embody support for particular forms of culture as is evident in the school's support for specific ways of speaking, the legitimating of distinct forms of knowledge, the privileging of certain histories and patterns of authority, and the confirmation of particular ways of experiencing and seeing the world. Schools often give the appearance of transmitting a common culture, but they, in fact, more often than not, legitimate what can be called a dominant culture. (p. 176)

Giroux goes on to state that:

> At issue here is understanding that student experience has to be understood as part of an interlocking web of power relations in which some groups of students are often privileged over others. But if we are to view this insight in an important way, we must understand that it is imperative for teachers to critically examine the cultural backgrounds and social formations out of which their students produce the categories they use to give meaning to the world. For teachers are not merely dealing with students who have individual interests, they are dealing primarily with individuals whose stories, memories, narratives, and readings of the world are inextricably related to wider social and cultural formations and categories. This issue here is not merely one of relevance but one of power. (p. 177)

Similarly, Apple (1992) has argued for nearly a decade that "it is naive to think of the school curriculum as neutral knowledge. . . . Rather, what counts as legitimate knowledge is the result of complex power relations and struggles among identifiable class, race, gender, and religious groups" (p. 4). Critical literacy draws attention to the historical, political, cultural, and social dimensions of literacy. Most importantly, this form of literacy focuses on power relations in society and how knowledge and power are interrelated. Educationalists, practitioners in particular, have not yet fully grasped this position on literacy. The other forms of literacy, functional/descriptive and cultural/prescriptive, do not include, among other things, the notion of power relations in literacy instruction.

Philosophically, social constructivist notions (a form of prescriptive/cultural literacy) may be seen as comparable to those espoused by critical literacy. From the schema theorists of the early 1980s to the social constructivist theories of the 1990s, literacy development is understood to be a "meaning making process" — that is, socially mediated (Meek, 1982). Drawing primarily on the work of Halliday (1975), Vygotsky (1978), and Goodman (1989), a number of literacy researchers have stressed the universality of language learning. For example, Goodman's (1989) discussion of the philosophical stance of whole language is that:

> At the same time that whole language sees common strengths and universals in human learning, it expects and recognizes differences among learners in culture, value systems, experience, needs, interests and language. Some of these differences are personal, reflecting the ethnic, cultural, and belief systems of the social groups pupils represent. Thus teachers in whole-language programs value differences among learners as they come to school and differences in objectives and outcomes as students progress through school. (p. 209)

However, I argue that the role of culture in the social constructivist theories is not as well defined as it needs to be in a pluralistic or multicultural society. While it is fair to say that unidimensional views of culture would not be supported by social constructivists, it is also fair to say that the multilayered complexity of culture, especially the cultures of historically oppressed groups, is not explicitly addressed by them either. By way of example, I will examine the prescriptive/cultural literacy foundation of whole language. Goodman (1986) argues that "language begins as means of communication between members of the group. Through it, however, each developing child acquires the life view, the cultural perspective, the ways of meaning particular to its own culture" (p. 11). But this definition fails to acknowledge that in addition to acquiring culturally "neutral" knowledge, some children must also acquire a Eurocentric cultural perspective to be successful in school. It is not sufficient to suggest that the language and culture of every student is welcomed, supported, and nurtured in school without explicitly addressing the power relations in institutions, social practice, and literature that advantage some and hinder others (Delpit, 1988; Reyes, 1992). School-based literacy, in its varying forms, fails to acknowledge explicitly the richness of the cultural ways of knowing, forms of language other than standard English, and the interwoven relationship among power, language, and literacy that silences kids like Jake.[7] To fail to attend to the plurality and diversity within the United States — and to fail to take seriously the historic past and the social and political contexts that have sustained it — is to dismiss the cultural ways of knowing, language, experiences, and voices of children from diverse linguistic and cultural backgrounds. This is not to imply that programs based on such theories need to be scrapped. It does mean that social constructivist theories need to be reworked to include the complexities of culture that are currently absent. It will also mean that teacher education will need to: 1) make explicit the relationship among culture, language, literacy and power; and 2) train teachers to use cultural information to support and nurture the literacy development of all the students who enter their classrooms.

When taken at face value, social constructivist theory would lead one to assume that new holistic approaches to literacy are culturally validating for all students. An examination of Jake's home and school contexts for his developing understanding of literacy illustrates that this is not always true. That is, we need to understand where he acquired language and his understanding of culture, as well as his history of literacy instruction, to understand how he is "reading the world" of school literacy and how his experiences with a variety of school literacy forms, including holistic approaches, have not addressed his cultural ways of knowing, experiences, language, and voice.

Literacy Contexts

Home Context

Literacy acquisition does not evolve in one context or through one type of event; rather, it is a complex endeavor that is mediated through culture. Jake's home literacy environment began with our preparations for him as a new baby. He was brought into a loving two-parent home in which two older brothers were awaiting his arrival. Jake also entered a print- and language-rich environment. He was read to when only a few months old, and continues to share reading (and now writing) with family members. Like the homes of many other middle-class children, Jake's is filled with language, and a range of standard and vernacular languages is used. Our talk centers around family issues, but also includes conversations about world events, neighborhood and school concerns, and personal interests. There are stories, prayers, niceties (manners), verbal games, family jokes, homework assignments, daily Bible reading and discussion, as well as family vacations and excursions to museums, zoos, concerts, and ball parks. Daily routines include reading and responding to mail, making schedules, appointments, grocery and chore lists, and taking telephone messages, all of which include opportunities for shared conversations. There is also a family library that consists of adult fiction, nonfiction, and reference materials. Conversations flow constantly and with ease as we enjoy sharing with each other.

Prior to Jake's entering school, we enjoyed music, games, songs, fingerplay, writing notes on unlined paper with lots of different writing tools, long nature walks, as well as trips to the store, library, barbershop, and church.[8] All these activities were accompanied by lots of talk to expand understanding and draw connections. In addition, Jake and his brothers all have their own bedroom library in which they keep their favorite books, collected since early childhood. Jake's written communications include telephone messages, calendar events, schedules, notes, recipes, invitations, thank-you notes, game brackets (Sega or Nintendo), and occasionally letters and poems.

Jake has a special interest in his collections of stickers, stamps, coins, puzzles, board games, maps, newspaper clippings, and baseball, football, and basketball cards. He also enjoys reading his bedtime story books, magazines (especially *Sports Illustrated for Kids*), and the newspaper (his favorite parts are the sports page, the comics, and the weather map).

What makes Jake's understanding of language and literacy so culturally different from his school's, although both are apparently based on middle-class standards, is that his home literacy events have been culturally defined and are mediated through his cultural understanding. Jake's world is African American; that is, his growing understanding of who and what he is has consciously and unconsciously been mediated through an African American perspective. We select our artwork, magazines, novels, television programs, music, videos, and movies to reflect interests in African American life and society.

School Context

Like most parents, I inquired about the kindergarten's literacy program before enrolling Jake in school.[9] I wanted to have some idea of how his teachers viewed literacy development and how they planned to conduct literacy instruction. My primary question was, "What approach to literacy will you use?" Jake's private, full-day kindergarten was founded by three Jewish women, two of whom taught the kindergarten class, while the third served as school administrator. The teachers informed me that they had taught for many years and were aware of the modern trends. They had therefore designed a program that included what they considered to be the strong points of several programs. Jake's classmates included twelve European Americans (eight were Jewish) and two African American children. His teachers tried to provide all the children with what they thought the children would need to know in order to be successful readers and writers in grade one. As a result, the classroom was colorful and full of print. Labels were placed on cubbyholes, activity centers, children's table chairs, and charts.[10] The reading material was an eclectic mix of basals, trade books, and a small library of children's classics.

In first grade, Jake attended a public elementary school. This classroom was a mixed-age group (grades one and two) of twenty-three children, including seventeen European Americans, four African Americans, and two Asian Americans. His teacher described her literacy program as literature-based, and she stressed reading and writing. This teacher read to the children, who also read individually or in small groups. The reading materials included recipients of the Caldecott award and other award-winning books, stories, and poems by children's favorite authors, classics of children's literature, and writing "published" by the students. The children especially liked to read folk tales. As they gained reading and writing skills, the children coauthored, published, and shared their own work. Students were also encouraged to read and write for pleasure. In all these works, I recall that very few were written about or authored by people of color, except for a few on the Caldecott list.

Jake attended a different elementary school for second grade. I eagerly met his new teacher and asked my standard question about literacy. She informed me that she used the basal approach, which she believed ensured that all the "skills" needed to be a successful reader would be covered. The particular basal series she used included "universal" themes and contained illustrations of various racial/ethnic groups but made little reference to the culture of the people. There were several "ethnic" stories, but I consider their authorship suspect, at best.[11] The series also included isolated skill development, vocabulary regulated text, several thematically organized stories, informational selections, and limited writing opportunities. This class of twenty-eight children included twenty European Americans, five African Americans, and three Asian Americans.

Not wishing Jake to repeat this basal approach in grade three, I spoke with other mothers in the neighborhood, soliciting information about the "good" third-grade teachers. After much prayer, I informed the principal of my choice. Now in third grade, Jake is experiencing what his teacher refers to as a whole language approach to literacy, which includes lots of reading and writing for meaning, working in cooperative groups, process writing, and having sustained time for reading and writing. Writing is a daily activity, and Thursday mornings are designated as Writing Workshop mornings with parent volunteers who assist students in a variety of ways, from brainstorming topics to editing their writing. The teacher allows time for individual and small group readings of trade books on a daily basis. Since my conversation with Jake, I have learned his teacher had selected the books she planned to use during the school year, ahead of time, and the children were allowed only to choose which of these books to read. All of the books were written by European American authors. Even the folk tales from other countries were rewritten by European Americans. Very few books by or about U.S. minorities have been read to students by the teacher, student teachers, or in the reading groups.

I cannot account for the moment-by-moment decisions Jake's teachers have had to make each day. However, I can review the philosophies behind the programs they use. Theoretically, each literacy program purports to be culturally neutral and not mediated by any dominant view of language, when, in fact, a Eurocentric, mainstream cultural view dominates. Darder (1991) argues that it is important to understand the historicity of knowledge:

> The dominant school culture functions not only to support the interests and values of the dominant society, but also to marginalize and invalidate knowledge forms and experiences that are significant to subordinate and oppressed groups. This function is best illustrated in the ways that curriculum often blatantly ignores the histories of women, people of color, and the working class. (p. 79)

Having held a conference with each of Jake's teachers and observed each class setting on several occasions, I can say without hesitation that each teacher believed that she was doing her best to meet the needs of each child in her classroom. That is, she was trying to foster a growing sense of literacy competence in each child. Yet, I don't believe that any of Jake's teachers were aware that they were also narrowly defining the cultural lens through which all children in the classroom were expected to understand literacy.

Thus, in four short years Jake has experienced a wide range of philosophies, approaches, and instruction in literacy, and, at the same time, a narrow ethnocentric view of school literacy. All of his teachers have meant to encourage his growth and development as a literate person. Why, then, have they failed to acknowledge an important part of who he is and what he *culturally* brings to the school literacy program? Reyes (1992) argues that teachers often fail to make adjustments in their approaches to literacy for culturally and linguistically diverse learners because

> the majority of [teachers] are members of the dominant culture, implementing programs designed primarily for mainstream students. Teachers implementing these programs tend to treat students of color as exceptions to the norm, as students who should be assimilated into the dominant group, rather than accommodated according to their own needs. (p. 437)

Some theorists, researchers, and teachers may suggest the counter argument; that is, that elements of the mainstream culture are apparent in all "parallel cultures" and that it is easiest to teach to the mainstream (Hamilton, 1989).[12] I would argue that to ignore, consciously or not, the culture and language that each child brings to the literacy table is to mis-educate him or her.

As the research by Au (1993), Morrow (1992), and Reyes and Laliberty (1992), among others, has shown, when cultural and linguistic adjustments are made to school literacy programs, all children benefit.

You may wonder if I have tried to inform Jake's teachers of the narrowness of the literacy lens through which they seem to be defining literacy development and instruction. I admit that I have failed miserably to take a strong stand. Rather than confront them about the lack of culturally responsive literacy instruction, I have expressed my concerns for Jake's personal literacy growth. For example, I have shared multicultural book lists with Jake's teachers and offered to serve as a resource. I have honestly wanted to inform Jake's teachers of two things: one, the need to be more sensitive in their approach to the language and cultural experiences that children bring to the classroom; and two, the need to incorporate more books written by people of color to legitimize the contributions of all literate people. Yet I have also believed that expressing my thoughts might jeopardize Jake's educational future with some kind of backlash.

A Status Report

While literacy theorists, researchers, and practitioners continue to suggest that school literacy is culturally neutral, Jake's literacy experiences offer an intimate and compelling argument that, as currently practiced, school literacy has been and still is narrowly defined in terms of culture. Only the packaging is new.

Descriptions of my conversation with Jake have met with lots of head nodding and similar stories from many of my non-White students. Delpit (1988) has shared similar insights into what she correctly describes as the "silenced dialogue." The commonsense response among some people of color to school literacy (and schooling in general) has been to take a "way things are" attitude. Many people of color understand that there are inequalities in the educational system; however, we also understand that little can be done without massive school reform. So, to be educated in our current system requires accepting that "this is the way things are. If you want to advance you must learn to play the game." That is, institutionalized racism is something we all know, but see as an unavoidable part of education in U.S. society.

In sharing my analysis with my graduate students, several European Americans have questioned why I refer to Jake's school literacy experiences as being narrowly defined and inquired what is so "acultural" about his literacy education. They ask, "Aren't literature-based and whole language programs built upon notions of constructivist theory that embrace notions of culture?" Of course, my students' understanding is correct: Current holistic school literacy programs support constructivist theory. I guess that's what is so frightening.

While the rhetoric of school literacy programs suggests that culture is part of the theoretical framework, "culture" has been narrowly defined to mean middle-class European American culture. The tacit assumption is, then, that all children are being well served by the new literacy programs that are built on the "natural" language acquisition of middle-class European American children. However, natural language acquisition is mediated through the particular culture in which the child lives. The reality, then, as shared in this article, is that theoreticians, researchers, teacher educators, practitioners, and publishers of literacy approaches and programs are frequently unaware of their assumptions.

Some may truly believe that they are delivering on their promise to build on the culture and language of the child, but what they have been unable, or unwilling, to acknowledge is that school literacy, as it exists, is not universal or reflective of the language and culture of many children. They claim that current school literacy programs and practices are acultural. These programs, however, clearly put some children at a disadvantage, while giving an advantage to others. It is clear, even to a nine-year-old, that school literacy is narrowly defined.

Discussion

In order to meet the needs of our U.S. society, which is rapidly becoming more culturally diverse, our literacy programs should offer more than sensitivity training, human relations, or attitudinal shifts to issues of culture and linguistic diversity. Programs are needed that will also help teachers transform their thinking about the role of language and culture in literacy development. It is simply not enough to inform teachers of what they do not know. Teachers need to question "cultural bumps," or mismatches in expectations of performance in literacy development (Garcia, 1994, personal communication). As Barnitz (1994) states, "Teachers must recognize difference as manifestations of cultural discourse which can be expanded rather than interrupted or suppressed" (p. 587).

What I see is an institutionalized racism that is grounded in the theories used to discuss literacy and to inform and educate teachers and teacher educators. I believe that we need to enhance pre-service teacher curricula and education. The current method of dispersing concepts of diversity, inclusivity, or multiculturalism across several courses, hoping students will synthesize these issues into a workable whole, has been ineffective. Pre-service teachers also need intensive education in understanding the dynamic role that culture plays in language and literacy development and in defining school literacy.

In a pre-service teacher education course I teach, I use literature authored by domestic minority men and women as a starting point for pre-service teachers to begin to reflect on their cultural assumptions about how they "read the word and the world" (Freire, 1985). The method has been effective in helping many students face their own, heretofore unvoiced, assumptions of their own culture and the cultures of other groups.

Most of my students are in their early twenties and have never really concerned themselves with issues of race. Even the students who are members of U.S. minority groups prefer not to discuss race, ethnicity, or culture openly. At the opening of class, for example, many of my students think that their cultural understanding will not affect the students they teach. They believe that their most important concern should be the subject matter and how to transmit effectively a love for their subject to their students. Some of my students also have difficulty understanding the notion of institutionalized racism in U.S. public education. It is at this point in the course that I begin to share the daily occurrences in the lives of my children. Further, some of my European American students see themselves only as "American" and do not wish to deal with their heritage. They want to minimize any tie to Europe and only concentrate on their "Americanness." Some students believe that most U.S. minority group members are poor people, and that most poor people (from all racial groups, but especially those seen most frequently in the media — African Americans and Latinos) really don't care about their children's education. Some also think that children from minority groups don't care about their own education. Most of my students have not even considered how to prepare to teach in multicultural or multilingual classrooms. They tend to live under the false assumption that they can get jobs in homogeneous, suburban school districts.

As in most pre-service teacher education courses nationwide, my students are predominantly European American women. However, in each of my classes, I have had at least one U.S. minority group member. The presence of members from these groups has helped give voice to the concerns of their various communities. My courses are elective, which I believe is important, because it means that the students in my class are interested in issues of diversity. In the best of all worlds, all students would be so inclined, but they are not.

One of the first things I do to help my students become aware of their own cultural understandings is to have them write an autobiographical essay. The essay requires them to trace their ancestry over four or five generations, and to explain their families' use of language, food traditions, and other interesting cultural habits. The essays are shared first in small groups and then with the whole class. In this way, students can readily understand that everyone is a product of their culture, knowingly or not. I too share my cultural and ethnic background. As a person of African, Native, and European American descent, yet who looks only African American, I use my background and life as a springboard for discussions of students' cultural diversity and the limited conception of "culture" in most schools. Since this is a semester-long course, we have the time to engage in many activities, such as community and faculty presentations, videos, and readings by U.S. minority members. However, I believe that some of the most productive work occurs in the small group discussions my students have with each other as they respond to literature written by U.S. minority group members. For example, recently we read a number of novels written by Asian Americans. Many of my students had not heard of the internment of Japanese Americans during World War II.

After my students and I have reflected upon the cultural assumptions from which we perceive our world (and those worlds that might differ from our own), we begin to address teachers' roles and how their cultural assumptions affect the decisions they make, their interactions with students, and their selection of teaching materials. I then give the students opportunities to use their growing understanding of cultural knowledge in lessons they design and teach. My students are all required to teach two literacy lessons during the semester. Many of them choose activities that require participants to work together in cooperative learning groups. Four examples come to mind. One student asked each of us to recall an event using the Native American concept of a "skin story" — drawing on animal pelts — to create pictograph symbols to relate that event. Another student separated class members by attributes they could not control (gender, hair color, size of feet). The "minority" group members (men in this case) were seated in the front of the classroom and were the only students the leader of the exercise asked to respond to her questions. In a third example, a student distributed a series of photographs to small groups and had each group classify the people in the photos, rating them on attributes such as who appeared most intelligent, most successful, and nicest. Finally, a student asked us to read current newspaper articles about war-torn countries and write a diary entry or letter to a government official from the perspective of someone in the country. Through such exercises and activities, my students have learned that culture is a complex issue, one that cannot be taken lightly. They learn to think and act reflectively and become predisposed to considering issues of race, class, gender, age, and sexual preference. Moreover, they understand that their decisions must be based on more than theory; they must also consider the interrelationship of power and knowledge.

I also design in-class lessons around students' responses to the authentic texts they have read. Throughout their field experiences, I have been impressed by the culturally responsive approach to literacy and literature that many of my students have taken with them into the field. For example, one of my students invited recent Asian immigrants to her eighth-grade class to be interviewed by her students. She believed that the face-to-face interactions her students had during the interviews allowed them to understand better the hardships endured by the new U.S. citizens. Another student taught *Huckleberry Finn*. She began the lesson by sharing the historical context in which the novel was written, a model I insist each student use in my class. When confronted by an African American student about the use of the word "nigger" in the novel, she was able to facilitate a group discussion on the use of derogatory terms. She believed that membership in my class enabled her to deal openly with the student and the offensive term. Her experience demonstrates that it is possible to create multicultural learning communities within classrooms that are based on critical literacy theory that validates and legitimizes all learners.

Conclusion

In this article, I have argued that for school literacy to begin to move beyond its "neutral" conception of culture, educators at all levels must acknowledge the role and importance of more than one culture in defining school literacy.

Educators have not effectively built upon the culture and language of every child, and have set arbitrary standards of acceptance and defined them as normative. I have also argued for the reconceptualization and program development of school literacy, not to dismantle, but to strengthen, literacy frameworks. We can and must do a better job of inviting all students to the literacy table and including them in conversations on school literacy.

I had initial misgivings about sharing my conversation with Jake, as I feared that my thinking would be misinterpreted. My fears lay with the "predictable inability" (West, 1993) of some European Americans to consider honestly the shortcomings of programs they espouse as universal. In addition, I was concerned that my colleagues would view the conversation as one isolated event, ignoring the fact that there are countless instances of narrow cultural constructions of literacy in the daily lives of culturally and linguistically diverse children. I was also reluctant to give such an intimate look into my private world. Therefore, I hope that sharing the incident opens conversations about reconceptualizing and reforming school literacy. When I wonder if I've done the right thing, I recall Jake saying to his older brothers, "I want to share a picture of my real self."

Notes

1. Going to the barbershop and getting a haircut is a bimonthly occurrence for many African American males. A number of Jake's classmates differed in their definition of what constituted a "part"; however, the other African American children in his class have a similar cultural understanding of the term.
2. As a Writing Workshop parent volunteer in his class, I know that Jake's class consists of ten European American boys, nine European American girls, four African American boys, two African American girls, and one Asian American girl. The class is taught by a European American woman with over twenty years of experience. Also, during this school year, there have been three student teachers (all European American women) and several other parent volunteers (also European American women).
3. In the fall of 1993 I taught a pilot course, which included multicultural education, reading methods for grades six–twelve, and literature for grades six–twelve with special emphasis on multicultural literature.
4. To me, "growing literateness" means an understanding of how language, reading, and writing fit into the communication patterns of home and school life. It can also mean the development of literate behaviors, the adoption of literate attitudes, and the confidence that allows one to define oneself as a reader and a writer.
5. Selfhood, as used in this article, means the awareness of oneself as a person, in particular as a person who belongs to a specific culturally and linguistically distinct group.
6. Cose's (1993) book, *The Rage of a Privileged Class*, gives examples of the frustration experienced by other middle-class African Americans who believed that by doing everything according to plan they would reap just rewards. For example, Cose quotes Darwin Davis, senior vice president of Equitable Life Assurance Society: "They [young Black managers] have an even worse problem [than I did] because they've got M.B.A.'s from Harvard. They did all the things that you're supposed to do . . . and things are supposed to happen" (p. 76).

    By "history," I mean how the inequalities that exist in schools reflect a much greater history of institutionalized inequalities. By "tradition," I mean teachers' ten-

dency to teach how they were taught. Whether history or tradition is the overriding factor in this instance, I am not sure.
7. Silencing, as used by Michelle Fine (1987), "constitutes a process of institutionalized policies and practices which obscure the very social, economic and therefore experiential conditions of students' daily lives, and which expel from written, oral, and nonverbal expression substantive and critical 'talk' about these conditions. . . . Silencing constitutes the process by which contradictory evidence, ideologies, and experiences find themselves buried, camouflaged, and discredited" (p. 157).
8. "Fingerplay" is a term often used to describe actions made with the fingers as children sing a song. For example, the motions used with the song "The Itsy Bitsy Spider" are fingerplay.
9. During my years as a classroom teacher, many parents asked what type of reading program I planned to use. While most parents do not use the term "literacy programs" or inquire about writing programs per se, they do inquire about reading. I have also found that parents are interested in the methods used to teach spelling and vocabulary.
10. Activity centers are areas set aside for special activities. For example, the science center, math center, etc., all have activities specifically designed for children interested in learning more about a selected topic.
11. Many stories contained in basals, like the one Jake used in second grade, are written by teams of authors seeking to control vocabulary or teach specific skills. Basal stories are often abridged or edited versions of original works, and in some instances, such as folk tales, legends, and fairy tales, are translations or a retelling of the original.
12. Recently, Hamilton (1989) used the term "parallel cultures" to refer to the historical experiences of domestic minorities in the United States. "Parallel" conveys a sense of coexistence with the more dominant European American culture so loosely referred to as American culture. The term "domestic minorities" is used to refer to minority groups that have a long history in this country (African Americans, Asian Americans, etc.) but whose forefathers and foremothers lived elsewhere — except in the case of Native Americans.

References

Apple, M. (1992). The text and cultural politics. *Educational Researcher, 21*(7), 4–11, 19.

Au, K. (1993). *Literacy instruction in multicultural settings.* Fort Worth, TX: Harcourt Brace Jovanovich.

Barnitz, J. (1994). Discourse diversity: Principles for authentic talk and literacy instruction. *Journal of Reading, 37,* 586–591.

Barrera, R. (1992). The cultural gap in literature-based literacy instruction. *Education and Urban Society, 24,* 227–243.

Cook-Gumperz, J. (Ed) (1986). *The social construction of literacy.* Cambridge, Eng.: Cambridge University Press.

Cose, E. (1993). *The rage of a privileged class.* New York: Harper Collins.

Darder, A. (1991). *Culture and power in the classroom: A critical foundation for bicultural education.* New York: Bergin & Garvey.

Delpit, L. (1986). Skills and other dilemmas of a progressive Black educator. *Harvard Educational Review, 56,* 379–385.

Delpit, L. (1988). The silenced dialogue: Power and pedagogy in educating other people's children. *Harvard Educational Review, 58,* 280–298.

Delpit, L. (1991). A conversation with Lisa Delpit. *Language Arts, 68,* 541–547.

Delpit, L. (1993). The politics of teaching literate discourse. In T. Perry & J. Fraser (Eds.), *Freedom's plow: Teaching in the multicultural classroom* (pp. 285–295). New York: Routledge.

DuBois, W. E. B. (1965). *The souls of Black folks*. New York: Bantam. (Original work published in 1903)

Ellison, R. (1952). *Invisible man*. New York: Random House.

Fine, M. (1987). Silencing in public schools. *Language Arts, 64,* 157–174.

Freire, P. (1985). Reading the world and the word: An interview with Paulo Freire. *Language Arts, 62,* 15–21.

Freire, P., & Macedo, D. (1987). *Literacy: Reading the world and the word*. South Hadley, MA: Bergin & Garvey.

Giroux, H. (1987). Critical literacy and student experience: Donald Graves' approach to literacy. *Language Arts, 64,* 175–181.

Goodman, K. (1986). *What's whole in whole language?* Portsmouth, NH: Heinemann.

Goodman, K. (1989). Whole-language research: Foundations and development. *Elementary School Journal, 90,* 207–221.

Gutierrez, K. (1992). A comparison of instructional contexts in writing process classrooms with Latino children. *Education and Urban Society, 24,* 244–262.

Halliday, M. (1975). *Learn how to mean*. London: Edward Arnold.

Hamilton, V. (1989). Acceptance speech, Boston Globe-Horn Book Award, 1988. *Horn Book, 65*(2), 183.

Heath, S. (1983). *Ways with words: Language, life and work in the communities and classrooms*. Cambridge, Eng.: Cambridge University Press.

Hirsch, E. (1987). *Cultural literacy: What every American needs to know*. Boston: Houghton Mifflin.

Hughes, L. (1951). Theme for English B. In L. Hughes, *Montage of a dream deferred* (pp. 39–40). New York: Henry Holt.

Labov, W. (1972). The logic of nonstandard English. In R. D. Abrahams & R. C. Troike (Eds.), *Language and cultural diversity in American education* (pp. 225–261). Englewood Cliffs, NJ: Prentice-Hall.

McLaren, P. (1988). Culture or canon? Critical pedagogy and the politics of literacy. *Harvard Educational Review, 58,* 213–234.

Meek, M. (1982). *Learning to read*. Portsmouth, NH: Heinemann.

Morrison, T. (1992). *Playing in the dark: Whiteness and the literary imagination*. Cambridge, MA: Harvard University Press.

Morrow, L. (1992). The impact of a literature-based program on literacy achievement, use of literature, and attitudes of children from minority backgrounds. *Reading Research Quarterly, 27,* 251–275.

Ovando, C., & Collier, V. (1985). *Bilingual and ESL classrooms: Teaching in multicultural contexts*. New York: McGraw-Hill.

Reyes, M. de la Luz. (1992). Challenging venerable assumptions: Literacy instruction for linguistically different students. *Harvard Educational Review, 62,* 427–446.

Reyes, M. de la Luz, & Laliberty, E. (1992). A teacher's "Pied Piper" effect on young authors. *Education and Urban Society, 24,* 263–278.

Reyes, M. de la Luz, & Molner, L. (1991). Instructional strategies for second-language learners in content areas. *Journal of Reading, 35,* 96–103.

Sawyer, D., & Rodriguez, C. (1992). How native Canadians view literacy: A summary of findings. *Journal of Reading, 36,* 284–293.

Scheurich, J. (1992). Toward a White discourse on White racism. *Educational Researcher, 22*(8), 5–10.

West, C. (1993). *Race matters*. Boston: Beacon Press.

Woodson, C. (1990). *The mis-education of the Negro*. Nashville, TN: Winston-Derek. (Original work published 1933)

Vygotsky, L. (1978). *Mind in society*. Cambridge, MA: Harvard University Press.

Why the "Monkeys Passage" Bombed: Tests, Genres, and Teaching

BONNY NORTON*
PIPPA STEIN

> Insurgent readings are not simply struggles over the sign — what a text means — but actually struggles over forms of life, struggles over how people's identities will be constituted and history lived. (Simon, 1992, p. 116)

We wish to relate a cautionary tale of an experience in a high school graduation class in Johannesburg, South Africa, in which we piloted a passage from a reading test to be used for admissions purposes at the University of the Witwatersrand (Wits), Johannesburg. The piloting of a reading passage about an encounter between monkeys and humans, what we call the "monkeys passage," began as a routine procedure and turned into a classroom experience that disrupted our assumptions about tests, texts, and teaching. We believe that the process we underwent provides a window onto a number of important issues in assessment, reading, and pedagogy that are of importance not only in the South African context, but also for many teachers in the wider educational community who are concerned about issues of educational equity.

Admissions Testing in Post-Apartheid South Africa

Educational assessment is a growing industry in post-apartheid South Africa. Institutions across the country, from schools and universities to businesses and corporations, are attempting to identify students of color who have the potential to succeed academically and professionally, despite the debilitating effects of an apartheid legacy (Yeld & Haeck, 1993).

---

*This article was originally published under the name Bonny Norton Peirce.

At the end of secondary school in South Africa, all students write a national matriculation examination based on the courses they have taken for graduation purposes. In the apartheid era, different racial groups had different matriculation examinations, a practice that is in the process of being dismantled. All students who pass these examinations receive a secondary school certificate. Some of these students will also qualify for a university entrance certificate. Because of high demand in some universities, such as Wits, some faculties and departments impose additional cutoff points for entry, over and above the government-stipulated criteria for university admission.

An additional barrier for Black students is the status of the English language, notwithstanding the fact that there are now eleven official languages in South Africa. Although English is the first language of less than 10 percent of the population, and only one of the official languages, it is de facto the most dominant language in the society. Black South Africans, who constitute the majority of the South African population, frequently speak two or three languages, but do not speak English as their first language. Of particular relevance to this article is the fact that English is the medium of instruction in the majority of universities in the country. Thus, the Wits University requirement (as stated in the General Information for Applicants, 1994) that students in all faculties must be proficient in English is a particularly onerous requirement for Black students.

The matriculation examination that most students write has been an unreliable predictor of Black student success, and has often served as a barrier to their admission to universities. Since 1985, the Faculty of Arts of Wits University has been administering an alternative admissions procedure to identify students who have fulfilled the requirements for university entrance, but who nevertheless fall below the cutoff point for automatic entry into the Faculty of Arts (Stack, 1994). Currently the three main components of the alternative admissions procedure are a test of English-language usage, a test of reasoning and table reading, and a biographical questionnaire. Students within the Black community who have been particularly disadvantaged by apartheid education are the main target group for the Faculty of Arts Admissions Committee.

The Faculty of Arts English test seeks to determine the extent to which applicants, most of whom are English Language Learners (ELLs), can cope with the language demands of an English-medium university.[1] The purpose of the test is to facilitate the admission of students into the Faculty of Arts who would otherwise be denied admission, based on their matriculation examination results.

In our respective capacities as teacher educator (Stein) and language testing specialist (Norton), we have participated in the development of this English proficiency test, currently referred to as the "Exercise in English Language Usage."[2] Pippa Stein is a White South African woman who has worked in English-language teacher education at the preservice and in-service level since 1980. She is based at Wits University, working at a preservice level with secondary school teachers who intend to teach in multicultural, multilingual secondary school classrooms. Bonny Norton is a White woman who has worked in language education in South Africa, Canada, and the United States. She received her training in language test development at the Educational Testing Service in Princeton, New Jersey, from 1984 to 1987, and was invited by the Faculty of Arts of Wits University in 1991 to help revise their English admissions test. At the time the research was conducted, Norton was a postdoctoral fellow in the Modern Language Centre, Ontario Institute for Studies in Education, Toronto, Canada. She spent several months in 1991, and again in 1993–1994, as a visiting scholar at Wits University. Norton and Stein have mutual interests in assessment, literacy, and educational equity, and were both members of the Faculty of Arts Admissions Committee in 1991.

The English proficiency test has undergone many revisions since it was first developed in 1985. Although the university is now in a post-apartheid era, it still needs to set criteria for admission because of high student demand for admission. The 1992 version of the English test had three components: a short, multiple-choice reading test, a longer comprehension test with short answer questions, and an essay question. The monkeys passage, based on a local Johannesburg newspaper article, and a set of multiple-choice questions on the text were to be included in the first component of the short, multiple-choice reading test. The purpose of the first component of the test was to serve as an initial screening device to identify the applicants who did not perform well on the monkeys passage test and exclude them from further consideration for alternative admission.

Below is the text of the monkeys passage, followed by the multiple-choice questions:

MONKEYS ON RAMPAGE*

A troop of about 80 monkeys, enraged after a mother monkey and her baby were caught in a trap, went on the rampage at a Durban home at the weekend attacking two policemen who were forced to flee and call for help. A 14-year-old boy also had to run for his life and reached the safety of a home split seconds before a full-grown monkey hurled itself against the door. The troop also attacked a house, banging windows and doors.

Mrs Kittie Lambrechts, 59, of Firdale Road, Sea View, told reporters how the monkeys' behaviour was sparked off by events on Saturday. She said her family had been pestered by monkeys for over a year.

"They come nearly every day, and they steal all the fruit from our fruit trees before it's ripe enough to pick," she complained. "We didn't know what to do, so we wrote a letter to the Durban Corporation. They said that it would be unsafe to use guns in the neighborhood, and that we should not poison the monkeys because sometimes dogs and cats eat the poison; rather, we should

---

*This material has been adapted from *The Star*, a Johannesburg-based newspaper within the Independent News & Media group.

set traps. On Saturday we bought a trap and put it in our garden. Shortly afterwards, the monkeys arrived and a mother and her baby were caught in the trap. The whole troop went into a raging fury and attacked us. Edwin Schultz, a young visitor from the Transvaal, had to run for his life and slammed the door closed just before a full-grown monkey could get hold of him. It jumped against the door. The troop attacked our home and hit against the doors and windows. It was terrifying."

Mrs Lambrechts telephoned the police and Const N M Moodley and Const E Coetzer of the Bellair police station went to investigate. But when they arrived, the troop turned on them and they had to run for cover as well. "The men ran to their van and called for help while monkeys surrounded them and jumped against the vehicle," Mrs. Lambrechts said. Police armed with shotguns arrived on the scene and four monkeys were shot dead. The troop then fled into the bushes, apparently because their leader had been among the monkeys shot dead.

1. This newspaper article is about
    (a) Edwin Schultz's visit to Durban from the Transvaal;
    (b) how Mrs Lambrechts runs her fruit business;
    (c) monkeys that attacked people;
    (d) the accidental poisoning of dogs and cats.
2. A "troop" of monkeys is
    (a) monkeys that live near people;
    (b) any group of monkeys living together;
    (c) any group of animals living together;
    (d) monkeys having the same mother.
3. Why were the monkeys considered pests?
    (a) The monkeys were dangerous and attacked people.
    (b) The monkeys made a lot of noise and disturbed the family.
    (c) The monkeys took unripe fruit from the garden.
    (d) The monkeys made a mess in the garden.
4. The Durban Corporation advised Mrs Lambrechts
    (a) to shoot dead the leader of the troop;
    (b) to set traps in her garden;
    (c) to poison the fruit in her trees;
    (d) to telephone the police.
5. When the monkeys went on their rampage,
    (a) Mrs Lambrechts was enraged;
    (b) Mrs Lambrechts' husband called the police;
    (c) Mrs Lambrechts' son was chased by a full-grown monkey;
    (d) Mrs Lambrechts was terrified.
6. Edwin Schultz, at the time of the story,
    (a) was visiting the Transvaal;
    (b) was 14 years old;
    (c) lived on Firdale Road in Sea View;
    (d) was caught by a full-grown monkey.

7. Const Moodley and Const Coetzer
   (a) shot dead the leader of the troop;
   (b) called for help;
   (c) never left their van;
   (d) interviewed Mrs Lambrechts.
8. Why did the monkeys flee into the bushes?
   (a) Police arrived with shotguns.
   (b) The monkeys had already chased the people inside.
   (c) Their leader had been shot dead.
   (d) Their leader led them into the bushes.
9. How many monkeys were shot dead by the police?
   (a) 1 (the leader)
   (b) 4
   (c) 5
   (d) all of them
10. This article was written by
    (a) Const E Coetzer;
    (b) a witness;
    (c) Kittie Lambrechts;
    (d) a journalist.

At a Faculty of Arts test development meeting in August 1991, Norton raised questions about the suitability of the monkeys passage text for Black students. She was concerned that in the prevailing political climate of violence and instability, the young adults whose communities had been most affected by violence might become distressed by the passage. Her primary concern was that if test takers became unduly disturbed by the content of the test, their performance might be compromised. This, in turn, would weaken the validity of the test and undermine the credibility of the alternative admissions procedure in the Faculty of Arts. Norton suggested that the text be piloted on a sample of the target population to determine whether the passage might be disturbing to test-takers. Stein volunteered to administer the test to a graduation class of Black students in a Johannesburg secondary school. The following section is Stein's personal narrative describing the testing event.

Stein: Piloting the Test

In August and September of 1991, I piloted the first section of the proposed 1992 English Proficiency Test with Black high school students whose first language was not English. I had been involved in preservice teacher development work in local Black high schools since 1986. Part of my job was to visit teacher-trainees who were completing their practicum in English-language teaching in local schools. Through this work, I had established connections with a large network of schools, particularly in downtown Johannesburg. It was in one of these schools that I wished to pilot this section of the test.

This secondary school had been recently established by a group of private individuals for students from the surrounding segregated townships whose schooling had been interrupted by the chronic instability and violence of the apartheid era. This was not a state-run school and it had no state subsidy. As a privately run enterprise, it was financially dependent on private funds from the commercial sector and tuition paid by students.

The school of four hundred students was housed in a building on a run-down office block. On the day I visited, a nearby building was being demolished. There was constant traffic outside the main classrooms. Material resources were scarce: there were no photocopying or reproduction facilities, few textbooks or exercise books, and no overhead projectors. During my visit, I learned that a group of students had been suspended from classes for not having paid their fees. In my view, the school environment, administratively and educationally, was not conducive to sustained and focused learning.

The principal allowed me to conduct the piloting procedure with the graduation class who, one month later, would be writing their matriculation examinations. I was introduced to the students' English teacher. I told her that I was evaluating the suitability of a reading comprehension passage that was possibly going to be used for examination. She introduced me to her nineteen students as a "lecturer from Wits" and asked if they would be prepared to take a short reading comprehension test for me. Even though the students' lunch break was about to begin, they agreed to take the test. From the expressions on students' faces, I was concerned that many were apprehensive. I assured them that I was in no way assessing their individual abilities, but rather the suitability of the test. I indicated that the results of the test would not affect their grades or be used against them in any way. This statement appeared to put them at ease. I also introduced the students to Jean Ure, a visiting colleague from Edinburgh, Scotland. A colleague of mine had asked me if Ure could accompany me on my school visits that day, and I asked Ure if she would help me to administer the test. Later, after the class, she commented on how interesting she had found the experience, and I asked her to record what she had observed. My main purpose for this was to have a written record from a different perspective to present at the Admissions Committee meeting the next day. The majority of the class took between nine and twelve minutes to complete the test.

After the students had completed the test, I wanted to initiate an informal discussion with them on their responses to the text. I have enough experience as a teacher to know that in order to do this successfully, I had to try to change the atmosphere in the classroom from the formality of the testing event to a more informal context that would facilitate open discussion. I had to shift my position from a subjective "tester" to that of a "conversational partner." For me, this shift is deeply connected to the spatial and body relationships in the classroom, so I knew I had to change my physical position in relationship to the students. I had to shift from the position of being the "surveillant" in the testing event, where I had stood and walked around the classroom, to one of conversational partner, where I sat informally on one of the desks. In retrospect, it is interesting to note that I was not ready to relinquish complete control — I was still sitting on the desks "above" the general sightline of the class.

I asked the students, "What did you think of the passage?"[3] The first student to answer said that it was "funny." "What do you mean, 'funny'?" I asked. At this point, other students started to participate in the discussion, which rapidly became centered on the topic of monkeys. It became clear to me as the discussion progressed that the use of the word "funny" specifically meant "strange" or "threatening." One woman explained the cultural significance of monkeys for her:

> I was offended by the passage because monkeys have a special significance in our culture. . . . They are associated with witchcraft.

Other students pointed out the racist associations:

> Black people are often thought of as monkeys.

Building on their readings of the monkeys as "Black people" in this text, several students interpreted the text as an extended metaphor for Black and White social relations:

> It's about Black people, who are the "monkeys" "on the rampage" in White people's homes.

This discussion led to an animated debate among the students on the issue of land ownership:

> It's about who owns the land — the monkeys think the land belongs to them but the Whites think they own the land.

> How are the monkeys supposed to know about private ownership of property?

Many students expressed sympathy for the monkeys and deep rejection of their violent treatment at the hands of the police:

> Why did they need to shoot the monkeys? The monkeys were hungry. Why don't they have the right to pick the fruit?

> I don't like the violence in this passage. We live with violence . . . why do we need to read about it?

> It was unnecessary to shoot the monkeys. They should have found other ways of dealing with the problem.

However, a few students rejected these alternative readings of the text:

> I think it's just a story about monkeys. It was nice and easy. I hope we get something like this in the final exam.

The atmosphere in the classroom became more and more charged as the students became increasingly interested in debating the moral issues raised in this text: Who owns the land? Why should the monkeys go hungry? Which parties have the right to the fruit? Why not seek nonviolent solutions to the problem? Most of the students entering the discussion read the monkeys passage as an example of racist discourse and appeared to identify with the plight of the dispossessed monkeys. Jean Ure described the atmosphere in the classroom in a written account:

> This test, which the students appeared to do quite carefully but without enthusiasm, led to an increasingly richer and more impressive discussion following questions pressed on them consistently and persistently by PS [Pippa Stein], which gradually broke down an initial reserve and which by the end, most of them seemed to find exciting. . . . The questions brought out a deeply felt rejection of the text, on a variety of grounds. . . . Two men, older than the rest, objected on the grounds both of the violence extended to the animals and to the reporting of violence in these terms. . . . I had the impression that, although this test proved excellent for discussion, and the discussion was cathartic, not only would it have been disastrous as a test, but that it worked as well as it did because of the shared, communal nature of the discussion.

My own response to what was emerging from the discussion was complex. I was completely taken by surprise at the students' reading of the text as racist. My reading of this text as a simple factual report about monkeys in Durban shot by the police was fundamentally challenged by the students. I was embarrassed that I had not been more sensitive to a possible reading of this text as racist.

I left the class feeling confused and disoriented. I had entered the classroom with what I assumed to be a "universal" understanding of the monkeys passage as a factual account of monkeys who are a nuisance to a Durban family and who are shot by the police. My assumptions about the meanings of a text were seriously challenged. Where does the meaning of a text lie? Is this text about monkeys or is it about the dispossessed? What discursive histories did each individual student bring to bear on that text in that particular place at that particular moment?

Another assumption was challenged as well: my assumption that high school students are relatively naive about the ways in which they might use the different readings of text to their advantage. In this classroom, students were extremely adept at juggling a series of different readings in their heads, which they used appropriately, according to the demands of the social occasion.

I reported back to the Faculty of Arts Admissions Committee on how the students had responded to the test. The monkeys passage was rejected by the committee on the grounds that it might be interpreted by test takers as a racist text.

Analysis: Texts and Genres

From such an impassioned discussion of the offensiveness of the passage, we were concerned that the students' performance on the test might be compromised. We were surprised that so many (63 percent of the students) scored high (80 percent correct). In order to address this paradox, we turned to recent developments in genre analysis. While genre analysis has been used in a wide variety of fields, such as literary studies, linguistics, and rhetoric (Swales, 1990), it has only recently been applied to the field of language testing, where the standardized reading test has been framed as a particular genre (Norton Peirce, 1992).

Our conception of "genre" is not the more conventional notion of "text type" as, for example, a sonnet, term paper, interview, or prayer. Drawing on Kress (1989, 1991, 1993), we conceive of a genre as a social process in which different texts — either oral or written — are socially constructed:

> Language always happens as text; and as text, it inevitably occurs in a particular generic form. That generic form arises out of the action of social subjects in particular social situations. (Kress, 1993, p. 27)

In Kress's terms, a genre is constituted within and by a particular social occasion that has a conventionalized structure, and that functions within the context of larger institutional and social processes. In this formulation, the social occasions that constitute a genre may be formulaic and ritualized, such as a wedding or committee meeting, or less ritualized, such as a casual conversation. The important point is that the conventionalized forms of these occasions, along with the organization, purpose, and intention of the participants within the occasion, give rise to the meanings associated with the specific genre.

A central aspect of Kress's formulation of genre concerns the differences between spoken language and written language:

> A social theory of genre will need to be closely attentive to the constantly shifting relations between the language in the spoken and in the written mode, and its relations to shifts in power. (1993, p. 37)

The immediate presence of an audience in speech makes it potentially interactional and spontaneous. Both speakers and listeners jointly construct a world of shared meanings, constantly modifying and elaborating according to the responses of the moment. Turn-taking patterns shift according to the power relations between the interlocutors. In a conversation, for example, where the power relations may be relatively equitable, turn-taking may be subject to negotiation. In a typical classroom lesson, on the other hand, the interaction between teacher and students may be controlled to a greater extent by the teacher.

Kress (1989) argues that the power relations between participants in an interaction have a particular effect on the social meanings of the texts constructed within a given genre. In essence, the *mechanism* of interaction — the conventionalized form of the genre — is of primary importance in genres where a greater power difference exists between the participants, while the *substance* of the interaction — the content — is of secondary importance. The power differences also affect the relative "closedness" or "openness" of an interaction — in other words, the extent to which the social meaning of an interaction is open to negotiation. In a lesson — a genre in which the power differentials are great — the interaction is more closed, whereas in a conversation — a genre in which power differentials are reduced — interaction is more open.

Norton Peirce (1992) argues that the standardized reading test is a genre. The value ascribed to texts within the standardized reading test genre is associated with a ritualized social occasion in which participants (test makers and test takers) share a common purpose and set of expectations, but whose relationship is constituted on inequitable terms. The social occasion is characterized by strict time limits in which test takers have little control over the rate at which information is transmitted or needs to be processed. The test takers are expected to be silent at all times, observe rigorous proctoring procedures, and read the text in solitude. Both test makers and test takers recognize that the purpose of the test is to discriminate among readers with reference to an arbitrary criterion established by the test makers. The shared expectations are that the personal experience of the test takers has little relevance to the items being tested, and that the test makers decide what an acceptable reading of the text should be. The relationship between test makers and test takers, a manifestly unequal one, has a direct bearing on the social meaning ascribed to texts in the standardized reading test.

Kress's conception of genre and Norton's conception of the standardized reading test help to make sense of the contrasting readings of the monkeys passage that occurred on September 19, 1991. The intended reading, which occurred during the written test-taking event, positioned the text as a story about monkeys who were a nuisance to a Durban family, and who were accordingly disciplined by the authorities. This intended reading — or what we call the "dominant reading" — was, in fact, partly an artifact of the test maker, as evidenced in the framing of multiple-choice questions and the optional answers provided. The very first question, for example, is phrased as follows: "This newspaper article is about . . ." The test-takers are provided with four options, including the intended answer, "monkeys that attacked people." Question three reinforces the view that the monkeys were "pests," while question five depicts the monkeys' actions as destructive and undisciplined. Although the students were presented with multiple choices, they were not given the option of considering whether the text had multiple meanings. This problem is inherent in the structure of multiple-choice tests.

The divergent reading, or "insurgent reading" (taken from Simon, 1992), which arose out of the discussions following the test-taking event, positioned the text as a metaphor for inequitable social relations between Blacks and Whites in South Africa. Simon's conception of an insurgent reading is a reading produced at a particular point in time and space that contests sets of meanings that hegemonically frame text interpretation. These "sets of meaning" are the taken-for-granted assumptions shared by the writer and the intended audience.

In the case of the monkeys passage, the newspaper reporter who wrote the story takes for granted that the rights of the powerless are secondary to the rights of the powerful, and uses language in such a way that it obscures the manner in which the powerful abuse power. For example, the author positions the actions of the monkeys who were defending a trapped mother and baby as violent and extreme through words such as "rampage," "attacking," and "hurled." Later, the writer does not use the active voice to state that the police "killed" the monkeys. Instead the writer uses the agentless passive voice to indicate that the monkeys were "shot dead." In the insurgent reading of the text, it is precisely such sets of meaning that are called into question.

Our central argument is that these two contrasting readings of the text were revealed within the context of two very different social occasions, albeit on the same day and in the same place. The first social occasion was the test-taking event, with its ritualized procedures and time constraints. Key features of the first occasion included the emphasis on the written mode, the individual nature of the reading event, the reductive characteristics of the multiple-choice format, and the imposition of direct control by a White adult "expert." The second social occasion was the subsequent class discussion about the text, which began as a typical teacher-initiated discussion but rapidly developed into a conversational interaction. The mode of communication was oral rather than written.

We argue that the difference in the power relations between the teacher (Stein) and the students on the two different social occasions is implicated in the production of two different readings of the monkeys passage. To support our argument, we will explore this dynamic in greater detail.

On the first social occasion, when Stein was introduced and administered the test, she was the "test maker" — a White, English-speaking professional from prestigious Wits University. The students were the "test takers" — Black, secondary school English Language Learners from a city school with scarce resources. Despite Stein's attempts to put students at ease, we believe that her race, class, and institutional position at that point in time put her in a position of power relative to the students. We assert that not one of the students was, in fact, in a position to refuse the request to give up their lunch break in order to take the test. In this context, the mechanism of the interaction — the conventionalized form of the test event — determined to a great extent how the students "read" the text. They understood that they were expected to comply with the dictates of the genre, and to reproduce the test maker's reading of the text. When Stein asked students, "What did you think of the passage?" it is significant that some students responded to her question by highlighting the *level of difficulty* of the passage and not its interest value. Those who said, "It was nice and easy. I hope we get something like this on the final exam," were responding to the text as test. In other words, their interest in the text was structured largely by the *mechanism* of the interaction and not the *substance* of the interaction. Many students voiced less of a concern about a critical analysis of the text than with how easy it was to ascertain a "legitimate" reading of the text — a reading that a lecturer from Wits University would validate.

On the second social occasion, after the tests had been duly collected, we believe that the power relations between Stein and the students altered dramatically. Stein was no longer the test maker nor the students the test takers. Stein sat informally on the desk, inviting comment and criticism. Although she may have positioned herself at the beginning of the discussion as the controller of knowledge and power, her subject position seems to have shifted in the course of the interaction. In Stein's view, the students were no longer apprehensive, and they appeared to become more confident as they verbalized their critical reading of the text. On this social occasion, the substance of the interaction — the content of the text — became more important than the mechanism of the interaction, and there was no longer a single, legitimate reading of the text voiced by the students. Students could draw on their background knowledge and experience to analyze the social meaning of the text, and there was space for multiple readings. Students no longer appeared isolated, silent, and unenthusiastic. They interacted with one another animatedly; they debated, argued, and laughed together. The predominantly *social* context in which this discussion took place allowed for the further development of an insurgent reading that gained widespread support in the class as the discussion deepened.

Given this social occasion, the value ascribed to the monkeys passage was complex and contested. For most students, the text reflected race and class interests at the expense of less powerful communities: "It's about Black people, who are the monkeys 'on the rampage' in White people's homes." "It's about who owns the land." "It's about violence in our society." For other students, the story remained simply a story about monkeys disturbing a family.

In sum, the piloting of the monkeys passage illustrates that the social meaning of a text is not fixed, but is a product of the social occasion in which it is read. This social occasion, in turn, is a complex tapestry in which the status of the participants, their use of body language, their race (among other characteristics), the time and place of interaction, and the purpose of interaction have a direct bearing on the social meaning of texts apprehended within the occasion. Our analysis of the two contrasting readings of the monkeys passage is, however, incomplete. We do not know what power relations existed among the students themselves — whose voices were taken up and whose were ignored. We do not know whether the women were silent, or whether the speakers of minority African language were marginalized, because such differences were not attended to by Stein during the test event.

Implications for Testing and Pedagogy

We have argued thus far that the shifting power relations between Stein and the students on the two different social occasions was an important factor in the construction of the two contrasting readings of the monkeys passage.

However, the debate raises two important questions that we wish to address. First, did the monkeys passage test really "bomb"? Second, what are the implications of the test event for pedagogy? The question of whether the monkeys passage really failed to achieve its objectives of measuring English reading comprehension is complex. It is difficult to determine from such a small sample whether the psychometric qualities of the test were satisfactory. The Admissions Committee rejected the text because committee members were concerned that the students had read the text as racist. The committee did not want Wits University, with its stated ideals of nonracialism, implicated in the use of a racist test.

While this issue is clearly an important one that should not be underestimated, there is another issue about the suitability of the text-as-test that should be addressed: the "washback" effect of a test. The washback effect of a test, sometimes referred to as the systemic validity of a test (Alderson & Wall, 1993), refers to the impact of a test on classroom pedagogy, curriculum development, and educational policy. If test developers are accountable only to administrators, then a test such as the monkeys passage, with more trials, might well have proved to be a successful instrument as an initial screening device. If, on the other hand, test developers are concerned about how texts and testing impact learning and teaching in the classroom, a more complex picture emerges (see, for example, Lacelle-Peterson & Rivera, 1994).

It would be paradoxical for a university to promote a student's passive and uncritical reading of a text in an admissions test, and then expect these same "successful" students to display an active and critical approach to learning and testing once they have passed through the university gates. If a student's academic potential is defined as the ability to recognize the assumptions and worldview of test makers, then the monkeys passage did not fail; if, on the other hand, a student's potential is defined as the ability to draw on experience and knowledge to understand and critique existing knowledge, then the monkeys passage has little utility as a testing instrument. In our view, the monkeys passage failed, not because of its psychometric qualities, but because it could not be justified on pedagogical grounds.

Furthermore, even if the ability to recognize the assumptions of test makers is considered acceptable for testing purposes, equity issues become a central concern. In essence, if test makers are drawn from a particular class, a particular race, and a particular gender, then test takers who share these characteristics will be at an advantage relative to other test takers. Clearly, such inequities are not restricted to the testing of English proficiency or language testing in South Africa (see, for example, Hanson, 1993). To promote equity in educational assessment, different stakeholders, such as testers, teachers, administrators, parents, and students should be able to contribute to the test development process.

This does not address our second question, however: What are the implications of the test event for pedagogy? More specifically, how does the teacher create the conditions that will enable students to draw on their experience and understanding of the world to engage with texts and become active, critical readers? We have found Simon's (1992) work on textual interpretation particularly helpful in addressing this question. Drawing on the work of Said (1982), Simon argues that all texts are apprehended within socially regulated discourses, and that there is an "inherent instability" of textual meaning. The very fact that the same students provided at least two different readings of the monkeys passage on the same day and in the same place testifies on behalf of this position. Simon believes, however, that although a text can be read in multiple ways, such a possibility does not mean that we are "adrift in a relativism that challenges nothing and takes us nowhere" (1992, p. 113). He argues that what is pedagogically productive is to ask ourselves what makes insurgent readings possible.

With reference to the monkeys passage, a wide range of social and pedagogical conditions enabled the students to construct an insurgent reading of the text. At one level, the inequitable social and economic conditions that regulated the students' day-to-day lives in South Africa led them to identify with the dispossessed protagonists in the monkeys passage. We question whether White, middle-class students would have been likely to construct a similar reading of this text because the White, middle-class Admissions Committee had not anticipated that the text might be read as racist. As Simon argues:

> [An insurgent reading] ruptures the taken-for-granted grounds of our own understanding and teaches us that the scars and wounds of history cannot be erased within our search for universal truths. (1992, p. 24)

At another level, the pedagogical conditions that made this insurgent reading possible were significant. From the learner's point of view, the context for reading had shifted from a focus on an individual, highly ritualized, and controlled reading event (in the case of the test) to an interactive, collective oral discussion.

Drawing on Simon, we suggest that the challenge for the teacher is to *reframe* the focus of classroom discourse from a consideration of what the text "really" means to a consideration of how multiple readings of the text are socially constructed:

> The question to be asked from an educator's point of view is what discourse is regulating an insurgent reading and whether it would be desirable and possible to support that as a counterdiscursive position. (1992, p. 115)

What this means in practice is that the teacher can use the range of readings produced to explore critically with the students what investments they have in the readings and how these investments intersect with the students' histories, their relationship to the social world, and their desires for the future.[4] It is not possible for a teacher to predict the many readings students may produce from a single text, nor is it easy to predict which text will ignite insurgent readings in which context (Janks, 1993). Clearly, however, when readers' investments and identities are at stake, they may go to great lengths to seek validation for their claims to knowledge and power. What becomes important, then, is that the teacher not uncritically privilege different readings, but instead create possibilities for discussion and analysis of the social construction of these readings.

Conclusion

In post-apartheid South Africa, both the National Educational and Policy Initiative reports (NEPI, 1993) and the African National Congress (ANC) draft framework on education and training (1994) promote fundamental principles of nonracism, non-sexism, democracy, and redress. In the wider educational community, both in South Africa and internationally, such principles are inseparable from the promotion of equity in assessment and pedagogical practices. In striving for educational equity, teachers, testers, parents, students, and politicians will be inextricably enmeshed in debates and struggles over the meaning of texts and the purposes of tests.

The struggle over the meaning of the monkeys passage and its place in a university admissions test is part of larger, related questions that have relevance in many international contexts. For example, if students from historically disadvantaged communities seek access to schools, universities, and workplaces, what forms of assessment would give them the best opportunity to demonstrate their talents and abilities? Are students being excluded from certain institutions because they do not share the worldview of test makers, or because they do not have the potential to succeed? Indeed, who determines criteria for "success?" Related questions concern the meaning of texts and the validity of insurgent readings. Who determines what an acceptable reading of a text should be? Which texts are considered works of art and which are relegated to the margins of social life? Such questions, in turn, are inseparable from struggles over the ownership of tests: to whom should test makers be accountable? How should test makers address the diverse interests of stakeholders such as administrators, teachers, students, parents? Who are the test makers?

Our chapter may have raised more questions than it has successfully addressed. However, drawing on our experience with the monkeys passage, we have demonstrated that consideration must be given to the way both tests and textual meanings are socially constructed, and whether these social constructions serve the interests of justice and equality. In addition, we have highlighted a fundamental validity paradox in some language tests that are used for university admissions purposes: While admissions officers may desire language tests that identify critical, independent learners, the testing instruments they use may not give test takers the opportunity to demonstrate such abilities. Furthermore, students of color may feel particularly constrained to draw on their background experience to engage with texts used in tests. We have suggested that both test developers and teachers should use their talents to validate the histories and identities of test takers and students, encouraging them to deconstruct their insurgent readings of texts. In this way, test takers from diverse backgrounds may have the opportunity to demonstrate the richness of their experience, and students may learn not only about their past, but also construct a hopeful vision for their future.

Notes

1. The term *English Language Learners* is taken from Lacelle-Peterson and Rivera (1994) and refers to students whose first language is not English. The term includes those who are beginning to learn English, as well as those who have considerable proficiency.
2. Many members of the academic staff at Wits have participated in the development of the test, including Norman Blight, Qedusizi Buthelezi, Lorraine Chaskalson, Hilary Janks, Tom Lodge, Debra Nails, Esther Ramani, and Louise Stack.
3. The following quotations are taken from the field notes that I wrote the evening after the testing event.
4. See Norton Peirce (1995) for a discussion of the relationship between investment and social identity.

References

African National Congress (ANC). (1994). *A policy framework for education and training.* Johannesburg: National ANC Office.
Alderson, C., & Wall, D. (1993). Does washback exist? *Applied Linguistics, 14,* 115–129.
Hanson, F. A. (1993). *Testing testing: Social consequences of the examined life.* Berkeley: University of California Press.
Janks, H. (1993). *Closed meanings in open schools.* Proceedings of the Australian Reading Association First International Conference, Melbourne, Australia.
Kress, G. (1989). *Linguistic processes in sociocultural practice.* Oxford, Eng.: Oxford University Press.
Kress, G. (1991). Critical discourse analysis. *Annual Review of Applied Linguistics, 11,* 84–89.
Kress, G. (1993). Genre as social process. In B. Cope & M. Kalantzis (Eds.), *The powers of literacy* (pp. 22–37). London: Falmer Press.
Lacelle-Peterson, W., & Rivera, C. (1994). Is it real for all kids? A framework for equitable assessment policies for English Language Learners. *Harvard Educational Review, 64,* 55–75.
National Educational and Policy Initiative. (1993). *Framework report.* Cape Town: Oxford University Press.
Norton Peirce, B. (1992). Demystifying the TOEFL reading test. *TESOL Quarterly, 26,* 665–691.
Norton Peirce, B. (1995). Social identity, investment and language learning. *TESOL Quarterly, 29*(1), 9–31.
Said, E. (1982). *The world, the text and the critic.* Cambridge, MA: Harvard University Press.
Simon, R. (1992). *Teaching against the grain: Texts for a pedagogy of possibility.* New York: Bergin & Garvey.
Stack, L. (1994). *Report to the Arts Faculty Admissions Committee.* Johannesburg: University of the Witwatersrand.
Swales, J. (1990). *Genre analysis: English in academic and research settings.* Cambridge, Eng.: Cambridge University Press.

Yeld, N., & Haeck, W. (1993). Educational histories and academic potential: Can tests deliver? In S. Angeli-Carter (Ed.), *Language in academic development at U.C.T.* Unpublished manuscript.

We would like to thank Heather Brookes, Hilary Janks, Gunther Kress, Nomsa Ngqakayi, Roger Simon, and Sue Starfield for their valuable comments on an earlier draft of this paper. In addition, the support of the Social Sciences and Humanities Research Council of Canada and the Academic Support Programme, University of the Witwatersrand, is gratefully acknowledged.

More than "Model Minorities" or "Delinquents": A Look at Hmong American High School Students

STACEY J. LEE

The first Southeast Asian refugees arrived in the United States in 1975, and within ten years the popular press identified Southeast Asian youth as "the new whiz kids" (Brand, 1987). Conspicuously absent from these reports were Hmong American youth, whose academic difficulties bumped up against the popular "model minority" image (Walker-Moffat, 1995). The first Hmong arrived in the United States as refugees from Laos over twenty-five years ago. Early scholarly and popular descriptions of Hmong refugees emphasized the differences between Hmong culture — described as rural, preliterate, patriarchal, and traditional — and mainstream American culture (e.g., Donnelly, 1994; Fass, 1991; Rumbaut & Ima, 1988; Sherman, 1988). These cultural differences were explained as the root of many of the social and economic problems Hmong refugees faced in the United States. For example, cultural barriers were identified as the reason behind the high dropout rates among Hmong refugee students in middle and high school (Cohn, 1986; Goldstein, 1985). Hmong girls, in particular, experienced high dropout rates, which were traced back to the Hmong cultural practices of early marriage and early childbearing (Goldstein, 1985; Rumbaut & Ima, 1988; Walker-Moffat, 1995).

While the early research on Hmong refugees painted a grim picture of Hmong student achievement, much of the recent research has highlighted the success of Hmong American students. Several researchers have argued that Hmong students as a group have overcome their early difficulties and are now managing to do well in school despite high rates of poverty, low levels of parental education, and the cultural practice of early marriage among teens (Call & McNall, 1992; Dunnigan, Olney, McNall, & Spring, 1996; Hutchinson,

1997; Hutchinson & McNall, 1994; Rumbaut, 1995). Scholars attribute the success of Hmong American students to the support of the immigrant community, family support, and adherence to traditional values such as respect for elders (Hutchinson, 1997; Rumbaut, 1995). Thus, in contrast to earlier portrayals of Hmong culture as problematic, current scholarship characterizes it as a positive influence on student achievement. In his recent study on Hmong students in Wisconsin, Hutchinson (1997) concluded that "Hmong youth will be more successful in their educational careers than any other immigrant or refugee group to ever come to the United States" (p. 1). It would appear that Hmong American students have joined the ranks of the model minority.

Although many Hmong American students appear to be successful, there is evidence that some Hmong youth are exhibiting serious adjustment problems. Truancy, rising dropout rates, and delinquency among teens have been identified by researchers as some of the major concerns within Hmong American communities (Faderman, 1998; Thao, 1999; Walker-Moffat, 1995). These problems have not gone unnoticed by the popular press, which has highlighted the rise of Southeast Asian gangs (e.g., Ingersoll, 1999; Kifner, 1991). The academic literature and the popular press convey a perception that Hmong American youth fall into two opposite groups: high-achieving model minorities, and delinquents, truants, and gang members.

Research on other Southeast Asian ethnic groups suggests that dropping out of school, truancy, and other forms of resistant behavior are more common among second- generation than first-generation youth (Rumbaut, 1995; Zhou & Bankston, 1998). Some researchers argue that the youth who experience trouble in school and with the law are those who have become disconnected from their families and culture and therefore become over-Americanized (Rumbaut, 1995; Zhou & Bankston, 1998). In his research on Hmong youth in Chicago, Thao (1999) asserts that youth who are over-Americanized are particularly vulnerable to gang involvement. Similarly, the popular explanation the media advances suggests that second-generation youth have lost their culture. One newspaper article, for example, referred to the rise in Southeast Asian gangs as evidence of the "cultural growing pains" (Ingersoll, 1999, p. 1) within immigrant communities. Such analysis, of course, oversimplifies the reasons youth engage in resistant behavior. This analysis assumes that "American" culture is inherently dangerous and that Hmong culture can protect its youth from harm. Furthermore, it places Hmong-ness and American-ness into mutually exclusive categories.

Other researchers have observed the impact of race, social context, and economic opportunities on the adjustment of second-generation youth (Ima, 1995; Portes, 1995, 1996; Portes & Rumbaut, 1996; Suárez-Orozco & Suárez-Orozco, 1995). Portes asserts, "There are three features of the social contexts encountered by today's newcomers that create vulnerability to downward assimilation. The first is color, the second is location, and the third is the absence of mobility ladders" (1995, p. 73). The strength of this selection of work is that it considers the impact of structural forces on student adjustment.

In this article, I explore the way economic forces, relationships with the dominant society, perceptions of opportunities, family relationships, culture, and educational experiences affect Hmong American students' attitudes toward school. Specifically, I compare the way 1.5-generation and second-generation Hmong American students respond to education.[1] Additionally, I focus attention on variations within each group. The following questions provide the focus for this piece: How do Hmong American students view education? Do responses to education vary between 1.5-generation and second-generation students? I pay particular attention to how the forces inside and outside of school affect attitudes toward education.

Data for this article was collected as part of a one and one-half academic year ethnographic study of Hmong American students at a Wisconsin public school, University Heights High School (UHS).[2] I visited UHS three days per week on average for three to five hours at a time. The primary means of data collection were participant observation of Hmong students in the high school (e.g., in classrooms, during lunch periods, during study hall, and during extracurricular activities) and interviews with Hmong students and school staff. Interviews lasted from one to three hours and were taped when possible. I also analyzed school documents, observed Hmong parents at meetings organized by the school district, and conducted participant observation at local Hmong community events. Although there are many places in the article where I provide verbatim quotes from interviews and describe individuals in detail, at other times I speak more generally about a group. My decision to speak generally reflects an effort to protect the identity of individuals who revealed sensitive information that they did not want traced back to them.

Located in a mid-size city in Wisconsin, UHS enjoys an excellent reputation in the city and the state. Mr. Schenk, the school social worker, explained that the faculty and staff at UHS are proud of its high academic standards and many consider UHS to be a "public prep school":

> It is a public school that has many, many qualities of a private prep school. It services a population in the community that are primarily university families or university-connected families, professional families. And then . . . about a fourth of . . . the student population . . . are special populations: African Americans, Asian Americans . . . probably . . . somewhat less a percentage of poor kids. But it really is . . . in terms of the traditions, in terms of the way it views itself, it's really kind of a prep school. It is invested in the academic standards . . . the quality of the students, in terms of the high achieving, it has a really broad selection. . . . And so it is kind of a secondary image, a secondary school, trying to become like a university, which it is very close to. Then I think that if you are looking for a sort of prep school attitude toward academics . . . that is what would capture University Heights High — a public prep school.

UHS enrolled 2,023 students during the 1999–2000 academic year, with 29 percent of these students classified as students of color and 14 percent listed as receiving free or reduced lunch. Several members of the staff commented that the percentage of students of color and lower income students had grown significantly in the last twenty years. A significant portion of the student population still comes from middle-class and professional families who live in the neighborhood of the school. Although there has been an increase in the diversity of the student population, Mr. Schenk's comments suggest that the school continues to reflect the culture of the middle-class students.

Since UHS and the school district classify all students of Asian descent into one category, "Asians," it was difficult to attain an exact count of the Hmong students. According to estimates by various school staff, there were fifty-four Hmong students enrolled at UHS during the 1998–1999 school year and approximately sixty-five enrolled during the 1999–2000 school year.[3] Most of the Hmong students were from low-income families and received free or reduced lunch. Many lived in low-income housing in the poorer sections of the city.

With few exceptions, Hmong American students at UHS were acutely aware of issues of identity and typically used ethnicity, race, gender, age, generation, and marital status to situate others. In my first encounters with Hmong students I was typically asked the following: "Are you Hmong?" "Where were you born?" and "Are you married?" As a third-generation Chinese American woman, I share a panethnic/racial identity with the Hmong students. This helped to facilitate our initial conversations, but the fact that I am not Hmong still branded me an ethnic outsider. Because the Hmong students saw me as an outsider they were initially very cautious around me. Many of my informants, for example, would switch to speaking Hmong when discussing potentially sensitive topics (e.g., marriage, funerals, ritual healing, etc.). Two of my primary informants hid their married status from me for several months until they felt that I was trustworthy. Significantly, these young women hid their married status from school officials, for fear of moral and even legal judgment.

Similarly, in her research on Hmong immigrants in Wisconsin, Koltyk (1998) discovered that most Hmong go to great lengths to protect their culture from the gaze and criticism of outsiders. Koltyk (1998) explains, "As the Hmong have learned that aspects of their culture seem primitive or offensive to many Americans, they have become reluctant to talk to outsiders about them" (p. 14). By keeping their secrets and sharing aspects of my Chinese cultural background, I was eventually able to gain the trust of many students, though they remained cautious in new situations.

"There are two groups of Hmong students at UHS"

During my first week at UHS, Mrs. Her, one of the Hmong bilingual resource specialists, informed me that there were basically two groups of Hmong students at UHS. Using language that could best be described as diplomatic, she referred to the first group as the English as a Second Language (ESL) students and the second group as the "Americanized" students. She explained that the ESL students were "newcomers" and the Americanized students were born in the United States, and that the Hmong student population at UHS had shifted over two decades. In the 1980s, Hmong American students were all first generation, while today they are mostly second generation. While ESL students were the norm in the 1980s, most Hmong American students at UHS today are in mainstream classes. Mrs. Her elaborated by saying that the newcomers "still keep and value Hmong traditions," and that the Americanized students had adopted more American ways. She added that the two groups of students had very different relationships to schooling. She explained:

> We don't have problems with those ESL kids. Because, they are, I don't know, they seem, maybe they're not Americanized, . . . so they are still thinking, like they said they are still, let's say, good kids. So they are working hard and trying to graduate from UHS. The other problems, I think the problem that most of the Hmong students face are students who are in the mainstream — they are facing truancy.

Like many scholars (Thao, 1999; Zhou & Bankston, 1998), Mrs. Her points to the negative impact of Americanization on student achievement. In a later interview, Mrs. Her stated that Hmong parents divided Hmong youth into the "good kids" and the "bad kids":

> The good kid will go back to the culture, whether it's a boy or a girl. When they come back home, they will, I guess help the parents, [by] doing housework, chores. I guess [they] dress differently too. . . . A normal kid . . . practicing some traditional culture, and going to school, attending school, getting good grades, will be . . . good, a good child, a good boy or girl. And also, I guess doing what the parents want them to do. . . . And, so the opposite is when the kids start to rebel or talk back to the parents, not obeying. And then wearing the baggy clothes, not attending school. Those are the bad kids.

At a school district–sponsored meeting for Southeast Asian parents, several Hmong parents stated (through interpreters) that they were afraid that they were losing their children to the American culture. Some parents explained that while their children were "good kids" they feared that "bad Hmong kids" at school would influence their children. Like Mrs. Her, these parents viewed students' wearing baggy clothes as the first sign of trouble. In this regard, Mrs. Her and the parents were in agreement: they all identify "good kids" and "bad kids" by their clothes, their relationship with adults, and their attitudes toward school.

The Hmong students at UHS also emphasized the differences between ESL and Americanized students. In my one and one-half academic years at UHS, the social boundaries between the 1.5-generation and second-generation groups of students were rarely crossed at school. Students in one group would admit to having cousins in the other group, but they maintained their distance. While 1.5-generation students were more likely to participate in the school's Asian Club, second-generation students dominated the school's

Hmong Club. While the Asian Club included students from various Asian ethnic groups (e.g., Chinese, Tibetan, Vietnamese, Hmong, etc.), all members of the Hmong Club were ethnically Hmong. When I asked 1.5-generation students why they chose to participate in the Asian Club instead of the Hmong Club, they explained that they wanted to be in a club that emphasized teaching others about their culture. These students suggested that the members of the Hmong Club were more interested in parties than in their culture. My observations of the Hmong Club revealed that its members were interested in organizing parties and other social events, but they were also interested in participating in a club where they could express their own identities. Although these second-generation students did not see themselves as being traditional, they participated in the club because they were proud of being Hmong.

Several 1.5-generation students reported that their parents warned them to stay away from "bad kids" who were "too Americanized." Echoing the sentiments of the parental generation, a 1.5-generation student compared the two groups like this: "We are more traditional. We speak Hmong and know the Hmong culture. The others speak more English — they want to be cool. They don't follow what adults say." For their part, second-generation Hmong students ridiculed 1.5-generation students for being too "traditional" and "old fashioned." They even used derogatory terms such as *FOB* or *FOBBIES* (i.e., Fresh Off the Boat) to describe 1.5-generation students. A second-generation student described 1.5-generation students like this: "FOBS don't care about clothes. They are stingy about clothes. They dress in out-of-date 1980s-style clothes. American-born Hmong are into clothes and cars."

1.5-Generation Students

During lunch hours, members of the 1.5 generation can be found sitting with other foreign-born Asians at the edge of the cafeteria. The more academically successful 1.5-generation students cluster in one group, and those who are struggling academically sit together in another. Observers are likely to hear 1.5-generation students speaking a combination of Hmong and English. Typical topics of conversations include family and school. Born in Thailand or Laos, most of these students have been in the United States for three to eight years. Those who remember life before the United States stress that things are better here than in their native countries. This dual frame of reference is typical of immigrant children and allows them to persist in the face of difficulties in the new country (Ogbu, 1993; Suárez-Orozco, 1989; Suárez-Orozco & Suárez-Orozco, 1995). In describing the significance of the dual frame of reference, Ogbu (1993) writes:

> The immigrants often compare themselves with the standard of their home country or with their peers "back home" or in the immigrants' neighborhood. When they make such a comparison they usually find plenty of evidence that they have made significant improvements in their lives. (p. 100)

In terms of cultural expression (e.g., dating, language), 1.5-generation students appear to many to be "traditionally Hmong." Mrs. Her described 1.5-generation students as "not Americanized," suggesting a kind of cultural purity. Although most 1.5-generation students live by their parents' rules, the Hmong culture has not remained static. Even as relative newcomers, 1.5-generation students and their families have made cultural adjustments in response to life in the United States. One of the biggest of these adjustments is their increased support for the education of girls and women (Goldstein, 1985; Koltyk, 1998; Lee, 1997). Furthermore, while 1.5-generation students in this study follow their parents' ways out of respect, many assert that that they will raise their own children in "Hmong *and* American ways." Such attitudes suggest a more complex embracing of Hmong culture than is evident at first glance.

Perceptions of Education

From their parents, 1.5-generation students have acquired a "folk theory of success" that links education to social mobility (Ogbu, 1993), a concept typical among immigrants from many cultures (Gibson, 1988; Suárez-Orozco, 1989). Many students who participated in this research study diligently because they, like their parents, believe that education is the route to ascending the socioeconomic ladder of American society. Most students dream of going to college or vocational school after graduating from high school. It is not uncommon to find members of the 1.5 generation studying in groups before school and during lunch. Some students seek out other hard-working foreign-born Asians as friends and study companions. Friendly competition over test scores on the latest French or chemistry test helps to further motivate the students. Many 1.5-generation students are well aware that UHS has a reputation for being an excellent school with high academic standards. In comparing UHS to schools in Thailand or Laos, they conclude that the educational opportunities in the United States are far superior and consider themselves to be fortunate to be attending such a school.

May, a sophomore, dreams of becoming a doctor. She firmly believes that as a woman her educational opportunities are greater in the United States than they would have been in Laos. Furthermore, she maintains that UHS is a particularly good school:

> This is a really good school. At this school if you want to be a success you can. There are harder and better classes here than at other schools. I feel lucky to go to school here and I tell my sister that she is lucky she will be coming here.

Family Obligations

Like other immigrant children, 1.5-generation Hmong youth report having significant family responsibilities that they must juggle along with their schoolwork (Portes & Rumbaut, 1996; Song, 1999). Many Hmong students at UHS are responsible for interpreting for their parents, driving their parents to appointments, performing various household chores, and even working to help support the family. Jackson, a senior in high school, misses school occasionally because he has to drive his parents to appointments. Cha, a sophomore, must work at a local supermarket in order to earn money to help support his mother, who is living on disability insurance. Cha explained, "It is my job to take care of my mother . . . my father is in Laos." Girls, in particular, are often expected to help cook, clean, and take care of younger siblings. May wakes up at 6:15 A.M. and helps her younger siblings get ready for school. She catches the bus at 7:00 A.M. and meets her friends to study in the school cafeteria for an hour before school starts. After a full day of academic classes, she attends an after-school tutoring program for academically talented students from disadvantaged backgrounds until 7:00 P.M. When she gets home, she cooks dinner and then helps her siblings with their homework before doing her own homework. By the time she goes to bed at midnight she is exhausted. Jackson, Cha, May, and others perform this caring work because they feel obliged to their parents and because they believe it is the right thing to do. Despite the fact that the traditional parent-child relationships are reversed within these families, parental authority is preserved.

In describing the conditions necessary to maintain parental authority, Portes and Rumbaut write:

> Parental authority is maintained in those admittedly rare instances where little acculturation takes place in either generation. More commonly, that authority is preserved where sufficient resources exist to guide second-generation acculturation. These resources are of two kinds: first, parental education, allowing the first generation to "keep up" with their children's learning and to monitor its course; second, ethnic bonds, creating incentives for youth to comply with community norms and to combine them with American cultural patterns. (1996, pp. 240–241)

Although the parents of 1.5-generation students have little formal education, most 1.5- generation students report that their parents have close ties to the Hmong community that support parental authority. May, for example, reports that the Hmong community monitors her actions and that this prevents her from straying from her parents' ways. May's parents' ability to maintain their authority also derives from their willingness to make certain cultural accommodations. In describing her parents, May says, "They are traditional, but they want me to go to college." May is quick to point out that her parents' support for her education distinguishes them from some Hmong parents, who fail to support higher education for their daughters. Because her parents support her dreams for higher education, she perceives them as reasonable. This judgment leads her to follow their rules with little resistance.

Although students rarely complained about their family responsibilities, it is important to note that family obligations can interfere with students' educational pursuits. In her research on Hmong college students, for example, Ngo (2000) discovered that students often had to choose between their education and their family responsibilities. In my study, students explained that family obligations often had to come before homework, which ultimately affected their grades. Cha, for example, explained that after work and household chores, he was often too tired to do his homework. Similarly, early marriage and childbearing can create obstacles for young women. Many immigrant parents now believe that their daughters should wait until after graduating from high school to get married, but there are still some parents who encourage their daughters to marry while in high school. On the subject of early marriage, Dunnigan, Olney, McNall, and Spring (1996) recently concluded that "early marriage and childbearing do not appear to serve as an impediment to young Hmong adults' pursuit of education" (p. 206). Unlike these researchers, I am less optimistic about the impact of early marriage on the educational persistence of Hmong girls. Although most parents value education for their daughters, once girls are married, the decision to pursue education is in the hands of their in-laws. Furthermore, even when in-laws support the idea of education it is often difficult for young women to successfully pursue an education when they are responsible for the care of the in-laws' family.

During my research at UHS, I learned about three girls who were pressured into getting married. The experiences of my respondents serve as cautionary tales regarding the impact of early marriage on the pursuit of education. One student explained that although she did not want to get married, she ultimately agreed to the marriage out of feelings of obligation to her parents. Her in-laws and parents have all agreed that she should be allowed to go to college when she graduates from high school, but her increased family obligations often interfere with her studies. This young woman now splits her time between her parents' house, where she continues to help cook and care for her siblings, and her in-laws' house, where she also cooks and cleans. Given the increase in her family responsibilities, she now fears that she will not be able to earn the grades to win a scholarship to go to school, but she has not given up. Such stories serve as a warning to researchers who would too blithely dismiss the impact of early marriage on girls.

Although my data suggests that early marriage may negatively affect girls' education, I would caution schools not to condemn early marriage. Early marriage is a highly political issue and one about which the Hmong community is very sensitive. The fact that many married Hmong girls at UHS choose to hide their married status suggests that they are well aware of the fact that school authorities would condemn their status. By condemning early marriage, schools may inadvertently be asking students to choose between their education and their families.

ESL as a Safe Space

Although UHS has an excellent reputation among the White, middle-class population of the city, some people of color have criticized the school for overlooking the specific needs of students of color. The ESL program at UHS, however, is led by a team of educators dedicated to serving students who are

English-language learners.[4] Most 1.5-generation students are enrolled in the ESL program, which offers courses in ESL, social studies, science, and math. The school offers guided-study courses to help students make the transition from ESL to mainstream classes. In addition to these course offerings, the department employs part-time bilingual resource specialists to assist with tutoring and translations, as well as a special guidance counselor to help students select courses. In ESL classes students are encouraged to draw on their cultural experiences. They are also afforded the freedom to develop their English-language skills without fear of being ridiculed by mainstream students (Olsen, 1997). Students who are 1.5 generation reported that they felt more comfortable talking in their ESL classes than in their mainstream classes. In short, the ESL program provides a safe space for its students in a large and often intimidating school. Ms. Heinemann, the chair of the ESL department during the 1998–1999 school year, believes that the mission of the ESL program is to teach students the academic and cultural skills to make the transition to mainstream classes. In her words:

> I think we're teaching language and culture, including the culture of an American high school and how to access that. I'm very concerned about holding kids separate because, for their learning, they need to be in contact with peers. And I think for our society, if we don't have different groups mixing at the high school level, some of those groups will never mix. So, for those two reasons, I've worked really hard to try to create joint courses between departments.

Despite the efforts of the ESL program to integrate ESL students into the mainstream of the school, ESL and former ESL students remain socially segregated from mainstream students. Several 1.5-generation students complained about the social environment of the school, where it is difficult to make "American" friends. Although they are frustrated by this, most of them also emphasize that they are getting superior educational opportunities in the United States. Many 1.5-generation students report having close relationships with their ESL teachers, which further confirms their faith in the American educational system. May, for example, said she even felt comfortable talking to Mrs. Heinemann about "private things."

Contrary to the model minority stereotype, most 1.5-generation students were not high achievers. In fact, achievement among 1.5-generation students ranged from high to low, with the majority passing their classes with average grades. According to some school personnel, a growing minority of ESL students are falling into a pattern of chronic truancy.

Mr. Thao, a bilingual resource specialist, explained that some students begin skipping classes because they cannot keep up with the material. According to Mr. Thao, these students are often overlooked because they are quiet and teachers assume that they are working hard. Unfortunately, these students do not receive the assistance they need in order to survive academically. Thus, the emerging stereotype of the hard-working, quiet model minority works against the students' best interests. Their quiet demeanor serves as a reminder that resistance to schooling is not always expressed through direct confrontation. Other chronic truants, however, have come to the attention of school authorities for engaging in what is characterized as "negative behaviors." Sam, like other 1.5-generation students who are chronically truant, began skipping classes because he could not understand the material. Since becoming a chronic truant he has been suspended for fighting on more than one occasion. According to the tenth-grade principal, the most recent suspension came after Sam hit a White student for calling him a derogatory name. Although the principal was sympathetic to Sam, he could not make exceptions to the rules regarding fighting.[5] For Sam, the suspension served to confirm his suspicions that UHS is a racist institution. Unlike the higher achieving ESL students, Sam cannot console himself with dreams of higher education because his high school grades are low. For students like Sam, UHS is a social and academic minefield. What is significant about Sam's case is that he only began to skip his classes after he had struggled academically. Skipping classes was a way for him to avoid further embarrassment and frustration caused by his academic difficulties. Students like Sam do not begin skipping classes out of a desire to resist authority or out of a rejection of school. Unfortunately, Sam's truancy exacerbated his academic difficulties and got him into other trouble.

At the other end of the spectrum are the few students who are successful enough to make the honor roll. Interestingly, the students with the highest educational aspirations and the highest levels of achievement (e.g., grade point average) are girls. They are also the most likely to participate in after-school tutorial programs for academically successful students, and to be identified by teachers as exceptionally hard workers. In my previous work on Hmong American college women, I discovered that high achievement among Hmong women was in part a response to cultural norms regarding gender, which have been described as patrilinear and patriarchal (Donnelly, 1994; Lynch, 1999; Rumbaut & Ima, 1988). In describing the role of Hmong women in Laos, Donnelly (1994) wrote, "Ultimately, each woman worked under the command of men of her own household — under her husband if married, under her father and brothers if unmarried, under her son if aged" (p. 32). Gender roles in Laos were also shaped by the agricultural lifestyle. For example, women were encouraged to marry as teens and bear many children, who could then work on the farm (Lynch, 1999). Hmong American girls and women perceive the United States as a place where they have the chance to gain gender equality. Hmong American women explained that Hmong men could get respect with or without an education, but education was one of the only ways for women to gain freedom (Lee, 1997). May, for example, is a high-achieving sophomore who works hard in school because she wants "a good life where I won't have to work as hard as my mother." May's mother works two jobs, maintains the family's vegetable garden, and takes care of the house.

Second-Generation Students

> For the young, there is no going back. For better or worse, they are Americans. (Faderman, 1998, p. 88)

At lunchtime, large groups of second-generation students gather at tables in the cafeteria. All American-born students are welcome, but the students they refer to as "FOBs" (1.5-generation Hmong American students) are not. After eating their lunch, some students run outside for a smoke while others stay inside and talk or study.

Although they proudly assert their American-born status, second-generation youth also express a strong sense of ethnic solidarity. Those who are active in extracurricular clubs choose to participate in the school's Hmong Club. During the 1999–2000 academic year, for instance, the Hmong Club had a difficult time finding an advisor. At one point a teacher suggested that the Hmong Club merge with the Asian Club, but the students dismissed this idea as being out of the question. The students explained that they wanted their own club. When I asked why they chose to participate in the Hmong Club, the girls responded by saying, "I love the Hmong people" and "I can relate to Hmong people."

In interviews, second-generation students consistently asserted that getting an education is important because it leads to a good job. Despite these professed beliefs regarding the instrumental value of education, their actual responses to education vary. Within the second generation are students who work hard, do well in school, and plan on going to college, and others who are chronically truant and on the brink of failing most of their courses. Like some of the 1.5-generation students who are chronic truants, some second-generation students begin skipping classes because of academic difficulties. For these students, truancy does not reflect a rejection of education but is a response to feelings of inadequacy and embarrassment. One such student, for example, stated that he hated going to class "because it makes me feel stupid." Other second-generation students begin to skip classes because of intergenerational conflicts at home. Still other second-generation students skip classes because they doubt that education will lead to social mobility.

Intergenerational Conflicts

Second-generation students routinely complain that their parents are too strict and do not understand life in the United States. According to them, immigrant parents want their American-born children to be "more traditional." However, second-generation youth, born and educated in the United States, inhabit a world apart from their immigrant parents. While many immigrant parents only speak Hmong, most second-generation youth are more fluent in English. Intergenerational conflict between immigrant parents and their American-born teens reflects the tension over how each group imagines the future of Hmong America. Like students of the 1.5 generation, many second-generation students are expected to perform caring work (e.g., interpreting and driving) and household chores. In second-generation families, however, these role reversals often lead to the weakening of parental authority. Portes and Rumbaut (1996) assert that the loss of parental authority is directly related to the fact that the parental generation has not acculturated at the same rate as their children. According to Portes and Rumbaut (1996), this "generational dissonance occurs when second-generation acculturation is neither guided nor accompanied by changes in the first generation. This situation leads directly to role reversal in those instances when first generation parents lack sufficient education or sufficient integration into the ethnic community to cope with the outside environment and hence must depend on their children's guidance" (p. 241). It is important to point out that second-generation students are not rejecting their Hmong backgrounds. Rather, they are trying to redefine what it means to be Hmong in the United States. Intergenerational conflict between immigrant parents and their American born teenagers reflects the tension over how each group imagines the future of Hmong America.

One of the most common conflicts between parents and adolescents often revolves around the issue of dating. Girls, in particular, lament that they are forbidden to spend time alone with boys. Jane, for example, complains that "it is so stupid. Parents think that if you are alone with a guy, you are fooling around." Many girls report that their parents expect their dates to come to the house to visit with the entire family, an idea that most second-generation girls find appalling. Many parents also prefer arranged marriages, while their second-generation daughters dream of marrying someone of their own choice. In an effort to circumvent their parents' rules, many second-generation youth have turned to the Internet as a way to meet members of the opposite sex. Adolescents report that it is becoming very common for young people to meet on the Internet in Hmong chat rooms. Once adolescents have established a relationship over the Internet, they go to considerable effort to arrange clandestine face-to-face meetings (Lee, 2001).

Another source of tension between second-generation youth and their parents involves the way teenagers dress. Many Hmong parents consider what their American-born children wear to be a sign of gang membership. Mrs. Her describes the way the adult Hmong community view youth who wear baggy clothes: "The kids start wearing the different clothes. Big clothes, loose clothes, baggy clothes. So they [Hmong adults] will start to call those kids 'gang'." Second-generation youth report that their parents learn about the dangers of Asian gangs from the television and from the larger Hmong community. The local school district has also tried to educate Hmong parents about the dangers of gangs. This attention to gang prevention contributes to the tension between parents and second-generation youth. For example, I attended a school district-sponsored meeting for Southeast Asian parents that focused on gangs. The day after this meeting, several students complained that such meetings stir up trouble by leading parents to believe that gangs are more prevalent than they actually are. Hope, a sophomore in high school, complained:

> They look at us as some bad kids. They call us some "little gang bangers" 'cause [of] the people around us, the way we dress and stuff. . . . People started dressing all baggy and they don't like it. People, like the old folks, they just say that we've forgotten our language a little bit, [and] we have a little bit, but then we still carry our traditions and stuff around.

Hope explains that she would like to learn more about her culture and history, but she finds communication with her parents frustrating. She asserts that she is proud of being Hmong, but she does not agree with all Hmong traditions. She understands that her clothes make her "look like a thug" in her parents' eyes, but she maintains that she and her friends are not in gangs. Because of their clothing, however, Hmong elders and many school authorities assume that she and her friends are involved with gangs. Criticized by adults, many second-generation students like Hope cling more tightly to their peers and turn away from adults.

Hmong immigrant parents view the changing family roles, their children's desire for increased independence, and their children's clothes as evidence that they are losing their second-generation children to "American ways." Research shows that immigrant parents have responded to the situation by trying to further control all aspects of their children's lives. Suárez-Orozco and Suárez-Orozco (1995) discovered that Latino immigrant parents may "over-restrict the activities of the children and attempt to minimize the host country's influence" (p. 65). Similarly, some Hmong parents attempted to control all aspects of their children's lives. Many second-generation Hmong American youth respond to their parents' hypercontrol by resisting parental authority. Resistance may come in the form of direct confrontation (e.g., talking back to parents) or in the form of indirect challenges to parental authority (e.g., sneaking around). Toua, a junior at UHS, has had problems with truancy for the past two years. She explains that she skips class because "school is the only time we can hang out with our friends." When she is not in school, Toua and her friends are expected to be at home helping with the chores, but at school she and her friends have figured out that they can control their own time. Thus, truancy is an indirect way to circumvent their parents' control.

Toua and Hope are examples of students who experience significant conflict with their parents. This intergenerational conflict is related to differences in opinion regarding how to respond to life in the United States. In other cases, however, the intergenerational conflict is less severe. Moua, for example, explains that her parents are "traditional, but not real traditional," and they are "strict, but not super strict." Although they do not really approve of the clothes their second-generation children wear, Moua's parents do allow their children to pick their own clothes. They have also allowed their oldest daughter to go away to college in California. Although many Hmong parents now support higher education for their daughters, most expect their daughters to attend colleges near home. The fact that Moua's parents have been willing to make compromises has, paradoxically, helped to limit the intergenerational conflict within the family and helped to maintain parental authority.

"All Americans Are Rich"

In contrast to the generally hopeful attitude of the 1.5 generation, most second-generation students are somewhat cynical about life in the United States, where ongoing experiences with poverty have contributed to their cynicism about opportunities. Unlike immigrants, second-generation youth do not have a dual frame of reference (Ogbu, 1993). All they know is life in the United States and they want to be treated like other Americans. They cannot relate to what their parents say about life in Laos. They are more likely to compare themselves to their White, middle-class peers than to relatives in Thailand or Laos. Based on their observations at UHS and the images from the media, second-generation students have concluded that most Whites are wealthy. Moua, for example, moved to Wisconsin from California with her parents because they heard that there were greater economic opportunities in Wisconsin. Moua imagines that the typical White family is economically well off and supportive. She says:

> When I think of the mainstream I think of a White family I guess. As both parents working . . . have really good jobs and maybe one kid or two kids, three at the most. And the kids are doing house chores and everything, they, like, have good grades and even when the girl grows up, the woman, the mom has a good job like a doctor or something. And the father supports the girl — she may go to college to be a doctor or major in business or something and the dad totally supports it.

Moua's father works at two jobs and her mother works one full-time job and takes in sewing. During her senior year Moua worked part-time on weekends to save money to attend community college. Students like Moua compare themselves to their White, middle-class peers, which makes them painfully aware that they are poor. For example, when I asked her why she did not participate in class discussions in her philosophy class, Moua said her experiences were "less interesting" than those of "White kids who have traveled all over." Another student, Toua, lives with her mother and two siblings in low-income housing. Her father died unexpectedly a few years ago. Toua bitterly expresses her resentment about being poor. She complained, "I hate being poor. . . . All Hmong people are poor and live in shabby houses." Toua and many of her peers have concluded that money is the most important thing in the United States, and they dream of being rich.

Some second-generation students see education as the route out of poverty. Like many immigrant youth, these students cling to a folk theory of success that links education to social mobility. Moua, for example, graduated from UHS with a B average. She plans to earn her associate's degree and then transfer to the local university to earn her bachelor's degree. Moua's parents have encouraged her and her two older siblings to pursue higher education in order to get better jobs. Other second-generation youth, however, have begun to question whether education will lead to social mobility. Like other working-class and poor youth, many second-generation youth do not see how academic subjects will help them get a job (Eckert, 1989; Willis, 1977). Furthermore, they question whether it makes sense to spend time in high school when they can be earning money at a job. Some chronic truants hold on to the belief that a high school diploma is important, but they have clearly prioritized their part-time jobs over their schooling. "G," for example, should be a senior in high school, but she has only earned enough credits to be a sophomore. "G" explains that her part-time job is more important than school because she earns money to buy herself clothes and to travel to Hmong soccer tournaments in cities throughout the Midwest.[6] She has dropped out of high school, but she still hopes to earn her high school equivalency degree.

"They think we are all lazy and on welfare"

Second-generation students complain that non-Hmong people mock their culture and stereotype them as lazy welfare recipients with big families. Tim, a senior in the class of 1999, complained that "a lot of Americans think all Asians eat dogs and cats. We don't. They think Hmong are all on welfare. We aren't." Other students tell stories about being treated like gang members by store clerks, police officers, and others. Second-generation students are unwilling to overlook instances of racism and discrimination. Sia, a graduate of the class of 1999, explains her distrust of White people:

> For me, I feel, I just feel like some White people neglect me. I mean as much as I try to be nice to them, give them respect, they don't give it back to me. Why should I even bother with them? Because I feel like I really don't need people like that. . . . I mean, if you're not Asian like me, you don't understand where I'm coming from either. Like White people, I mean, they may say they do, but I don't see it. They don't really know how it feels.

Sia's distrust for White people extends to White teachers as well. During her senior year in high school Sia was having serious family problems and she almost flunked out of school. When I suggested that she tell her teachers or counselors about her problems, she refused because she did not trust them to treat her problems with respect. Many second-generation Hmong American students at UHS share a similar distrust of teachers. One semester there was a rumor that one of the vice principals had made racist comments about Hmong students. Although the students were angry about the alleged comment, most were not shocked to hear that a school authority might have made racist comments. Previous experiences inside and outside of school led students to be suspicious of White authority figures.

Most second-generation students were in ESL classes during elementary and middle school, but have been mainstreamed at UHS. Unlike the ESL students who have a somewhat sheltered experience at UHS, students in the mainstream find themselves in an impersonal and highly competitive culture. Mr. Schenk, like other faculty and staff who work closely with students of color, points out that the culture of UHS reflects and favors those same White, middle-class students. Furthermore, they assert that the needs of poorer students and students of color are often sacrificed to protect the interests of White, middle-class students. Mr. Burns, one of the vice-principals, says:

> I think . . . any time you have . . . this diverse group, this heterogeneous culture . . . I think just by default, there's some pecking order to that. And I think that exists here at UHS. I mean . . . we have a diverse student population. . . . I think there's still . . . some sort of elemental power relative to those subsets. . . . There has to be some sort of . . . system in place, or some sort of order by which . . . things are [done] . . . at the school. And I think that exists here at UHS. For example . . . I think the school is very responsive to . . . our talented students, the ones who are honor students. It doesn't necessarily mean that the school isn't responsive to the students at the other end of the spectrum. But, you know, the school is set up in a sense to be very responsive to the kids . . . who are achieving.

What Mr. Burns does not say here is that the majority of "honor students" at UHS are White. His comments do suggest, however, that lower achieving students and students who are outside of the mainstream experience a kind of benign neglect at UHS.

Despite these conditions, some second-generation students manage to survive and even thrive at UHS. Each semester a few second-generation students earn high enough grades to make the honor roll. Most of these "successful" students had been identified as "good" students by their elementary school teachers, and they had maintained good relationships with their teachers into high school. The majority of the second-generation students, however, become disconnected from school. They complain that they cannot relate to the curriculum or their teachers. As noted earlier, many question whether classes like algebra, chemistry, or Shakespeare can lead to a job. Tim, for example, believes that the vocational high school he attended when his family lived in California was superior to UHS because it offered job skills. He explains:

> My school in California gave a lot of electives and stuff. Back there, they give you vocational classes already and everything. So, you know what part of the field you're going to go into already and get experience and all that. Here is just really academic classes and stuff like that. So I would say I like it there a lot better than here.

Many students also distrust their teachers, assuming that they are racist or at the very least critical of Hmong culture. As mentioned earlier, girls who are married hide their marital status from school authorities. Referring to the impact of isolation of Hmong American students, Mr. Schenk says,

> Every kid that I have talked to, whether they are sort of these hard gang members or whomever, that are Hmong, they feel like this place just doesn't fit them. If you listen to the actual words, you know, "the teacher doesn't like me," "I don't have any place to go," "I don't like the principals," "if I am in the hall somebody's . . ." it is all about whether or not they are invited or included in some way. Those are the words. Whether they are angry or whether they are depressed or sad or whatever, those are still the words and the words have to do with being included or excluded.

Several second-generation students remarked that the content of their classes is simply boring and that they crave a curriculum that reflects their culture and history. They asserted that they would take any class that focused on Hmong culture. Hope, a chronic truant who failed ninth grade, said that she would welcome a class in Hmong culture, history, or language so she could learn about "her people." When she was in elementary school she took Hmong language classes at the community center. She still uses some of that Hmong when she participates in Hmong chat rooms.

Like the low-achieving 1.5-generation students, some second-generation students start skipping class because they're having academic difficulties. These students often hide their problems until it becomes apparent to teachers that their grades are dropping and they are failing exams. By that time, of course, much of the damage is already done. Some low-achieving students have internalized their shame and simply accept that they are "stupid." Jane, for example, is one year behind in school because she failed her sophomore year. When she revealed this to me she said sarcastically that it was "the Hmong way" to be at least one year behind.

Many UHS educators blame students for their own academic problems. Some members of the staff have concluded that Hmong American students simply lack motivation. One guidance counselor came to this conclusion after comparing Southeast Asian students with East Asian students.[7] She says, "An East Asian student might be number three in the class and going to Yale, but the Southeast Asians aren't very motivated." What this counselor fails to recognize and address, however, is the possibility that the school may or may not be doing something to affect underachievement among some Hmong youth. The fact that some Asians are successful proves to her that success is possible for Asians at UHS. The fact that many of the East Asians are from highly educated backgrounds is not factored into the equation of their success — the perception is that their success is just an issue of motivation.

Other UHS educators assume that Hmong students' cultural differences create problems for them. Although cultural issues no doubt play a role, many educators use the cultural explanation to free themselves of responsibility for guiding these students toward achievement at UHS. According to many of these educators, cultural issues are the responsibility of the ESL department. Most second-generation Hmong are not in ESL, but as soon as they have problems they are referred there. It should be noted that this is not an official school policy, but rather an unofficial practice.

Ms. Heinemann, the chair of ESL, complained that the school often abdicates responsibility for culturally different students. She argues that

> the school needs to recognize the population of students who are born and educated here and still don't feel part of the mainstream curriculum, the mainstream school activities. . . . I don't think those students should be counted as ESL students, because that makes them more different, that separates them more. They don't want that.

Ms. Heinemann's comments are echoed in the words of second-generation students themselves, who say that they do not want to be in ESL and that ESL is just for "FOBs." Kim, a senior, complained, "They always put Hmong students in ESL, which is racist. My cousin was put in ESL here and he doesn't even need it. I told him not to let them do that."

As in the 1.5-generation group, there are second-generation students who begin to skip classes in response to academic difficulties. Although second-generation Hmong students speak about the importance of education, some are beginning to question whether education is the most efficient method of achieving social mobility. In short, second-generation students' attitudes regarding education are shaped by their experiences inside and outside of school. Intergenerational relationships, experiences with racism, economic circumstances, relationships with school authorities, and academic achievement all influence their reactions to school.

Conclusions

The Hmong American students at UHS embody a complexity that challenges simplistic representations of Hmong youth as either model minorities or juvenile delinquents. Additionally, descriptions of Hmong students as either traditional or Americanized fail to fully appreciate the extent to which those who are described as traditional have acculturated and those who are described as Americanized have maintained a distinct identity as Hmong Americans. Although Mrs. Her and many Hmong students at UHS characterized Hmong students as falling into two distinct groups — 1.5-generation students, who are traditional (i.e., "good kids"), and second-generation students, who are Americanized (i.e., "bad kids") — my data suggests a more complex picture.

Although 1.5-generation youth are characterized as being traditional, some of them embrace aspects of mainstream American society and many indicate that they will raise their children to follow both Hmong and American ways. On the other hand, while second-generation students appear to be Americanized (e.g., in their clothes and language), most continue to identify strongly as Hmong. There are high-achieving and hard-working students in both the 1.5-generation and second-generation groups, and there are chronic truants in both groups. While intergenerational conflict between second-generation youth and their parents is common, some second-generation youth, like their 1.5-generation counterparts, obey their parents' authority with little resistance. One significant difference between 1.5-generation and second-generation students concerns their respective responses to racism. While both groups complained about the way non-Hmong people treat them, 1.5-generation students were more willing to overlook instances of discrimination and to focus on the positive aspects of life in the United States.

My ethnographic data challenges work that suggests a simplistic one-to-one relationship between the maintenance of traditional culture and high achievement, and Americanization and low achievement and delinquency (Hutchinson, 1997; Thao, 1999). Arguments regarding the positive impact of traditional culture on achievement underestimate the extent of cultural transformation in the Hmong community. Hmong culture, like all cultures, is fluid and dynamic. What researchers describe as traditional is in fact a culture that has changed and adapted in response to external conditions.

Rather than seeing the maintenance of traditional culture as being at the root of success, my data suggests that it is the practice of "accommodation and acculturation without assimilation" (Gibson, 1988, p. 24) that supports success. This strategy involves conforming to certain rules of the dominant society (i.e., accommodation) and making certain cultural adaptations while maintaining the group's own cultural identity (pp. 24–25). The experiences of 1.5-generation and second-generation students suggest that their parents' willingness and ability to adopt aspects of the dominant culture are directly related to their ability to maintain aspects of the Hmong culture. May (1.5 generation) and Moua (second generation), for example, accept their parents' authority because their parents have made certain cultural adjustments. In other words, my data suggests that academic success is the result of both cultural transformation and cultural preservation.

Although Hmong culture certainly plays a role in school achievement, a sole focus on the role of culture in achievement fails to adequately consider the impact of structural forces on students' attitudes toward education. My data supports the previous research that points to the impact of racism and economic opportunities on students' responses to school and their perceptions of life opportunities (Portes, 1995; Suárez-Orozco & Suárez-Orozco, 1995). Second-generation youth, in particular, had long-term experiences with racism and poverty that challenged their faith in education. These students are not resisting school because they are Americanized, but because they do not perceive school to offer real opportunities.

Additionally, my research highlights the significance of the local school culture in the lives of these students and in their levels of school achievement. Unlike many poor immigrants and second-generation youth, the Hmong American youth in my study attend a relatively well-funded school with a reputation for academic excellence. Despite this reputation and perhaps even because of it, students of color and those from other marginal categories often fall through the cracks and fail to see themselves as part of the larger community of the school. The one major exception to this is the ESL program, which serves as a major source of support for many 1.5-generation students. For second-generation students there is no comparable source of support or inclusion.

To make these students full citizens in the schools that are intended to serve them, a number of things are necessary: educators who understand and respect their culture and the difficulties they face in their homes as they try to straddle the gulf between their culture and the larger American society; a curriculum that reflects their history; and a sense of inclusion in the school community at large. In sum, the school success or failure of 1.5- and second-generation Hmong students does not hinge on any one thing, but rather on a marriage of both external and internal forces.

Notes

1. The term *1.5 generation* is used to describe foreign-born individuals who arrive in the United States as children and are largely educated and socialized in the United States (see Portes, 1996).
2. The name of the school and individuals quoted are pseudonyms.
3. School staff estimated the number of Hmong students at UHS by searching the school roster for Hmong surnames.
4. It is important to point out that not all teachers in the ESL program were equally dedicated and/or qualified to work with ESL students. For example, two teachers had reputations among the students for being "nice, but too easy." Other ESL teachers criticized these "easy teachers" in hushed tones. Furthermore, some of the very dedicated ESL teachers complained that their efforts to improve the ESL program were often thwarted by school district regulations.
5. According to the school district's conduct and discipline plan, middle and high school students charged with hitting another student are subject to suspension.
6. Hmong soccer and volleyball tournaments are popular among 1.5- and second-generation youth. Like the Hmong New Year celebrations, the sports tournaments offer Hmong American youth an opportunity to meet and socialize with other Hmong youth. While most 1.5-generation youth report attending tournaments with their parents, second-generation youth attend with families or peers.
7. At UHS, the Southeast Asian category includes Hmong, Cambodian, Vietnamese, and Laotian students, while the East Asian category includes Chinese and Korean students.

References

Brand, D. (1987, August 31). The new whiz kids. *Time*, pp. 42–51.
Call, K., & McNall, M. (1992). Poverty, ethnicity and youth adjustment: A comparison of poor Hmong and non-Hmong adolescents. In W. Meeus, M. de Goede, W. Kox, & K. Hurrelmann (Eds.), *Adolescence, careers, and cultures* (pp. 373–392). Berlin, NY: Degruyter.
Cohn, M. (1986). Hmong youth and the Hmong future in America. In G. Hendricks, B. Downing, & A. Deinard (Eds.), *The Hmong in transition* (pp. 197–201). Staten Island, NY: Center for Migration Studies.
Donnelly, N. (1994). *Changing lives of refugee Hmong women*. Seattle: University of Washington Press.

Dunnigan, T., Olney, D., McNall, M., & Spring, M. (1996). Hmong. In D. W. Haines (Ed.), *Refugees in America in the 1990s: A reference handbook* (pp. 191–212). Westport, CT: Greenwood Press.

Eckert, P. (1989). *Jocks and burnouts: Social categories and identity in the highschool.* New York: Teachers College Press.

Faderman, L. (1998). *"I begin my life all over": The Hmong and the American experience.* Boston: Beacon Press.

Fass, S. (1991). *The Hmong in Wisconsin: On the road to self-sufficiency.* Milwaukee: Wisconsin Policy Research Institute.

Gibson, M. (1988). *Accommodation without assimilation: Sikh immigrants in an American high school.* Ithaca, NY: Cornell University Press.

Goldstein, B. (1985). *Schooling for cultural transitions: Hmong girls and boys in American high schools.* Unpublished doctoral dissertation, University of Wisconsin, Madison.

Hutchinson, R. (1997). *The educational performance of Hmong students in Wisconsin.* Thiensville: Wisconsin Policy Research Institute.

Hutchinson, R., & McNall, M. (1994). Early marriage in a Hmong cohort. *Journal of Marriage and Family, 56,* 579–590.

Ima, K. (1995). Testing the American dream: Case studies of Southeast Asian refugee students in secondary schools. In R. Rumbaut & W. Cornelius (Eds.), *California's immigrant children: Theory, research, and implications for educational policy* (pp. 191–208). San Diego: Center for U.S.-Mexican Studies.

Ingersoll, B. (1999, November 19). Cultural growing pains. *Wisconsin State Journal,* pp. 1A, 3A.

Kifner, J. (1991, January 6). Immigrant waves from Asia bring an underworld ashore. *New York Times,* p. 11A.

Koltyk, J. (1998). *New pioneers in the heartland: Hmong life in Wisconsin.* Boston: Allyn & Bacon.

Lee, S. (1997). The road to college: Hmong American women's pursuit of higher education. *Harvard Educational Review, 67,* 803–831.

Lee, S. J. (2001). Transforming and exploring the landscape of gender and sexuality: Hmong American teenaged girls. *Race, Gender and Class, 8(2),* 35–46.

Lynch, A. (1999). *Dress, gender, and cultural change: Asian American and African American rites of passage.* New York: Berg.

Ngo, B. (2000). *Obstacles, miracles, and the pursuit of higher education: The experiences of Hmong American college students.* Unpublished master's thesis, University of Wisconsin, Madison.

Ogbu, J. U. (1993). Variability in minority school performance: A problem in search of an explanation. In E. Jacob & C. Jordan (Eds.), *Minority education: Anthropological perspectives* (pp. 83–107). Norwood, NJ: Ablex.

Olsen, L. (1997). *Made in America: Immigrant students in our public schools.* New York: New Press.

Portes, A. (1995). Segmented assimilation among new immigrant youth: A conceptual framework. In R. Rumbaut & W. Cornelius (Eds.), *California's immigrant children: Theory, research, and implications for educational policy* (pp. 71–76). San Diego: Center for U.S.-Mexican Studies.

Portes, A. (1996). *The new second generation.* New York: Russell Sage Foundation.

Portes, A., & Rumbaut, R. (1996). *Immigrant America: A portrait* (2nd ed.) Berkeley: University of California Press.

Rumbaut, R. (1995). The new Californians: Comparative research findings on the educational progress of immigrant children. In R. Rumbaut & W. Cornelius (Eds.), *California's immigrant children: Theory, research and implications for educational policy* (pp. 17–69), La Jolla, CA: Center for U.S.-Mexican Studies.

Rumbaut, R., & Ima, K. (1988). *The adaptation of Southeast Asian refugee youth: A comparative study.* Washington, DC: U.S. Office of Refugee Resettlement.

Sherman, S. (1988). The Hmong: Laotian refugees in the land of the giants. *National Geographic, 174*, 586–610.

Song, M. (1999). *Helping out: Children's labor in ethnic businesses.* Philadelphia: Temple University Press.

Suárez-Orozco, M. (1989). *Central American refugees and U.S. high schools: A psychosocial study of motivation and achievement.* Stanford, CA: Stanford University Press.

Suárez-Orozco, M., & Suárez-Orozco, C. (1995). The cultural patterning of achievement motivation: A comparison of Mexican, Mexican immigrant, Mexican American, and non-Latino White American students. In R. Rumbaut & W. Cornelius (Eds.), *California's immigrant children: Theory, research, and implications for educational policy* (pp. 161–190). San Diego: Center for U.S.-Mexican Studies.

Thao, P. (1999). *Hmong education at the crossroads.* New York: University Press of America.

Walker-Moffat, W. (1995). *The other side of the Asian American success story.* San Francisco: Jossey-Bass.

Willis, P. E. (1977) *Learning to labor: How working class kids get working class jobs.* New York: Columbia University Press.

Zhou, M., & Bankston, C. L. (1998). *Growing up American: How Vietnamese children adapt to life in the United States.* New York: Russell Sage Foundation.

PART TWO
(De)Constructing Racism

—■—■—■—

> The whole history of the progress of human liberty shows that all concessions . . . have been born of earnest struggle. . . . If there is no struggle, there is no progress. . . . Power concedes nothing without a demand. It never did, and it never will. Find out just what people will submit to, and you have found out the exact amount of injustice and wrong which will be imposed upon them; and these will continue till they are resisted with either words or blows, or with both.
>
> — *Frederick Douglass*[1]

The right to equal educational opportunities for all people has been contested terrain virtually since the founding of the United States in the eighteenth century. Now, more than two hundred years later, the struggle for access to quality education continues for those who come from marginalized and underrepresented groups in American society. Much of this struggle has been predicated on deconstructing the racist assumptions that have infused many of our nation's social institutions and that have persisted, albeit often in subtle forms, into the twenty-first century. As a result, it is important to understand the ways that opposition to educational equity is constructed and operates in order to best devise strategies to combat it. The three authors in Part Two bring to light some of the individual and institutional barriers that tacitly or explicitly impede the goal of providing quality education for all our nation's children.

In her foundational piece, "The Silenced Dialogue: Power and Pedagogy in Educating Other People's Children," Lisa Delpit uses the debate between skills-based and process-based approaches to writing instruction to frame her analysis of the absence of the voices of parents of color from educational dialogue, and the larger messages about privilege and power that this silence reveals. Delpit identifies a "culture of power" that functions in schools and influences the spoken and unspoken dialogue, norms, and expectations that operate in this context. When students come from outside of this culture of power, their unfamiliarity with its rules may limit their academic and personal success because they lack knowledge of the communicative and behavioral forms needed to conform to this context. Furthermore, to the extent that teachers deny students access to the forms of knowledge needed to succeed in the culture of power, they become benignly complicit in maintaining the status quo. Delpit challenges teachers to redefine their roles as gatekeepers to educational success in a way that respects the cultural attributes that students bring with them to school and equips them with the knowledge and skills necessary to function successfully within larger mainstream society.

In "The Politics of Culture: Understanding Local Political Resistance to Detracking in Racially Mixed Schools," Amy Stuart Wells and Irene Serna give life to Delpit's culture of power theory with their portrait of the "ideology of entitlement" that underlies the systems of inequality that persist within schools. Using qualitative data from interviews with school personnel, students, parents, and community leaders in ten racially and socioeconomically mixed communities, Wells and Serna uncover some of the ways in which White elites mount political resistance to detracking in order to preserve the benefits that this practice confers to their children. Drawing from social reproduction theory, the authors reveal the subtle assumptions about privilege, merit, and entitlement upon which elites' tacit attitudes about tracking are based. Moreover, by elucidating the relationship between cultural capital and educational achievement, Wells and Serna reveal the arbitrary nature of the educational knowledge and standards propagated by schools, and in so doing, they expose these standards as subjective reflections of the experiences and ways of knowing held and valued by the elite. In this way, they contend that tracking serves as a tool for legitimizing and maintaining the privileged place of elites in the educational system. In response, Wells and Serna call for greater awareness among parents, educators, and policymakers about the individual, institutional, and societal barriers to detracking reform in order to deconstruct the arbitrary systems of privilege that exist in schools and provide greater learning opportunities for all students.

Finally, in "Bilingual Education for Puerto Ricans in New York City: From Hope to Compromise," Sandra Del Valle describes how Puerto Ricans have used legislative and judicial means to dismantle linguistic barriers to equal opportunity in education. Del Valle presents this push for educational equity as a civil rights issue in which the New York City Puerto Rican constituency demanded effective language instruction in schools and contested schools' efforts to mold Latino students into mainstream White images of success. Del Valle points out, however, that early bilingual education policies ignored Spanish fluency as a cultural and cognitive asset and cast it instead as an English-language deficit in need of remediation. Although New York City Puerto Ricans' fight for bilingual education began more than twenty-five years ago, Del Valle notes that the issue remains hotly contested between groups with competing ideas about what the goals of bilingual education should be — a transitional program that seeks to establish English-language dominance for non-English-speaking students or a developmental program that encourages both native- and English-language abilities simultaneously. As a result of this ongoing debate and questions about bilingual education programs' continued viability in general, Del Valle urges advocates to look beyond a singular focus on mainstream national efforts to protect these programs and to take a more inclusive approach that reaches out to parents, students, and grassroots organizations committed to bilingual education and to the improvement of educational quality for all students.

Note

1. From the West India Emancipation speech delivered in Canandaigua, New York, August 4, 1857. In *The Life and Writings of Frederick Douglass*, ed. Philip S. Foner (New York: International Publishers, 1950), vol. 2, p. 437.

The Silenced Dialogue:
Power and Pedagogy in Educating
Other People's Children

LISA D. DELPIT

A Black male graduate student who is also a special education teacher in a predominantly Black community is talking about his experiences in predominantly White university classes:

> There comes a moment in every class where we have to discuss "The Black Issue" and what's appropriate education for Black children. I tell you, I'm tired of arguing with those White people, because they won't listen. Well, I don't know if they really don't listen or if they just don't believe you. It seems like if you can't quote Vygotsky or something, then you don't have any validity to speak about your *own* kids. Anyway, I'm not bothering with it anymore, now I'm just in it for a grade.

A Black woman teacher in a multicultural urban elementary school is talking about her experiences in discussions with her predominantly White fellow teachers about how they should organize reading instructions to best serve students of color:

> When you're talking to White people they still want it to be their way. You can try to talk to them and give them examples, but they're so headstrong, they think they know what's best for *everybody*, for *everybody's* children. They won't listen, White folks are going to do what they want to do *anyway*.
>
> It's really hard. They just don't listen well. No, they listen, but they don't *hear* — you know how your mama used to say you listen to the radio, but you *hear* your mother? Well they don't *hear* me.
>
> So I just try to shut them out so I can hold my temper. You can only beat your head against a brick wall for so long before you draw blood. If I try to stop arguing with them I can't help myself from getting angry. Then I end up

walking around praying all day "Please Lord, remove the bile I feel for these people so I can sleep tonight." It's funny, but it can become a cancer, a sore.

So, I shut them out. I go back to my own little cubby, my classroom, and I try to teach the way I know will work, no matter what those folk say. And when I get Black kids, I just try to undo the damage they did.

I'm not going to let any man, woman, or child drive me crazy — White folks will try to do that to you if you let them. You just have to stop talking to them, that's what I do. I just keep smiling, but I won't talk to them.

A soft-spoken Native Alaskan woman in her forties is a student in the Education Department of the University of Alaska. One day she storms into a Black professor's office and very uncharacteristically slams the door. She plops down in a chair and, still fuming, says, "Please tell people, just don't help us anymore! I give up. I won't talk to them again!"

And finally, a Black woman principal who is also a doctoral student at a well-known university on the West Coast is talking about her university experiences, particularly about when a professor lectures on issues concerning educating Black children:

If you try to suggest that that's not quite the way it is, they get defensive, then you get defensive, then they'll start reciting research.

I try to give them my experiences, to explain. They just look and nod. The more I try to explain, they just look and nod, just keep looking and nodding. They don't really hear me.

Then, when it's time for class to be over, the professor tells me to come to his office to talk more. So I go. He asks for more examples of what I'm talking about, and he looks and nods while I give them. Then he says that that's just my experiences. It doesn't really apply to most Black people.

It becomes futile because they think they know everything about everybody. What you have to say about your life, your children, doesn't mean anything. They don't really want to hear what you have to say. They wear blinders and earplugs. They only want to go on research they've read that other White people have written.

It just doesn't make any sense to keep talking to them.

Thus was the first half of the title of this text born — "The Silenced Dialogue." One of the tragedies in the field of education is that scenarios such as these are enacted daily around the country. The saddest element is that the individuals that the Black and Native American educators speak of in these statements are seldom aware that the dialogue *has* been silenced. Most likely, the White educators believe that their colleagues of color did, in the end, agree with their logic. After all, they stopped disagreeing, didn't they?

I have collected these statements since completing a recently published article (Delpit, 1986). In this somewhat autobiographical account, entitled "Skills and Other Dilemmas of a Progressive Black Educator," I discussed my perspective as a product of a skills-oriented approach to writing and as a teacher of process-oriented approaches. I described the estrangement that I and many teachers of color feel from the progressive movement when writing-process advocates dismiss us as too "skills oriented." I ended the article suggesting that it was incumbent upon writing-process advocates — or indeed, advocates of any progressive movement — to enter into dialogue with teachers of color who may not share their enthusiasm about so-called new, liberal, or progressive ideas.

In response to this article, which presented no research data and did not even cite a reference, I received numerous calls and letters from teachers, professors, and even state school personnel from around the country, both Black and White. All of the White respondents, except one, have wished to talk more about the question of skills versus process approaches — to support or reject what they perceive to be my position. On the other hand, *all* of the non-White respondents have spoken passionately on being left out of the dialogue about how best to educate children of color.

How can such complete communication blocks exist when both parties truly believe they have the same aims? How can the bitterness and resentment expressed by the educators of color be drained so that the sores can heal? What can be done?

I believe the answer to these questions lies in ethnographic analysis, that is, in identifying and giving voice to alternative world views. Thus, I will attempt to address the concerns raised by White and Black respondents to my article "Skills and Other Dilemmas" (Delpit, 1986). My charge here is not to determine the best instructional methodology; I believe that the actual practice of good teachers of all colors typically incorporates a range of pedagogical orientations. Rather, I suggest that the differing perspectives on the debate over "skills" versus "process" approaches can lead to an understanding of the alienation and miscommunication, and thereby to an understanding of the "silenced dialogue."

In thinking through these issues, I have found what I believe to be a connecting and complex theme: what I have come to call "the culture of power." There are five aspects of power I would like to propose as given for this presentation:

1. Issues of power are enacted in classrooms.
2. There are codes or rules for participating in power; that is, there is a "culture of power."
3. The rules of the culture of power are a reflection of the rules of the culture of those who have power.
4. If you are not already a participant in the culture of power, being told explicitly the rules of that culture makes acquiring power easier.
5. Those with power are frequently least aware of — or least willing to acknowledge — its existence. Those with less power are often most aware of its existence.

The first three are by now basic tenets in the literature of the sociology of education, but the last two have seldom been addressed. The following discussion will explicate these aspects of power and their relevance to the schism between liberal educational movements and that of non-White, non-middle-class teachers and communities.[1]

1. Issues of power are enacted in classrooms.
These issues include: the power of the teacher over the students; the power of the publishers of textbooks and of the developers of the curriculum to determine the view of the world presented; the power of the state in enforcing compulsory schooling; and the power of an individual or group to determine another's intelligence or "normalcy." Finally, if schooling prepares people for jobs, and the kind of job a person has determines her or his economic status and, therefore, power, then schooling is intimately related to that power.

2. There are codes or rules for participating in power; that is, there is a "culture of power."
The codes or rules I'm speaking of relate to linguistic forms, communicative strategies, and presentation of self; that is, ways of talking, ways of writing, ways of dressing, and ways of interacting.

3. The rules of the culture of power are a reflection of the rules of the culture of those who have power.
This means that success in institutions — schools, workplaces, and so on — is predicated upon acquisition of the culture of those who are in power. Children from middle-class homes tend to do better in school than those from non-middle-class homes because the culture of the school is based on the culture of the upper and middle classes — of those in power. The upper and middle classes send their children to school with all the accoutrements of the culture of power; children from other kinds of families operate within perfectly wonderful and viable cultures but not cultures that carry the codes or rules of power.

4. If you are not already a participant in the culture of power, being told explicitly the rules of that culture makes acquiring power easier.
In my work within and between diverse cultures, I have come to conclude that members of any culture transmit information implicitly to co-members. However, when implicit codes are attempted across cultures, communication frequently breaks down. Each cultural group is left saying, "Why don't those people say what they mean?" as well as, "What's wrong with them, why don't they understand?"

Anyone who has had to enter new cultures, especially to accomplish a specific task, will know of what I speak. When I lived in several Papua New Guinea villages for extended periods to collect data, and when I go to Alaskan villages for work with Alaskan Native communities, I have found it unquestionably easier — psychologically and pragmatically — when some kind soul has directly informed me about such matters as appropriate dress, interactional styles, embedded meanings, and taboo words or actions. I contend that it is much the same for anyone seeking to learn the rules of the culture of power. Unless one has the leisure of a lifetime of "immersion" to learn them, explicit presentation makes learning immeasurably easier.

And now, to the fifth and last premise:

5. Those with power are frequently least aware of — or least willing to acknowledge — its existence. Those with less power are often most aware of its existence.

For many who consider themselves members of liberal or radical camps, acknowledging personal power and admitting participation in the culture of power is distinctly uncomfortable. On the other hand, those who are less powerful in any situation are most likely to recognize the power variable most acutely. My guess is that the White colleagues and instructors of those previously quoted did not perceive themselves to have power over the non-White speakers. However, either by virtue of their position, their numbers, or their access to that particular code of power of calling upon research to validate one's position, the White educators had the authority to establish what was to be considered "truth" regardless of the opinions of the people of color, and the latter were well aware of that fact.

A related phenomenon is that liberals (and here I am using the term "liberal" to refer to those whose beliefs include striving for a society based upon maximum individual freedom and autonomy) seem to act under the assumption that to make any rules or expectations explicit is to act against liberal principles, to limit the freedom and autonomy of those subjected to the explicitness.

I thank Fred Erickson for a comment that led me to look again at a tape by John Gumperz[2] on cultural dissonance in cross-cultural interactions. One of the episodes showed an East Indian interviewing for a job with an all-White committee. The interview was a complete failure, even though several of the interviewers appeared to really want to help the applicant. As the interview rolled steadily downhill, these "helpers" became more and more indirect in their questioning, which exacerbated the problems the applicant had in performing appropriately. Operating from a different cultural perspective, he got fewer and fewer clear clues as to what was expected of him, which ultimately resulted in his failure to secure the position.

I contend that as the applicant showed less and less aptitude for handling the interview, the power differential became ever more evident to the interviewers. The "helpful" interviewers, unwilling to acknowledge themselves as having power over the applicant, became more and more uncomfortable. Their indirectness was an attempt to lessen the power differential and their discomfort by lessening the power-revealing explicitness of their questions and comments.

When acknowledging and expressing power, one tends toward explicitness (as in yelling to your ten-year-old, "Turn that radio down!"). When de-emphasizing power, there is a move toward indirect communication. Therefore, in the interview setting, those who sought to help, to express their egalitarianism with the East Indian applicant, became more and more indirect — and less and less helpful — in their questions and comments.

In literacy instruction, explicitness might be equated with direct instruction. Perhaps the ultimate expression of explicitness and direct instruction in the primary classroom is Distar. This reading program is based on a behaviorist model in which reading is taught through the direct instruction of phonics generalizations and blending. The teacher's role is to maintain the full attention of the group by continuous questioning, eye contact, finger snaps, hand claps, and other gestures, and by eliciting choral responses and initiating some sort of award system.

When the program was introduced, it arrived with a flurry of research data that "proved" that all children — even those who were "culturally deprived" — could learn to read using this method. Soon there was a strong response, first from academics and later from many classroom teachers, stating that the program was terrible. What I find particularly interesting, however, is that the primary issue of the conflict over Distar has not been over its instructional efficacy — usually the students did learn to read — but the expression of explicit power in the classroom. The liberal educators opposed the methods — the direct instruction, the explicit control exhibited by the teacher. As a matter of fact, it was not unusual (even now) to hear of the program spoken of as "fascist."

I am not an advocate of Distar, but I will return to some of the issues that the program — and direct instruction in general — raises in understanding the differences between progressive White educators and educators of color.

To explore those differences, I would like to present several statements typical of those made with the best of intentions by middle-class liberal educators. To the surprise of the speakers, it is not unusual for such content to be met by vocal opposition or stony silence from people of color. My attempt here is to examine the underlying assumptions of both camps.

"I want the same thing for everyone else's children as I want for mine."
To provide schooling for everyone's children that reflects liberal, middle-class values and aspirations is to ensure the maintenance of the status quo, to ensure that power, the culture of power, remains in the hands of those who already have it. Some children come to school with more accoutrements of the culture of power already in place — "cultural capital," as some critical theorists refer to it (for example, Apple, 1979) — some with less. Many liberal educators hold that the primary goal for education is for children to become autonomous, to develop fully who they are in the classroom setting without having arbitrary, outside standards forced upon them. This is a very reasonable goal for people whose children are already participants in the culture of power and who have already internalized its codes.

But parents who don't function within that culture often want something else. It's not that they disagree with the former aim, it's just that they want something more. They want to ensure that the school provides their children with discourse patterns, interactional styles, and spoken and written language codes that will allow them success in the larger society.

It was the lack of attention to this concern that created such a negative outcry in the Black community when well-intentioned White liberal educators introduced "dialect readers." These were seen as a plot to prevent the schools from teaching the linguistic aspects of the culture of power, thus dooming Black children to a permanent outsider caste. As one parent demanded, "My kids know how to be Black — you all teach them how to be successful in the White man's world."

Several Black teachers have said to me recently that as much as they'd like to believe otherwise, they cannot help but conclude that many of the "progressive" educational strategies imposed by liberals upon Black and poor children could only be based on a desire to ensure that the liberals' children get sole access to the dwindling pool of American jobs. Some have added that the liberal educators believe themselves to be operating with good intentions, but that these good intentions are only conscious delusions about their unconscious true motives. One of Black anthropologist John Gwaltney's (1980) informants reflects this perspective with her tongue-in-cheek observation that the biggest difference between Black folks and White folks is that Black folks *know* when they're lying!

Let me try to clarify how this might work in literacy instruction. A few years ago I worked on an analysis of two popular reading programs, Distar and a progressive program that focused on higher-level critical thinking skills. In one of the first lessons of the progressive program, the children are introduced to the names of the letter *m* and *e*. In the same lesson they are then taught the sound made by each of the letters, how to write each of the letters, and that when the two are blended together they produce the word *me*.

As an experienced first-grade teacher, I am convinced that a child needs to be familiar with a significant number of these concepts to be able to assimilate so much new knowledge in one sitting. By contrast, Distar presents the same information in about forty lessons.

I would not argue for the pace of the Distar lessons; such a slow pace would only bore most kids — but what happened in the other lesson is that it merely provided an opportunity for those who already knew the content to exhibit that they knew it, or at most perhaps to build one new concept onto what was already known. This meant that the child who did not come to school already primed with what was to be presented would be labeled as needing "remedial" instruction from day one; indeed, this determination would be made before he or she was ever taught. In fact, Distar was "successful" because it actually *taught* new information to children who had not already acquired it at home. Although the more progressive system was ideal for some children, for others it was a disaster.

I do not advocate a simplistic "basic skills" approach for children outside of the culture of power. It would be (and has been) tragic to operate as if these children were incapable of critical and higher-order thinking and reasoning. Rather, I suggest that schools must provide these children the content that other families from a different cultural orientation provide at home. This does not mean separating children according to family background, but instead, ensuring that each classroom incorporate strategies appropriate for all the children in its confines.

And I do not advocate that it is the school's job to attempt to change the homes of poor and non-White children to match the homes of those in the culture of power. That may indeed be a form of cultural genocide. I have frequently heard schools call poor parents "uncaring" when parents respond to the school's urging that they change their home life in order to facilitate their children's learning by saying, "But that's the school's job." What the school personnel fail to understand is that if the parents were members of the culture of power and lived by its rules and codes, then they would transmit those codes to their children. In fact, they transmit another culture that children must learn at home in order to survive in their communities.

"Child-centered, whole language, and process approaches are needed in order to allow a democratic state of free, autonomous, empowered adults, and because research has shown that children learn best through these methods."

People of color are, in general, skeptical of research as a determiner of our fates. Academic research has, after all, found us genetically inferior, culturally deprived, and verbally deficient. But beyond that general caveat, and despite my or others' personal preferences, there is little research data supporting the major tenets of process approaches over other forms of literacy instruction, and virtually no evidence that such approaches are more efficacious for children of color (Siddle, 1986).

Although the problem is not necessarily inherent in the method, in some instances adherents of process approaches to writing create situations in which students ultimately find themselves held accountable for knowing a set of rules about which no one has ever directly informed them. Teachers do students no service to suggest, even implicitly, that "product" is not important. In this country, students will be judged on their product regardless of the process they utilized to achieve it. And that product, based as it is on the specific codes of a particular culture, is more readily produced when the directives of how to produce it are made explicit.

If such explicitness is not provided to students, what it feels like to people who are old enough to judge is that there are secrets being kept, that time is being wasted, that the teacher is abdicating his or her duty to teach. A doctoral student in my acquaintance was assigned to a writing class to hone his writing skills. The student was placed in the section led by a White professor who utilized a process approach, consisting primarily of having the students write essays and then assemble into groups to edit each others' papers. That procedure infuriated this particular student. He had many angry encounters with the teacher about what she was doing. In his words:

I didn't feel she was teaching us anything. She wanted us to correct each others' papers and we were there to learn from her. She didn't teach anything, absolutely nothing.

Maybe they're trying to learn what Black folks knew all the time. We understand how to improvise, how to express ourselves creatively. When I'm in a classroom, I'm not looking for that, I'm looking for structure, the more formal language.

Now my buddy was in [a] Black teacher's class. And that lady was very good. She went through and explained and defined each part of the structure. This [White] teacher didn't get along with that Black teacher. She said that she didn't agree with her methods. But *I* don't think that White teacher *had* any methods.

When I told this gentleman that what the teacher was doing was called a process method of teaching writing, his response was, "Well, at least now I know that she *thought* she was doing *something*. I thought she was just a fool who couldn't teach and didn't want to try."

This sense of being cheated can be so strong that the student may be completely turned off to the educational system. Amanda Branscombe, an accomplished White teacher, recently wrote a letter discussing her work with working-class Black and White students at a community college in Alabama. She had given these students my "Skills and Other Dilemmas" article (Delpit, 1986) to read and discuss, and wrote that her students really understood and identified with what I was saying. To quote her letter:

> One young man said that he had dropped out of high school because he failed the exit exam. He noted that he had then passed the GED without a problem after three weeks of prep. He said that his high school English teacher claimed to use a process approach, but what she really did was hide behind fancy words to give herself permission to do nothing in the classroom.

The students I have spoken of seem to be saying that the teacher has denied them access to herself as the source of knowledge necessary to learn the forms they need to succeed. Again, I tentatively attribute the problem to teachers' resistance to exhibiting power in the classroom. Somehow, to exhibit one's personal power as expert source is viewed as disempowering one's students.

Two qualifiers are necessary, however. The teacher cannot be the only expert in the classroom. To deny students their own expert knowledge *is* to disempower them. Amanda Branscombe, when she was working with Black high school students classified as "slow learners," had the students analyze rap songs to discover their underlying patterns. The students became the experts in explaining to the teacher the rules for creating a new rap song. The teacher then used the patterns the students identified as a base to begin an explanation of the structure of grammar, and then of Shakespeare's plays. Both student and teacher are experts at what they know best.

The second qualifier is that merely adopting direct instruction is not the answer. Actual writing for real audiences and real purposes is a vital element in helping students to understand that they have an important voice in their own learning processes. Siddle (1988) examines the results of various kinds of interventions in a primarily process-oriented writing class for Black students. Based on readers' blind assessments, she found that the intervention that produced the most positive changes in the students' writing was a "mini-lesson" consisting of direct instruction about some standard writing convention. But what produced the *second* highest number of positive changes was a subsequent student-centered conference with the teacher. (Peer conferencing in this group of Black students who were not members of the culture of power produced the least number of changes in students' writing. However, the classroom teacher maintained — and I concur — that such activities are necessary to introduce the elements of "real audience" into the task, along with more teacher-directed strategies.)

"It's really a shame but she (that Black teacher upstairs) seems to be so authoritarian, so focused on skills and so teacher directed. Those poor kids never seem to be allowed to really express their creativity. (And she even yells at them.)"

This statement directly concerns the display of power and authority in the classroom. One way to understand the difference in perspective between Black teachers and their progressive colleagues on this issue is to explore culturally influenced oral interactions.

In *Ways With Words,* Shirley Brice Heath (1983) quotes the verbal directives given by the middle-class "townspeople" teachers (p. 280):

- "Is this where the scissors belong?"
- "You want to do your best work today."

By contrast, many Black teachers are more likely to say:

- "Put those scissors on that shelf."
- "Put your name on the papers and make sure to get the right answer for each question."

Is one oral style more authoritarian than another?

Other researchers have identified differences in middle-class and working-class speech to children. Snow et al. (1976), for example, report that working-class mothers use more directives to their children than do middle- and upper-class parents. Middle-class parents are likely to give the directive to a child to take his bath as, "Isn't it time for your bath?" Even though the utterance is couched as a question, both child and adult understand it as a directive. The child may respond with "Aw Mom, can't I wait until . . . ," but whether or not negotiation is attempted, both conversants understand the intent of the utterance.

By contrast, a Black mother, in whose house I was recently a guest, said to her eight-year-old son, "Boy, get your rusty behind in that bathtub." Now I happen to know that this woman loves her son as much as any mother, but she would never have posed the directive to her son to take a bath in the form of a question. Were she to ask, "Would you like to take your bath now?" she would not have been issuing a directive but offering a true alternative. Consequently, as Heath suggests, upon entering school the child from such a family may not understand the indirect statement of the teacher as a direct command. Both White and Black working-class children in the communities Heath studied "had difficulty interpreting these indirect requests for adherence to an unstated set of rules" (p. 280).

But those veiled commands are commands nonetheless, representing true power, and with true consequences for disobedience. If veiled commands are ignored, the child will be labeled a behavior problem and possibly officially classified as behavior disordered. In other words, the attempt by the teacher to reduce an exhibition of power by expressing herself in indirect terms may remove the very explicitness that the child needs to understand the rules of the new classroom culture.

A Black elementary school principal in Fairbanks, Alaska, reported to me that she has a lot of difficulty with Black children who are placed in some White teachers' classrooms. The teachers often send the children to the office for disobeying teacher directives. Their parents are frequently called in for conferences. The parents' response to the teacher is usually the same: "They do what I say; if you just *tell* them what to do, they'll do it. I tell them at home that they have to listen to what you say." And so, does not the power still exist? Its veiled nature only makes it more difficult for some children to respond appropriately, but that in no way mitigates its existence.

I don't mean to imply, however, that the only time the Black child disobeys the teacher is when he or she misunderstands the request for certain behavior. There are other factors that may produce such behavior. Black children expect an authority figure to act with authority. When the teacher instead acts as a "chum," the message sent is that this adult has no authority, and the children react accordingly. One reason this is so is that Black people often view issues of power and authority differently than people from mainstream middle-class backgrounds.[3] Many people of color expect authority to be earned by personal efforts and exhibited by personal characteristics. In other words, "the authoritative person gets to be a teacher because she is authoritative." Some members of middle-class cultures, by contrast, expect one to achieve authority by the acquisition of an authoritative role. That is, "the teacher is the authority because she is the teacher."

In the first instance, because authority is earned, the teacher must consistently prove the characteristics that give her authority. These characteristics may vary across cultures, but in the Black community they tend to cluster around several abilities. The authoritative teacher can control the class through exhibition of personal power; establishes meaningful interpersonal relationships that garner student respect; exhibits a strong belief that all students can learn; establishes a standard of achievement and "pushes" the students to achieve that standard; and holds the attention of the students by incorporating interactional features of Black communicative style in his or her teaching.

By contrast, the teacher whose authority is vested in the role has many more options of behavior at her disposal. For instance, she does not need to express any sense of personal power because her authority does not come from anything she herself does or says. Hence, the power she actually holds may be veiled in such questions/commands as "Would you like to sit down now?" If the children in her class understand authority as she does, it is mutually agreed upon that they are to obey her no matter how indirect, soft-spoken, or unassuming she may be. Her indirectness and soft-spokenness may indeed be, as I suggested earlier, an attempt to reduce the implication of overt power in order to establish a more egalitarian and non-authoritarian classroom atmosphere.

If the children operate under another notion of authority, however, then there is trouble. The Black child may perceive the middle-class teacher as weak, ineffectual, and incapable of taking on the role of being the teacher; therefore, there is no need to follow her directives. In her dissertation, Michelle Foster (1987) quotes one young Black man describing such a teacher:

> She is boring, bo::ing.* She could do something creative. Instead she just stands there. She can't control the class, doesn't know how to control the class. She asked me what she was doing wrong. I told her she just stands there like she's meditating. I told her she could be meditating for all I know. She says that we're supposed to know what to do. I told her I don't know nothin' unless she tells me. She just can't control the class. I hope we don't have her next semester. (pp. 67–68)

But of course the teacher may not view the problem as residing in herself but in the student, and the child may once again become the behavior-disordered Black boy in special education.

What characteristics do Black students attribute to the good teacher? Again, Foster's dissertation provides a quotation that supports my experience with Black students. A young Black man is discussing a former teacher with a group of friends:

> We had fu::an in her class, but she was mean. I can remember she used to say, "Tell me what's in the story, Wayne." She pushed, she used to get on me and push me to know. She made us learn. We had to get in the books. There was this tall guy and he tried to take her on, but she was in charge of that class and she didn't let anyone run her. I still have this book we used in her class. It's a bunch of stories in it. I just read one on Coca-Cola again the other day (p. 68).

To clarify, this student was *proud* of the teacher's "meanness," an attribute he seemed to describe as the ability to run the class and pushing and expect-

---

* *Editor's note:* The colons [:::] refer to elongated vowels.

ing students to learn. Now, does the liberal perspective of the negatively authoritarian Black teacher really hold up? I suggest that although all "explicit" Black teachers are not also good teachers, there are different attitudes in different cultural groups about which characteristics make for a good teacher. Thus, it is impossible to create a model for the good teacher without taking issues of culture and community context into account.

And now to the final comment I present for examination:

"Children have the right to their own language, their own culture. We must fight cultural hegemony and fight the system by insisting that children be allowed to express themselves in their own language style. It is not they, the children, who must change, but the schools. To push children to do anything else is repressive and reactionary."

A statement such as this originally inspired me to write the "Skills and Other Dilemmas" article. It was first written as a letter to a colleague in response to a situation that had developed in our department. I was teaching a senior-level teacher education course. Students were asked to prepare a written autobiographical document for the class that would also be shared with their placement school prior to their student teaching.

One student, a talented young Native American woman, submitted a paper in which the ideas were lost because of technical problems — from spelling to sentence structure to paragraph structure. Removing her name, I duplicated the paper for a discussion with some faculty members. I had hoped to initiate a discussion about what we could do to ensure that our students did not reach the senior level without getting assistance in technical writing skills when they needed them.

I was amazed at the response. Some faculty implied that the student should never have been allowed into the teacher education program. Others, some of the more progressive minded, suggested that I was attempting to function as gatekeeper by raising the issue and had internalized repressive and disempowering forces of the power elite to suggest that something was wrong with a Native American student just because she had another style of writing. With few exceptions, I found myself alone in arguing against both camps.

No, this student should not have been denied entry to the program. To deny her entry under the notion of upholding standards is to blame the victim for the crime. We cannot justifiably enlist exclusionary standards when the reason this student lacked the skills demanded was poor teaching at best and institutionalized racism at worst.

However, to bring this student into the program and pass her through without attending to obvious deficits in the codes needed for her to function effectively as a teacher is equally criminal — for though we may assuage our own consciences for not participating in victim blaming, she will surely be accused and convicted as soon as she leaves the university. As Native Alaskans were quick to tell me, and as I understood through my own experience in the Black community, not only would she not be hired as a teacher, but those who did not hire her would make the (false) assumption that the university was putting out only incompetent Natives and that they should stop looking seriously at any Native applicants. A White applicant who exhibits problems is an individual with problems. A person of color who exhibits problems immediately becomes a representative of her cultural group.

No, either stance is criminal. The answer is to *accept* students but also to take responsibility to *teach* them. I decided to talk to the student and found out she had recognized that she needed some assistance in the technical aspects of writing soon after she entered the university as a freshman. She had gone to various members of the education faculty and received the same two kinds of responses I met with four years later: faculty members told her either that she should not even attempt to be a teacher, or that it didn't matter and that she shouldn't worry about such trivial issues. In her desperation, she had found a helpful professor in the English Department, but he left the university when she was in her sophomore year.

We sat down together, worked out a plan for attending to specific areas of writing competence, and set up regular meetings. I stressed to her the need to use her own learning process as insight into how best to teach her future students those "skills" that her own schooling had failed to teach her. I gave her some explicit rules to follow in some areas; for others, we devised various kinds of journals that, along with readings about the structure of the language, allowed her to find her own insights into how the language worked. All that happened two years ago, and the young woman is now successfully teaching. What the experience led me to understand is that pretending that gatekeeping points don't exist is to ensure that many students will not pass through them.

Now you may have inferred that I believe that because there is a culture of power, everyone should learn the codes to participate in it, and that is how the world should be. Actually, nothing could be further from the truth. I believe in a diversity of style, and I believe the world will be diminished if cultural diversity is ever obliterated. Further, I believe strongly, as do my liberal colleagues, that each cultural group should have the right to maintain its own language style. When I speak, therefore, of the culture of power, I don't speak of how I wish things to be but of how they are.

I further believe that to act as if power does not exist is to ensure that the power status quo remains the same. To imply to children or adults (but of course the adults won't believe you anyway) that it doesn't matter how you talk or how you write is to ensure their ultimate failure. I prefer to be honest with my students. Tell them that their language and cultural style is unique and wonderful but that there is a political power game that is also being played, and if they want to be in on that game there are certain games that they too must play.

But don't think that I let the onus of change rest entirely with the students. I am also involved in political work both inside and outside of the educational system, and that political work demands that I place myself to influence as many gatekeeping points as possible. And it is there that I agitate for change — pushing gatekeepers to open their doors to a variety of styles and codes. What I'm saying, however, is that I do not believe that political change toward diversity can be effected from the bottom up, as do some of my colleagues. They seem to believe that if we accept and encourage diversity within classrooms of children, then diversity will automatically be accepted at gatekeeping points.

I believe that will never happen. What will happen is that the students who reach the gatekeeping points — like Amanda Branscombe's student who dropped out of high school because he failed his exit exam — will understand that they have been lied to and will react accordingly. No, I am certain that if we are truly to effect societal change, we cannot do so from the bottom up, but we must push and agitate from the top down. And in the meantime, we must take the responsibility to *teach*, to provide for students who do not already possess them, the additional codes of power.[4]

But I also do not believe that we should teach students to passively adopt an alternate code. They must be encouraged to understand the value of the code they already possess as well as to understand the power realities in this country. Otherwise they will be unable to work to change these realities. And how does one do that?

Martha Demientieff, a masterly Native Alaskan teacher of Athabaskan Indian students, tells me that her students, who live in a small, isolated, rural village of less than two hundred people, are not aware that there are different codes of English. She takes their writing and analyzes it for features of what has been referred to by Alaskan linguists as "Village English," and then covers half a bulletin board with words or phrases from the students' writing, which she labels "Our Heritage Language." On the other half of the bulletin board she puts the equivalent statements in "standard English," which she labels "Formal English."

She and the students spend a long time on the "Heritage English" section, savoring the words, discussing the nuances. She tells the students, "That's the way we say things. Doesn't it feel good? Isn't it the absolute best way of getting that idea across?" Then she turns to the other side of the board. She tells the students that there are people, not like those in their village, who judge others by the way they talk or write.

> We listen to the way people talk, not to judge them, but to tell what part of the river they come from. These other people are not like that. They think everybody needs to talk like them. Unlike us, they have a hard time hearing what people say if they don't talk exactly like them. Their way of talking and writing is called "Formal English."
>
> We have to feel a little sorry for them because they have only one way to talk. We're going to learn two ways to say things. Isn't that better? One way will be our Heritage way. The other will be Formal English. Then, when we go to get jobs, we'll be able to talk like those people who only know and can only really listen to one way. Maybe after we get the jobs we can help them to learn

how it feels to have another language, like ours, that feels so good. We'll talk like them when we have to, but we'll always know our way is best.

Martha then does all sorts of activities with the notions of Formal and Heritage or informal English. She tells the students,

> In the village, everyone speaks informally most of the time unless there's a potlatch or something. You don't think about it, you don't worry about following any rules — it's sort of like how you eat food at a picnic — nobody pays attention to whether you use your fingers or a fork, and it feels *so* good. Now, Formal English is more like a formal dinner. There are rules to follow about where the knife and fork belong, about where people sit, about how you eat. That can be really nice, too, because it's nice to dress up sometimes.

The students then prepare a formal dinner in the class, for which they dress up and set a big table with fancy tablecloths, china, and silverware. They speak only Formal English at this meal. Then they prepare a picnic where only informal English is allowed.

She also contrasts the "wordy" academic way of saying things with the metaphoric style of Athabaskan. The students discuss how book language always uses more words, but in Heritage language, the shorter way of saying something is always better. Students then write papers in the academic way, discussing with Martha and with each other whether they believe they've said enough to sound like a book. Next, they take those papers and try to reduce the meaning to a few sentences. Finally, students further reduce the message to a "saying" brief enough to go on the front of a T-shirt, and the sayings are put on little paper T-shirts that the students cut out and hang throughout the room. Sometimes the students reduce other authors' wordy texts to their essential meanings as well.

The following transcript provides another example. It is from a conversation between a Black teacher and a Southern Black high school student named Joey, who is a speaker of Black English. The teacher believes it very important to discuss openly and honestly the issues of language diversity and power. She has begun the discussion by giving the student a children's book written in Black English to read.

Teacher: What do you think about that book?
Joey: I think it's nice.
Teacher: Why?
Joey: I don't know. It just told about a Black family, that's all.
Teacher: Was it difficult to read?
Joey: No.
Teacher: Was the text different from what you have seen in other books?
Joey: Yeah. The writing was.
Teacher: How?
Joey: It use more of a southern-like accent in this book.

Teacher: Uhm-hmm. Do you think that's good or bad?
Joey: Well, uh, I don't think it's good for people down this a way, cause that's the way they grow up talking anyway. They ought to get the right way to talk.
Teacher: Oh. So you think it's wrong to talk like that?
Joey: Well . . . [*Laughs.*]
Teacher: Hard question, huh?
Joey: Uhm-hmm, that's a hard question. But I think they shouldn't make books like that.
Teacher: Why?
Joey: Because they not using the right way to talk and in school they take off for that and li'l chirren grow up talking like that and reading like that so they might think that's right and all the time they getting bad grades in school, talking like that and writing like that.
Teacher: Do you think they should be getting bad grades for talking like that?
Joey: [*Pauses, answers very slowly.*] No . . . No.
Teacher: So you don't think that it matters whether you talk one way or another?
Joey: No, not long as you understood.
Teacher: Uhm-hmm. Well, that's a hard question for me to answer, too. It's ah, that's a question that's come up in a lot of schools now as to whether they should correct children who speak the way we speak all the time. Cause when we're talking to each other we talk like that even though we might not talk like that when we get into other situations, and who's to say whether it's —
Joey: [*Interrupting.*] Right or wrong.
Teacher: Yeah.
Joey: Maybe they ought to come up with another kind of . . . maybe Black English or something. A course in Black English. Maybe Black folks would be good in that cause people talk, I mean Black people talk like that, so . . . but I guess there's a right way and wrong way to talk, you know, not regarding what race. I don't know.
Teacher: But who decided what's right or wrong?
Joey: Well that's true . . . I guess White people did.
[*Laughter. End of tape.*]

Notice how throughout the conversation Joey's consciousness has been raised by thinking about codes of language. This teacher further advocates having students interview various personnel officers in actual workplaces about their attitudes toward divergent styles in oral and written language. Students begin to understand how arbitrary language standards are, but also how politically charged they are. They compare various pieces written in different styles, discuss the impact of different styles on the message by making translations and back translations across styles, and discuss the history, apparent purpose, and contextual appropriateness of each of the technical writing rules presented by their teacher. *And* they practice writing different forms to different audiences based on rules appropriate for each audience. Such a program not only "teaches" standard linguistic forms, but also explores aspects of power as exhibited through linguistic forms.

Tony Burgess, in a study of secondary writing in England by Britton, Burgess, Martin, McLeod, and Rosen (1975/1977), suggests that we should not teach "iron conventions . . . imposed without rationale or grounding in communicative intent, . . . [but] critical and ultimately cultural awareness" (p. 54). Courtney Cazden (1987) calls for a two-pronged approach:

1. Continuous opportunities for writers to participate in some authentic bit of the unending conversation . . . thereby becoming part of a vital community of talkers and writers in a particular domain, and
2. Periodic, temporary focus on conventions of form, taught as cultural conventions expected in a particular community. (p. 20)

Just so that there is no confusion about what Cazden means by a focus on conventions of form, or about what I mean by "skills," let me stress that neither of us is speaking of page after page of "skill sheets" creating compound words or identifying nouns and adverbs, but rather about helping students gain a useful knowledge of the conventions of print while engaging in real and useful communicative activities. Kay Rowe Grubis, a junior high school teacher in a multicultural school, makes lists of certain technical rules for her eighth graders' review and then gives them papers from a third grade to "correct." The students not only have to correct other students' work, but also tell them why they have changed or questioned aspects of the writing.

A village teacher, Howard Cloud, teaches his high school students the conventions of formal letter writing and the formulation of careful questions in the context of issues surrounding the amendment of the Alaska Land Claims Settlement Act. Native Alaskan leaders hold differing views on this issue, critical to the future of local sovereignty and land rights. The students compose letters to leaders who reside in different areas of the state seeking their perspectives, set up audioconference calls for interview/debate sessions, and, finally, develop a videotape to present the differing views.

To summarize, I suggest that students must be *taught* the codes needed to participate fully in the mainstream of American life, not by being forced to attend to hollow, inane, decontextualized subskills, but rather within the context of meaningful communicative endeavors; that they must be allowed the resource of the teacher's expert knowledge, while being helped to acknowledge their own "expertness" as well; and that even while students are assisted in learning the culture of power, they must also be helped to learn about the arbitrariness of those codes and about the power relationships they represent.

I am also suggesting that appropriate education for poor children and children of color can only be devised in consultation with adults who share their culture. Black parents, teachers of color, and members of poor communities must be allowed to participate fully in the discussion of what kind of instruction is in their children's best interest. Good liberal intentions are not enough. In an insightful study entitled "Racism without Racists: Institutional Racism in Urban Schools," Massey, Scott, and Dornbusch (1975) found that under the pressures of teaching, and with all intentions of "being nice," teachers had essentially stopped attempting to teach Black children. In their words: "We have shown that oppression can arise out of warmth, friendliness, and concern. Paternalism and a lack of challenging standards are creating a distorted system of evaluation in the schools" (p. 10). Educators must open themselves to, and allow themselves to be affected by, these alternative voices.

In conclusion, I am proposing a resolution for the skills/process debate. In short, the debate is fallacious; the dichotomy is false. The issue is really an illusion created initially not by teachers but by academics whose world view demands the creation of categorical divisions — not for the purpose of better teaching, but for the goal of easier analysis. As I have been reminded by many teachers since the publication of my article, those who are most skillful at educating Black and poor children do not allow themselves to be placed in "skills" or "process" boxes. They understand the need for both approaches, the need to help students to establish their own voices, but to coach those voices to produce notes that will be heard clearly in the larger society.

The dilemma is not really in the debate over instructional methodology, but rather in communicating across cultures and in addressing the more fundamental issue of power, of whose voice gets to be heard in determining what is best for poor children and children of color. Will Black teachers and parents continue to be silenced by the very forces that claim to "give voice" to our children? Such an outcome would be tragic, for both groups truly have something to say to one another. As a result of careful listening to alternative points of view, I have myself come to a viable synthesis of perspectives. But both sides do need to be able to listen, and I contend that it is those with the most power, those in the majority, who must take the greater responsibility for initiating the process.

To do so takes a very special kind of listening, listening that requires not only open eyes and ears, but open hearts and minds. We do not really see through our eyes or hear through our ears, but through our beliefs. To put our beliefs on hold is to cease to exist as ourselves for a moment — and that is not easy. It is painful as well, because it means turning yourself inside out, giving up your own sense of who you are, and being willing to see yourself in the unflattering light of another's angry gaze. It is not easy, but it is the only way to learn what it might feel like to be someone else and the only way to start the dialogue.

There are several guidelines. We must keep the perspective that people are experts on their own lives. There are certainly aspects of the outside world of which they may not be aware, but they can be the only authentic chroniclers of their own experience. We must not be too quick to deny their interpretations, or accuse them of "false consciousness." We must believe that people are rational beings, and therefore always act rationally. We may not understand their rationales, but that in no way militates against the existence of these rationales or reduces our responsibility to attempt to apprehend them. And finally, we must learn to be vulnerable enough to allow our world to turn upside down in order to allow the realities of others to edge themselves into our consciousness. In other words, we must become ethnographers in the true sense.

Teachers are in an ideal position to play this role, to attempt to get all of the issues on the table in order to initiate true dialogue. This can only be done, however, by seeking out those whose perspectives may differ most, by learning to give their words complete attention, by understanding one's own power, even if that power stems merely from being in the majority, by being unafraid to raise questions about discrimination and voicelessness with people of color, and to listen, no, to *hear* what they say. I suggest that the results of such interactions may be the most powerful and empowering coalescence yet seen in the educational realm — for *all* teachers and for *all* the students they teach.

Notes

1. Such a discussion, limited as it is by space constraints, must treat the intersection of class and race somewhat simplistically. For the sake of clarity, however, let me define a few terms: "Black" is used herein to refer to those who share some or all aspects of "core black culture" (Gwaltney, 1980, p. xxiii), that is, the mainstream of Black America — neither those who have entered the ranks of the bourgeoisie nor those who are participants in the disenfranchised underworld. "Middle-class" is used broadly to refer to the predominantly. White American "mainstream." There are, of course, non-White people who also fit into this category; at issue is their cultural identification, not necessarily the color of their skin. (I must add that there are other non-White people, as well as poor White people, who have indicated to me that their perspectives are similar to those attributed herein to Black people.)
2. *Multicultural Britain: "Crosstalk,"* National Centre of Industrial Language Training, Commission for Racial Equality, London, England, John Twitchin, Producer.
3. I would like to thank Michelle Foster, who is presently planning a more in-depth treatment of the subject, for her astute clarification of the idea.
4. Bernstein (1975) makes a similar point when he proposes that different educational frames cannot be successfully institutionalized in the lower levels of education until there are fundamental changes at the post-secondary levels.

References

Apple, M. W. (1979). *Ideology and curriculum.* Boston: Routledge & Kegan Paul.
Bernstein, B. (1975). Class and pedagogies: Visible and invisible. In B. Bernstein, *Class, codes, and control* (Vol. 3). Boston: Routledge & Kegan Paul.
Britton, J., Burgess, T., Martin, N., McLeod, A., & Rosen, H. (1975/1977). *The development of writing abilities.* London: Macmillan Education for the Schools Council, and Urbana, IL: National Council of Teachers of English.
Cazden, C. (1987, January). *The myth of autonomous text.* Paper presented at the Third International Conference on Thinking, Hawaii.
Delpit, L. D. (1986). Skills and other dilemmas of a progressive Black educator. *Harvard Educational Review, 56,* (4), 379–385.
Foster, M. (1987). *It's cookin' now: An ethnographic study of the teaching style of a successful Black teacher in an urban community college.* Unpublished doctoral dissertation, Harvard University.

Gwaltney, J. (1980). *Drylongso*. New York: Vintage Books.
Heath, S. B. (1983). *Ways with words*. Cambridge: Cambridge University Press.
Massey, G. C., Scott, M. V., & Dornbusch, S. M. (1975). Racism without racists: Institutional racism in urban schools. *Black Scholar,* 7(3), 2–11.
Siddle, E. V. (1986). *A critical assessment of the natural process approach to teaching writing*. Unpublished qualifying paper, Harvard University.
Siddle, E. V. (1988). *The effect of intervention strategies on the revisions ninth graders make in a narrative essay*. Unpublished doctoral dissertation, Harvard University.
Snow, C. E., Arlman-Rup, A., Hassing, Y., Josbe, J., Joosten, J., & Vorster, J. (1976). Mother's speech in three social classes. *Journal of Psycholinguistic Research,* 5, 1–20.

I take full responsibility for all that appears herein; however, aside from those mentioned by name in this text, I would like to thank all of the educators and students around the country who have been so willing to contribute their perspectives to the formulation of these ideas, especially Susan Jones, Catherine Blunt, Dee Stickman, Sandra Gamble, Willard Taylor, Mickey Monteiro, Denise Burden, Evelyn Higbee, Joseph Delpit Jr., Valerie Montoya, Richard Cohen, and Mary Denise Thompson.

The Politics of Culture:
Understanding Local Political Resistance to Detracking in Racially Mixed Schools

—■—■—■—

AMY STUART WELLS
IRENE SERNA

Research on tracking, or grouping students into distinct classes for "fast" and "slow" learners, has demonstrated that this educational practice leads to racial and socioeconomic segregation within schools, with low-income, African American, and Latino students frequently placed in the lowest level classes, even when they have equal or higher test scores or grades (see Oakes, 1985; Welner & Oakes, 1995). Furthermore, being placed in the low track often has long-lasting negative effects on these students, as they fall further and further behind their peers and become increasingly bored in school. Partly in response to this research and partly in response to their own uneasiness with the separate and unequal classrooms created by tracking, educators across the country are beginning to respond by testing alternatives to tracking, a reform we call "detracking."

Over the last three years, our research team studied ten racially and socioeconomically mixed schools undergoing detracking reform, and attempted to capture the essence of the political struggles inherent in such efforts.[1] We believe that an important aspect of our qualitative, multiple case study is to help educators and policymakers understand the various manifestations of local political resistance to detracking — not only who instigates it, but also the ideology of opposition to such reforms and the political practices employed (see Oakes & Wells, 1995).

This article focuses on how forces outside the school walls shaped the ability of educators to implement "detracking reform" — to question existing track structures and promote greater access to challenging classes for all students. More specifically, we look at those actors whom we refer to as the "local elites" — those with a combination of economic, political, and cultural capital that is highly valued within their particular school community.[2] These elites are most likely to resist detracking reform because their children often enjoy privileged status in a tracked system. The capital of the elites enables them to engage in political practices that can circumvent detracking reform.

In order to understand the influence of local elites' political practices on detracking reform, we examine their ideology of entitlement, or how they make meaning of their privilege within the educational system and how others come to see such meanings as the way things "ought to be." According to Gramsci (cited in Boggs, 1984), insofar as ruling ideas emanating from elites are internalized by a majority of individuals within a given community, they become a defining motif of everyday life and appear as "common sense" — that is, as the "traditional popular conception of the world" (p. 161).

Yet we realize that the high-status cultural capital — the valued tastes and consumption patterns — of local elites and the resultant ideologies are easily affected by provincial social contexts and the particular range of class, race, and culture at those sites (Bourdieu, 1984). In a study of social reproduction in a postmodern society, Harrison (1993) notes that "the task is not so much to look for the global correspondences between culture and class, but to reconstruct the peculiarly local and material micrologic of investments made in the intellectual field" (p. 40). Accordingly, in our study, we particularize the political struggles and examine the specific ideologies articulated at each school site. Because we were studying ten schools in ten different cities and towns, we needed to contextualize each political struggle over detracking reform within its local school community. These local contexts are significant because the relations of power and domination that affect people most directly are those shaping the social contexts within which they live out their everyday lives: the home, the workplace, the classroom, the peer group. As Thompson (1990) states, "These are the contexts within which individuals spend the bulk of their time, acting and interacting, speaking and listening, pursuing their aims and following the aims of others" (p. 9).

Our research team used qualitative methods to examine technical aspects of detracking — school organization, grouping practices, and classroom pedagogy — as well as cultural norms and political practices that legitimize and support tracking as a "commonsense" approach to educating students (Oakes & Wells, 1995). Our research question was, What happens when someone with power in a racially mixed secondary school decides to reduce tracking? Guided by this question, we selected ten sites — six high schools and four middle schools — from a pool of schools that were undergoing detracking reform and volunteered to be studied. We chose these particular schools because of their diversity and demonstrated commitment to detracking. The schools we studied varied in size from more than three thousand to less than five hundred students. One school was in the Northeast, three were in the Midwest, one in the South, two in the Northwest, and three in various regions of California. Each school drew from a racially and socioeconomically diverse community and served significant but varied mixes of White, African American, Latino, Native American/Alaska Native, and/or Asian students. We visited each school three times over a two-year period. Data collection during our site visits included in-depth, semi-structured tape-recorded interviews with administrators, teachers, students, parents, and community leaders, including school board members. In total, more than four hundred participants across all ten schools were interviewed at least once. We also observed classrooms, as well as faculty, PTA, and school board meetings. We reviewed documents and wrote field notes about our observations within the schools and the communities. Data were compiled extensively from each school to form the basis of cross-case analysis. Our study ran from the spring of 1992 through the spring of 1995.[3]

Descriptions of the "Local Elites"

The struggles over tracking and detracking reforms are, to a large extent, concerned with whose culture and lifestyle is valued, and, thus, whose way of knowing is equated with "intelligence." Traditional hierarchical track structures in schools have been validated by the conflation of culture and intelligence. When culturally biased "truths" about ability and merit confront efforts to "detrack," political practices are employed either to maintain the status quo or to push toward new conceptions of ability that would render a rigid and hierarchical track structure obsolete (see Oakes, Lipton, & Jones, 1995).

While we acknowledge that many agents contribute to the maintenance of a rigid track structure, this article examines the political practices of local elites in the school communities we studied. The elites discussed here had children enrolled in the detracking schools and thus constitute the subgroup of local elites active in shaping school policies. Their practices were aimed at maintaining a track structure, with separate and unequal educational opportunities for "deserving" elite students and "undeserving" or non-elite students. Our analysis of elite parents' ideology of privilege and the resultant political practices therefore includes an examination of "corresponding institutional mechanisms" (Bourdieu & Wacquant, 1992, p. 188) employed to prevent structural change that would challenge their status and privilege.

Our intention is not to criticize these powerful parents in an unsympathetic manner. Yet, we believe that too often the cultural forces that shape such parents' agency as they try to do what is best for their children remain hidden from view and thus unquestioned. Our effort to unpack the "knapsack" of elite privilege will expose the tight relationship between the "objective" criteria of the schools and the cultural forces of the elite (McIntosh, 1992).

Detracking, or the process of moving schools toward a less rigid system of assigning students to classes and academic programs, is a hotly contested educational reform. In racially mixed schools, the controversy surrounding detracking efforts is compounded by beliefs about the relationship among race, culture, and academic ability. In virtually all racially mixed secondary schools, tracking resegregates students, with mostly White and Asian students in the high academic tracks and mostly African American and Latino students in the low tracks (Oakes, 1985; Oakes, Oraseth, Bell, & Camp, 1990). To the extent that elite parents have internalized dominant, but often unspoken, beliefs about race and intelligence, they may resist "desegregation" within racially mixed schools — here defined as detracking — because they do not want their children in classes with Black and Latino students.

Efforts to alter within-school racial segregation via detracking, then, are generally threatening to elites, in that they challenge their position at the top of the hierarchy. The perceived stakes, from an elite parent's perspective, are quite high. They argue, for instance, that their children will not be well served in detracked classes. And while these stakes are most frequently discussed in academic terms — for example, the dumbing down of the curriculum for smart students — the real stakes, we argue, are generally not academics at all, but, rather, status and power. For example, if a school does away with separate classes for students labeled "gifted" but teachers continue to challenge these students with the same curriculum in a detracked setting, the only "losses" the students will incur are their label and their separate and unequal status. Yet in a highly stratified society, such labels and privileged status confer power.

In looking at the ability of the upper strata of society to maintain power and control, Bourdieu (1977) argues that economic capital — that is, income, wealth, and property — is not the only form of capital necessary for social reproduction. He describes other forms of capital, including political, social, and cultural (Bourdieu & Wacquant, 1992). In our analysis of resistance to detracking reforms, we focus on cultural capital and its relationship to dominant ideologies within our school communities because of the explicit connections between cultural capital and educational achievement within Bourdieu's work. According to Bourdieu (1984), cultural capital consists of culturally valued tastes and consumption patterns, which are rewarded within the educational system. Bourdieu discusses "culture" not in its restricted, normative sense, but rather from a more anthropological perspective. Culture is elaborated in a "taste" for refined objects, which is what distinguishes the culture of the dominant class or upper social strata from that of the rest of society. In order for elites to employ their cultural capital to maintain power, emphasis must be placed on subtleties of taste — for example, form over function, manner over matter. Within the educational system, Bourdieu argues, students are frequently rewarded for their taste, and for the cultural knowledge that informs it. For instance, elite students whose status offers them the opportunity to travel to other cities, states, and countries on family vacations are often perceived to be more "intelligent" than other students, simply because the knowledge they have gained from these trips is reflected in what is valued in schools. When high-status, elite students' taste is seen as valued knowledge within the educational system, other students' taste and the knowledge that informs it is devalued (Bourdieu & Passeron, 1979). In this way, high-status culture is socially constructed as "intelligence" — a dubious relationship that elites must strive to conceal in order to legitimize their merit-based claim to privileged status. In other words, what is commonly referred to as "objective" criteria of intelligence and achievement is actually extremely biased toward the subjective experience and ways of knowing of elite students. Similarly, Delpit (1995) describes the critical role that power plays in our society and educational system, as the worldviews of those in privileged positions are "taken as the only reality, while the worldviews of those less powerful are dismissed as inconsequential" (p. xv). The education system is the primary field in which struggles over these cultural meanings take place and where, more often than not, high-status cultural capital is translated into high-status credentials, such as academic degrees from elite institutions (Bourdieu & Passeron, 1977).

Thus, socially valuable cultural capital — form and manner — is the property many upper class and, to a lesser extent, middle-class families transmit to their offspring that substitutes for, or supplements, the transmission of economic capital as a means of maintaining class, status, and privilege across generations (Bourdieu, 1973). Academic qualifications and high-status educational titles are to cultural capital what money and property titles are to economic capital. The form and manner of academic qualifications are critical. Students cannot simply graduate from high school; they must graduate with the proper high-status qualifications that allow them access to the most selective universities and to the credentials those institutions confer.

Through the educational system, elites use their economic, political, and cultural capital to acquire symbolic capital — the most highly valued capital in a given society or local community. Symbolic capital signifies culturally important attributes, such as status, authority, prestige, and, by extension, a sense of honor. The social construction of symbolic capital may vary from one locality to another, but race and social class consistently play a role, with White, wealthy, well-educated families most likely to be at the top of the social strata (Harrison, 1993).

Because the cultural capital of the elite is that which is most valued and rewarded within the educational system, elite status plays a circular role in the process of detracking reform: parents with high economic, political, and cultural capital are most likely to have children in the highest track and most prestigious classes, which in turn gives them more symbolic capital in the community. The elite parents can then employ their symbolic capital in the educational decision-making arena to maintain advantages for their children. Educational reforms that, like detracking, challenge the advantages bestowed upon children of the elite are resisted not only by the elites themselves, but also by educators and even other parents and community members who may revere the cultural capital of elite families. The school and the community thus bestow elite parents with the symbolic capital, or honor, that allows them political power.

The status of the local elites in the ten school communities we studied derived in part from the prestige they and their children endowed to public schools simply by their presence. The elite are the most valued citizens, those the public schools do not want to lose, because the socially constructed status of institutions such as schools is dependent upon the status of the individuals attending them. These are also the families most likely to flee public schools if they are denied what they want from them. For example, at Grant High School, an urban school in the Northwest, the White, upper-middle-class parents who sent their children to public schools held tremendous power over the district administration. Many of them were highly educated and possessed the economic means to send their children to private schools if they so chose.

While the elites at each of the schools we studied held economic, social, and political capital, the specific combination of these varied at each site in relation to the cultural capital valued there. Thus, who the elites were and their particular rationale for tracking varied among locations, based on the distinctive mix of race, class, and culture. For instance, at Liberty High School, located in a West Coast city, many of the White parents were professors at a nearby university. As "professional intellectuals," they strongly influenced the direction of Liberty High; although they were generally not as wealthy as business executives, they were nevertheless imbued with a great deal of high-status cultural capital. Meanwhile, educators and White parents at Liberty noted that most of the Black and Latino students enrolled in the school came from very low-income families. Many of the people we interviewed said there was a sizable number of middle-class Black families in this community, but that they did not send their children to public schools. This school's social class divide, which some educators and Black students argued was a caricature, allowed White parents to blame the school's resegregation through tracking on the "family backgrounds" of the students, rather than on racial prejudice.

In the midwestern town of Plainview, the local White elites worked in private corporations rather than universities. Here, the high-status cultural capital was, in general, far more conservative, pragmatic, and less "intellectual" than at Liberty. Nonetheless, the elite parents here and at each of the schools we studied strove for the same advantages that the elite parents at Liberty High demanded for their children.

The African American students in Plainview comprised two groups — those who lived in a small, working-class Black neighborhood in the district and those who transferred into Plainview from the "inner city" through an interdistrict desegregation plan. At this site, however, the social class distinctions between the two groups of Black students were blurred by many White respondents, particularly in their explanations of why Black students from both groups were consistently found in the lowest track classes. For instance, teachers could not tell us which Black students lived in Plainview and which rode the bus in from the city. Some teachers also spoke of Black students' — all Black students' — low levels of achievement as the result of their families' culture of poverty, and not the result of what the school offered them. Despite the relative economic advantages of many African American students who lived in the Plainview district as compared to those who lived in the city, all

Black students in this mostly White, wealthy suburban school were doing quite poorly. While African Americans constituted 25 percent of the student population, less than 5 percent of the students in the highest level courses were Black. Furthermore, a district task force on Black achievement found that more than half of the Black students in the high school had received at least one D or F over the course of one school year.

In other schools, the interplay between race and class was more complex, especially when the local elite sought to distinguish themselves from other, lower income Whites. For instance, in the small midwestern Bearfield School District, which is partly rural and partly suburban, wealthy, well-educated, White suburban parents held the most power over the educational system because they possessed more economic and highly valued cultural capital than rural Whites or African Americans. When a desegregation plan was instituted in the 1970s, it was Black and poor rural White children who were bused. As the Bearfield Middle School principal explained, "As our business manager/superintendent once told me, the power is neither Black nor White; it's green — as in money. And that's where the power is. Rich people have clout. Poor people don't have clout."

Still, the less wealthy and less educated rural Whites in Bearfield, while not as politically powerful as the suburban Whites, remained more influential than the African American families. When the two middle schools in the district were consolidated in 1987, Whites — both wealthy suburban and poor rural — were able to convince the school board to close down the newly built middle school located in the African American community and keep open the older middle school on the White side of the town.

Although the interplay between class and culture within a racially mixed community is generally defined along racial lines, we found that was not always the case. For example, King Middle School, a magnet school in a large northeastern city, was designed to attract students of many racial groups and varied socioeconomic status. A teacher explained that the parents who are blue-collar workers do not understand what's going on at the school, but the professional and middle-class parents frequently call to ask for materials to help their children at home. Educators at King insisted that middle-class and professional parents were not all White, and that there was very little correlation between income and race at the school, with its student body composed of more than twenty racial/ethnic groups, including Jamaican, Chinese, Armenian, Puerto Rican, African American, and various European ethnic groups. While we found it difficult to believe that there was no correlation between race/ethnicity and income in this city with relatively poor African American and Latino communities, it is clear that not all of the local elites at King were White.

Thus, the layers of stratification in some schools were many, but the core of the power elite in all ten communities consisted of a group of parents who were more White, wealthy, and well-educated relative to others in their community. They were the members of the school communities with the greatest economic and/or high-status cultural capital, which they have passed on to their children. The schools, in turn, greatly rewarded the children of these elite for their social distinctions, which were perceived to be distinctions of merit (DiMaggio, 1979).

The Political Ideology of Tracking and Detracking: "Deserving" High-Track Students

Bourdieu's concepts of domination and social reproduction are particularly useful in understanding the education system, because education is the field in which the elite both "records and conceals" its own privilege. Elites "record" privilege through formal educational qualifications, which then serve to "conceal" the inherited cultural capital needed to acquire them. According to Harrison (1993), "What is usually referred to as equality of opportunity or meritocracy is, for Bourdieu, a "sociodicy"; that is, a sacred story that legitimates the dominant class' own privilege" (p. 43).

The political resistance of the local elite to detracking reforms cannot, therefore, be understood separately from the "sociodicy" or ideology employed to legitimize the privileged place elites and their children hold in the educational system. Ideology, in a Gramscian sense, represents ideas, beliefs, cultural preferences, and even myths and superstitions, which possess a certain "material" reality of their own (Gramsci, 1971). In education, societal ideas, beliefs, and cultural preferences of intelligence have found in tracking structures their own material reality. Meanwhile, tracking reinforces and sustains those ideas, beliefs, and cultural preferences.

According to Thompson (1990), ideology refers to the ways in which meaning serves, in particular circumstances, to establish and sustain relations of power that are systematically asymmetrical. Broadly speaking, ideology is *meaning in the service of power.* Thompson suggests that the study of ideology requires researchers to investigate the ways in which meaning is constructed and conveyed by symbolic forms of various kinds, "from everyday linguistic utterances to complex images and texts; it requires us to investigate the social contexts within which symbolic forms are employed and deployed" (p. 7).

The ideology of the local elites in the schools we studied was often cloaked in the "symbolic form" that Thompson describes. While the symbols used by politically powerful people to express their resistance to detracking differed from one site to the next, race consistently played a central, if not explicit, role. Although local elites rarely expressed their dissatisfaction with detracking reform in overtly racial terms, their resistance was couched in more subtle expressions of the politics of culture that have clear racial implications. For example, they said they liked the concept of a racially mixed school, as long as the African American or Latino students acted like White, middle-class children, and their parents were involved in the school and bought into the American Dream. At Central High, a predominantly Latino school on the West Coast with a 23 percent White student body, the local elite consisted of a relatively small middle class of mostly White and a few Latino families. No real upper middle class existed, and most of the Latino students came from very low-income families; many were recent immigrants to the United States. A White parent whose sons were taking honors classes explained her opposition to detracking efforts at Central, exposing her sense of entitlement this way:

> I think a lot of those Latinos come and they're still Mexicans at heart. They're not American. I don't care what color you are, we're in America here and we're going for this country. And I think their heart is in Mexico and they're with that culture still. It's one thing to come over and bring your culture and to use it, but it's another thing to get into that . . . and I'm calling it the American ethic. They're not into it and that's why they end up so far behind. They get in school, and they are behind.

This construct of the "deserving minority" denies the value of non-White students' and parents' own culture or of their sometimes penetrating critique of the American creed (see Yonesawa, Williams, & Hirshberg, 1995), and implies that only those students with the cultural capital and underlying elite ideology deserve to be rewarded in the educational system. Yet because the political arguments put forth by powerful parents in the schools we studied sounded so benign, so "American," the cultural racism that guided their perspective was rarely exposed. Consequently, both the racial segregation within the schools and the actions of parents to maintain it were perceived as natural.

We found many instances in which elite parents attempted to distance their children from students they considered to be less deserving of special attention and services. For instance, at Rolling Hills Middle School, located in a southeastern metropolitan area with a large, county-wide desegregation plan, one wealthy White parent said she and her husband purchased a home in the nearby neighborhood because Rolling Hills and its feeder high school are two of the handful of schools in the district that offer an "advanced program." She said several people had told her that in the advanced program the curriculum was better, fewer behavior problems occurred in the classes, and students received more individualized attention from teachers. She also said that had her children not been accepted into the advanced program, she and her family would not have moved into this racially mixed school district, but would have purchased a home in one of the Whiter suburbs east of the county line. Interestingly enough, this parent did not know whether or not the White suburban schools offered an advanced program. Also of interest in this district is the creation of the advanced program in the same year as the implementation of the desegregation plan.

The White, well-educated parents at Grant High School often stated that the racial diversity of the student body was one characteristic they found most appealing about the school. They said that such a racially mixed environment better prepared their children for life in "the real world." One parent noted that "the positive mixing of racial groups is important to learning to live in society." But some teachers argued that while these parents found Grant's diversity acceptable — even advantageous — their approval was conditioned by their understanding that "their children [would] only encounter Black students in the hallways and not in their classrooms." Grant's assistant principal noted that "many upper class, professional parents hold occupational positions in which they work toward equity and democracy, but expect their children to be given special treatment at Grant."

This ideology of "diversity at a distance" is often employed by White parents at strategic moments when the privileged status of their children appears to be threatened (Lareau, 1989). In our study, the parents of honors students at Grant successfully protested the school's effort to eliminate the "tennis shoe" registration process by which students and teachers jointly negotiated access to classes.[4] Some of the faculty had proposed that the school switch to a computer registration program that would guarantee Black and Latino students greater access to high-track classes. The parents of the honors students stated that they were not protesting the registration change because they were opposed to having their children in racially mixed classes, but because "they [felt] that their children [would] learn more in an environment where all students are as motivated to learn as they are — in a homogeneous ability classroom."

Respondents at Grant said that parents assumed that if any student was allowed into an honors class, regardless of his or her prior track, it must not be a good class. The assumption here was that if there was no selectivity in placing students in particular classes, then the learning and instruction in those classes could not be good. Parents of the most advanced students "assumed" that since the language arts department had made the honors and regular curriculum the same and allowed more students to enroll in honors, the rigor of these classes had probably diminished, despite the teachers' claims that standards had remained high.

At Liberty High School, where the intellectual elite were more "liberal" than the elite in most of the other schools, parents also frequently cited the racial diversity of the school as an asset. For instance, one parent commented that it was the racial and cultural mix — "the real range of people here" — that attracted her to Liberty High. She liked the fact that her daughter was being exposed to people of different cultures and different socioeconomic backgrounds: "We took her out of private school, where there's all these real upper middle-class White kids." Yet, despite this espoused appreciation for diversity among White liberal parents at Liberty, they strongly resisted efforts to dismantle the racially segregated track system. According to another White parent of a high-track student at Liberty:

> I think the one thing that really works at Liberty High is the upper track. It does. And to me, I guess my goal would be for us to find a way to make the rest of Liberty High work as well as the upper track. But it's crucial that we not destroy the upper track to do that, and that can happen . . . it really could. . . . I feel my daughter will get an excellent education if the program continues the way it is, if self-scheduling continues so that they aren't all smoothed together.

In all of the schools we studied, the most interesting aspect of elites' opposition to detracking is that they based their resistance on the symbolic mixing of high "deserving" and low "undeserving" students, rather than on information about what actually happens in detracked classrooms. For instance, an English teacher at Plainview High School who taught a heterogeneous American Studies course in which she academically challenged all her students said that the popularity of the Advanced Placement classes among the elite parents was in part based upon a "myth" that "they're the only classes that offer high standards, that they're the only courses that are interesting and challenging. And the myth is that that's where the best learning takes place. That's a myth."

At Explorer Middle School, located in a mid-sized northwestern city, the identified gifted students — nearly all White, despite a school population that was 30 percent American Indian — were no longer segregated into special classes or teams. Rather, "gifted" students were offered extra "challenge" courses, which other "non-gifted" students could choose to take as well. The day after a grueling meeting with parents of the "gifted" students, the designated gifted education teacher who works with these and other students in the challenge classes was upset by the way in which the parents had responded to her explanation of the new challenge program and the rich educational opportunities available in these classes:

> And they didn't ask, "well what are our kids learning in your classes?" Nobody asked that. I just found that real dismaying, and I was prepared to tell them what we do in class and here's an example. I had course outlines. I send objectives home with every class, and goals and work requirements, and nobody asked me anything about that . . . like they, it's . . . to me it's like I'm dealing with their egos, you know, more than what their kids really need educationally.

What this and other teachers in our study told us is that many elite parents are more concerned about the labels placed on their children than what actually goes on in the classroom. This is a powerful illustration of what Bourdieu (1984) calls "form over function" and "manner over matter."

Notions of Entitlement

Symbols of the "deserving," high-track students must be juxtaposed with conceptions of the undeserving, low-track students in order for strong protests against detracking to make sense in a society that advocates equal opportunity. Bourdieu argues that "impersonal domination" — the sociocultural form of domination found in free, industrial societies where more coercive methods of domination are not allowed — entails the rationalization of the symbolic. When symbols of domination are rationalized, the *entitlement* of the upper strata of society is legitimized, and thus this impersonal domination is seen as natural (Harrison, 1993, p. 42).

In our study, we found that elite parents rationalized their children's entitlement to better educational opportunities based upon the resources that they themselves brought to the system. For instance, parents from the White, wealthy side of Bearfield Middle School's attendance zone perceived that the African American students who attended the school and lived on the "other" side of town benefited from the large tax burden shouldered by the White families. One White parent noted, "I don't feel that our school should have, you know, people from that far away coming to our school. I don't think it's right as far as the taxes we pay. . . . They don't pay the taxes that we pay, and they're at our schools also. Um, I just don't feel they belong here, no." According to the superintendent of the school district, this statement reflects the widely held belief among Whites that they are being taxed to pay for schools for Black students, "and therefore, the White community . . . should make the decisions about the schools . . . because they are paying the bill." These perspectives explain in part why the consolidation of the district's two middle schools resulted in the closing of the mostly Black but much more recently built school, and favored the old, dilapidated Bearfield building as the single middle school site.

At the same time, these parents balked at the suggestion that their own social privilege and much of their children's advantages had less to do with objective merit or intellectual ability than it had to do with their families' economic and cultural capital. Harrison (1993) expands upon Bourdieu's notion that culture functions to deny or disavow the economic origins of capital by gaining symbolic credit for the possessors of economic and political capital. Harrison argues that the seemingly legitimate and meritocratic basis upon which students "earn" academic credentials is an important aspect of the dominant class' denial of entitlement as a process in which inherited economic and political power receives social consecration. In other words, the elite parents must convince themselves and others that the privileges their children are given in the educational system were earned in a fair and meritocratic way, and are not simply a consequence of the parents' own privileged place in society. "The demonstration that the belief of merit is a part of the process of social consecration in which the dominant class's power is both acknowledged and misrecognized, is at the core of Bourdieu's analysis of culture" (Harrison, 1993, p. 44).

There is strong evidence from the schools we studied that students frequently end up in particular tracks and classrooms more on the basis of their parents' privilege than of their own "ability." A school board member in the district in which Rolling Hills Middle School is located explained that students are placed in the advanced program depending on who their parents happen to know. Because the advanced program was implemented at the same time as the county-wide desegregation plan, it has become a sophisticated form of resegregation within racially mixed schools supported by conceptions of "deserving" advanced students. The school board member said that parents of the advanced students are very much invested in labels that their children acquire at school. When children are labeled "advanced," it means their parents are "advanced" as well. In fact, said the board member, some of these parents refer to themselves as the "advanced parents": "There is still an elitist aspect as far as I am concerned. I also think it is an ego trip for parents. They love the double standard that their children are in Advanced Placement programs."

Similarly, several elite parents of students in the advanced program at Grant High School expressed regret that the school had such a poor vocational education department for the "other" students — those who were not advanced. Their lament for vocational education related to their way of understanding the purpose of the high school in serving different students. One of these parents, for example, stated that the role of the honors classes was to groom students to become "managers and professionals" and that something else should be done for those kids who would grow up to be "workers."

According to Harrison (1993), the elite seek to deny the arbitrary nature of the social order that culture does much to conceal. This process, which he calls "masking," occurs when what is culturally arbitrary is "essentialized, absolutized or universalized" (p. 45). Masking is generally accomplished via symbols — culturally specific as opposed to materially specific symbols (Bourdieu & Wacquant, 1992). For example, standardized test scores become cultural symbols of intelligence that are used to legitimize the track structure in some instances while they are "masked" in other instances.

An example of this "masking" process was revealed to us at Grant High School, where elite parents of the most advanced students approved of using test scores as a measure of students' intelligence and worthiness to enroll in the highest track classes. But when children of the elite who were identified as "highly able" in elementary school did not make the test score cutoffs for high school honors classes, the parents found ways to get their children placed in these classes anyway, as if the tests in that particular instance were not valid. The educators usually gave in to these parents' demands, and then cited such instances as evidence of a faulty system. The so-called faults within the system, however, did not lead to broad-based support among powerful parents or educators to dismantle the track structure.

Similarly, at Explorer Middle School, where the wealthy White "gifted" students were all placed in regular classes and then offered separate challenge classes along with other students who chose to take such a class, the principal collected data on the achievement test scores for the identified gifted students and other students in the school. She found huge overlaps in the two sets of scores, with some identified "non-gifted" students scoring in the 90th percentile and above, and some "gifted" students ranking as low as the 58th percentile. Yet, when the mostly White parents of children identified by the district as "gifted" were presented with these data, they attributed the large number of low test scores among the pool of gifted students to a handful of non-White students participating in that program, although the number of non-White "gifted" students was far lower than the number of low test scores within the gifted program. The White parents simply would not admit that any of their children did not deserve a special label (and the extra resources that come with it). According to the teacher of the challenge classes, one of the most vocal and demanding "gifted" parents was the mother of a boy who was not even near the top of his class: "I still can't figure out how he got in the gifted program; he doesn't perform in any way at that high a level. . . . She is carrying on and on and on . . ."

Despite evidence that the "gifted" label may be more a form of symbolic capital than a true measure of innate student ability, the parents of students who had been identified as gifted by this school district maintained a strong sense of entitlement. For instance, a White, upper middle-class father of two so-called gifted boys told us he was outraged that the "gifted and talented" teacher at Explorer spent her time teaching challenge classes that were not exclusively for gifted students. This father was adamant that the state's special funding for gifted and talented (G/T) programs should be spent exclusively on identified G/T students. He noted that at the other middle school in the district, the G/T teacher worked with a strictly G/T class, "whereas at Explorer, the G/T teacher works with a class that is only 50 percent G/T." In other words, "precious" state resources for gifted and talented students were being spent on "non-deserving" students — many of whom had higher middle school achievement test scores than the students who had been identified by the school district as gifted many years earlier.

At Plainview High School, the English teacher who created the heterogeneous American Studies class began reading about the social science research on intelligence, and concluded that our society and education system do not really understand what intelligence is or how to measure it. When the principal asked her to present her research to parents at an open house, her message was not well received, particularly by those parents whose children were in the Advanced Placement classes. According to this teacher, "If you were raised under the system that said you were very intelligent and high achieving, you don't want anyone questioning that system, OK? That's just the way it is." She said that what some of the parents were most threatened by was how this research on intelligence was going to be used and whether the high school was going to do away with Advanced Placement classes. She recalled, "I used the word 'track' once and debated whether I could weave that in because I knew the power of the word, and I didn't want to shut everyone down. It was very interesting."

Political Practices:
How the Local Elite Undermined Detracking

The ideology and related symbols that legitimate local elites' sense of entitlement are critical to educational policy and practice. As Harrison (1993) and Harker (1984) note, Bourdieu's work is ultimately focused on the strategic practices employed when conflicts emerge. In this way, Bourdieu identifies "practices" — actions that maintain or change the social structures — within strategically oriented forms of conflict. These strategic actions must be rooted back into the logic or sense of entitlement that underlies these practices. In other words, we examined political practices that are intended to be consistent with an ideology of "deserving" high-track students. These practices were employed by elite parents when educators posed a threat to the privileged status of their children by questioning the validity and objectivity of a rigid track structure (Useem, 1990).

According to Bourdieu, when seemingly "objective" structures, such as tracking systems, are faithfully reproduced in the dispositions or ways of knowing of actors, then the "arbitrary" nature of the existing structure can go completely unrecognized (Bourdieu & Wacquant, 1992). For instance, no one questions the existence of the separate and unequal "gifted and talented" or "highly advanced" program for children of the local elites, despite the fact that the supposedly "objective" measures that legitimize these programs — standardized tests scores — do not always support the somewhat "arbitrary" nature of student placement. This arbitrary placement system is more sensitive to cultural capital than academic "ability."

In the case of tracking, so-called objective and thus non-arbitrary standardized tests are problematic on two levels. First, the tests themselves are culturally biased in favor of wealthy, White students, and therefore represent a poor measure of "ability" or "intelligence." Second, scores on these exams tend to count more for some students than others. Elite students who have low achievement test scores are placed in high tracks, while non-White and non-wealthy students with high test scores are bound to the lower tracks (see Oakes et al., 1995; Welner & Oakes, 1995). Still, test scores remain an undisclosed and undisputed "objective" measure of student track placement and thus a rationale for maintaining the track structure in many schools.

When these undisclosed or undisputed parts of the universe are questioned, conflicts arise that call for strategic political practices on the part of elites. As Harrison (1993) states, "Where the fit can no longer be maintained and where, therefore, the arbitrary nature of the objective structure becomes evident, the dominant class must put into circulation a discourse in which this arbitrary order is misrecognized as such" (p. 41). When the arbitrary nature of the "objective" tracking structure becomes evident, detracking efforts are initiated, often by educators who have come to realize the cultural basis of the inequalities within our so-called meritocratic educational system.

Within each of our ten schools, when educators penetrated the ideology that legitimizes the track structure (and the advantages that high-track students have within it), elite parents felt that their privileges were threatened. We found that local elites employed four practices to undermine and co-opt meaningful detracking efforts in such a way that they and their children would continue to benefit disproportionately from educational policies. These four overlapping and intertwined practices were threatening flight, co-opting the institutional elites, soliciting buy-in from the "not-quite elite," and accepting detracking bribes.

Threatening Flight

Perhaps nowhere in our study was the power of the local elite and their ideology of entitlement more evident than when the topic of "elite flight" was broached, specifically when these parents threatened to leave the school. Educators in the ten schools we studied were acutely aware that their schools, like most institutions, gain their status, or symbolic capital, from the social status of the students who attend (Wells & Crain, 1992). They know they must hold onto the local elites in order for their schools to remain politically viable institutions that garner broad public support. As a result, the direct or indirect threat of elite flight can thwart detracking efforts when local elite parents have other viable public or private school options.

At Liberty High School, the liberal ideals and principles that are the cornerstone of this community were challenged when local elites were asked to embrace reforms that they perceived to be removing advantages held by their children. In fact, discussions and implementation of such reforms — for example, the creation of a heterogeneous ninth-grade English/social studies core — caused elite parents to "put into circulation a discourse" that legitimized their claim to something better than what other students received. Without this special attention for high-track students, elite parents said, they had little reason to keep their children at Liberty. As one parent of a high-track student noted in discussing the local elite's limits and how much of the school's equity-centered detracking reforms they would tolerate before abandoning the school:

> I think it happens to all of us; when you have children, you confront all your values in a totally different way. I mean, I did all this work in education, I knew all these things about it, and it's very different when it's your own child 'cause when it's your own child your real responsibility is to advocate for that child. I mean, I might make somewhat different decisions about Liberty High, though probably not terribly different, because as I say, I would always have in mind the danger of losing a big chunk of kids, and with them the community support that makes this school work well.

The power of the threat of elite flight is evident in the history of the creation of tracking structures in many of our schools, where advanced and gifted programs began to appear and proliferate at the same time that the schools in these districts were becoming more racially mixed, either through a desegregation plan or demographic shifts. This shift toward more tracking as schools became increasingly racially mixed follows the long history of tracking in the U.S. educational system. Tracking became more systematized at the turn of the century, as non-Anglo immigrant students enrolled in urban high schools (Oakes, 1985). At Grant High School, which is located in a racially diverse urban school district surrounded by separate Whiter and more affluent districts, the highly advanced and "regular" advanced programs were started shortly after desegregation at the insistence of local elite parents who wanted separate classes for their children. One teacher noted that the advanced programs were designed to respond to a segment of the White community that felt, "Oh, we'll send our kids to public school, but only if there's a special program for them."

At Grant, the chair of the language arts department, an instigator of detracking reform efforts, said that the parents of the "advanced" students run the school district:

> They scare those administrators the same way they scare us. They're the last vestiges of middle-class people in the public schools in some sense. And they know that. And they flaunt that sometimes. And they scare people with that. And the local media would spit [the deputy superintendent] up in pieces if she did something to drive these parents out of the school district. So, yeah. I'm sure she's nervous about anything we're doing.

Similarly, at Rolling Hills Middle School, where the Advanced Program began in the late 1970s, shortly after the county-wide desegregation plan was implemented, the mother of two White boys in the program noted, "If I heard they were going to eliminate the Advanced Program, I would be very alarmed, and would seriously consider if I could afford a private school." She indicated that she thought that most parents of students at Rolling Hills felt this way.

At Central High School, White flight consistently paralleled the influx of Latino immigrant students into the school. Administrators said they hoped that the relocation of the school to a new site in a more middle-class area of the district would allow Central to maintain its White population. But many educators said they felt that what keeps White students at Central is the honors program, which would have been scaled back under detracking reform. This reform effort has been almost completely derailed by political roadblocks from both inside the school and the surrounding community.

Suburban, midwestern Plainview High School was the school in which we perhaps noted the perceived threat of elite flight to be most powerful. There, the concept of "community stability" was foremost on the minds of the educators. Many of the teachers and administrators in the Plainview district, particularly at the high school, came to Plainview from the nearby Hamilton School District, which experienced massive White flight two decades earlier. Essentially, the population of the Hamilton district shifted from mostly White, upper middle class to all Black and poor in a matter of ten years — roughly between 1968 and 1978. According to these educators and many other respondents in Plainview, the status of the Hamilton district and its sole high school plummeted, as each incoming freshman class became significantly darker and poorer. Once regarded as the premier public high school in the metropolitan area, Hamilton suddenly served as a reminder of the consequences of White flight. The large numbers of White residents and educators who came to Plainview after fleeing Hamilton kept the memory of White flight alive, and used Hamilton as a symbol of this threat.

Of all the educators in the district, it was the Plainview High School principal, Mr. Fredrick, who appeared most fixated on issues of community "stability" and the role of the schools in maintaining it:

> Here's my problem, what I'm doing at Plainview High School is essentially trying to make it stable enough so that other people can integrate the neighborhood. Now if other people aren't integrating the neighborhood, I'm not doing it either. I'm not out there working on that, I don't have time to be out there working on that, I've got to be making sure that what we're doing in Plainview High School is strong, we're strong enough, and have the reputation of, so that as we integrate, which I'm hoping is happening, that Whites won't get up and flee . . . when they come in and say, I hope you're here in eight years, that is a commitment those White people are gonna be there in eight years.

Fredrick argues that an academically strong high school led by a principal who maintains a good relationship with the community will help stabilize the whole community. As he explains, "I believe we can keep stability in Plainview while still being out in front of education. Now that's what I feel my job is." Fredrick's goal of maintaining racial stability in the community is noble in many respects, but we learned during our visits to Plainview that his focus on White flight has resulted in intense efforts to please the elite White parents. These efforts to cater to elite parents have consistently worked against detracking reforms in the school. While some of the teachers and other administrators continued to push for more innovative grouping and instructional strategies, Fredrick has advocated more Advanced Placement courses and encouraged more students to take these classes. In this way, the threat of White elite flight has helped maintain the hierarchical track structure and an Advanced Placement curriculum that many teachers, students, and less elite parents argue is not creative or instructionally sound.

Co-opting the Institutional Elites

The threat of flight is one of the ways in which local elites provoke responses to their institutional demands. This threat, and the fear it creates in the hearts of educators, is related to the way in which the "institutional elites" — that is, educators with power and authority within the educational system — become co-opted by the ideology of the local elites. Both Domhoff (1983, 1990) and Mills (1956) write about institutional elites as "high-level" employees in institutions (either private corporations or governmental agencies, such as the U.S. Treasury Department) who see their roles as serving the upper, capitalist-based class. At a more micro or local level, we find that the institutional elites are the educational administrators who see their roles as serving the needs and demands of the local elites. Indeed, in most situations, their professional success and even job security depend on their ability to play these roles.

For instance, in small-town Bearfield, the new superintendent, who is politically very popular with elite parents and community members, has developed a less than positive impression of detracking efforts at the middle school. Yet his view is based less on first-hand information about the reform through visits to the school or discussions with the teachers than on the input he has received from White parents who have placed their children in private schools. To him, the educators at Bearfield Middle School have "let the academics slide just a little bit." Because of the superintendent's sense of commitment to the powerful White, wealthy parents, the principal of Bearfield indicated that he feels intense pressure to raise standardized test scores and prove that academics are not sliding at the school. Thus, some degree of "teaching to the test" has come at the expense of a more creative and innovative curriculum that facilitates detracking efforts by acknowledging, for example, different ways of knowing material. In a symbolic move, the teaching staff has rearranged the Black History Month curriculum to accommodate standardized test prepping in the month of February.

The relationship among the institutional elites at urban Grant High School, its school district office, and the local elite parents, however, demonstrates one of the most severe instances of "co-optation" that we observed. At the district's main office and at the high school, many of the educational administrators are African American. Still, these administrators frequently have failed to push for the kinds of reforms that would benefit the mostly African American students in the lowest track classes. Several respondents noted that Black educators who have been advocates for democratic reform have not survived in this district, and that those who cater to the demands of powerful White parents have been promoted within the system.

At the end of the 1993–1994 school year, the African American principal of Grant, Mr. Phillips, rejected the language arts department's proposal to detrack ninth-grade English by putting "honors" and "regular" students together in the same classes and offering honors as an extra credit option for all students. The principal claimed that it was not fair to do away with separate honors classes when the proposal had not been discussed with parents. His decision, he explained, was based on frequent complaints he received from the mostly White parents of high-track students that changes were being made at the school, particularly in the language arts department, without their prior knowledge or consent. According to the language arts department chair, when her department detracked twelfth-grade electives, it "really pissed people off." Also, when these elite parents were not consulted about the proposal to change the school schedule to an alternative four-period schedule, they protested and were successful in postponing the change.

Furthermore, a recent attempt by Grant's history department to do away with separate honors classes at the request of some students was thwarted by the parents of honors students, who, according to one teacher, "went through the roof." Some of the teachers in other departments indicated that they suspected that the history department's move to eliminate honors classes was not sincere, but rather a political tactic designed to generate support among powerful elite parents for the honors program. In fact, the history department chair, who opposes detracking, noted that his only recourse to stop the detracking reform was to go to the parents and get them upset "because they had the power to do things at school."

At Grant, administrators at the district office have historically been very responsive to the concerns of White parents, and thus regularly implement policies designed to retain the White students. For instance, the district leadership convened an all-White "highly capable parent task force" to examine issues surrounding the educational advanced programs for "highly capable" students. The task force strongly recommended self-contained classrooms for advanced students, making detracking efforts across the district more problematic. According to one of the teachers at Grant, school board members would not talk about the elitism around this program because they were "feeling under siege."

At several schools in our study, educational administrators, especially principals, have lost their jobs since detracking efforts began, in part because they refused co-optation and advocated detracking. At Liberty High School, despite the principal's efforts to make detracking as politically acceptable to the elite parents as possible, in the end he was "done in" by the institutional elites at the district office who would not give him the extra resources he needed to carry out detracking in a manner local elites would have considered acceptable.

Buy-in of the "Not-Quite Elite"

In an interesting article about the current political popularity of decentralized school governance and growth of school-site councils with broad decisionmaking power, Beare (1993) writes that the middle class is a very willing accomplice in the strategy to create such councils and "empower" parents to make important decisions about how schools are run. He notes that it is the middle-class parents who put themselves forward for election to such governing bodies. Yet he argues that in spite of this new-found participatory role for middle-class parents, they actually have little control over the course of their children's schools, because such courses are chartered by a larger power structure. As Beare states, "In one sense, then, participative decision-making is a politically diversionary tactic, a means of keeping activist people distracted by their own self-inflicted, busy work. The middle class are willing accomplices, for they think they are gaining access to the decision-making of the power structures" (p. 202).

The ideology of the local elite's entitlement is so pervasive and powerful that the elites do not necessarily have to be directly involved in the decision-making processes at schools, although they often are. But between the local elites' threats to flee, co-optation of institutional elites, and ability to make their privilege appear as "common sense," such school-site councils will most likely simply reflect, as Beare (1993) points out, the broader power structure. In this way, the "self-inflicted busy work" of the not-quite elites, which, depending on the context of the schools, tend to be the more middle- or working-class parents, is just that — busy work that helps the schools maintain the existing power relations and a highly tracked structure. This is what Gramsci (1971) would refer to as the "consensual" basis of power, or the consensual side of politics in a civil society (see Boggs, 1984; Gramsci, 1971).

We saw a clear example of how this co-optation plays out at Plainview High School, where a group of about thirty predominantly White parents served on the advisory board for the most visible parent group, called the Parent-Teacher Organization, or PTO (even though there were no teachers in this organization). The PTO advisory board met with the principal once a month to act as his "sounding board" on important school-site issues, particularly those regarding discipline. We found through in-depth interviews with many of the parents on the PTO board that these parents were not the most powerful or most elite parents in the one-high-school district. In fact, as the former president of the advisory board and the mother of a not-quite-high-track student explained, "The Advanced Placement parents don't run the president of the PTO. As a matter of fact, I'm trying to think when the last time [was] we had a president of the PTO whose kids were on the fast track in Advanced Placement. I don't think we've had one in quite a few years."

She did note, however, that there were "a lot of parents on the [district-wide] school board whose kids are in the Advanced Placement classes." Interestingly, in the Plainview school district, the school board and the central administration, and not the school-site councils such as the PTO advisory board, have the power to change curricular and instructional programs — the areas most related to detracking reform — in the schools.

Furthermore, despite the past president's assertion that the Advanced Placement parents do not run the PTO advisory board, the board members we interviewed told us they were unwilling to challenge the pro-Advanced Placement stance of the principal. Still, several of the PTO board members said they believed there was too much emphasis on Advanced Placement at Plainview, and that they were at times uncomfortable with the principal's constant bragging about the number of Advanced Placement classes the school offers, the number of students taking Advanced Placement exams, and the number of students who receive 3's, 4's, or 5's on these exams. Some of these parents said that, in their opinion, a heavy load of Advanced Placement classes is too stressful for high school students; others said the curriculum in the Advanced Placement classes is boring rote memorization. But none of these parents had ever challenged the principal in his effort to boost the number of Advanced Placement classes offered and students enrolling in them. According to one mother on the PTO board:

> I think parents have seen that there are so many pressures in the world, they realize that this is high school and they're fed up with all the competition. At the same time they know you have to play the game, you know.... And again, it's hard to evaluate with some of the top, top students, you know, what's appropriate.... I think a lot of this has to do with Plainview as a community, too.

Now, for example, where I live right here is in Fillburn, and that is a more upscale community [within the Plainview district]. Two houses from me is the Doner school district, which is a community of wealthier homes, wealthier people, many of whom have children in private schools.

During interviews, most of the not-quite-elite parents at all of the schools in our study discussed their awareness of the demands that families with high economic and cultural capital placed on the schools. They cited these demands as reasons why they themselves did not challenge the push for more Advanced Placement or gifted classes and why they were not supporters of detracking efforts — even when they suspected that such changes might be beneficial for their own children. For instance, at Grant High School, the chair of the language arts department formed a parent support group to focus on issues of tracking and detracking. This group consisted mostly of parents of students in the regular and honors classes, with only a handful of parents of very advanced students in the highest track. The department chair said she purposefully postponed "the fight" with more of the advanced parents. "We thought if we could get a group of parents who are just as knowledgeable . . . as we were, they should be the ones that become the advocates with the other parents. So that's probably our biggest accomplishment this year is getting this group of parents that we have together." But one of the few parents of advanced students left the group because she said her concerns were not being addressed, and the advisory group disbanded the following spring.

We saw other examples of "not-quite-elite" buy-in at schools where middle-class minority parents had become advocates of tracking practices and opponents of detracking efforts, despite their lament that their children were often the only children of color in the high-track classes. For instance, a Black professional parent at Rolling Hills Middle School, whose two children were in the advanced program, noted that a growing number of African American parents in the district were upset with the racial composition of the nearly all-White "advanced" classes and the disproportionately Black "comprehensive" tracks within racially mixed schools. He said, "So you have segregation in a supposedly desegregated setting. So what it is, you have a growing amount of dissatisfaction within the African American community about these advanced programs that are lily White." Despite his dissatisfaction, this father explained that he is not against tracking per se. "I think tracking has its merits. I just think they need to be less rigid in their standards."

Similarly, at Green Valley High School, a rural West Coast school with a 43 percent White and 57 percent Latino student population, a professional, middle-class Latino couple who had sent their children to private elementary and middle schools before enrolling them in the public high school said that the students at Green Valley should be divided into three groups: those at the top, those in the middle, and those at the bottom. The father added that those students in the middle should be given more of a tech prep education, and that an alternative school might be good for a lot of kids who won't go to college.

Detracking Bribes

Another political practice employed by local elites in schools that are attempting detracking reforms is their use of symbolic capital to bribe the schools to give them some preferential treatment in return for their willingness to allow some small degree of detracking to take place. These detracking bribes tend to make detracking reforms very expensive and impossible to implement in a comprehensive fashion.

Bourdieu (in Harrison, 1993) would consider such detracking bribes to be symbolic of the irreversible character of gift exchange. In exchange for their political buy-in to the detracking efforts, elite parents must be assured that their children are still getting something more than other children. In the process of gift exchange, according to Bourdieu, gifts must be returned, but this return represents neither an exchange of equivalents nor a case of cash on delivery:

> What is returned must be both different in kind and deferred in time. It is within this space opened up by these two elements of non-identity [of the gifts] and temporality [deferred time] that strategic actions can be deployed through which either one actor or another tries to accumulate some kind of profit. The kind of profit accumulated is, of course, more likely to be either symbolic or social, rather than economic. (p. 39)

In the case of the detracking bribes, the elite parents tend to profit at the expense of broad-based reform and restructuring. Yet, detracking bribes take on a different shape and character in different schools, depending upon the bargaining power of the local elite parents and the school's resources. As Bourdieu notes, in the case of the gift exchange, it is the agent's sense of honor that regulates the moves that can be made in the game (Harrison, 1993).

For instance, at King Middle School, located in a large northeastern city, the bribe is the school itself — a well-funded magnet program with formal ties to a nearby college and a rich art program that is integrated into the curriculum. Because King is a school of choice for parents who live in the surrounding area of the city, it is in many ways automatically perceived to be "better than" regular neighborhood schools, where students end up by default. Still, an administrator noted that King must still work at getting elite parents to accept the heterogeneous grouping within the school: "The thing is to convince the parents of the strong students that [heterogeneous grouping] is a good idea and not to have them pull children out to put them in a gifted program. It is necessary to really offer them a lot. You need parent education, along with offering a rich program for the parents so that they don't feel their children are being cheated."

At Rolling Hills Middle School, where African American students are bused to this otherwise White, wealthy school, the detracking bribe comes in the form of the best sixth-grade teachers and a "heterogeneous" team of students, which is skewed toward a disproportionate number of advanced program students. For instance, the heterogeneous team is comprised of 50 percent "advanced" students, 25 percent "honors" students, and 25 percent "regular" students, while the sixth grade as a whole is only about one-third "advanced" students and about one-half "regular" students. Thus, detracking at Rolling Hills is feasible when it affects only one of four sixth-grade teams, and that one team enrolls a disproportionate number of advanced students and is taught by the teachers whom the local elite consider to be the best. The generosity of the "gifts" that the school gives the elite parents who agree to enroll their children in the heterogeneous team are such that this team has become high status itself. The "parent network" of local elites at this school now promotes the heterogeneous team and advises elite mothers of incoming sixth-graders to choose that team. According to one wealthy White parent, "the heterogeneous team is 'hand-picked'." Another White parent whose daughter is on the heterogeneous team noted, "It's also been good to know that it's kind of like a private school within a public school. And that's kind of fair, I hate to say that, but it's kind of a fair evaluation."

Of course, Rolling Hills does not have enough of these "gifts" to bribe all of the local elite parents to place their children on a heterogeneous team. In other words, Rolling Hills will never be able to detrack the entire school as long as the cost of the bribe remains so high and the elite parental profit is so great. By definition, the "best" teachers at any given school are scarce; there are not enough of them to go around. In addition, the number of Advanced Placement students in the school is too small to assure that more heterogeneous teams could be created with the same skewed proportion of advanced, honors, and comprehensive tracks.

At Grant High School, the bribe for detracking the marine science program consists of this unique science offering, coupled with the school's excellent science and math departments and one of the two best music programs in the city. These are commodities that elite parents cannot get in other schools — urban or suburban. As one teacher explained, "So what options do these parents have? Lift their kids out of Grant, which they love? They can't get a science program like this anywhere else in the city." Although the school itself is highly tracked, especially in the history department, the marine science classes enroll students from all different tracks. A marine science teacher noted that parents of the advanced students never request that their kids be placed in separate classes because curricula in this program are both advanced and unique.

Interestingly, the detracking bribe at Liberty High, as the school moved toward the ninth-grade English/social studies core classes, was to be smaller class sizes and ongoing staff development. Unfortunately, the district administration withheld much of the promised funding to allow the school to deliver these gifts to the parents of high-track students. Whether or not these parents were ever committed to this bribe — whether they thought the school was offering them enough in return — is not really clear. What we do know is that the principal who offered the gift was, as we mentioned, recently "let go" by the district. His departure may have been the ultimate bribe with the local elites, because, as Bourdieu (in Harrison, 1993) argues, the kind of profit accumulated is, of course, more likely to be either symbolic or social, rather than economic.

Conclusions

When our research team began this study in 1992, we initially focused on what was happening within the racially mixed schools we were to study. Yet as we visited these schools, it became increasingly evident to us that the parents had a major impact on detracking reform efforts. Over the course of the last three years, we came to appreciate not only the power of this impact but its subtleties as well. In turning to the literature on elites and cultural capital, we gained a deeper understanding of the barriers educators face in their efforts to detrack schools.

As long as elite parents press the schools to perpetuate their status through the intergenerational transmission of privilege that is based more on cultural capital than "merit," educators will be forced to choose between equity-based reforms and the flight of elite parents from the public school system.

The intent of this article is not simply to point fingers at the powerful, elite parents or the educators who accommodate them at the ten schools we studied. We understand that these parents are in many ways victims of a social system in which the scarcity of symbolic capital creates an intense demand for it among those in their social strata. We also recognize the role that the educational system writ large — especially the higher education system — plays in shaping their actions and their understanding of what they must do to help their children succeed.

Still, we hope that this study of ten racially mixed schools undertaking detracking reform is helpful to educators and policymakers who struggle to understand more clearly the political opposition to such reform efforts. Most importantly, we have learned that in a democratic society, the privilege, status, and advantage that elite students bring to school with them must be carefully deconstructed by educators, parents, and students alike before meaningful detracking reforms can take place.

References

Beare, H. (1993). Different ways of viewing school-site councils: Whose paradigm is in use here? In H. Beare & W. L. Boyd (Eds.), *Restructuring schools: An international perspective on the movement to transform the control and performance of schools* (pp. 200–214). Washington, DC: Falmer Press.

Boggs, C. (1984). *The two revolutions: Gramsci and the dilemmas of western Marxism.* Boston: South End Press.

Bourdieu, P. (1973). Cultural reproduction and social reproduction. In R. Brown (Ed.), *Knowledge, education, and cultural change* (pp. 487–501). New York: Harper & Row.

Bourdieu, P. (1977). *Outline of a theory of practice.* Cambridge, Eng.: Cambridge University Press.

Bourdieu, P. (1984). *Distinction: A social critique of the judgment of taste.* Cambridge, MA: Harvard University Press.
Bourdieu, P., & Passeron, J. C. (1977). *Reproduction in education, society and culture.* Beverly Hills, CA: Sage.
Bourdieu, P., & Passeron, J. C. (1979). *The inheritors: French students and their relation to culture.* Chicago: University of Chicago Press.
Bourdieu, P., & Wacquant, L. J. D. (1992). *An invitation to reflexive sociology.* Chicago, IL: University of Chicago Press.
Delpit, L. (1995). *Other people's children: Cultural conflict in the classroom.* New York: New Press.
DiMaggio, P. (1979). Review essay: On Pierre Bourdieu. *American Journal of Sociology, 84,* 1460–1472.
Domhoff, W. G. (1983). *Who rules America now? A view for the 80s.* Englewood Cliffs, NJ: Prentice-Hall.
Domhoff, W. G. (1990). *The power elite and the state: How policy is made in America.* New York: A. deGruyter.
Gramsci, A. (1971). *Selections from the prison notebooks.* New York: International Publishers.
Harker, K. (1984). On reproduction, habitus and education. *British Journal of Sociology of Education, 5*(2), 117–127.
Harrison, P. R. (1993). Bourdieu and the possibility of a postmodern sociology. *Thesis Eleven, 35,* 36–50.
Lareau, A. (1989). *Home advantage.* London: Falmer Press.
McIntosh, P. (January/February, 1992). White privilege: Unpacking the invisible knapsack. *Creation Spirituality,* pp. 33–35.
Mills, C. W. (1956). *The power elite.* London: Oxford University Press.
Oakes, J. (1985). *Keeping track: How schools restructure inequalities.* New Haven, CT: Yale University Press.
Oakes, J., Oraseth, T., Bell, R., & Camp, P. (1990). *Multiplying inequalities: The effects of race, social class, and tracking on opportunities to learn mathematics and science.* Santa Monica, CA: Rand.
Oakes, J., Lipton, M., & Jones, M. (1995, April). *Changing minds: Deconstructing intelligence in detracking schools.* Paper presented at the annual meeting of the American Educational Research Association, San Francisco.
Oakes, J., & Wells, A. S. (1995, April) *Beyond sorting and stratification: Creative alternatives to tracking in racially mixed secondary schools.* Paper presented at the annual meeting of the American Educational Research Association, San Francisco.
Thompson, J. B. (1990). *Ideology and modern culture.* Stanford, CA: Stanford University Press.
Useem, B. (1990, April). *Social class and ability group placement in mathematics in transition to seventh grade: The role of parental involvement.* Paper presented at the annual meeting of the American Educational Research Conference, Boston.
Wells, A. S., & Crain, R. L. (1992). Do parents choose school quality or school status? A sociological theory of free-market education. In P. W. Cookson (Ed.), *The choice controversy* (pp. 65–82). Newbury Park, CA: Corwin Press.
Welner, K., & Oakes, J. (1995, April). *Liability grouping: The new susceptibility of school tracking systems to legal challenges.* Paper presented at the annual meeting of the American Educational Research Association, San Francisco.
Yonesawa, S., Williams, E., & Hirshberg, D. (1995, April). *Seeking a new standard: Minority parent and community involvement in detracking schools.* Paper presented at the annual meeting of the American Educational Research Association, San Francisco.

An earlier version of this article was presented at the American Educational Research Association's 1995 annual meeting in San Francisco.

Bilingual Education for Puerto Ricans in New York City: From Hope to Compromise

SANDRA DEL VALLE

In 1975, the U.S. Commission on Civil Rights quoted a leading Puerto Rican educator on the issue of education and language:

> Our definition of cultural pluralism must include the concept that our language and culture will be given equal status to that of the majority population. It is not enough simply to say that we should be given the opportunity to share in the positive benefits of modern American life. Instead, we must insist that this sharing will not be accomplished at the sacrifice of all those traits which make us what we are as Puerto Ricans. (U.S. Commission on Civil Rights, 1975, p. 103)

In looking for "equal status" on the mainland for the Spanish language and Puerto Rican culture, this educator reflected a popular attitude among Puerto Ricans that gave rise to their support for bilingual education. Bilingual education is a method of teaching a language to speakers of another language using the students' native language to some extent. The extent to which native language is used depends on the nature and goals of the program. For example, developmental bilingual education (DBE) is contrasted with transitional bilingual education programs (TBE). In this article, TBE is considered an assimilationist program in which the educational system usually takes a top-down approach that leaves the affected community with no real decisionmaking power. Teachers are trained to teach the "standard variety" of the minority language. The student body is usually exclusively language minority and the program usually lasts three years. While it may begin with the use of the native language, this language is phased out in a short time in favor of the majority (target) language. The oppositional model to this assimilationist model is the pluralistic model, or DBE, in which the native language is developed along with the target language (Dicker, 1996).

Mainland Puerto Ricans see bilingual education not only as a method to educate language-minority students, but also as a means to realize the promise of equal citizenship in the educational arena. Their vision of bilingual education was one in which the native language — that is, Spanish — was a valuable building block with which they could learn English without sacrificing academic achievement or their native language.

By 1995, the character of Puerto Rican demands for bilingual education had changed dramatically. In *Bushwick Parents Organization v. Mills,* the Bushwick Parents Organization (BPO), a Puerto Rican–dominated parents' organization, supported a lawsuit against Richard P. Mills, New York State's Education Commissioner, which stated that:

> [A] forbidding system of bilingual education has been permitted to emerge in New York City which fails to provide [limited English proficient] children with adequate instruction in English, the critical skill they need to participate fully in the educational and economic opportunities American society offers. (*Bushwick Parents Organization v. Mills*, 1995)

Support for bilingual education and the maintenance of native languages as a goal for Puerto Ricans was no longer to be taken for granted. In the twenty years between these two statements — that is, the U.S. Commission on Civil Rights and the BPO lawsuit — bilingual education has suffered on the local and national level from a variety of factors, including compromised decisionmaking by professionals, lack of information about the goals and methods of bilingual education among language-minority communities, a gap between professional policymakers and the grassroots communities they served, a suspicion by the majority culture of bilingual education's goals, and the perception that it is a failed practice that only serves the entrenched self-interest of professional Latinos (Moran, 1986).

In this article, I discuss the struggle for bilingual education as a fight for civil rights in which lawyers and litigation have played a large role. I specifically examine the role of Puerto Ricans in New York City in these struggles. An important issue to be examined is the fatal gap between two visions of bilingual education — the vision of the grassroots Puerto Rican community that saw bilingual education as educational enrichment, and the remedial model that was ultimately adopted and advanced by lawyers and other professionals in the courts. I also examine the effects of that gap today and its contributions to the development of *BPO v. Mills*. Finally, I discuss the current antibilingual climate, the growth in immigration from Central and South America and Asia to cities like New York, the school reform movement, and the implications these hold for the future of bilingual education.

Federal Decisionmaking and Its Implications for Bilingual Education

Federal decisionmaking in language and education has operated on the legislative and judicial levels. The first and earliest interventions were legislative and sought to fund special English-language instructional programs for language-minority students. The second set of interventions, never fully defined, attempted to define the contours and prohibitions of language-based discrimination. Both tracks, however, shared and have been defined by a vision of bilingual education as a "deficit" and have assumed, if not a "blame the victim" mentality, at least a "change the victim" mentality. The first track found its expression in Title VII of the Elementary and Secondary Education Act (1968), also known as the Bilingual Education Act. The judicial track can be seen in the U.S. Supreme Court case, *Lau v. Nichols* (1974). The development and implications for bilingual education of both tracks are discussed below.

The Legislative Track: The Bilingual Education Act

The national audience first became aware of the educational underachievement of language-minority students in the late 1960s, with the issuance of the National Education Association (NEA) report entitled, "The Invisible Minority, *Pero No Vencibles*," which focused on the educational plight of Mexican American children. The NEA report focused on Arizona's educational neglect of its Mexican American students in Tucson and became the impetus for a later Tucson conference that involved influential congressmen. José Cardenas, a southwestern educator, spoke about the terrible quality of education for Tucson's Mexican American students, saying that "almost anything is better" than what they were receiving (Crawford, 1991, p. 41). The increasing political clout of Mexican American students and the emergence of radical groups, such as the Crusade for Justice, that grew out of the community's frustrations in dealing with an unresponsive government made education a priority issue (Baez, 1995). The Tucson conference proposed developmental bilingual education programs extending from preschool into the high school years as at least one remedy for the "miseducation" of Mexican American children.

The growing Puerto Rican community in New York also received attention. Although Puerto Ricans had been officially recognized as U.S. citizens since 1917, those who migrated to the U.S. were subjected to the same type of racial, ethnic, socioeconomic, and linguistic discrimination as were Mexican Americans in the Southwest. When they entered the U.S. schools with only limited English ability and a poor rural education, they encountered schools unprepared for their needs, teachers untrained to educate "foreign" pupils, outdated textbooks with no bearing on their lives or histories, and a school system generally prepared only to conform students to a White, middle-class model of success (Castellanos, 1985). Meanwhile, the Puerto Rican community was already experimenting with bilingual education. The Puerto Rican Study conducted in 1958 by the Board of Education of the City of New York recommended the use of the native language, and even native-language retention, as a way to address the high Puerto Rican dropout rate (Board of Education of the City of New York, 1958). By the mid-1960s, groups like ASPIRA,[1] United

Bronx Parents, and the Puerto Rican Educators Association were promoting bilingualism and multiculturalism as goals for the system's bilingual education programs (Baez, 1995).

Responding to the increased attention given to Latino education issues, Congress passed the 1968 Bilingual Education Act. The legislation was lauded by education advocates and Latino supporters for placing the educational needs of language-minority children at the forefront of national education policymaking. However, it defined the problem in terms of English-language proficiency rather than the educational under-attainment of all language-minority children. Not surprisingly, the legislation defined simply teaching children English as the solution. The Bilingual Education Act defined bilingual education as a remedial effort to make students dominant in English only, thereby a de facto squelching of possibilities for the development of bilingualism. In other words, "remedial" was defined as compensatory in terms of not knowing English, as opposed to viewing proficiency in a native language as an asset to which English could be added. The compromised nature of what was won through this legislation was not lost on Puerto Rican bilingual education advocates:

> I wish to stress that I realize the importance of learning English by Puerto Ricans and other minority groups living in the United States. But I do not feel that our educational abilities are so limited and our educational vision so shortsighted that we must teach one language at the expense of another, that we must sacrifice the academic potential of thousands of youngsters in order to promote the learning of English, that we must jettison and reject ways of life that are our own. (S. Polanco-Abreu, quoted in Crawford, 1991, p. 38)

The act also issued no guidelines in the development of programs; instead, it relied on local districts, which often had little expertise or incentive, to address the "special" needs of language-minority students. Congress also prioritized poor families as program recipients and, by injecting an unnecessary poverty criteria, stamped the "compensatory" label firmly on bilingual education. The act also appeared to condone the racial segregation of language-minority children. Without guidance and with only limited funding, districts and parents accepted the segregation of these students as programatically necessary (children needed to be grouped together by language in order to be served) and fiscally required (the inclusion of Anglos, who were difficult to attract anyway would water down the funds available to language-minority students) (Castellanos, 1985). Housed in poor, already-segregated Latino schools, bilingual programs were new, underfunded, and already seen as remedial efforts rather than as magnets to draw students not zoned for these schools (Castellanos, 1985; Crawford, 1992). These early decisions, which reflect an ambivalence toward bilingual education and federal educational interventions, reverberate even today in the heated debate over bilingual education.

The Judicial Track: Lau v. Nichols

Bilingual education *seemed* to receive another boost in 1974 when the U.S. Supreme Court held in *Lau v. Nichols* that schools must address the English-language "deficiencies" of English Language Learners (ELLs),[2] who, according to the decision, could not simply be allowed to sit in the classroom and neither comprehend nor participate. The Court ruled that such a state of affairs was the denial of equal educational opportunity.

Lau began as a reaction by Chinese parents to a San Francisco education desegregation case that they feared would jeopardize their bilingual programs. Approximately half of the Chinese schoolchildren who needed language support services were receiving them, prompting parents to go to court to demand bilingual education programs in their neighborhood schools. Controversy over exactly what the Chinese parents were demanding marked the lower court proceedings. The parents' lawyers asked for "bilingual compensatory education in English" (Baez, 1995, p. 129). The court interpreted this as demanding special non-English courses, and circuit judges responded by stating that

> the State's use of English as the language of instruction in its schools is intimately and properly related to the educational and socializing purposes for which schools were established. This is an English-speaking nation. (*Lau*, 1974)

A dissenting judge resisted this interpretation that translated the parents' demands as a plea for their children to learn only English. Even sympathetic judges were confused, however, finding that "the children do not seek to have their classes taught in both English and Chinese. All they ask is that they receive instruction in the English language" (*Lau*, 1974, p. 801).

When the Supreme Court reviewed the case, the lawyers decided not to request that the Court mandate any particular educational methodology. Although the Court essentially precluded rampant "sink or swim" methods of education, it did not explicitly endorse bilingual education either. In fact, it endorsed no particular methodology, but left that choice up to school administrators. The Federal Office of Civil Rights read *Lau* as requiring transitional bilingual education programs and developed "Lau Guidelines" that were to be used by school districts when developing programs for language-minority schoolchildren. Although hailed for acknowledging the legitimate educational needs of these children, *Lau* did not find a constitutional violation of the children's rights. For instance, the Court could have found that it was a violation of the Fourteenth Amendment's Equal Protection Clause not to provide special language programs for these children. Such a ruling would have put *Lau* on the same footing as *Brown v. Board of Education* and would have raised the moral stakes for providing language-minority students a proper education, not to mention raising the national visibility of these students. A decision based on the Constitution might have been used to strengthen programs and substantially increase spending for language-minority students. Most significantly, such a decision could have led to the use of a results-based approach to the education of these students, in which program effectiveness would be measured by the academic success of students. Instead, it decided the case on the basis of Title VI of the Civil Rights Laws, which precluded recipients of federal funds from discriminating on the basis of national origin. Further, equal educational opportunity was defined by the Court as a mechanism for ensuring access to English-language instruction only; the Chinese community's aspirations for a truly bilingual, bicultural education got no real hearing and were not reflected in the Court's decision. Despite its limitations, *Lau* became the template used for fashioning bilingual education litigation and its consequent remedies.

New York City

Latino education litigation began in New York City and elsewhere as a grassroots movement to address the inequities in schooling for Puerto Rican students regardless of their language dominance. The Puerto Rican agenda for education reform was comprehensive and holistic — it demanded respect for the language and culture and home life of Puerto Rican children. It further demanded that Puerto Rican children's home language be used as an asset in building toward bilingualism rather than as a deficit. It went beyond these cultural issues to seek greater numbers of Latino teachers, better links between schools and families and communities, and far greater community control of schools than the large, bureaucratic, Anglo-dominated school system offered (National Puerto Rican Taskforce on Educational Policy, 1982; Pedraza, 1997).

In the early 1970s, the energetic and politically active Puerto Rican community in New York had enjoyed a series of educational victories because of grassroots activism. For example, in 1973, in the middle of a school redistricting fight, community pressure kept East Harlem, a Puerto Rican stronghold, in a single school district rather than allowing its divisions to divide the neighborhood into two districts (Pedraza, 1997). The East Harlem Puerto Rican community was not new to educational struggles; from the 1920s to the 1960s, it had been involved in progressive educational reform that brought about the East Harlem Block School, an innovative school founded by Black and Puerto Rican parents.

ASPIRA of New York v. Board of Education

ASPIRA of New York was founded in 1961 as a nonprofit educational and leadership development agency dedicated to serving the Puerto Rican community in New York City (*ASPIRA v. Board of Education,* 1973). Clearly, the existing educational system was failing Puerto Rican students in 1970; 51 percent of non-Hispanic Whites over the age of twenty-five had graduated from high school, as opposed to 20 percent of Puerto Ricans; only 1 percent of Puerto Ricans were college graduates (Wagenheim, 1975). In 1947, an estimated 25,000

Puerto Rican students were in the New York City school system (Falk & Wang, 1990); by 1972, that number had risen to 245,000, with an additional 38,000 students from non-Puerto Rican Spanish-speaking nationalities. About 40 percent of the Puerto Rican children spoke Spanish only, requiring an unprepared school system to quickly develop approaches and curricula to properly educate them (Falk & Wang, 1990). In 1966, with Puerto Ricans constituting 21 percent of New York City's public school enrollment, ASPIRA issued *The Losers* (Margolis, 1968), a report documenting the system's failure to educate its Puerto Rican students. In creating its agenda for education reform, ASPIRA decided to press for bilingual education as a method, not only as a means of addressing the miseducation of Puerto Rican children, but also as an organizing tool and a means of "preserving community identity" (Falk & Wang, 1990, p. 6).

The Puerto Rican grassroots community wanted to see a revitalized educational experience for their children that respected their cultural and linguistic backgrounds and that developed students' Spanish literacy, while at the same time giving those students who needed it the opportunity to learn English. Most importantly, the problem was not defined as one resting within Spanish-dominant children. It instead framed the problem as a school system that did not respond to the needs of all Puerto Rican children, regardless of their dominant language. Although bilingual education was deemed a worthy goal in itself, it was seen as part and parcel of what the educator Jim Cummins (1986) would later call a "framework for intervention" for language-minority students. By itself, bilingual education could not address the underachievement of language-minority children in the United States. Cummins argued that a theory of intervention addressing the power relations between majority and minority cultures was needed. Since school culture simply reflected the imbalance of power between majorities and minorities in society generally, it required a mediating construct to help minority children succeed in school despite their subjugated status. The extent to which minority students' language and culture were valued and incorporated in the school was one factor in empowering minority students. In 1973, Latino educators defined cultural pluralism as their rationale for bilingual education. By "cultural pluralism" they meant a respect for cultures other than the majority, other-than-English language acquisition, development of a positive self-image, and equality of educational opportunity (Cardenas, 1995).

To achieve this goal, individual Puerto Rican parents and ASPIRA decided to go to court to press for reforms in the school system. ASPIRA was represented in court by the newly formed Puerto Rican Legal Defense and Education Fund (PRLDEF), an organization formed in response to the outcry over the education of Puerto Rican children and the demand for litigation. The resulting case was one of the earliest to establish a legal federal mandate for bilingual education as a method of ensuring an equal educational opportunity for students who were not proficient in English. It was also notable because the case involved the largest school system in the nation at that time, as well as the largest plaintiff group, with over 80,000 children potentially affected (Santiago-Santiago, 1986). The case was settled with a court-monitored consent decree setting up a transitional bilingual education program that became a model for school districts facing similar litigation throughout the nation.[3]

The available research, the spirit of educational innovation, and the Puerto Rican community's activism could have turned the case into not just landmark but legendary litigation for bilingual education. Instead, the litigation, following the parameters of *Lau,* closely defined the class-action group only as those Spanish-surnamed children who needed English-language remediation. Afraid that *Lau* would not succeed in the Supreme Court, lawyers stopped short of asking for a developmental model of bilingual education and instead urged and secured a transitional model. One commentator noted that, given the high level of energy in the Latino community in New York City at the time, the "professional class managing the litigation" should not have "held back" by allowing the recently decided *Lau* case to dominate the bilingual litigation strategy (Baez, 1995, p. 179). As a result, these grassroots organizations would not see their vision for a truly transformative education secured. Instead, in the consent decree and subsequent rulings, Judge Marvin E. Frankel described plaintiffs' monolingual non-English-speaking children as "disturbed, deprived, culturally ghettoized" since they were not academically successful (*ASPIRA v. Board of Education,* 1975, p. 1164).

The dissonance between community wishes and litigation objectives in ASPIRA was marked. While ASPIRA's leaders and the lawyers agreed on following a modest strategy to secure transitional services, other community members wanted bilingual programs that would maintain and further develop the Spanish language and culture in addition to academic support programs that would help all Puerto Rican/Latino students (Baez, 1995). Although ASPIRA's leaders, the lawyers, and university professionals worked together on the case, neither front-line teachers nor average parents whose children would be affected by the outcome even knew of the litigation or of the resulting consent decree (Santiago-Santiago, 1986).

After the decree, community activists and bilingual education advocates stressed the continuing need for struggle in this area, particularly since the consent decree had only partially fulfilled their demands:

> Many [ASPIRA and other advocates, as well] fully realized that the decree would not ensure equal educational opportunity for all 253,452 Puerto Rican children in the City's schools. At best, the decree had the potential of assisting those most in need — Puerto Rican and Hispanic LEP children. This meant that equal educational opportunity for approximately 60 percent of the population, which had varying degrees of proficiency in English and were not eligible for the [consent decree] program, remained virtually unaddressed. (Santiago-Santiago, 1986, p. 161)

Many felt that the decree represented an assimilationist model of education that did not address the essential concerns of the Puerto Rican community —

that is, the need, as expressed by Cummins, to have schools respect the Spanish language and the social, familial, and civic culture of Puerto Rican students. The decree did not attempt to realize these broader goals, and there remains a sense that the professionals handling the litigation compromised a visionary idea of education for a quicker legal victory (Falk & Wang, 1990).

Ten years after the litigation, ASPIRA convinced the Educational Priorities Panel (EPP), a fiscal educational watchdog in New York City, that the consent decree's promise was still not being fulfilled. As a result of their collaborative efforts, EPP issued an influential report, *Ten Years of Neglect: The Failure to Serve Language Minority Children in the New York City Public Schools* (Willner, 1986), which documented the decree's inadequacies, reporting that 40 percent of the ELLs entitled to bilingual services were not receiving them. Their report became the fountainhead from which more negotiations with the Board of Education sprang.

Indeed, despite its attempt to promote Puerto Rican empowerment, *ASPIRA v. Board of Education* is one of the least community empowering of the bilingual education litigation cases of the 1970s (Baez, 1995). It did little to change power relations in the school system, did not address the unequal learning opportunities of Latino/Puerto Rican children as a whole, did not change schools into centers for community learning and empowerment, and did not address the low expectations often held for Latino/Puerto Rican students. The litigation, however, did force the New York City public school system to acknowledge at least some of the needs of Puerto Rican children, increased the influence of ASPIRA on educational policymaking, and continues to force the Board of Education to offer bilingual education programs. Further, the requirement that the school system hire teachers proficient in English and Spanish created a cadre of teachers within the system to help monitor the consent decree and develop more holistic linguistic programs. Unfortunately, the emphasis on bilingual education has continued to obscure the need for greater systemic reform. Twenty years after the ASPIRA consent decree, with Latino children comprising 35 percent of the school system and growing, Latinos are still concentrated in the worst performing schools in the city and are subjected to poor, underfunded, remedial bilingual programs (Latino Commission on Educational Reform, 1992).

Effects of the Litigation Model on Bilingual Education Nationally

The flawed legal strategy pursued in bilingual education litigation was exemplified but not confined to New York City.[4] Given the narrow parameters of litigation within which complex community needs must be fitted into the technical strictures of a complaint, Latino education litigation nationally devolved within a short time into litigation *only* over the needs of non-English-dominant students, or ELLs, at the expense of the majority of English-speaking, second- and third-generation Latino children, who were also being neglected by the educational establishment. The litigation model pursued in New York City and nationally had three interrelated and unfortunate results that are still being felt today. Discussed in greater detail below, these results have helped increase the vulnerability of bilingual education programs. From allowing bilingual education to be treated as a panacea for school systems' failing to educate language-minority students to then limiting the scope and goals of the programs, these factors have had a corrosive effect on public support for bilingual education.

1. *An artificial and unworkable limitation on the kind of educational litigation that could be fashioned for language-minority children.* By developing cases that relied exclusively on the educational needs of ELLs, lawyers ended up without a legal strategy that addressed the legitimate and compelling educational needs of all other Latino and language-minority children — that is, children who come from a language-minority background but are proficient in English. TBE ended up being used as a panacea to cure the ills of an educational system that consistently failed to address the needs of language-minority children. Rather than seeing *Lau* as a small and hopeful sign that the needs of language-minority children could be addressed in courts, lawyers took *Lau* as the last word on equal educational opportunities for these schoolchildren and failed to continue to push for a Constitutional guarantee for bilingual education.

The status of Puerto Ricans as migratory citizens caught between two cultures was likewise never explored as a possible legal hook. For at least a decade, Puerto Ricans had argued that their status as citizens of both Puerto Rican and Anglo cultures and languages required that mainland schools incorporate their linguistic needs in their instructional methods. Unfortunately, these possibilities were never fully explored by lawyers leading bilingual education litigation, and there are still no viable legal strategies today that place the language-minority children's educational needs generally before courts or policymakers.

2. *Dysfunction between community wishes and litigation obligations.* While the Latino community in New York City and elsewhere called for the transformation of schools into nurturing environments in which their children could succeed, the litigation focused exclusively on ELLs. Prior to 1974, Latino education litigation nationally was notable for its grassroots foundation (Baez, 1995). Nationalist Latino groups from the Northeast and Southwest, and parents' groups such as the United Bronx Parents, headed by Puerto Rican Evelina Antonetti and *El Comité de Padres* in Boston, were instrumental in raising parents' consciousness of the need for concerted community action, as well as in educating them about democratic education principles (Baez, 1995). The litigation that occurred until the mid-1970s transformed the greater Latino community precisely because it sprang from that community, changed parents through the litigation process, and created a new educa-

tional experience for all — that is, for parents and students, English proficient or not.

After *Lau*, however, the community's vision of educational reform was lost in the push by leaders and lawyers for "quick fix" remedies that ignored the complex issues raised by parents. Some commentators have argued that the role of lawyers, judges, and national policymakers undermines the necessary community choice over and control of bilingual education policy (Baker & de Kanter, 1986). Naturally, it can also be argued that lawyers, judges, and national policymakers are the only people small minority communities can turn to if their larger political subdivision — that is, their school district or local government — does not value their language heritage (Teitelbaum & Hiller, 1977). Either way, the impact of federal litigation on a community's voice and empowerment can be substantial.

3. *Institutionalization of transitional bilingual education (TBE)*. Finally, lawyers and national policymakers did succeed in raising the awareness of the needs of ELLs to a previously unheard of level (Baker & de Kanter, 1986). Unfortunately, lawyers also ended up institutionalizing TBE and shaping a deficit-based, remedial type of bilingual education that begins with the premise that the most important educational objective for a language-minority student is to learn English, and then measures program success by how quickly students are transitioned into English (Puerto Rican Legal Defense and Education Fund, 1972). Yet, that shape neither fulfills the promise of bilingual education nor consequently serves the vibrant and multifaceted communities that still await the transformative educational litigation they originally sought.

From 1974 to 1981, the presumed legal mandate for bilingual education was lost. In 1983, the Supreme Court withdrew from *Lau*'s interpretation of Title VI, which only required that the challenged action or policy have a negative effect on the protected group. The Court decided that Title VI required that a plaintiff show that the recipient of federal funds *intended* to discriminate (*Guardians Association v. Civil Service Commission of New York*, 1983). In 1974, the Equal Educational Opportunities Act (EEOA) was passed, a statute generally intended to address busing for desegregative purposes. The statute, however, contained a provision that mandated equal educational opportunities for ELLs.[5] With the waning influence of *Lau*, the EEOA became the prime vehicle for bilingual education litigation. The EEOA allowed plaintiffs to proceed with an "effects test" of discrimination; that is, they would not have to prove intentional discrimination. However, the EEOA's provisions have been read as giving local educational agencies (LEAs) wide latitude in their decisionmaking without providing penalties for abuse of discretion.[6]

Further, Reagan and Bush federal court appointees began retreating from a federalist approach to civil rights and relying more on LEAs' discretion. Despite the landmark that *Lau* represented, the case served as a viable precedent for a bilingual education mandate for only seven years, from 1974 to 1981. In 1981, in *Castañeda v. Pickard*, the Fifth Circuit Court of Appeals, which has jurisdiction over six states, including Texas and Florida, read civil rights laws as requiring only that districts somehow meet the language needs of ELLs, but not necessarily through bilingual education.[7] As the means of doing so in *Castañeda*, the Fifth Circuit Court of Appeals outlined a three-pronged test to determine whether a local educational agency was meeting its requirements towards ELLs under the EEOA: 1) the LEA must use a methodology for teaching English that is supported by some experts in the field or that is considered a legitimate experimental strategy; 2) the LEA must dedicate sufficient resources to the program to make it work; and 3) after a reasonable trial period, the program must indeed succeed in teaching the students English. *Castañeda* signaled a federal retreat from bilingual education and a continuing reluctance on the part of courts to mandate educational policymaking for local districts.

Although *Castañeda* is not a Supreme Court decision and technically does not overrule *Lau*, it has been cited or referred to by courts throughout the nation as reflecting the legal standards for serving ELLs.[8] Given *Lau*'s weakness and the lack of political support for bilingual education, *Castañeda* has generally been taken as the best bilingual education advocates can hope for in the foreseeable future. Ultimately, this means that litigation cannot force school districts with no specific bilingual education consent decrees or state laws to develop these programs in cities such as New York. Consent decrees that predate *Castañeda* are increasingly open to attack as inflexible mandates at a time when the federal government is looking to expand school districts' autonomy. With the federal retreat from bilingual education and its growing unpopularity, consent decrees like ASPIRA, once seen as minimal starting points for greater educational reform, become the ceiling for litigatively enforceable rights.

Current Climate

Today, many effective and operational bilingual education programs are being lost because language has long been seen as a proxy for ethnicity, and the maintenance of minority languages as a threat to a national identity (Fishman, 1989). In 1981, Joseph Califano, then Secretary of Health, Education, and Welfare, remarked that bilingual programs had become "captives of the professional Hispanic and other ethnic groups, with their understandably emotional but often exaggerated political rhetoric of biculturalism" (Califano, 1981, p. 313). Indeed, in 1985, U.S. Secretary of Education William Bennett said that the "original purposes" of the Bilingual Education Act of 1968 had been "perverted and politicized," and that a "sense of cultural pride cannot come at the price of proficiency in English, our common language" (Moran, 1993, p. 274). Educator Sonia Nieto notes that

> bilingual education is a political issue because both the proponents and opponents of bilingual education have long recognized its potential for empow-

ering these traditionally powerless groups. Because it represents the class and ethnic group interest of traditionally subordinate groups and comes out on the side of education as an emancipatory proposition, it is no mystery that bilingual education has been characterized by great controversy. (Nieto, 1996, p. 194)

Sociolinguist Joshua Fishman, linking bilingual education with ethnolinguistic diversity, has found that

from the very beginning of speculative social theory, ethnicity has been primarily associated with its debits, rather than with its assets. The view [that] ethnolinguistic diversity is itself nothing but a byproduct of poverty and backwardness is a recurring theme in both modern liberal and conservative thought. Why are such destructive myths so hard to combat? Myths are vested interests and vested interests produce their own intellectual blinders, even when they are entertained and adopted by folks who are modern, progressive and even intellectual. Power is a scarce commodity and power-sharing is never engaged in voluntarily. Ethnolinguistic aggregates are suspected of power aspirations and ethnolinguistic pluralism is considered a bad risk, insofar as potentially fostering such aspirations rather than overcoming them. (Fishman, 1989, pp. 561–563)

The attacks on bilingual education today are based not only on ethnicity principles, but on the popular issue of "standards" as well. Since the program is seen as benefiting only minorities, it is assumed that it coddles students and lowers their threshold of success rather than ensuring educational excellence in two languages.[9] This new tactic has had a divisive effect on Latinos, who are left insisting that they want the very best for their children — that is, to learn English as a way into the middle class. Bilingual education detractors have used these protestations as "proof" that Latinos don't support bilingual education (Center for Equal Opportunity [CEO], 1996b). Using Latinos as opponents of bilingual education is very valuable to these detractors, as it helps insulate critics from charges of discrimination. Indeed, they can charge that bilingual education or a failing segregated system is itself discriminating against Latinos, the single largest ethnic group receiving bilingual education services, nationally and in New York City (Garvin, 1998; Meyers, 1998). This is not surprising, since the limitations of bilingual education that have made it vulnerable to attack were embedded in its defining moments more than twenty years ago.

Bushwick Parents Organization v. Mills

Many of these issues were reflected in a lawsuit that arose in New York City when the Bushwick Parents Organization (BPO) filed a lawsuit attempting to dismantle bilingual education in the city (*BPO v. Mills*, 1995). Latino parents — including mostly Puerto Ricans who were backed by a large church-run parents' organization that, in turn, was helped in its lawsuit by conservative think tanks and a large private law firm — filed the suit. BPO complained that their members' children were being misplaced in bilingual classes, were learning neither English nor Spanish adequately in those classes, and were unable to remove themselves from the program without having their loyalty to their "ethnicity" questioned.

Sadly, the Bushwick school district in Brooklyn, New York, with a poverty rate of over 90 percent, is like many other districts in which Puerto Rican and Latino students predominate (Board of Education of the City of New York, 1997a). According to state standards, its boundaries contain four "failing" schools. In half the middle schools, less than a quarter of the students read at grade level; in no middle school were half the children reading at grade level (Public Education Association, 1994). Despite these glaring inadequacies throughout a failing school system, the lawsuit focused only on the failures of the bilingual education programs.

One year prior to the filing of this lawsuit, former schools chancellor Ramón Cortines issued results of a longitudinal study that severely undermined the credibility of bilingual education in New York City because of its finding that ELLs in ESL-only classrooms learned English faster and academically outperformed their counterparts receiving bilingual education (Board of Education, 1994). The methodologically flawed study received enormous media attention, as the *New York Times* featured the findings on a front page usually reserved for national and international news. The study has since been repeatedly cited as the last word on the state of bilingual education in New York (Berman, 1998; CEO, 1996a; Garvin, 1998).

The repercussions of the report reverberated through the BPO lawsuit. The report was used to argue that any state practices that allowed children to remain in bilingual education for longer than three years was tantamount to educational malpractice and was attached to the complaint as support for the plaintiff's contentions. The BPO sued the State Commissioner of Education, saying that enforcement of a fortieth percentile cutoff score on English-language assessments before a child was no longer considered an ELL, and therefore no longer eligible for English-language support services, was "arbitrary and capricious," as it allowed students to remain too long in bilingual education classes. The lawsuit, however, was legally meritless. The commissioner's reliance on individual student performance on the assessments was appropriate, and the use of a fortieth percentile was a codified educational decision that no court, lacking pedagogical expertise, would second guess. The court ruled that how the assessments were being used were appropriate.

Although quickly dismissed, the lawsuit grabbed national headlines, as moderate and liberal press rushed to cover a story where Puerto Rican parents criticized bilingual education (Amselle, 1996; "Parents worried," 1996; Steinberg, 1995). The press, however, did not cover the strong support that existed for bilingual education in the Bushwick community among Puerto Ricans, and even among the Puerto Rican leadership of the BPO (M. Diaz, personal communiction, 1995). The lawsuit had a corrosive effect on the Bushwick community, with support for bilingual education becoming the driving issue in school board elections and people within BPO resigning over the lawsuit. The activist Latino parents whom BPO attracted could have used the opportunity of community mobilization to shift its emphasis to achieve a more systemic reform in District 32, which would have addressed the educational failures of the district as a whole rather than focusing only on bilingual education programs. Instead, national conservative groups, such as the Center for Equal Opportunity (CEO, 1996a),[10] used the lawsuit to further their own agendas in opposition to bilingual education by attempting to intervene in the lawsuit.

The growing lethargy among the Puerto Rican and Latino community in New York about bilingual education helped create the climate for filing the lawsuit. The battle for bilingual education was considered won with the signing of the ASPIRA consent decree. In fact, new, younger heads of Puerto Rican organizations, as well as newly immigrating parents and new teachers, had no notion of the history and, most importantly, did not even know of the decree's existence, let alone its significance. After the decree was signed it continued to be monitored — and still is — by lawyers at the Puerto Rican Legal Defense and Education Fund: community monitoring, such as was done by ASPIRA to gather data for the building of the ASPIRA lawsuit, would not become a feature of the decree. By the time the Bushwick parents' unhappiness with their district was translated into a bilingual education lawsuit, there were no other parents or alternatives on the grassroots level to BPO's divisive guidance. Never truly allowed to take its form from the aspirations of parents, bilingual education in New York City was now being attacked by Puerto Rican parents.

Bilingual education at the college level was made the scapegoat in a battle over graduation requirements at Hostos Community College in the South Bronx in spring 1997. There, a contest of wills between the former chancellor of the City University of New York and newly appointed, conservative Board of Trustee members erupted into a controversy over whether the college, with a mission to educate poor, immigrant students and use bilingual education, was undermining graduation standards. Although the issues surrounding the graduation standards, especially the writing assessments, were complex, the media concentrated only on the issue of whether the use of bilingual education was necessary, appropriate, or standards-eroding (Chan, 1997; "Short-changing students," 1997; "Failure at Hostos," 1997; "No substitute," 1997).

The same concern over erosion of standards was used in the debate over new high school graduation standards proposed by New York State Commissioner of Education Richard P. Mills. Under Commissioner Mills's proposal, all graduating seniors would have been required to take and pass more rigorous exams in a variety of subject areas before being allowed to graduate. Previously, seniors could have chosen to take less rigorous exams and graduate with a lesser "local" diploma rather than the more prestigious "Regents" diploma. The tests for the local diploma, however, were available in a variety of languages. The debate over whether to even offer the new exams in languages other than English was a hot one. Over and over, there was a concern that translation of tests would somehow lower standards rather than ensuring that all children were actually meeting the high standards expected of all seniors. After being repeatedly tabled by Board of Regents member Saul Cohen, the chair of the Committee on Elementary and Secondary Education who opposed the translations, the translations were finally approved only for those students entering the New York State school system after ninth grade and only after the commissioner issued a statement stressing the need for intensive English-language instruction. How the plan to effect this statement will interact or collide with the ASPIRA consent decree in New York City remains to be seen. However, one could argue that it was again this aged decree that was used to stop the commissioner from issuing a statement that would have promised total English-language immersion for all ELLs in exchange for the translation of the tests and in direct violation of the decree.

Despite this modest victory, bilingual education throughout New York State is in jeopardy. Although the state currently has a strong bilingual education law, the Board of Regents recently indicated that it wanted to "massage" the law to allow for "intensive English-language instruction." This terminology has not yet been defined by the Board of Regents or Commissioner Mills, but unhappiness with the current levels of English-language instruction in bilingual education programs is palpable.[11] If the state moves away from bilingual education, as many other states already have done, it will be looking for major compromises from ASPIRA on its consent decree, the only legal impediment to the statewide elimination of bilingual education. In the ensuing political and legal struggle, ASPIRA and its lawyers at PRLDEF cannot be perceived as only representing a handful of elites or the interests of bilingual teachers. The support for bilingual education and the consent decree must return to the grassroots level, to students in the programs and their parents.

The transitional nature of bilingual education programs also makes it difficult to develop a movement. By its nature, those most affected by the elimination of bilingual programs are the most recent immigrants — those who have been in the school system for less than three years. A population generally economically vulnerable and dealing with the social and cultural dislocations involved in immigrating, they usually have little time and energy for involvement in educational struggles that are not directly personal, especially when the need for English-language support services is seen as a temporary measure to be exhausted within one to three years. The reputation of bilingual education as a remedial program for poor children who cannot meet the same expectations as Anglo students hardly makes it a sympathetic cause. Already, bilingual programs are seen as stigmatizing and the first step to a lower academic track. In summarizing immigrant students' educational experiences in New York City, Francisco Rivera-Batiz noted that

> the participation of students in . . . programs [for limited English proficient students] frequently places them in a separate track in schools, a track which

often has lower expectations of their students, and lower outcomes. The progress of the students is not monitored adequately, and many wind up graduating from high school without ever attending the regular school program. Furthermore, LEP students do not have the same access to the services available to students in mainstream programs. (Rivera-Batiz, 1996, p. 29)

Regardless of the accuracy of this assessment, the public perceives "LEP programs," especially bilingual education programs, as palatably negative.

Recommendations and Future Possibilities

Bilingual education is being attacked not only by conservatives who fear its capacity to empower minorities, but by liberals as well, who see poorly devised and implemented programs as a hindrance to the academic success and assimilation of language-minority, especially Latino, students. Turning the tide for bilingual education will be difficult; given the political nature of bilingual education, simply strengthening programs, as at least one commentator has suggested, will not be sufficient (Krashen, 1996). Instead, a reinvigorated, multitiered advocacy strategy must be pursued that should weave together the following elements:

Develop committed bilingual education teachers. Bilingual education was funded and mandated before there were sufficient numbers of teachers to make it a reality. Poorly implemented programs, implemented either by hostile, uninterested teachers and districts or by well-meaning but untrained staff has had a negative impact on the ability of many to wholeheartedly support bilingual education. Community monitoring of bilingual education's implementation and the professional development of teachers can help ensure that we have defensible programs. Community-based organizations that operate youth programs should be sharing the history, politics, and empowering nature of bilingual education with their students. Even if the students do not want to become bilingual education teachers, they can become a resource to the greater community on the ideas and ideals of bilingual education.

Respond to the changing Latino demographics in New York City. Recent immigrants have been arriving at New York City's schools in record numbers over the past several years. In 1989, New York City's public schools had 36,000 recent immigrant enrollees; by 1995 that number had increased to 134,875 (Rivera-Batiz, 1996).[12] The percentage of immigrant children enrolled in the city's schools rose from 20 percent in 1989 to over 30 percent in 1995; the number identified as "recent" immigrants (three years or less in the state's schools) rose from 3.8 percent in 1989 to 12.8 percent in 1995 (Rivera-Batiz, 1996). The range of languages now represented in bilingual education and ESL classes in the state is over 172, with Spanish, Haitian Creole, Chinese, Russian, and Korean as the largest language groups (Kadamus, 1997).

Generally, immigrants, especially Latino immigrants, experience the same poor education as Puerto Ricans. They attend overcrowded, highly segregated schools within Anglo-dominated school systems. There is a threat that low-literacy ELLs who need intensive instruction in their own languages before they can learn English will instead be referred to special education classes, as was done with Puerto Rican children decades ago. After much pressure, the Board of Education released a study in 1997 documenting that Latino children are the most underrepresented ethnic group in gifted and talented programs (Board of Education, 1997b). The vast majority of the districts do not even have a way to measure giftedness in ELLs, and thereby automatically exclude them from New York City's best programs. In short, the civil rights issues that confronted Puerto Ricans in the 1950s and 1960s are still being felt today by the newer Latino subgroups.

Puerto Ricans can play a role in shaping the terrain of a possible new movement by sharing their history of struggle and educational activism to pushing for holistic school reform. Rather than continuing to push for remedial bilingual education as an end in itself or simply monitoring the consent decree, the emphasis needs to be on bilingual education as a component of remaking schools. Providing bilingual education alone will not address immigrant children's needs, which may range from having access to schools that prepare them for the Regents exams to ensuring that their classrooms are small enough to handle the diversity in languages and literacy levels that they present.

Contextualize bilingual education within a struggle for educational reform. Some advances have already been made in placing bilingual education as an enrichment model in a variety of smaller, dual-language, developmental schools throughout the city. Backed by a large grant from the Annenberg Foundation, these schools have a greater autonomy and can develop creative curriculum and hire teachers who are dedicated to serving a particular school population.

Since 1994, six new small schools for predominantly Latino schoolchildren with an emphasis on bilingualism have been or are in the process of being created in New York City. The first of these schools, the Leadership Secondary School, was opened in 1994 on the basis of recommendations by the Latino Commission on Educational Reform, a commission of thirty-five parents, students, teachers, administrators, researchers, and concerned citizens chaired by Manhattan Board of Education member Luís O. Reyes.

After the commission created five more schools with an emphasis on the education of ELLs and Latinos, a Latino education network, funded by the Annenberg grant, was created to provide a forum in which the schools can share their technical and pedagogical knowledge with each other. Most importantly, the schools' leaders are trying to develop a curriculum to achieve biliteracy on a high school level that could be used city-wide. These leaders, overwhelmingly Puerto Rican, are unabashedly using bilingual education and the goal of biliteracy as a central piece in the creation of their schools. The schools also are striving to create "a sharing, supportive, nurturing learning environment in our schools that is student-centered and encourages a holistic approach to education; educational excellence to cope with and succeed according to and beyond traditional 'standards'; bilingual literacy; proactive participation in the movement for civil and human rights; empowering and creating new leaders" (Latino Network Members, 1997, p. 1).

These schools, however, serve only a portion of the thousands of Latino children in New York City's public schools. Further, as unzoned schools of choice, only the most educated and politically savvy parents will be able to negotiate their children's way into them. The schools and their creators, however, can be a rich resource for remaking the image of bilingual education from the "forbidding" system the Bushwick parents felt they had to fight their way out of into a magnet for all children.

Develop support for bilingual education among various ethnic and linguistic minority groups. Since its inception, the general public has viewed bilingual education as a special education component for Latino children. This perspective is not coincidental, since the Bilingual Education Act was intended to redress the educational under-achievement of Latino children. Advocates expanded the potential beneficiaries to include other language groups when they realized that the act would have greater support if it included other groups; they also felt morally obligated to include other groups suffering the same educational neglect (Crawford, 1992, p. 41).

Other linguistic groups besides Latinos support bilingual education and benefit from these programs. New York City hosts transitional and developmental bilingual programs in a rainbow of languages, reflecting a concern for native-language retention among other language groups. If the base of support for bilingual programs is to widen, which seems critical, then Latinos and other language groups must highlight and nurture cross-cultural support for these programs. Latinos have to be willing to share leadership in this area with other groups, and other language groups have to make advocacy for bilingual education a visible priority for their organizations.

Puerto Ricans can be instrumental in this area, since they have been at the forefront of the bilingual education struggle. Puerto Ricans have established organizations for which bilingual education is a top agenda item. Unfortunately, many of these organizations have either been overwhelmed by their own needs or lulled into a false sense of security by the provision of federal and state laws on bilingual education. These organizations need to reinvigorate their bilingual education strategies by reaching down to the grassroots level, as well as across to other language groups. To date, that outreach has either not been done or done halfheartedly. Collaboration — sharing of strategies, joint events, sessions on cross-cultural understanding — needs to be developed by grassroots organizations on the local level. Latino bilingual education teachers can be especially helpful as they reach out to their colleagues in ESL or other bilingual programs to share information on building successful programs. Recognizing the political nature of bilingual education, they can strategize with each other, their parents, and their students on building cross-cultural support for bilingual education in their own communities.

Build coalitions with mainstream, nonethnic education groups such as the National Education Association (NEA), the Educational Priorities Panel (EPP), and the recently created Campaign for Fiscal Equity in New York City. Wade Henderson of the Leadership Conference on Civil Rights has declared that "coalition politics is the politics of the future."[13] These national groups usually have access to larger audiences and are not perceived as having a particular ethnic special interest to promote. Both the EPP and the NEA were significantly involved in raising the profile of the education of language-minority children, both nationally and locally. No single civil rights issue calls for such coalition-building as bilingual education. Hampered by the public's perception of it as remedial, segregatory, failing, and promoting the special interests of professional Latinos, the investment and support of mainstream education agencies is critical to reshaping public perception.

Develop leadership among parents and students who benefit from bilingual programs. Bilingual education opponents have successfully painted a portrait of bilingual education advocates as self-interested elites who think they "know better" than immigrant parents about educating their children, often to the detriment of the child and against the parents' best instincts. If the advocacy for bilingual education continues to rest on the shoulders of professionals alone, it will not succeed (Callaghan, 1997; CEO, 1996b; Garvin, 1998).

Involve lawyers to the extent necessary to prevent the dismantling of community-supported bilingual programs currently in existence. Lawyers can help communities in building organizations and coalitions to advance the goals of bilingual education, as well as in devising legal strategies that might address a community's educational issues. However, the legal role cannot and should not dominate the strategic thinking of a community seeking empowerment. The past struggles in New York City and elsewhere have taught us that lawyering should take place within a context of community support, mobilization, and leadership, or it may cause as much damage as good.

Conclusion

National policymakers, federal courts, and advocacy organizations have raised the nation's consciousness on issues affecting language-minority students. The fact that the merits of bilingual education are even heatedly debated owes much to their efforts to keep the pedagogy viable in even the most politically conservative times. However, these forces, perhaps because of their very nature — institutionalized, mainstream, national in scope — have also contributed to the compromised nature of bilingual education, making it especially vulnerable to attack.

The current sociopolitical and legal climate requires that national policymakers, federal courts, and advocacy organizations continue to play a role in defending bilingual education programs. However, that role must be constructed differently than it has been; it must take its cues from parents, students, and local grassroots organizations. These entities must make more extensive efforts to educate the communities they wish to represent, and they must be willing to be as radical and hopeful, as daring and as resourceful as the Puerto Ricans who fought for bilingual education twenty-five years ago and the new immigrants who will continue to fight for it in the future.

Notes

1. ASPIRA is Spanish for "aspire" and is intended to convey the hopes of young Puerto Ricans, as well as to serve as a symbol of their struggle to attain those hopes and dreams. ASPIRA, which was established in 1961 in New York City, organizes Puerto Rican high school and college youth into clubs, where they learn leadership and problem-solving skills while engaged in community action projects. Youth also use ASPIRA resources to develop and implement a plan for completing their education.
2. "English Language Learner" (ELL) denotes someone who does not speak, read, and/or write in English at the academic level of their peers. Most school districts and the federal government use the more pejorative "limited English proficient" (LEP) to designate the same population. The "ELL" designation, however, stresses that the student already has native-language strengths and should not be defined solely in relation to their need to learn English.
3. A consent decree is an agreement between two parties to a litigation that is monitored by a court. A violation of a term in the consent decree enables the original party to seek relief in the court. A consent decree can be modified by the agreement of all parties or by the court after a hearing.
4. For instance, in *Serna v. Portales* (1974), elementary-grade Spanish-surnamed children in Texas were to receive between forty-five and sixty minutes of bilingual instruction per day. High school students were to be given access to "ethnic studies" only. In *Otero v. Mesa County Valley School District* (1975), the court completely rejected bilingual education programs as a remedy for the academic failure of Chicano schoolchildren in Colorado, finding instead that socioeconomic factors, not school districts, were to blame.
5. The Equal Educational Opportunities Act (1968) states: "No state shall deny equal educational opportunity to an individual on account of his or her race, color, sex or national origin by the failure of an educational agency to take appropriate action to overcome language barriers that impede equal participation by its students in its instructional programs."
6. The Elementary and Secondary Education Act states, "the term 'local educational agency' means a public board of education or other public authority legally constituted within a State for either administrative control or direction of or to perform a service function for, public elementary or secondary schools in a city, county, township, school district, or other political subdivision of a State, or such combination of school districts or counties as are recognized in a State as an administrative agency for its public elementary or secondary schools."
7. A federal Circuit Court of Appeals is the highest federal court in a region just below the U.S. Supreme Court. It interprets and defines the law for the states within its jurisdiction. However, because of common law principles of comity, other federal circuits

8. See, for example, *Teresa P. v. Berkeley* (1989). In 1985, *Castañeda*'s standards were also adopted by the OCR as the measure for compliance with Title VI when proceeding with a disparate impact theory (Williams, 1991).
9. For instance, in a *New York Post* editorial, one commentator noted that the bilingual education mission of Hostos Community College in the South Bronx really meant that "[y]ou can't expect poor immigrants to do college-level work." The Hostos attitude recalls the enslaving mentality of the 1960s welfare movement (Berman, 1998).
10. Founded by Linda Chavez, formerly of U.S. English, the Center for Equal Opportunity is a right-wing think tank opposing bilingual education, affirmative action, and other minority benefit programs.
11. These remarks are based on the author's attendance at the January 14, 1998, meeting of the Board of Regents Subcommittee on Elementary and Secondary Education.
12. These are conservative estimates based on the number of children eligible for Emergency Immigrant Education assistance.
13. Remarks made at the NAACP Legal Defense and Educational Fund's Civil Rights Conference at Airlie, Virginia, in October 1997.

References

Amselle, J. (1996, September 30). Ingles si! *National Review, 18*, 52.
ASPIRA of New York, Inc. v. Board of Education, 58 F.R.D. 62 (S.D.N.Y. 1973).
ASPIRA of New York, Inc. v. Board of Education, 394 F. Supp. 1161 (S.D.N.Y. 1975).
Baez, L. A. (1995). *From transformative school goals to assimilationist and remedial bilingual education: A critical review of key precedent-setting Hispanic bilingual litigation decided by federal courts between 1974 and 1983.* Unpublished manuscript.
Baker, K., & de Kanter, A. (1986). Assessing the legal profession's contribution to the education of bilingual students. *La Raza Law Journal, 1*, 295–329.
Berman, R. (1998, January 9). Hostos' war on English and success. *New York Post*, p. 27.
Board of Education of the City of New York. (1958). *The Puerto Rican Study, 1953–1957.* New York: Author.
Board of Education of the City of New York. (1994). *Educational progress of students in bilingual and ESL programs: A longitudinal study, 1990–1994.* Brooklyn, NY: Author.
Board of Education of the City of New York. (1997a). *Facts and figures.* New York: Author.
Board of Education of the City of New York. (1997b). *Programs serving gifted and talented students in New York City public schools, 1995–1996* (Division of Assessment and Accountability). New York: Author.
Bushwick Parents Organization v. Mills, 5181 Civ. 95 (Sup. Ct. New York.) Verified Petition (1995).
Califano, J. A., Jr. (1981). *Governing America: An insider's report from the White House and the cabinet.* New York: Simon & Schuster.
Callaghan, A. (1997, August 15). Desperate to learn English. *New York Times*, p. 31.
Cardenas, J. A. (1995). *Multicultural education: A generation of advocacy.* Needham, MA: Simon & Schuster.
Castañeda v. Pickard, 648 F. 2d 989 (5th Cir. 1981).
Castellanos, D. (1985). *The best of two worlds: Bilingual-bicultural education in the U.S.* Trenton: New Jersey Department of Education.
Center for Equal Opportunity. (1996a). *The failure of bilingual education.* Washington, DC: Author.
Center for Equal Opportunity. (1996b). *The importance of learning English: A national survey of Hispanic parents.* Washington, DC: Author.

Chan, Y. (1997, May 21). CUNY flap as school lowers bar on English. *New York Daily News*, p. 6.
Crawford, J. (1991). *Bilingual education: History, politics, theory and practice* (3d ed.) Los Angeles: Bilingual Educational Services.
Crawford, J. (Ed.). (1992). *Language loyalties: A source book on the official English controversy.* Chicago: University of Chicago Press.
Cummins, J. (1986). Empowering minority students: A framework for intervention. *Harvard Educational Review, 56,* 18–36.
Dicker, S. J. (1996). *Languages in America: A pluralist view.* Clevedon, Eng.: Multilingual Matters.
Elementary and Secondary Education Act, Chap. 47, 20 U.S.C.A. § 2891.
Equal Educational Opportunities Act, 20 U.S.C.A. § 1703(f) (1968).
Failure at Hostos College. (1997, May 23). *New York Post,* p. 34.
Falk, R., & Wang, T. (1990). ASPIRA v. Board of Education: *La lucha para la lengua: The slow vindication of educational rights.* Unpublished manuscript.
Fishman, J. (1989). *Language and ethnicity in minority sociolinguistic perspective.* Clevedon, Eng.: Multilingual Matters.
Garvin, G. (1998, January). Loco, completamente loco: The many failures of bilingual education. *REASON Magazine Online.*
Guardians Association v. Civil Service Commission of New York, 463 U.S. 582 (1983).
Kadamus, J. (1997, April 14). *Building capacity: Addressing the needs of limited English proficient students.* Albany: New York State Education Department.
Krashen, S. D. (1996). *Under attack: The case against bilingual education.* Culver City, CA: Language Education Associates.
Latino Commission on Educational Reform. (1992). *Toward a vision for the education of Latino students: Community voices, student voices.* Brooklyn: Board of Education of the City of New York.
Latino Network Members. (1997, June) Memorandum to Beth Lief, Sara Schwabacher, and Michael Webb.
Lau v. Nichols, 414 U.S. 563 (1974).
Margolis, R. J. (1968). *The losers: A report on Puerto Ricans and the public schools.* New York: ASPIRA.
Meyers, M. (1998, February 17). The bilingual dead-end. *New York Post,* p. 25.
Moran, R. F. (1986). Foreword — the lesson of Keyes: How do you translate "The American dream"? *La Raza Law Journal, 26,* 255–319.
Moran, R. F. (1993). Of democracy, devaluation and bilingual education. *Creighton Law Review, 26,* 274.
National Puerto Rican Taskforce on Educational Policy. (1982). *Toward a language policy for Puerto Ricans in the U.S.: An agenda for a community in movement.* New York: Research Foundation of the City University of New York.
Nieto, S. (1996). *Affirming diversity: The socio-political context of multicultural education* (2nd ed.). White Plains, NY: Longman.
No substitute for English. (1997, May 23). *New York Daily News,* p. 42.
Otero v. Mesa County Valley School District, 408 F. Supp. 162 (D.C. Colo. 1975).
Parents worried bilingual ed hurts students. (1996, February 28). *Education Week,* p. 1.
Pedraza, P. (1996–1997). Puerto Ricans and the politics of school reform. *Journal of El Centro de Estudios Puertorriqueños, Winter, 74*–85.
Public Education Association. (1994). *A consumer's guide to middle schools in District 32, Brooklyn.* New York: Author.
Puerto Rican Legal Defense and Education Fund. (1972). Brief *Amicus Curiae* in support of petitioners in *Lau v. Nichols.*
Rivera-Batiz, F. (1996). *The education of immigrant children: The case of New York City* (Working Paper No. 2). New York: International Center for Migration, Ethnicity and Citizenship of the New School for Social Research.

Santiago-Santiago, I. (1986). *ASPIRA v. Board of Education* revisited. *American Journal of Education, 95,* 149–199.

Serna v. Portales, 499 F. 2d 1147 (10th Cir. 1974).

Shortchanging students at Hostos. (1997, May 23). *New York Times,* p. 30.

Steinberg, J. (1995, September 19). Lawsuit is filed accusing state of overuse of bilingual classes. *New York Times,* p. A1.

Teitelbaum, H., & Hiller, R. (1977). Bilingual education: The legal mandate. *Harvard Educational Review, 47,* 138–170.

Teresa P. v. Berkeley, U.S.D., 724 F. Supp. 698 (N.D. Cal. 1989).

U.S. Commission on Civil Rights. (1975). *Report on Puerto Ricans in the United States: An uncertain future.* Washington, DC: Author.

Wagenheim, K. (1975). *A survey of Puerto Ricans on the U.S. mainland in the 1970s.* New York: Praeger.

Williams, M. L. (1991). *Policy update on schools' obligations toward national origin minority students with limited English proficiency.* Washington, DC: U.S. Dept. Of Education, Office for Civil Rights.

Willner, R. (1986). *Ten years of neglect: The failure to serve language-minority students in the New York City public schools.* New York: Educational Priorities Panel.

PART THREE
The Practice of Anti-Racism

—■—■—■—

> The academy is not paradise. But learning is a place where paradise can be created. The classroom, with all its limitations, remains a location of possibility. In that field of possibility we have the opportunity to labor for freedom, to demand of ourselves and our comrades, an openness of mind and heart that allows us to face reality even as we collectively imagine ways to move beyond boundaries, to transgress. This is education as the practice of freedom.
>
> — *bell hooks*[1]

This last section calls on teachers and students to have the courage to challenge racism in schools and enact "practices of freedom" in their classrooms. The following four articles echo the insights of the previous two sections as they encourage teachers to engage with each other, as well as students, and to learn what the "labor for freedom" might require. Teachers and students must learn to recognize and critique the systemic racism present in classrooms and schools, and to move past denial of the social relations of power that manifest in teacher-student relationships. These articles both challenge teachers and encourage them, offering them examples of practices that risk relationships and pedagogies that enact antiracist teaching and learning. Lastly, these articles remind all teachers that unlearning dominance and challenging oppression necessarily involves a commitment to what Myles Horton calls the "long haul" of teaching for freedom.

Part Three opens with "Talking about Race, Learning about Racism: The Application of Racial Identity Development Theory in the Classroom," Beverly Daniel Tatum's foundational work that establishes that processes of racialization that shape all students' experiences in a White racist society. The lens of racial identity development, her experiences as a university professor of psychology, and her students' journal writings all reveal the need for both White students and students of color to grapple with racism as it is deeply embedded in the practices and policies of U.S. social institutions. Tatum shows that classrooms that support and challenge this learning can be sites for personal change in terms of antiracist thoughts and behavior. In turn, this learning can lead teachers and students individually and collectively to dismantle racism in schools and classrooms.

Lilia Bartolomé's "Beyond the Methods Fetish: Toward a Humanizing Pedagogy" moves from critique to possibility as it takes up the question of what constitutes a "liberating pedagogy." Bartolomé identifies the damage done when White teachers and teacher educators assume that finding the "right methods" will necessarily lead them to successfully teach other people's children. She reminds teachers that, without understanding schools as institutions that reproduce U.S. society's unequal power relations and the impact that a deficit characterization of students of color have on teaching and learning, educators' thinking and practices will continue to perpetuate racism in schools and classrooms. Her "humanizing pedagogy" requires teachers to examine their purposes for teaching, develop a political awareness of their relationships with students, and create teaching practices and curricula that draw on the experiences of students and respect them as active participants in their own learning.

In "Violence, Nonviolence and the Lessons of History: Project HIP-HOP Journeys South," Nancy Uhlar Murray and her student Marco Garrido give teachers a powerful example of what it means to enact a "humanizing pedagogy," as laid out by Bartolomé. The first part, authored by Murray, describes the impetus for a civil rights tour that grew out of her commitment to engage the realities and questions of race and racism present in young people's daily lives. Murray's teaching through this project challenges the ahistorical assumption that violence is unique to this generation of youth. Moreover, both Murray's discussion and the reflections of Marco Garrido, a 17-year-old participant on the 1994 Project HIP-HOP tour, shows that as students deepen their understandings of history they gain new understandings of themselves, while also embracing new possibilities for change in their own communities and schools.

By the year 2009, some 2.2 million new teachers will enter the classrooms and hallways of U.S. schools. If current patterns persist, the large majority of those teachers (86%) will be White. While teacher-education programs alone cannot "fix" the racist inequities in schools, they do influence teachers and the roles they may or may not choose to play, individually and collectively, in dismantling racism in their classrooms and schools. In "Blind Vision: Unlearning Racism in Teacher Education," Marilyn Cochran-Smith lays bare her own learning as a White teacher educator and what it means for her to "labor for freedom." She deconstructs her own complicity in practices that maintain systems of White privilege and racial oppression, and names the new and difficult questions she and other teachers must ask themselves and their students. Using narrative as a way to organize and understand experience, she identifies this as one approach that can create new possibilities for unlearning racism in teacher education. Yet, she also names the limitations of the narrative approach and resists giving teacher educators and beginning teachers a new "methods fetish" — a quick-fix technique for unlearning racism.

Note

1. From bell hooks, *Teaching to Trangress: Education as the Practice of Freedom* (New York: Routledge, 1994), p. 207.

Talking about Race, Learning about Racism: The Application of Racial Identity Development Theory in the Classroom

BEVERLY DANIEL TATUM

As many educational institutions struggle to become more multicultural in terms of their students, faculty, and staff, they also begin to examine issues of cultural representation within their curriculum. This examination has evoked a growing number of courses that give specific consideration to the effect of variables such as race, class, and gender on human experience — an important trend that is reflected and supported by the increasing availability of resource manuals for the modification of course content (Bronstein & Quina, 1988; Hull, Scott, & Smith, 1982; Schuster & Van Dyne, 1985).

Unfortunately, less attention has been given to the issues of process that inevitably emerge in the classroom when attention is focused on race, class, and/or gender. It is very difficult to talk about these concepts in a meaningful way without also talking and learning about racism, classism, and sexism.[1] The introduction of these issues of oppression often generates powerful emotional responses in students that range from guilt and shame to anger and despair. If not addressed, these emotional responses can result in student resistance to oppression-related content areas. Such resistance can ultimately interfere with the cognitive understanding and mastery of the material. This resistance and potential interference is particularly common when specifically addressing issues of race and racism. Yet, when students are given the opportunity to explore race-related material in a classroom where both their affective and intellectual responses are acknowledged and addressed, their level of understanding is greatly enhanced.

This article seeks to provide a framework for understanding students' psychological responses to race-related content and the student resistance that can result, as well as some strategies for overcoming this resistance. It is informed by more than a decade of experience as an African American engaged in teaching an undergraduate course on the psychology of racism, by thematic analyses of student journals and essays written for the racism class, and by an understanding and application of racial identity development theory (Helms, 1990).

Setting the Context

As a clinical psychologist with a research interest in racial identity development among African American youth raised in predominantly White communities, I began teaching about racism quite fortuitously. In 1980, while I was a part-time lecturer in the Black Studies department of a large public university, I was invited to teach a course called Group Exploration of Racism (Black Studies 2). A requirement for Black Studies majors, the course had to be offered, yet the instructor who regularly taught the course was no longer affiliated with the institution. Armed with a folder full of handouts, old syllabi that the previous instructor left behind, a copy of *White Awareness: Handbook for Anti-racism Training* (Katz, 1978), and my own clinical skills as a group facilitator, I constructed a course that seemed to meet the goals already outlined in the course catalogue. Designed "to provide students with an understanding of the psychological causes and emotional reality of racism as it appears in everyday life," the course incorporated the use of lectures, readings, simulation exercises, group research projects, and extensive class discussion to help students explore the psychological impact of racism on both the oppressor and the oppressed.

Though my first efforts were tentative, the results were powerful. The students in my class, most of whom were White, repeatedly described the course in their evaluations as one of the most valuable educational experiences of their college careers. I was convinced that helping students understand the ways in which racism operates in their own lives, and what they could do about it, was a social responsibility that I should accept. The freedom to institute the course in the curriculum of the psychology departments in which I would eventually teach became a personal condition of employment. I have successfully introduced the course in each new educational setting I have been in since leaving that university.

Since 1980, I have taught the course (now called the Psychology of Racism) eighteen times, at three different institutions. Although each of these schools is very different — a large public university, a small state college, and a private, elite women's college — the challenges of teaching about racism in each setting have been more similar than different.

In all of the settings, class size has been limited to thirty students (averaging twenty-four). Though typically predominantly White and female (even in coeducational settings), the class make-up has always been mixed in terms of both race and gender. The students of color who have taken the course include Asians and Latinos/as, but most frequently the students of color have been Black. Though most students have described themselves as middle class, all socioeconomic backgrounds (ranging from very poor to very wealthy) have been represented over the years.

The course has necessarily evolved in response to my own deepening awareness of the psychological legacy of racism and my expanding awareness of other forms of oppression, although the basic format has remained the same. Our weekly three-hour class meeting is held in a room with movable chairs, arranged in a circle. The physical structure communicates an important premise of the course — that I expect the students to speak with each other as well as with me.

My other expectations (timely completion of assignments, regular class attendance) are clearly communicated in our first class meeting, along with the assumptions and guidelines for discussion that I rely upon to guide our work together. Because the assumptions and guidelines are so central to the process of talking and learning about racism, it may be useful to outline them here.

Working Assumptions

1. Racism, defined as a "system of advantage based on race" (see Wellman, 1977), is a pervasive aspect of U.S. socialization. It is virtually impossible to live in U.S. contemporary society and not be exposed to some aspect of the personal, cultural, and/or institutional manifestations of racism in our society. It is also assumed that, as a result, all of us have received some misinformation about those groups disadvantaged by racism.

2. Prejudice, defined as a "preconceived judgment or opinion, often based on limited information," is clearly distinguished from racism (see Katz, 1978). I assume that all of us may have prejudices as a result of the various cultural stereotypes to which we have been exposed. Even when these preconceived ideas have positive associations (such as "Asian students are good in math"), they have negative effects because they deny a person's individuality. These attitudes may influence the individual behaviors of people of color as well as of Whites, and may affect intergroup as well as intragroup interaction. However, a distinction must be made between the negative racial attitudes held by individuals of color and White individuals, because it is only the attitudes of Whites that routinely carry with them the social power inherent in the systematic cultural reinforcement and institutionalization of those racial prejudices. To distinguish the prejudices of students of color from the racism of White students is *not* to say that the former is acceptable and the latter is not; both are clearly problematic. The distinction is important, however, to identify the power differential between members of dominant and subordinate groups.

3. In the context of U.S. society, the system of advantage clearly operates to benefit Whites as a group. However, it is assumed that racism, like other forms

of oppression, hurts members of the privileged group as well as those targeted by racism. While the impact of racism on Whites is clearly different from its impact on people of color, racism has negative ramifications for everyone. For example, some White students might remember the pain of having lost important relationships because Black friends were not allowed to visit their homes. Others may express sadness at having been denied access to a broad range of experiences because of social segregation. These individuals often attribute the discomfort or fear they now experience in racially mixed settings to the cultural limitations of their youth.

4. Because of the prejudice and racism inherent in our environments when we were children, I assume that we cannot be blamed for learning what we were taught (intentionally or unintentionally). Yet as adults, we have a responsibility to try to identify and interrupt the cycle of oppression. When we recognize that we have been misinformed, we have a responsibility to seek out more accurate information and to adjust our behavior accordingly.

5. It is assumed that change, both individual and institutional, is possible. Understanding and unlearning prejudice and racism is a lifelong process that may have begun prior to enrolling in this class, and which will surely continue after the course is over. Each of us may be at a different point in that process, and I assume that we will have mutual respect for each other, regardless of where we perceive one another to be.

To facilitate further our work together, I ask students to honor the following guidelines for our discussion. Specifically, I ask students to demonstrate their respect for one another by honoring the confidentiality of the group. So that students may feel free to ask potentially awkward or embarrassing questions, or share race-related experiences, I ask that students refrain from making personal attributions when discussing the course content with their friends. I also discourage the use of "zaps," overt or covert put-downs often used as comic relief when someone is feeling anxious about the content of the discussion. Finally, students are asked to speak from their own experience, to say, for example, "I think . . ." or "In my experience, I have found . . ." rather than generalizing their experience to others, as in "People say . . ."

Many students are reassured by the climate of safety that is created by these guidelines and find comfort in the nonblaming assumptions I outline for the class. Nevertheless, my experience has been that most students, regardless of their class and ethnic background, still find racism a difficult topic to discuss, as is revealed by these journal comments written after the first class meeting (all names are pseudonyms):

> The class is called Psychology of Racism, the atmosphere is friendly and open, yet I feel very closed in. I feel guilt and doubt well up inside of me. (Tiffany, a White woman)

Class has started on a good note thus far. The class seems rather large and disturbs me. In a class of this nature, I expect there will be many painful and emotional moments. (Linda, an Asian woman)

I am a little nervous that as one of the few students of color in the class people are going to be looking at me for answers, or whatever other reasons. The thought of this inhibits me a great deal. (Louise, an African American woman)

I had never thought about my social position as being totally dominant. There wasn't one area in which I wasn't in the dominant group.... I first felt embarrassed.... Through association alone I felt in many ways responsible for the unequal condition existing in the world. This made me feel like shrinking in a hole in a class where I was surrounded by 27 women and 2 men, one of whom was Black and the other was Jewish. I felt that all these people would be justified in venting their anger upon me. After a short period, I realized that no one in the room was attacking or even blaming me for the conditions that exist. (Carl, a White man)

Even though most of my students voluntarily enroll in the course as an elective, their anxiety and subsequent resistance to learning about racism quickly emerge.

Sources of Resistance

In predominantly White college classrooms, I have experienced at least three major sources of student resistance to talking and learning about race and racism. They can be readily identified as the following:

1. Race is considered a taboo topic for discussion, especially in racially mixed settings.
2. Many students, regardless of racial-group membership, have been socialized to think of the United States as a just society.
3. Many students, particularly White students, initially deny any personal prejudice, recognizing the impact of racism on other people's lives, but failing to acknowledge its impact on their own.

Race as Taboo Topic

The first source of resistance, race as a taboo topic, is an essential obstacle to overcome if class discussion is to begin at all. Although many students are interested in the topic, they are often most interested in hearing other people talk about it, afraid to break the taboo themselves.

One source of this self-consciousness can be seen in the early childhood experiences of many students. It is known that children as young as three notice racial differences (see Phinney & Rotheram, 1987). Certainly preschoolers talk about what they see. Unfortunately, they often do so in ways that make adults uncomfortable. Imagine the following scenario: A White child in a public place points to a dark-skinned African American child and says loudly, "Why is that boy Black?" The embarrassed parent quickly responds, "Sh! Don't say that." The child is only attempting to make sense of a new observation (Derman-Sparks, Higa, & Sparks, 1980), yet the parent's attempt to silence the perplexed child sends a message that this observation is not okay to talk about. White children quickly become aware that their questions about race raise adult anxiety, and as a result, they learn not to ask questions.

When asked to reflect on their earliest race-related memories and the feelings associated with them, both White students and students of color often report feelings of confusion, anxiety, and/or fear. Students of color often have early memories of name-calling or other negative interactions with other children, and sometimes with adults. They also report having had questions that went both unasked and unanswered. In addition, many students have had uncomfortable interchanges around race-related topics as adults. When asked at the beginning of the semester, "How many of you have had difficult, perhaps heated conversations with someone on a race-related topic?", routinely almost everyone in the class raises his or her hand. It should come as no surprise then that students often approach the topic of race and/or racism with both curiosity and trepidation.

The Myth of the Meritocracy

The second source of student resistance to be discussed here is rooted in students' belief that the United States is a just society, a meritocracy where individual efforts are fairly rewarded. While some students (particularly students of color) may already have become disillusioned with that notion of the United States, the majority of my students who have experienced at least the personal success of college acceptance still have faith in this notion. To the extent that these students acknowledge that racism exists, they tend to view it as an individual phenomenon, rooted in the attitudes of the "Archie Bunkers" of the world or located only in particular parts of the country.

After several class meetings, Karen, a White woman, acknowledged this attitude in her journal:

> At one point in my life — the beginning of this class — I actually perceived America to be a relatively racist free society. I thought that the people who were racist or subjected to racist stereotypes were found only in small pockets of the U.S., such as the South. As I've come to realize, racism (or at least racially orientated stereotypes) is rampant.

An understanding of racism as a system of advantage presents a serious challenge to the notion of the United States as a just society where rewards are based solely on one's merit. Such a challenge often creates discomfort in students. The old adage "ignorance is bliss" seems to hold true in this case; students are not necessarily eager to recognize the painful reality of racism.

One common response to the discomfort is to engage in denial of what they are learning. White students in particular may question the accuracy or currency of statistical information regarding the prevalence of discrimination (housing, employment, access to health care, and so on). More qualitative data, such as autobiographical accounts of experiences with racism, may be challenged on the basis of their subjectivity.

It should be pointed out that the basic assumption that the United States is a just society for all is only one of many basic assumptions that might be challenged in the learning process. Another example can be seen in an interchange between two White students following a discussion about cultural racism, in which the omission or distortion of historical information about people of color was offered as an example of the cultural transmission of racism.

"Yeah, I just found out that Cleopatra was actually a Black woman."

"What?"

The first student went on to explain her newly learned information. Finally, the second student exclaimed in disbelief, "That can't be true. Cleopatra was beautiful!" This new information and her own deeply ingrained assumptions about who is beautiful and who is not were too incongruous to allow her to assimilate the information at that moment.

If outright denial of information is not possible, then withdrawal may be. Physical withdrawal in the form of absenteeism is one possible result; it is for precisely this reason that class attendance is mandatory. The reduction in the completion of reading and/or written assignments is another form of withdrawal. I have found this response to be so common that I now alert students to this possibility at the beginning of the semester. Knowing that this response is a common one seems to help students stay engaged, even when they experience the desire to withdraw.

Following an absence in the fifth week of the semester, one White student wrote, "I think I've hit the point you talked about, the point where you don't want to hear any more about racism. I sometimes begin to get the feeling we are all hypersensitive." (Two weeks later she wrote, "Class is getting better. I think I am beginning to get over my hump.")

Perhaps not surprisingly, this response can be found in both White students and students of color. Students of color often enter a discussion of racism with some awareness of the issue, based on personal experiences. However, even these students find that they did not have a full understanding of the widespread impact of racism in our society. For students who are targeted by racism, an increased awareness of the impact in and on their lives is painful, and often generates anger.

Four weeks into the semester, Louise, an African American woman, wrote in her journal about her own heightened sensitivity:

> Many times in class I feel uncomfortable when White students use the term
> Black because even if they aren't aware of it they say it with all or at least a lot

of the negative connotations they've been taught goes along with Black. Sometimes it just causes a stinging feeling inside of me. Sometimes I get real tired of hearing White people talk about the conditions of Black people. I think it's an important thing for them to talk about, but still I don't always like being around when they do it. I also get tired of hearing them talk about how hard it is for them, though I understand it, and most times I am very willing to listen and be open, but sometimes I can't. Right now I can't.

For White students, advantaged by racism, a heightened awareness of it often generates painful feelings of guilt. The following responses are typical:

After reading the article about privilege, I felt very guilty. (Rachel, a White woman)

Questions of racism are so full of anger and pain. When I think of all the pain White people have caused people of color, I get a feeling of guilt. How could someone like myself care so much about the color of someone's skin that they would do them harm? (Terri, a White woman)

White students also sometimes express a sense of betrayal when they realize the gaps in their own education about racism. After seeing the first episode of the documentary series *Eyes on the Prize*, Chris, a White man, wrote:

I never knew it was really that bad just 35 years ago. Why didn't I learn this in elementary or high school? Could it be that the White people of America want to forget this injustice? . . . I will never forget that movie for as long as I live. It was like a big slap in the face.

Barbara, a White woman, also felt anger and embarrassment in response to her own previous lack of information about the internment of Japanese Americans during World War II. She wrote:

I feel so stupid because I never even knew that these existed. I never knew that the Japanese were treated so poorly. I am becoming angry and upset about all of the things that I do not know. I have been so sheltered. My parents never wanted to let me know about the bad things that have happened in the world. After I saw the movie (*Mitsuye and Nellie*), I even called them up to ask them why they never told me this. . . . I am angry at them too for not teaching me and exposing me to the complete picture of my country.

Avoiding the subject matter is one way to avoid these uncomfortable feelings.

"I'm Not Racist, But . . ."

A third source of student resistance (particularly among White students) is the initial denial of any personal connection to racism. When asked why they have decided to enroll in a course on racism, White students typically explain their interest in the topic with such disclaimers as, "I'm not racist myself, but I know people who are, and I want to understand them better."

Because of their position as the targets of racism, students of color do not typically focus on their own prejudices or lack of them. Instead they usually express a desire to understand why racism exists, and how they have been affected by it.

However, as all students gain a better grasp of what racism is and its many manifestations in U.S. society, they inevitably start to recognize its legacy within themselves. Beliefs, attitudes, and actions based on racial stereotypes begin to be remembered and are newly observed by White students. Students of color as well often recognize negative attitudes they may have internalized about their own racial group or that they have believed about others. Those who previously thought themselves immune to the effects of growing up in a racist society often find themselves reliving uncomfortable feelings of guilt or anger.

After taping her own responses to a questionnaire on racial attitudes, Barbara, a White woman previously quoted, wrote:

> I always want to think of myself as open to all races. Yet when I did the interview to myself, I found that I did respond differently to the same question about different races. No one could ever have told me that I would have. I would have denied it. But I found that I did respond differently even though I didn't want to. This really upset me. I was angry with myself because I thought I was not prejudiced and yet the stereotypes that I had created had an impact on the answers that I gave even though I didn't want it to happen.

The new self-awareness, represented here by Barbara's journal entry, changes the classroom dynamic. One common result is that some White students, once perhaps active participants in class discussion, now hesitate to continue their participation for fear that their newly recognized racism will be revealed to others:

> Today I did feel guilty, and like I had to watch what I was saying (make it good enough), I guess to prove I'm really *not* prejudiced. From the conversations the first day, I guess this is a normal enough reaction, but I certainly never expected it in me. (Joanne, a White woman)

This withdrawal on the part of White students is often paralleled by an increase in participation by students of color who are seeking an outlet for what are often feelings of anger. The withdrawal of some previously vocal White students from the classroom exchange, however, is sometimes interpreted by students of color as indifference. This perceived indifference often serves to fuel the anger and frustration that many students of color experience, as awareness of their own oppression is heightened. For example, Robert, an African American man, wrote:

> I really wish the White students would talk more. When I read these articles, it makes me so mad and I really want to know what the White kids think. Don't they care?

Sonia, a Latina, described the classroom tension from another perspective:

> I would like to comment that at many points in the discussions I have felt uncomfortable and sometimes even angry with people. I guess I am at the stage where I am tired of listening to Whites feel guilty and watch their eyes fill up with tears. I do understand that everyone is at their own stage of development and I even tell myself every Tuesday that these people have come to this class by choice. Some days I am just more tolerant than others. . . . It takes courage to say things in that room with so many women of color present. It also takes courage for the women of color to say things about Whites.

What seems to be happening in the classroom at such moments is a collision of developmental processes that can be inherently useful for the racial identity development of the individuals involved. Nevertheless, the interaction may be perceived as problematic to instructors and students who are unfamiliar with the process. Although space does not allow for an exhaustive discussion of racial identity development theory, a brief explication of it here will provide additional clarity regarding the classroom dynamics when issues of race are discussed. It will also provide a theoretical framework for the strategies for dealing with student resistance that will be discussed at the conclusion of this article.

Stages of Racial Identity Development

Racial identity and racial identity development theory are defined by Janet Helms (1990) as

> a sense of group or collective identity based on one's *perception* that he or she shares a common racial heritage with a particular racial group . . . racial identity development theory concerns the psychological implications of racial-group membership, that is belief systems that evolve in reaction to perceived differential racial-group membership. (p. 3)

It is assumed that in a society where racial-group membership is emphasized, the development of a racial identity will occur in some form in everyone. Given the dominant/subordinate relationship of Whites and people of color in this society, however, it is not surprising that this developmental process will unfold in different ways. For purposes of this discussion, William Cross's (1971, 1978) model of Black identity development will be described along with Helms's (1990) model of White racial identity development theory. While the identity development of other students (Asian Latino/a, Native American) is not included in this particular theoretical formulation, there is evidence to suggest that the process for these oppressed groups is similar to that described for African Americans (Highlen, et al., 1988; Phinney, 1990).[2] In each case, it is assumed that a positive sense of one's self as a member of one's group (which is not based on any assumed superiority) is important for psychological health.

Black Racial Identity Development

According to Cross's (1971, 1978, 1991) model of Black racial identity development, there are five stages in the process, identified as Preencounter, Encounter, Immersion/Emersion, Internalization, and Internalization-Commitment. In the first stage of Preencounter, the African American has absorbed many of the beliefs and values of the dominant White culture, including the notion that "White is right" and "Black is wrong." Though the internalization of negative Black stereotypes may be outside of his or her conscious awareness, the individual seeks to assimilate and be accepted by Whites, and actively or passively distances him/herself from other Blacks.[3]

Louise, an African American woman previously quoted, captured the essence of this stage in the following description of herself at an earlier time:

> For a long time it seemed as if I didn't remember my background, and I guess in some ways I didn't. I was never taught to be proud of my African heritage. Like we talked about in class, I went through a very long stage of identifying with my oppressors. Wanting to be like, live like, and be accepted by them. Even to the point of hating my own race and myself for being a part of it. Now I am ashamed that I ever was ashamed. I lost so much of myself in my denial of and refusal to accept my people.

In order to maintain psychological comfort at this stage of development, Helms writes:

> The person must maintain the fiction that race and racial indoctrination have nothing to do with how he or she lives life. It is probably the case that the Preencounter person is bombarded on a regular basis with information that he or she cannot really be a member of the "in" racial group, but relies on denial to selectively screen such information from awareness. (1990, p. 23)

This de-emphasis on one's racial-group membership may allow the individual to think that race has not been or will not be a relevant factor in one's own achievement, and may contribute to the belief in a U.S. meritocracy that is often a part of a Preencounter worldview.

Movement into the Encounter phase is typically precipitated by an event or series of events that forces the individual to acknowledge the impact of racism in one's life. For example, instances of social rejection by White friends or colleagues (or reading new personally relevant information about racism) may lead the individual to the conclusion that many Whites will not view him or her as an equal. Faced with the reality that he or she cannot truly be White, the individual is forced to focus on his or her identity as a member of a group targeted by racism.

Brenda, a Korean American student, described her own experience of this process as a result of her participation in the racism course:

> I feel that because of this class, I have become much more aware of racism that exists around. Because of my awareness of racism, I am now bothered by

acts and behaviors that might not have bothered me in the past. Before when racial comments were said around me I would somehow ignore it and pretend that nothing was said. By ignoring comments such as these, I was protecting myself. It became sort of a defense mechanism. I never realized I did this, until I was confronted with stories that were found in our reading, by other people of color, who also ignored comments that bothered them. In realizing that there is racism out in the world and that there are comments concerning race that are directed towards me, I feel as if I have reached the first step. I also think I have reached the second step, because I am now bothered and irritated by such comments. I no longer ignore them, but now confront them.

The Immersion/Emersion stage is characterized by the simultaneous desire to surround oneself with visible symbols of one's racial identity and an active avoidance of symbols of Whiteness. As Thomas Parham describes, "At this stage, everything of value in life must be Black or relevant to Blackness. This stage is also characterized by a tendency to denigrate White people, simultaneously glorifying Black people. . . ." (1989, p. 190). The previously described anger that emerges in class among African American students and other students of color in the process of learning about racism may be seen as part of the transition through these stages.

As individuals enter the Immersion stage, they actively seek out opportunities to explore aspects of their own history and culture with the support of peers from their own racial background. Typically, White-focused anger dissipates during this phase because so much of the person's energy is directed toward his or her own group- and self-exploration. The result of this exploration is an emerging security in a newly defined and affirmed sense of self.

Sharon, another African American woman, described herself at the beginning of the semester as angry, seemingly in the Encounter stage of development. She wrote after our class meeting:

> Another point that I must put down is that before I entered class today I was angry about the way Black people have been treated in this country. I don't think I will easily overcome that and I basically feel justified in my feelings.

At the end of the semester, Sharon had joined with two other Black students in the class to work on their final class project. She observed that the three of them had planned their project to focus on Black people specifically, suggesting movement into the Immersion stage of racial identity development. She wrote:

> We are concerned about the well-being of our own people. They cannot be well if they have this pinned-up hatred for their own people. This internalized racism is something that we all felt, at various times, needed to be talked about. This semester it has really been important to me, and I believe Gordon [a Black classmate], too.

The emergence from this stage marks the beginning of Internalization. Secure in one's own sense of racial identity, there is less need to assert the

"Blacker than thou" attitude often characteristic of the Immersion stage (Parham, 1989). In general, "pro-Black attitudes become more expansive, open, and less defensive" (Cross, 1971, p. 24). While still maintaining his or her connections with Black peers, the internalized individual is willing to establish meaningful relationships with Whites who acknowledge and are respectful of his or her self-definition. The individual is also ready to build coalitions with members of other oppressed groups. At the end of the semester, Brenda, a Korean American, concluded that she had in fact internalized a positive sense of racial identity. The process she described parallels the stages described by Cross:

> I have been aware for a long time that I am Korean. But through this class I am beginning to really become aware of my race. I am beginning to find out that White people can be accepting of me and at the same time accept me as a Korean.
>
> I grew up wanting to be accepted and ended up almost denying my race and culture. I don't think I did this consciously, but the denial did occur. As I grew older, I realized that I was different. I became for the first time, friends with other Koreans. I realized I had much in common with them. This was when I went through my "Korean friend" stage. I began to enjoy being friends with Koreans more than I did with Caucasians.
>
> Well, ultimately, through many years of growing up, I am pretty much in focus about who I am and who my friends are. I knew before I took this class that there were people not of color that were understanding of my differences. In our class, I feel that everyone is trying to sincerely find the answer of abolishing racism. I knew people like this existed, but it's nice to meet with them weekly.

Cross suggests that there are few psychological differences between the fourth stage, Internalization, and the fifth stage, Internalization-Commitment. However, those at the fifth stage have found ways to translate their "personal sense of Blackness into a plan of action or a general sense of commitment" to the concerns of Blacks as a group, which is sustained over time (Cross, 1991, p. 220). Whether at the fourth or fifth stage, the process of Internalization allows the individual, anchored in a positive sense of racial identity, both to proactively perceive and transcend race. Blackness becomes "the point of departure for discovering the universe of ideas, cultures and experiences beyond blackness in place of mistaking blackness as the universe itself" (Cross, Parham, & Helms, 1991, p. 330).

Though the process of racial identity development has been presented here in linear form, in fact it is probably more accurate to think of it in a spiral form. Often a person may move from one stage to the next, only to revisit an earlier stage as the result of new encounter experiences (Parham, 1989), though the later experience of the stage may be different from the original experience. The image that students often find helpful in understanding this concept of recycling through the stages is that of a spiral staircase. As a person ascends a spiral staircase, she may stop and look down at a spot below. When she reaches the next level, she may look down and see the same spot, but the vantage point has changed.[4]

White Racial Identity Development

The transformations experienced by those targeted by racism are often paralleled by those of White students. Helms (1990) describes the evolution of a positive White racial identity as involving both the abandonment of racism and the development of a nonracist White identity. In order to do the latter,

> he or she must accept his or her own Whiteness, the cultural implications of being White, and define a view of Self as a racial being that does not depend on the perceived superiority of one racial group over another. (p. 49)

She identifies six stages in her model of White racial identity development: Contact, Disintegration, Reintegration, Pseudo-Independent, Immersion/Emersion, and Autonomy.

The Contact stage is characterized by a lack of awareness of cultural and institutional racism, and of one's own White privilege. Peggy McIntosh (1989) writes eloquently about her own experience of this state of being:

> As a white person, I realized I had been taught about racism as something which puts others at a disadvantage, but had been taught not to see one of its corollary aspects, white privilege, which puts me at an advantage. . . . I was taught to see racism only in individual acts of meanness, not in invisible systems conferring dominance on my group. (p. 10)

In addition, the Contact stage often includes naive curiosity about or fear of people of color, based on stereotypes learned from friends, family, or the media. These stereotypes represent the framework in use when a person at this stage of development makes a comment such as, "You don't act like a Black person" (Helms, 1990, p. 57).

Those Whites whose lives are structured so as to limit their interaction with people of color, as well as their awareness of racial issues, may remain at this stage indefinitely. However, certain kinds of experiences (increased interaction with people of color or exposure to new information about racism) may lead to a new understanding that cultural and institutional racism exist. This new understanding marks the beginning of the Disintegration stage.

At this stage, the bliss of ignorance or lack of awareness is replaced by the discomfort of guilt, shame, and sometimes anger at the recognition of one's own advantage because of being White and the acknowledgment of the role of Whites in the maintenance of a racist system. Attempts to reduce discomfort may include denial (convincing oneself that racism doesn't really exist, or if it does, it is the fault of its victims).

For example, Tom, a White male student, responded with some frustration in his journal to a classmate's observation that the fact that she had never read any books by Black authors in any of her high school or college English classes was an example of cultural racism. He wrote, "It's not my fault that Blacks don't write books."

After viewing a film in which a psychologist used examples of Black children's drawings to illustrate the potentially damaging effect of negative cultural messages on a Black child's developing self-esteem, David, another White male student, wrote:

> I found it interesting the way Black children drew themselves without arms. The psychologist said this is saying that the child feels unable to control his environment. It can't be because the child has notions and beliefs already about being Black. It must be built in or hereditary due to the past history of the Blacks. I don't believe it's cognitive but more biological due to a long past history of repression and being put down.

Though Tom's and David's explanations seem quite problematic, they can be understood in the context of racial identity development theory as a way of reducing their cognitive dissonance upon learning this new race-related information. As was discussed earlier, withdrawal (accomplished by avoiding contact with people of color and the topic of racism) is another strategy for dealing with the discomfort experienced at this stage. Many of the previously described responses of White students to race-related content are characteristic of the transition from the Contact to the Disintegration stage of development.

Helms (1990) describes another response to the discomfort of Disintegration, which involves attempts to change significant others' attitudes toward African Americans and other people of color. However, as she points out,

> due to the racial naivete with which this approach may be undertaken and the person's ambivalent racial identification, this dissonance-reducing strategy is likely to be met with rejection by Whites as well as Blacks. (p. 59)

In fact, this response is also frequently observed among White students who have an opportunity to talk with friends and family during holiday visits. Suddenly they are noticing the racist content of jokes or comments of their friends and relatives and will try to confront them, often only to find that their efforts are, at best, ignored or dismissed as a "phase," or, at worst, greeted with open hostility.

Carl, a White male previously quoted, wrote at length about this dilemma:

> I realized that it was possible to simply go through life totally oblivious to the entire situation or, even if one realizes it, one can totally repress it. It is easy to fade into the woodwork, run with the rest of society, and never have to deal with these problems. So many people I know from home are like this. They have simply accepted what society has taught them with little, if any, question. My father is a prime example of this.... It has caused much friction in our relationship, and he often tells me as a father he has failed in raising me cor-

rectly. Most of my high school friends will never deal with these issues and propagate them on to their own children. It's easy to see how the cycle continues. I don't think I could ever justify within myself simply turning my back on the problem. I finally realized that my position in all of these dominant groups gives me power to make change occur. . . . It is an unfortunate result often though that I feel alienated from friends and family. It's often played off as a mere stage that I'm going through. I obviously can't tell if it's merely a stage, but I know that they say this to take the attention off of the truth of what I'm saying. By belittling me, they take the power out of my argument. It's very depressing that being compassionate and considerate are seen as only phases that people go through. I don't want it to be a phase for me, but as obvious as this may sound, I look at my environment and often wonder how it will not be.

The societal pressure to accept the status quo may lead the individual from Disintegration to Reintegration. At this point the desire to be accepted by one's own racial group, in which the overt or covert belief in White superiority is so prevalent, may lead to a reshaping of the person's belief system to be more congruent with an acceptance of racism. The guilt and anxiety associated with Disintegration may be redirected in the form of fear and anger directed toward people of color (particularly Blacks), who are now blamed as the source of discomfort.

Connie, a White woman of Italian ancestry, in many ways exemplified the progression from the Contact stage to Reintegration, a process she herself described seven weeks into the semester. After reading about the stages of White identity development, she wrote:

> I think mostly I can find myself in the disintegration stage of development. . . . There was a time when I never considered myself a color. I never described myself as a "White, Italian female" until I got to college and noticed that people of color always described themselves by their color/race. While taking this class, I have begun to understand that being White makes a difference. I never thought about it before but there are many privileges to being White. In my personal life, I cannot say that I have ever felt that I have had the advantage over a Black person, but I am aware that my race has the advantage.
>
> I am feeling really guilty lately about that. I find myself thinking: "I didn't mean to be White, I really didn't mean it." I am starting to feel angry towards my race for ever using this advantage towards personal gains. But at the same time I resent the minority groups. I mean, it's not our fault that society has deemed us "superior." I don't feel any better than a Black person. But it really doesn't matter because I am a member of the dominant race. . . . I can't help it . . . and I sometimes get angry and feel like I'm being attacked.
>
> I guess my anger toward a minority group would enter me into the next stage of Reintegration, where I am once again starting to blame the victim. This is all very trying for me and it has been on my mind a lot. I really would like to be able to reach the last stage, autonomy, where I can accept being White without hostility and anger. That is really hard to do.

Helms (1990) suggests that it is relatively easy for Whites to become stuck at the Reintegration stage of development, particularly if avoidance of people of color is possible. However, if there is a catalyst for continued self-examination, the person "begins to question her or his previous definition of Whiteness and the justifiability of racism in any of its forms . . ." (p. 61). In my experience, continued participation in a course on racism provides the catalyst for this deeper self-examination.

This process was again exemplified by Connie. At the end of the semester, she listened to her own taped interview of her racial attitudes that she had recorded at the beginning of the semester. She wrote:

> Oh wow! I could not believe some of the things that I said. I was obviously in different stages of the White identity development. As I listened and got more and more disgusted with myself when I was at the Reintegration stage, I tried to remind myself that these are stages that all (most) White people go through when dealing with notions of racism. I can remember clearly the resentment I had for people of color. I feel the one thing I enjoyed from listening to my interview was noticing how much I have changed. I think I am finally out of the Reintegration stage. I am beginning to make a conscious effort to seek out information about people of color and accept their criticism. . . . I still feel guilty about the feeling I had about people of color and I always feel bad about being privileged as a result of racism. But I am glad that I have reached what I feel is the Pseudo-Independent stage of White identity development.

The information-seeking that Connie describes often marks the onset of the Pseudo-Independent stage. At this stage, the individual is abandoning beliefs in White superiority, but may still behave in ways that unintentionally perpetuate the system. Looking to those targeted by racism to help him or her understand racism, the White person often tries to disavow his or her own Whiteness through active affiliation with Blacks, for example. The individual experiences a sense of alienation from other Whites who have not yet begun to examine their own racism, yet may also experience rejection from Blacks or other people of color who are suspicious of his or her motives. Students of color moving from the Encounter to the Immersion phase of their own racial identity development may be particularly unreceptive to the White person's attempts to connect with them.

Uncomfortable with his or her own Whiteness, yet unable to be truly anything else, the individual may begin searching for a new, more comfortable way to be White. This search is characteristic of the Immersion/Emersion stage of development. Just as the Black student seeks to redefine positively what it means to be of African ancestry in the United States through immersion in accurate information about one's culture and history, the White individual seeks to replace racially related myths and stereotypes with accurate information about what it means and has meant to be White in U.S. society

(Helms, 1990). Learning about Whites who have been antiracist allies to people of color is a very important part of this process.

After reading articles written by antiracist activists describing their own process of unlearning racism, White students often comment on how helpful it is to know that others have experienced similar feelings and have found ways to resist the racism in their environments.[5] For example, Joanne, a White woman who initially experienced a lot of guilt, wrote:

> This article helped me out in many ways. I've been feeling helpless and frustrated. I know there are all these terrible things going on and I want to be able to do something. . . . Anyway this article helped me realize, again, that others feel this way, and gave me some positive ideas to resolve my dominant class guilt and shame.

Finally, reading the biographies and autobiographies of White individuals who have embarked on a similar process of identity development (such as Barnard, 1985/1987) provides White students with important models for change.

Learning about White antiracists can also provide students of color with a sense of hope that they can have White allies. After hearing a White antiracist activist address the class, Sonia, a Latina who had written about her impatience with expressions of White guilt, wrote:

> I don't know when I have been more impressed by anyone. She filled me with hope for the future. She made me believe that there are good people in the world and that Whites suffer too and want to change things.

For White students, the internalization of a newly defined sense of oneself as White is the primary task of the Autonomy stage. The positive feelings associated with this redefinition energize the person's efforts to confront racism and oppression in his or her daily life. Alliances with people of color can be more easily forged at this stage of development than previously because the person's antiracist behaviors and attitudes will be more consistently expressed. While Autonomy might be described as "racial self-actualization, . . . it is best to think of it as an ongoing process . . . wherein the person is continually open to new information and new ways of thinking about racial and cultural variables" (Helms, 1990, p. 66).

Annette, a White woman, described herself in the Autonomy stage, but talked at length about the circular process she felt she had been engaged in during the semester:

> If people as racist as C. P. Ellis (a former Klansman) can change, I think anyone can change. If that makes me idealistic, fine. I do not think my expecting society to change is naive anymore because I now *know* exactly what I want. To be naive means a lack of knowledge that allows me to accept myself both as a White person and as an idealist. This class showed me that these two are not mutually exclusive but are an integral part of me that I cannot deny. I realize now that through most of this class I was trying to deny both of them.

While I was not accepting society's racism, I was accepting society's telling me as a White person, there was nothing I could do to change racism. So, I told myself I was being naive and tried to suppress my desire to change society. This is what made me so frustrated — while I saw society's racism through examples in the readings and the media, I kept telling myself there was nothing I could do. Listening to my tape, I think I was already in the Autonomy stage when I started this class. I then seemed to decide that being White, I also had to be racist which is when I became frustrated and went back to the Disintegration stage. I was frustrated because I was not only telling myself there was nothing I could do but I also was assuming society's racism was my own which made me feel like I did not want to be White. Actually, it was not being White that I was disavowing but being racist. I think I have now returned to the Autonomy stage and am much more secure in my position there. I accept my Whiteness now as just a part of me as is my idealism. I will no longer disavow these characteristics as I have realized I can be proud of both of them. In turn, I can now truly accept other people for their unique characteristics and not by the labels society has given them as I can accept myself that way.

While I thought the main ideas that I learned in this class were that White people need to be educated to end racism and everyone should be treated as human beings, I really had already incorporated these ideas into my thoughts. What I learned from this class is being White does not mean being racist and being idealistic does not mean being naive. I really did not have to form new ideas about people of color; I had to form them about myself — and I did.

Implications for Classroom Teaching

Although movement through all the stages of racial identity development will not necessarily occur for each student within the course of a semester (or even four years of college), it is certainly common to witness beginning transformations in classes with race-related content. An awareness of the existence of this process has helped me to implement strategies to facilitate positive student development, as well as to improve interracial dialogue within the classroom.

Four strategies for reducing student resistance and promoting student development that I have found useful are the following:

1. the creation of a safe classroom atmosphere by establishing clear guidelines for discussion;
2. the creation of opportunities for self-generated knowledge;
3. the provision of an appropriate developmental model that students can use as a framework for understanding their own process;
4. the exploration of strategies to empower students as change agents.

Creating a Safe Climate

As was discussed earlier, making the classroom a safe space for discussion is essential for overcoming students' fears about breaking the race taboo, and will also reduce later anxieties about exposing one's own internalized racism. Establishing the guidelines of confidentiality, mutual respect, "no zaps," and speaking from one's own experience on the first day of class is a necessary step in the process.

Students respond very positively to these ground rules, and do try to honor them. While the rules do not totally eliminate anxiety, they clearly communicate to students that there is a safety net for the discussion. Students are also encouraged to direct their comments and questions to each other rather than always focusing their attention on me as the instructor, and to learn each other's names rather than referring to each other as "he," "she," or "the person in the red sweater" when responding to each other.[6]

The Power of Self-Generated Knowledge

The creation of opportunities for self-generated knowledge on the part of students is a powerful tool for reducing the initial stage of denial that many students experience. While it may seem easy for some students to challenge the validity of what they read or what the instructor says, it is harder to deny what they have seen with their own eyes. Students can be given hands-on assignments outside of class to facilitate this process.

For example, after reading *Portraits of White Racism* (Wellman, 1977), some students expressed the belief that the attitudes expressed by the White interviewees in the book were no longer commonly held attitudes. Students were then asked to use the same interview protocol used in the book (with some revision) to interview a White adult of their choice. When students reported on these interviews in class, their own observation of the similarity between those they had interviewed and those they had read about was more convincing than anything I might have said.

After doing her interview, Patty, a usually quiet White student, wrote:

> I think I learned a lot from it and that I'm finally getting a better grip on the idea of racism. I think that was why I participated so much in class. I really felt like I knew what I was talking about.

Other examples of creating opportunities for self-generated knowledge include assigning students the task of visiting grocery stores in neighborhoods of differing racial composition to compare the cost and quality of goods and services available at the two locations, and to observe the interactions between the shoppers and the store personnel. For White students, one of the most powerful assignments of this type has been to go apartment hunting with an African American student and to experience housing discrimination firsthand. While one concern with such an assignment is the effect it will have on the student(s) of color involved, I have found that those Black students who choose this assignment rather than another are typically eager to have their White classmates experience the reality of racism, and thus participate quite willingly in the process.

Naming the Problem

The emotional responses that students have to talking and learning about racism are quite predictable and related to their own racial identity development. Unfortunately, students typically do not know this; thus they consider their own guilt, shame, embarrassment, or anger an uncomfortable experience that they alone are having. Informing students at the beginning of the semester that these feelings may be part of the learning process is ethically necessary (in the sense of informed consent), and helps to normalize the students' experience. Knowing in advance that a desire to withdraw from classroom discussion or not to complete assignments is a common response helps students to remain engaged when they reach that point. As Alice, a White woman, wrote at the end of the semester:

> You were so right in saying in the beginning how we would grow tired of racism (I did in October) but then it would get so good! I have *loved* the class once I passed that point.

In addition, sharing the model of racial identity development with students gives them a useful framework for understanding each other's processes as well as their own. This cognitive framework does not necessarily prevent the collision of developmental processes previously described, but it does allow students to be less frightened by it when it occurs. If, for example, White students understand the stages of racial identity development of students of color, they are less likely to personalize or feel threatened by an African American student's anger.

Connie, a White student who initially expressed a lot of resentment at the way students of color tended to congregate in the college cafeteria, was much more understanding of this behavior after she learned about racial identity development theory. She wrote:

> I learned a lot from reading the article about the stages of development in the model of oppressed people. As a White person going through my stages of identity development, I do not take time to think about the struggle people of color go through to reach a stage of complete understanding. I am glad that I know about the stages because now I can understand people of color's behavior in certain situations. For example, when people of color stay to themselves and appear to be in a clique, it is not because they are being rude as I originally thought. Rather they are engaged perhaps in the Immersion stage.

Mary, another White student, wrote:

> I found the entire Cross model of racial identity development very enlightening. I knew that there were stages of racial identity development before I entered this class. I did not know what they were, or what they really entailed. After reading through this article I found myself saying, "Oh. That explains why she reacted this way to this incident instead of how she would have a year ago." Clearly this person has entered a different stage and is working through

different problems from a new viewpoint. Thankfully, the model provides a degree of hope that people will not always be angry, and will not always be separatists, etc. Although I'm not really sure about that.

Conversely, when students of color understand the stages of White racial identity development, they can be more tolerant or appreciative of a White student's struggle with guilt, for example. After reading about the stages of White identity development, Sonia, a Latina previously quoted, wrote:

> This article was the one that made me feel that my own prejudices were showing. I never knew that Whites went through an identity development of their own.

She later told me outside of class that she found it much easier to listen to some of the things White students said because she could understand their potentially offensive comments as part of a developmental stage.

Sharon, an African American woman, also found that an understanding of the respective stages of racial identity development helped her to understand some of the interactions she had had with White students since coming to college. She wrote:

> There is a lot of clash that occurs between Black and White people at college which is best explained by their respective stages of development. Unfortunately schools have not helped to alleviate these problems earlier in life.

In a course on the psychology of racism, it is easy to build in the provision of this information as part of the course content. For instructors teaching courses with race-related content in other fields, it may seem less natural to do so. However, the inclusion of articles on racial identity development and/or class discussion of these issues in conjunction with the other strategies that have been suggested can improve student receptivity to the course content in important ways, making it a very useful investment of class time. Because the stages describe kinds of behavior that many people have commonly observed in themselves, as well as in their own intraracial and interracial interactions, my experience has been that most students grasp the basic conceptual framework fairly easily, even if they do not have a background in psychology.

Empowering Students as Change Agents

Heightening students' awareness of racism without also developing an awareness of the possibility of change is a prescription for despair. I consider it unethical to do one without the other. Exploring strategies to empower students as change agents is thus a necessary part of the process of talking about race and learning about racism. As was previously mentioned, students find it very helpful to read about and hear from individuals who have been effective change agents. Newspaper and magazine articles, as well as biographical or autobiographical essays or book excerpts, are often important sources for this information.

I also ask students to work in small groups to develop an action plan of their own for interrupting racism. While I do not consider it appropriate to require students to engage in antiracist activity (since I believe this should be a personal choice the student makes for him/herself), students are required to think about the possibility. Guidelines are provided (see Katz, 1978), and the plans that they develop over several weeks are presented at the end of the semester. Students are generally impressed with each other's good ideas; and, in fact, they often do go on to implement their projects.

Joanne, a White student who initially struggled with feelings of guilt, wrote:

> I thought that hearing others' ideas for action plans was interesting and informative. It really helps me realize (reminds me) the many choices and avenues there are once I decided to be an ally. Not only did I develop my own concrete way to be an ally, I have found many other ways that I, as a college student, can be an active anti-racist. It was really empowering.

Another way all students can be empowered is by offering them the opportunity to consciously observe their own development. The taped exercise to which some of the previously quoted students have referred is an example of one way to provide this opportunity. At the beginning of the semester, students are given an interview guide with many open-ended questions concerning racial attitudes and opinions. They are asked to interview themselves on tape as a way of recording their own ideas for future reference. Though the tapes are collected, students are assured that no one (including me) will listen to them. The tapes are returned near the end of the semester, and students are asked to listen to their own tapes and use their understanding of racial identity development to discuss it in essay form.

The resulting essays are often remarkable and underscore the psychological importance of giving students the chance to examine racial issues in the classroom. The following was written by Elaine, a White woman:

> Another common theme that was apparent in the tape was that, for the most part, I was aware of my own ignorance and was embarrassed because of it. I wanted to know more about the oppression of people in the country so that I could do something about it. Since I have been here, I have begun to be actively resistant to racism. I have been able to confront my grandparents and some old friends from high school when they make racist comments. Taking this psychology of racism class is another step toward active resistance to racism. I am trying to educate myself so that I have a knowledge base to work from.
>
> When the tape was made, I was just beginning to be active and just beginning to be educated. I think I am now starting to move into the redefinition stage. I am starting to feel ok about being White. Some of my guilt is dissipating, and I do not feel as ignorant as I used to be. I think I have an understanding of racism; how it effects [sic] myself, and how it effects this country. Because of this I think I can be more active in doing something about it.

In the words of Louise, a Black female student:

> One of the greatest things I learned from this semester in general is that the world is not only Black and White, nor is the United States. I learned a lot about my own erasure of many American ethnic groups. . . . I am in the (immersion) stage of my identity development. I think I am also dangling a little in the (encounter) stage. I say this because a lot of my energies are still directed toward White people. I began writing a poem two days ago and it was directed to White racism. However, I have also become more Black-identified. I am reaching to the strength in Afro-American heritage. I am learning more about the heritage and history of Afro-American culture. Knowledge = strength and strength = power.

While some students are clearly more self-reflective and articulate about their own process than others, most students experience the opportunity to talk and learn about these issues as a transforming process. In my experience, even those students who are frustrated by aspects of the course find themselves changed by it. One such student wrote in her final journal entry:

> What I felt to be a major hindrance to me was the amount of people. Despite the philosophy, I really never felt at ease enough to speak openly about the feelings I have and kind of watched the class pull farther and farther apart as the semester went on. . . . I think that it was your attitude that kept me intrigued by the topics we were studying despite my frustrations with the class time. I really feel as though I made some significant moves in my understanding of other people's positions in our world as well as of my feelings of racism, and I feel very good about them. I feel like this class has moved me in the right direction. I'm on a roll I think, because I've been introduced to so much.

Facilitating student development in this way is a challenging and complex task, but the results are clearly worth the effort.

Implications for the Institution

What are the institutional implications for an understanding of racial identity development theory beyond the classroom? How can this framework be used to address the pressing issues of increasing diversity and decreasing racial tensions on college campuses? How can providing opportunities in the curriculum to talk about race and learn about racism affect the recruitment and retention of students of color specifically, especially when the majority of the students enrolled are White?

The fact is, educating White students about race and racism changes attitudes in ways that go beyond the classroom boundaries. As White students move through their own stages of identity development, they take their friends with them by engaging them in dialogue. They share the articles they have read with roommates, and involve them in their projects. An example of this involvement can be seen in the following journal entry, written by Larry, a White man:

> Here it is our fifth week of class and more and more I am becoming aware of the racism around me. Our second project made things clearer, because while watching T.V. I picked up many kinds of discrimination and stereotyping. Since the project was over, I still find myself watching these shows and picking up bits and pieces every show I watch. Even my friends will be watching a show and they will say, "Hey, Larry, put that in your paper." Since they know I am taking this class, they are looking out for these things. They are also watching what they say around me for fear that I will use them as an example. For example, one of my friends has this fascination with making fun of Jewish people. Before I would listen to his comments and take them in stride, but now I confront him about his comments.

The heightened awareness of the White students enrolled in the class has a ripple effect in their peer group, which helps to create a climate in which students of color and other targeted groups (Jewish students, for example) might feel more comfortable. It is likely that White students who have had the opportunity to learn about racism in a supportive atmosphere will be better able to be allies to students of color in extracurricular settings, like student government meetings and other organizational settings, where students of color often feel isolated and unheard.

At the same time, students of color who have had the opportunity to examine the ways in which racism may have affected their own lives are able to give voice to their own experience, and to validate it rather than be demoralized by it. An understanding of internalized oppression can help students of color recognize the ways in which they may have unknowingly participated in their own victimization, or the victimization of others. They may be able to move beyond victimization to empowerment, and share their learning with others, as Sharon, a previously quoted Black woman, planned to do.

Campus communities with an understanding of racial identity development could become more supportive of special-interest groups, such as the Black Student Union or the Asian Student Alliance, because they would recognize them not as "separatist" but as important outlets for students of color who may be at the Encounter or Immersion stage of racial identity development. Not only could speakers of color be sought out to add diversity to campus programming, but Whites who had made a commitment to unlearning their own racism could be offered as models to those White students looking for new ways to understand their own Whiteness, and to students of color looking for allies.

It has become painfully clear on many college campuses across the United States that we cannot have successfully multiracial campuses without talking about race and learning about racism. Providing a forum where this discussion can take place safely over a semester, a time period that allows personal and group development to unfold in ways that day-long or weekend programs do not, may be among the most proactive learning opportunities an institution can provide.

Notes

1. A similar point could be made about other issues of oppression, such as anti-Semitism, homophobia and heterosexism, ageism, and so on.
2. While similar models of racial identity development exist, Cross and Helms are referenced here because they are among the most frequently cited writers on Black racial identity development and on White racial identity development, respectively. For a discussion of the commonalities between these and other identity development models, see Phinney (1989, 1990) and Helms (1990).
3. Both Parham (1989) and Phinney (1989) suggest that a preference for the dominant group is not always a characteristic of this stage. For example, children raised in households and communities with explicitly positive Afrocentric attitudes may absorb a pro-Black perspective, which then serves as the starting point for their own exploration of racial identity.
4. After being introduced to this model and Helms's model of White identity development, students are encouraged to think about how the models might apply to their own experience or the experiences of people they know. As is reflected in the cited journal entries, some students resonate to the theories quite readily, easily seeing their own process of growth reflected in them. Other students are sometimes puzzled because they feel as though their own process varies from these models, and may ask if it is possible to "skip" a particular stage, for example. Such questions provide a useful departure point for discussing the limitations of stage theories in general, and the potential variations in experience that make questions of racial identity development so complex.
5. Examples of useful articles include essays by McIntosh (1988), Lester (1987), and Braden (1987). Each of these combines autobiographical material, as well as a conceptual framework for understanding some aspect of racism that students find very helpful. Bowser and Hunt's (1981) edited book, *Impacts of Racism on Whites,* though less autobiographical in nature, is also a valuable resource.
6. Class size has a direct bearing on my ability to create safety in the classroom. Dividing the class into pairs or small groups of five or six students to discuss initial reactions to a particular article or film helps to increase participation, both in the small groups and later in the large group discussions.

References

Barnard, H. F. (Ed.). (1987). *Outside the magic circle: The autobiography of Virginia Foster Durr.* New York: Simon & Schuster. (Original work published 1985)

Bowser, B. P., & Hunt, R. G. (1981). *Impacts of racism on Whites.* Beverly Hills: Sage.

Braden, A. (1987). Undoing racism: Lessons for the peace movement. *Nonviolent Activist* (April-May), 3–6.

Bronstein, P. A., & Quina, K. (Eds.). (1988). *Teaching a psychology of people: Resources for gender and sociocultural awareness.* Washington, DC: American Psychological Association.

Cross, W. E., Jr. (1971). The Negro to Black conversion experience: Toward a psychology of black liberation. *Black World, 20*(9), 13–27.

Cross, W. E., Jr. (1978). The Cross and Thomas models of psychological nigrescence. *Journal of Black Psychology, 5*(1), 13–19.

Cross, W. E., Jr. (1991). *Shades of Black: Diversity in African-American identity.* Philadelphia: Temple University Press.

Cross, W. E., Jr., Parham, T. A., & Helms, J. E. (1991). The stages of black identity development: Nigrescence models. In R. Jones (Ed.), *Black psychology* (3rd ed., pp. 319–338). San Francisco: Cobb and Henry.

Derman-Sparks, L., Higa, C. T., & Sparks, B. (1980). Children, race and racism: How race awareness develops. *Interracial Books for Children Bulletin, 11*(3/4), 3–15.

Helms, J. E. (Ed.). (1990). *Black and White racial identity: Theory, research and practice.* Westport, CT: Greenwood Press.

Highlen, P. S., Reynolds, A. L., Adams, E. M., Hanley, T. C., Myers, L. J., Cox, C., and Speight, S. (1988, August 13). *Self-identity development model of oppressed people: Inclusive model for all?* Paper presented at the American Psychological Association Convention, Atlanta, GA.

Hull, G. T., Scott, P. B., & Smith, B. (Eds.). (1982). *All the women are White, all the Blacks are men, but some of us are brave: Black women's studies.* Old Westbury, NY: Feminist Press.

Katz, J. H. (1978). *White awareness: Handbook for anti-racism training.* Norman: University of Oklahoma Press.

Lester, J. (1987). *What happens to the mythmakers when the myths are found to be untrue?* Unpublished paper, Equity Institute, Emeryville, CA.

McIntosh, P. (1988). *White privilege and male privilege: A personal a account of coming to see correspondences through work in women's studies.* Working paper, Wellesley College Center for Research on Women, Wellesley, MA.

McIntosh, P. (1989, July/August). White privilege: Unpacking the invisible knapsack. *Peace and Freedom,* pp. 10–12.

Parham, T. A. (1989). Cycles of psychological nigrescence. *Counseling Psychologist, 17*(2), 187–226.

Phinney, J. (1989). Stages of ethnic identity in minority group adolescents. *Journal of Early Adolescence, 9,* 34–39.

Phinney, J. (1990). Ethnic identity in adolescents and adults: Review of research. *Psychological Bulletin, 108*(3), 499–514.

Phinney, J. S., & Rotheram, M. J. (Eds.). (1987). *Children's ethnic socialization: Pluralism and development.* Newbury Park, CA: Sage.

Schuster, M. R., & Van Dyne, S. R. (Eds.). (1985). *Women's place in the academy: Transforming the liberal arts curriculum.* Totowa, NJ: Towman & Allanheld.

Wellman, D. (1977). *Portraits of White racism.* New York: Cambridge University Press.

Beyond the Methods Fetish:
Toward a Humanizing Pedagogy

LILIA I. BARTOLOMÉ

Much of the current debate regarding the improvement of minority student academic achievement occurs at a level that treats education as a primarily technical issue (Giroux, 1992).[1] For example, the historical and present day academic underachievement of certain culturally and linguistically subordinated student populations in the United States (e.g., Mexican Americans, Native Americans, Puerto Ricans) is often explained as resulting from the lack of cognitively, culturally, and/or linguistically appropriate teaching methods and educational programs.[2] As such, the solution to the problem of academic underachievement tends to be constructed in primarily methodological and mechanistic terms dislodged from the sociocultural reality that shapes it. That is, the solution to the current underachievement of students from subordinated cultures is often reduced to finding the "right" teaching methods, strategies, or prepackaged curricula that will work with students who do not respond to so-called "regular" or "normal" instruction.

Recent research studies have begun to identify educational programs found to be successful in working with culturally and linguistically subordinated minority student populations (Carter & Chatfield, 1986; Lucas, Henze, & Donato, 1990; Tikunoff, 1985; Webb, 1987). In addition, there has been specific interest in identifying teaching strategies that more effectively teach culturally and linguistically "different" students and other "disadvantaged" and "at-risk" students (Knapp & Shields, 1990; McLeod, in press; Means & Knapp, 1991; Tinajero & Ada, 1993). Although it is important to identify useful and promising instructional programs and strategies, it is erroneous to assume that blind replication of instructional programs or teacher mastery of particular teaching methods, in and of themselves, will guarantee successful student learning, especially when we are discussing populations that historically have been mistreated and miseducated by the schools.

This focus on methods as solutions in the current literature coincides with many of my graduate students' beliefs regarding linguistic minority education improvement. As a Chicana professor who has taught anti-racist multicultural education courses at various institutions, I am consistently confronted at the beginning of each semester by students who are anxious to learn the latest teaching methods — methods that they hope will somehow magically work on minority students.[3] Although my students are well-intentioned individuals who sincerely wish to create positive learning environments for culturally and linguistically subordinated students, they arrive with the expectation that I will provide them with easy answers in the form of specific instructional methods. That is, since they (implicitly) perceive the academic underachievement of subordinated students as a technical issue, the solutions they require are also expected to be technical in nature (e.g., specific teaching methods, instructional curricula and materials). They usually assume that: 1) they, as teachers, are fine and do not need to identify, interrogate, and change their biased beliefs and fragmented views about subordinated students; 2) schools, as institutions, are basically fair and democratic sites where all students are provided with similar, if not equal, treatment and learning conditions; and 3) children who experience academic difficulties (especially those from culturally and linguistically low-status groups) require some form of "special" instruction since they obviously have not been able to succeed under "regular" or "normal" instructional conditions. Consequently, if nothing is basically wrong with teachers and schools, they often conclude, then linguistic minority academic underachievement is best dealt with by providing teachers with specific teaching methods that promise to be effective with culturally and linguistically subordinated students. To further complicate matters, many of my students seek *generic* teaching methods that will work with a variety of minority student populations, and they grow anxious and impatient when reminded that instruction for any group of students needs to be tailored or individualized to some extent. Some of my students appear to be seeking what María de la Luz Reyes (1992) defines as a "one size fits all" instructional recipe. Reyes explains that the term refers to the assumption that instructional methods that are deemed effective for mainstream populations will benefit *all* students, no matter what their backgrounds may be.[4] She explains that the assumption is

> similar to the "one size fits all" marketing concept that would have buyers believe that there is an average or ideal size among men and women. . . . Those who market "one size fits all" products suggest that if the article of clothing is not a good fit, the fault is not with the design of the garment, but those who are too fat, too skinny, too tall, too short, or too high-waisted. (p. 435)

I have found that many of my students similarly believe that teaching approaches that work with one minority population should also fit another (see Vogt, Jordan, & Tharp, 1987, for an example of this tendency). Reyes argues that educators often make this "one size fits all" assumption when discussing instructional approaches, such as process writing. For example, as Lisa Delpit

(1988) has convincingly argued, the process writing approach that has been blindly embraced by mostly White liberal teachers often produces a negative result with African-American students. Delpit cites one Black student:

> I didn't feel she was teaching us anything. She wanted us to correct each other's papers and we were there to learn from her. She didn't teach anything, absolutely nothing.
>
> Maybe they're trying to learn what Black folks knew all the time. We understand how to improvise, how to express ourselves creatively. When I'm in a classroom, I'm not looking for that, I'm looking for structure, the more formal language.
>
> Now my buddy was in a Black teacher's class. And that lady was very good. She went through and explained and defined each part of the structure. This [White] teacher didn't get along with that Black teacher. She said she didn't agree with her methods. But *I* don't think that White teacher *had* any methods. (1988, p. 287)

The above quote is a glaring testimony that a "one size fits all" approach often does not work with the same level of effectiveness with all students across the board. Such assumptions reinforce a disarticulation between the embraced method and the sociocultural realities within which each method is implemented. I find that this "one size fits all" assumption is also held by many of my students about a number of teaching methods currently in vogue, such as cooperative learning and whole language instruction. The students imbue the "new" methods with almost magical properties that render them, in and of themselves, capable of improving students' academic standing.

One of my greatest challenges throughout the years has been to help students to understand that a myopic focus on methodology often serves to obfuscate the real question — which is why in our society, subordinated students do not generally succeed academically in schools. In fact, schools often reproduce the existing asymmetrical power relations among cultural groups (Anyon, 1988; Gibson & Ogbu, 1991; Giroux, 1992; Freire, 1985). I believe that by taking a sociohistorical view of present-day conditions and concerns that inform the lived experiences of socially perceived minority students, prospective teachers are better able to comprehend the quasi-colonial nature of minority education. By engaging in this critical sociohistorical analysis of subordinated students' academic performance, most of my graduate students (teachers and prospective teachers) are better situated to reinterpret and reframe current educational concerns so as to develop pedagogical structures that speak to the day-to-day reality, struggles, concerns, and dreams of these students. By understanding the historical specificities of marginalized students, these teachers and prospective teachers come to realize that an uncritical focus on methods makes invisible the historical role that schools and their personnel have played (and continue to play), not only in discriminating against many culturally different groups, but also in denying their humanity. By robbing students of their culture, language, history, and values, schools often reduce these students to the status of subhumans who need to be rescued from their "savage" selves. The end result of this cultural and linguistic eradication represents, in my view, a form of dehumanization. Therefore, any discussion having to do with the improvement of subordinated students' academic standing is incomplete if it does not address those discriminatory school practices that lead to dehumanization.

In this article, I argue that a necessary first step in reevaluating the failure or success of particular instructional methods used with subordinated students calls for a shift in perspective — a shift from a narrow and mechanistic view of instruction to one that is broader in scope and takes into consideration the sociohistorical and political dimensions of education. I discuss why effective methods are needed for these students, and why certain strategies are deemed effective or ineffective in a given sociocultural context. My discussion will include a section that addresses the significance of teachers' understanding of the political nature of education, the reproductive nature of schools, and the schools' continued (yet unspoken) deficit views of subordinated students. By conducting a critical analysis of the sociocultural realities in which subordinated students find themselves at school, the implicit and explicit antagonistic relations between students and teachers (and other school representatives) take on focal importance.

As a Chicana and a former classroom elementary and middle school teacher who encountered negative race relations that ranged from teachers' outright rejection of subordinated students to their condescending pity, fear, indifference, and apathy when confronted by the challenges of minority student education, I find it surprising that little minority education literature deals explicitly with the very real issue of antagonistic race relations between subordinated students and White school personnel (see Ogbu, 1987, and Giroux, 1992, for an in-depth discussion of this phenomenon).

For this reason, I also include in this article a section that discusses two instructional methods and approaches identified as effective in current education literature: culturally responsive education and strategic teaching. I examine the methods for pedagogical underpinnings that — under the critical use of politically clear teachers — have the potential to challenge students academically and intellectually while treating them with dignity and respect. More importantly, I examine the pedagogical foundations that serve to humanize the educational process and enable both students and teachers to work toward breaking away from their unspoken antagonism and negative beliefs about each other and get on with the business of sharing and creating knowledge. I argue that the informed way in which a teacher implements a method can serve to offset potentially unequal relations and discriminatory structures and practices in the classroom and, in doing so, improve the quality of the instructional process for both student and teacher. In other words, politically informed teacher use of methods can create conditions that enable subordinated students to move from their usual passive position to one of active and critical engagement. I am convinced that creating pedagogical spaces that enable students to move *from object to subject position* produces more far-reaching, positive effects than the implementation of a particular teaching methodology, regardless of how technically advanced and promising it may be.

The final section of this article will explore and suggest the implementation of what Donaldo Macedo (1994) designates as an

> anti-methods pedagogy that refuses to be enslaved by the rigidity of models and methodological paradigms. An anti-methods pedagogy should be informed by a critical understanding of the sociocultural context that guides our practices so as to free us from the beaten path of methodological certainties and specialisms. (p. 8)

Simply put, it is important that educators not blindly reject teaching methods across the board, but that they reject uncritical appropriation of methods, materials, curricula, etc. Educators need to reject the present methods fetish so as to create learning environments informed by both action and reflection. In freeing themselves from the blind adoption of so-called effective (and sometimes "teacher-proof") strategies, teachers can begin the reflective process, which allows them to recreate and reinvent teaching methods and materials by always taking into consideration the sociocultural realities that can either limit or expand the possibilities to humanize education. It is important that teachers keep in mind that methods are social constructions that grow out of and reflect ideologies that often prevent teachers from understanding the pedagogical implications of asymmetrical power relations among different cultural groups.

The Significance of Teacher Political Clarity[5]

In his letter to North American educators, Paulo Freire (1987) argues that technical expertise and mastery of content area and methodology are insufficient to ensure effective instruction of students from subordinated cultures. Freire contends that, in addition to possessing content area knowledge, teachers must possess political clarity so as to be able to effectively create, adopt, and modify teaching strategies that simultaneously respect and challenge learners from diverse cultural groups in a variety of learning environments.

Teachers working on improving their political clarity recognize that teaching is not a politically neutral undertaking. They understand that educational institutions are socializing institutions that mirror the greater society's culture, values, and norms. Schools reflect both the positive and negative aspects of a society. Thus, the unequal power relations among various social and cultural groups at the societal level are usually reproduced at the school and classroom level, unless concerted efforts are made to prevent their reproduction. Teachers working toward political clarity understand that they can either maintain the status quo, or they can work to transform the sociocultural reality at the classroom and school level so that the culture at this micro-level does not reflect macro-level inequalities, such as asymmetrical power relations that relegate certain cultural groups to a subordinate status.

Teachers can support positive social change in the classroom in a variety of ways. One possible intervention can consist of the creation of heterogeneous learning groups for the purpose of modifying low-status roles of individuals or groups of children.[6] Elizabeth Cohen (1986) demonstrates that when teachers create learning conditions where students, especially those perceived as low status (e.g., limited English speakers in a classroom where English is the dominant language, students with academic difficulties, or those perceived by their peers for a variety of reasons as less able), can demonstrate their possession of knowledge and expertise, they are then able to see themselves, and be seen by others, as capable and competent. As a result, contexts are created in which peers can learn from each other as well.

A teacher's political clarity will not necessarily compensate for structural inequalities that students face outside the classroom; however, teachers can, to the best of their ability, help their students deal with injustices encountered inside and outside the classroom. A number of possibilities exist for preparing students to deal with the greater society's unfairness and inequality that range from engaging in explicit discussions with students about their experiences, to more indirect ways (that nevertheless require a teacher who is politically clear), such as creating democratic learning environments where students become accustomed to being treated as competent and able individuals. I believe that the students, once accustomed to the rights and responsibilities of full citizenship in the classroom, will come to expect respectful treatment and authentic estimation in other contexts. Again, it is important to point out that it is not the particular lesson or set of activities that prepares the student; rather, it is the teacher's politically clear educational philosophy that underlies the varied methods and lessons/activities she or he employs that make the difference.

Under ideal conditions, competent educators simultaneously translate theory into practice *and* consider the population being served and the sociocultural reality in which learning is expected to take place. Let me reiterate that command of a content area or specialization is necessary, but it is not sufficient for effectively working with students. Just as critical is that teachers comprehend that their role as educators is a political act that is never neutral (Freire, 1985, 1987, 1993; Freire & Macedo, 1987). In ignoring or negating the political nature of their work with these students, teachers not only reproduce the status quo and their students' low status, but they also inevitably legitimize schools' discriminatory practices. For example, teachers who uncritically follow school practices that unintentionally or intentionally serve to promote tracking and segregation within school and classroom contexts continue to reproduce the status quo. Conversely, teachers can become conscious of, and subsequently challenge, the role of educational institutions and their own roles as educators in maintaining a system that often serves to silence students from subordinated groups.

Teachers must also remember that schools, similar to other institutions in society, are influenced by perceptions of socioeconomic status (SES), race/ethnicity, language, and gender (Anyon, 1988; Bloom, 1991; Cummins, 1989; Ogbu, 1987). They must begin to question how these perceptions influence classroom dynamics. An important step in increasing teacher political clarity is recognizing that, despite current liberal rhetoric regarding the equal value of all cultures, low SES and ethnic minority students have historically (and currently) been perceived as deficient. I believe that the present methods-restricted discussion must be broadened to reveal the deeply entrenched deficit orientation toward "difference" (i.e., non-Western European race/ethnicity, non-English language use, working-class status, femaleness) that prevails in the schools in a deeply "cultural" ideology of White supremacy. As educators, we must constantly be vigilant and ask how the deficit orientation has affected our perceptions concerning students from subordinated populations and created rigid and mechanistic teacher-student relations (Cummins, 1989; Flores, Cousin, & Diaz, 1991; Giroux & McLaren, 1986). Such a model often serves to create classroom conditions in which there is very little opportunity for teachers and students to interact in meaningful ways, establish positive and trusting working relations, and share knowledge.

Our Legacy: A Deficit View of Subordinated Students

As discussed earlier, teaching strategies are neither designed nor implemented in a vacuum. Design, selection, and use of particular teaching approaches and strategies arise from perceptions about learning and learners. I contend that the most pedagogically advanced strategies are sure to be ineffective in the hands of educators who implicitly or explicitly subscribe to a belief system that renders ethnic, racial, and linguistic minority students at best culturally disadvantaged and in need of fixing (if we could only identify the right recipe!), or, at worst, culturally or genetically deficient and beyond fixing.[7] Despite the fact that various models have been proposed to explain the academic failure of certain subordinated groups — academic failure described as *historical, pervasive,* and *disproportionate* — the fact remains that these views of difference are deficit-based and deeply imprinted in our individual and collective psyches (Flores, 1982, 1993; Menchaca & Valencia, 1990; Valencia, 1986, 1991).

The deficit model has the longest history of any model discussed in the education literature. Richard Valencia (1986) traces its evolution over three centuries:

> Also known in the literature as the "social pathology" model or the "cultural deprivation" model, the deficit approach explains disproportionate academic problems among low status students as largely being due to pathologies or deficits in their sociocultural background (e.g., cognitive and linguistic deficiencies, low self-esteem, poor motivation). . . . To improve the

educability of such students, programs such as compensatory education and parent-child intervention have been proposed. (p. 3)

Barbara Flores (1982, 1993) documents the effect this deficit model has had on the schools' past and current perceptions of Latino students. Her historical overview chronicles descriptions used to refer to Latino students over the last century. The terms range from "mentally retarded," "linguistically handicapped," "culturally and linguistically deprived," and "semilingual," to the current euphemism for Latino and other subordinated students: the "at-risk" student.

Similarly, recent research continues to lay bare our deficit orientation and its links to discriminatory school practices aimed at students from groups perceived as low status (Anyon, 1988; Bloom, 1991; Diaz, Moll, & Mehan, 1986; Oaks, 1986). Findings range from teacher preference for Anglo students, to bilingual teachers' preference for lighter skinned Latino students (Bloom, 1991), to teachers' negative perceptions of working-class parents as compared to middle-class parents (Lareau, 1990), and, finally, to unequal teaching and testing practices in schools serving working-class and ethnic minority students (Anyon, 1988; Diaz et al., 1986; Oaks, 1986; U.S. Commission on Civil Rights, 1973). Especially indicative of our inability to consciously acknowledge the deficit orientation is the fact that the teachers in these studies — teachers from all ethnic groups — were themselves unaware of the active role they played in the differential and unequal treatment of their students.

The deficit view of subordinated students has been critiqued by numerous researchers as ethnocentric and invalid (Boykin, 1983; Diaz et al., 1986; Flores, 1982; Flores et al., 1991; Sue & Padilla, 1986; Trueba, 1989; Walker, 1987). More recent research offers alternative models that shift the source of school failure away from the characteristics of the individual child, their families, and their cultures, and toward the schooling process (Au & Mason, 1983; Heath, 1983; Mehan, 1992; Philips, 1972). Unfortunately, I believe that many of these alternative models often unwittingly give rise to a kinder and more liberal, yet more concealed version of the deficit model that views subordinated students as being in need of "specialized" modes of instruction — a type of instructional "coddling" that mainstream students do not require in order to achieve in school. Despite the use of less overtly ethnocentric models to explain the academic standing of subordinated students, I believe that the deficit orientation toward difference, especially as it relates to low socioeconomic and ethnic minority groups, is very deeply ingrained in the ethos of our most prominent institutions, especially schools, and in the various educational programs in place at these sites.

It is against this sociocultural backdrop that teachers can begin to seriously question the unspoken but prevalent deficit orientation used to hide SES, racial/ethnic, linguistic, and gender inequities present in U.S. classrooms. And it is against this sociocultural backdrop that I critically examine two teaching approaches identified by the educational literature as effective with subordinated student populations.

Potentially Humanizing Pedagogy: Two Promising Teaching Approaches

Well-known approaches and strategies such as cooperative learning, language experience, process writing, reciprocal teaching, and whole language activities can be used to create humanizing learning environments where students cease to be treated as objects and yet receive academically rigorous instruction (Cohen, 1986; Edelsky, Altwerger, & Flores, 1991; Palinscar & Brown, 1984; Pérez & Torres-Guzmán, 1992; Zamel, 1982). However, when these approaches are implemented uncritically, they often produce negative results, as indicated by Lisa Delpit (1986, 1988). Critical teacher applications of these approaches and strategies can contribute to discarding deficit views of students from subordinated groups, so that they are treated with respect and viewed as active and capable subjects in their own learning.

Academically rigorous, student-centered teaching strategies can take many forms. One may well ask, is it not merely common sense to promote approaches and strategies that respect, recognize, utilize, and build on students' existing knowledge bases? The answer would be, of course, yes, it is. However, it is important to recognize, as part of our effort to increase our political clarity, that these practices have *not* typified classroom instruction for students from marginalized populations. The practice of learning from and valuing student language and life experiences *often* occurs in classrooms where students speak a language and possess cultural capital that more closely matches that of the mainstream (Anyon, 1988; Lareau, 1990; Winfield, 1986).[8]

Jean Anyon's (1988) classic research suggests that teachers of affluent students are more likely than teachers of working-class students to utilize and incorporate student life experiences and knowledge into the curriculum. For example, in Anyon's study, teachers of affluent students often designed creative and innovative lessons that tapped students' existing knowledge bases; one math lesson, designed to teach students to find averages, asked them to fill out a possession survey inquiring about the number of cars, television sets, refrigerators, and games owned at home so as to teach students to average. Unfortunately, this practice of tapping students' already existing knowledge and language bases is not commonly utilized with student populations traditionally perceived as deficient. Anyon reports that teachers of working-class students viewed them as lacking the necessary cultural capital, and therefore imposed content and behavioral standards with little consideration and respect for student input. Although Anyon did not generalize beyond her sample, other studies suggest the validity of her findings for ethnic minority student populations (Diaz et al., 1986; Moll, 1986; Oaks, 1986).

The creation of learning environments for low SES and ethnic minority students, similar to those for more affluent and White populations, requires that teachers discard deficit notions and genuinely value and utilize students' existing knowledge bases in their teaching. In order to do so, teachers must confront and challenge their own social biases so as to honestly begin to perceive their students as capable learners. Furthermore, they must remain open to the fact that they will also learn from their students. Learning is not a one-way undertaking.

It is important for educators to recognize that no language or set of life experiences is inherently superior, yet our social values reflect our preferences for certain language and life experiences over others. Student-centered teaching strategies such as cooperative learning, language experience, process writing, reciprocal teaching, and whole language activities (if practiced consciously and critically) can help to offset or neutralize our deficit-based failure and recognize subordinated student strengths. Our tendency to discount these strengths occurs whenever we forget that learning only occurs when prior knowledge is accessed and linked to new information.

Beau Jones, Annemarie Palinscar, Donna Ogle, and Eileen Carr (1987) explain that learning *is* the act of linking new information to prior knowledge. According to their framework, prior knowledge is stored in memory in the form of knowledge frameworks. New information is understood and stored by calling up the appropriate knowledge framework and then integrating the new information. Acknowledging and using existing student language and knowledge makes good pedagogical sense, and it also constitutes a humanizing experience for students traditionally *de*humanized and disempowered in the schools. I believe that strategies identified as effective in the literature have the potential to offset reductive education in which "the educator as *the one who knows* transfers existing knowledge to the learner as *the one who does not know*" (Freire, 1985, p. 114, emphasis added). It is important to repeat that mere implementation of a particular strategy or approach identified as effective does not guarantee success, as the current debate in process writing attests (Delpit, 1986, 1988; Reyes, 1991, 1992).

Creating learning environments that incorporate student language and life experiences in no way negates teachers' responsibility for providing students with particular academic content knowledge and skills. It is important not to link teacher respect and use of student knowledge and language bases with a laissez-faire attitude toward teaching. It is equally necessary not to confuse academic rigor with rigidity that stifles and silences students. The teacher is the authority, with all the resulting responsibilities that entails; however, it is not necessary for the teacher to become authoritarian in order to challenge students intellectually. Education can be a process in which teacher and students mutually participate in the intellectually exciting undertaking we call learning. Students *can* become active subjects in their own learning, instead of passive objects waiting to be filled with facts and figures by the teacher.

I would like to emphasize that teachers who work with subordinated populations have the responsibility to assist them in appropriating knowledge bases and discourse styles deemed desirable by the greater society. However, this process of appropriation must be additive, that is, the new concepts and new discourse skills must be added to, not subtracted from, the students' existing background knowledge. In order to assume this additive stance, teachers must discard deficit views so they can use and build on life experiences and language styles too often viewed and labeled as "low class" and undesirable. Again, there are numerous teaching strategies and methods that can be employed in this additive manner. For the purposes of illustration, I will briefly discuss two approaches currently identified as promising for students from subordinated populations. The selected approaches are referred to in the literature as culturally responsive instructional approaches and strategic teaching.

Culturally Responsive Instruction: The Potential to Equalize Power Relations

Culturally responsive instruction grows out of cultural difference theory, which attributes the academic difficulties of students from subordinated groups to cultural incongruence or discontinuities between the learning, language use, and behavioral practices found in the home and those expected by the schools. Ana María Villegas (1988, 1991) defines culturally responsive instruction as attempts to create instructional situations where teachers use teaching approaches and strategies that recognize and build on culturally different ways of learning, behaving, and using language in the classroom.

A number of classic ethnographic studies document culturally incongruent communication practices in classrooms where students and teachers may speak the same language but use it in different ways. This type of incongruence is cited as a major source of academic difficulties for subordinated students and their teachers (see Au, 1980; Au & Mason, 1983; Cazden, 1988; Erickson & Mohatt, 1982; Heath, 1983; Philips, 1972). For the purposes of this analysis, one form of culturally responsive instruction, the Kamehameha Education Project reading program, will be discussed.

The Kamehameha Education Project is a reading program developed as a response to the traditionally low academic achievement of native Hawaiian students in Western schools. The reading program was a result of several years of research that examined the language practices of native Hawaiian children in home and school settings. Observations of native Hawaiian children showed them to be bright and capable learners; however, their behavior in the classroom signaled communication difficulties between them and their non-Hawaiian teachers. For example, Kathryn Hu-Pei Au (1979, 1980) reports that native Hawaiian children's language behavior in the classroom was often misinterpreted by teachers as being unruly and without educational value. She found that the children's preferred language style in the classroom was linked to a practice used by adults in their homes and community called "talk story." She discusses the talk story phenomenon and describes it as a major speech event in the Hawaiian community, where individuals speak almost simultaneously and where little attention is given to turn taking. Au explains that this practice may inhibit students from speaking out as individuals because of their familiarity with and preference for simultaneous group discussion.

Because the non-Hawaiian teachers were unfamiliar with talk story and failed to recognize its value, much class time was spent either silencing the children or prodding unwilling individuals to speak. Needless to say, very little class time was dedicated to other instruction. More important, the children were constrained and not allowed to demonstrate their abilities as speakers and possessors of knowledge. Because the students did not exhibit their skills in mainstream accepted ways (e.g., competing as individuals for the floor), they were prevented from exhibiting knowledge via their culturally preferred style. However, once the children's interaction style was incorporated into classroom lessons, time on task increased and, subsequently, students' performance on standardized reading tests improved. This study's findings conclude that educators can successfully employ the students' culturally valued language practices while introducing the student to more conventional and academically acceptable ways of using language.

It is interesting to note that many of the research studies that examine culturally congruent and incongruent teaching approaches also inadvertently illustrate the equalization of previous asymmetrical power relations between teachers and students. These studies describe classrooms where teachers initially imposed participation structures upon students from subordinated linguistic minority groups and later learned to negotiate with them rules regarding acceptable classroom behavior and language use (Au & Mason, 1983; Erickson & Mohatt, 1982; Heath, 1983; Philips, 1972). Thus these studies, in essence, capture the successful negotiation of power relations, which resulted in higher student academic achievement and increased teacher effectiveness. Yet there is little explicit discussion in these studies of the greater sociocultural reality that renders it perfectly normal for teachers to automatically disregard and disrespect subordinated students' preferences and to allow antagonistic relations to foment until presented with empirical evidence that legitimizes the students' practices. Instead, the focus of most of these studies rests entirely on the cultural congruence of the instruction and not on the humanizing effects of a more democratic pedagogy. Villegas (1988) accurately critiques the cultural congruence literature when she states:

> It is simplistic to claim that differences in languages used at home and in school are the root of the widespread academic problems of minority children. Admittedly, differences do exist, and they can create communication difficulties in the classroom for both teachers and students. Even so, those differences in language must be viewed in the context of a broader struggle for power within a stratified society. (p. 260)

Despite the focus on the cultural versus the political dimensions of pedagogy, some effort is made to link culturally congruent teaching practices with equalization of classroom power relations. For example, Kathryn Au and Jana Mason (1983) explain that "one means of achieving cultural congruence in lessons may be to *seek a balance between the interactional rights of teachers and students, so that the children can participate in ways comfortable to them*" (p. 145, emphasis added). Their study compared two teachers and showed that the teacher who was willing to negotiate with students either the topic of discussion or the appropriate participation structure was better able to implement her lesson. Conversely, the teacher who attempted to impose both topic of discussion *and* appropriate interactional rules was frequently diverted because of conflicts with students over one or the other.

Unfortunately, as mentioned earlier, interpretations and practical applications of this body of research have focused on the *cultural* congruence of the approaches. I emphasize the term *cultural* because in these studies the term "culture" is used in a restricted sense devoid of its dynamic, ideological, and political dimensions. Instead, culture is treated as synonymous with ethnic culture, rather than as "the representation of lived experiences, material artifacts and practices *forged within the unequal and dialectical relations* that different groups establish in a given society at a particular point in historical time" (Giroux, 1985, p. xxi, emphasis added). I use this definition of culture because, without identifying the political dimensions of culture and subsequent unequal status attributed to members of different ethnic groups, the reader may conclude that teaching methods simply need to be ethnically congruent to be effective — without recognizing that not all ethnic and linguistic cultural groups are viewed and treated as equally legitimate in classrooms. Interestingly enough, there is little discussion of the various socially perceived minority groups' subordinate status vis-B-vis White teachers and peers in these studies. All differences are treated as ethnic cultural differences and not as responses of subordinated students to teachers from dominant groups, and vice versa.

Given the sociocultural realities in the above studies, the specific teaching strategies may not be what made the difference. Indeed, efforts to uncritically export the Kamehameha Education Project reading program to other student populations resulted in failure (Vogt et al., 1987). It could well be that the teachers' effort to negotiate and share power by treating students as equal participants in their own learning is what made the difference in Hawaii. Just as important is the teachers' willingness to critically interrogate their deficit views of subordinated students. By employing a variety of strategies and techniques, the Kamehameha students were allowed to interact with teachers in egalitarian and meaningful ways. More importantly, the teachers also learned to recognize, value, use, and build upon students' previously acquired knowledge and skills. In essence, these strategies succeeded in creating a comfort zone so students could exhibit their knowledge and skills and, ultimately, empower themselves to succeed in an academic setting. Teachers also benefitted from using a variety of student-centered teaching strategies that humanized their perceptions of treatment of students previously perceived as deficient. Ray McDermott's (1977) classic research reminds us that numerous teaching approaches and strategies can be effective, so long as trusting relations between teacher and students are established and power relations are mutually set and agreed upon.

Strategic Teaching: The Significance of Teacher-Student Interaction and Negotiation

Strategic teaching refers to an instructional model that explicitly teaches students learning strategies that enable them consciously to monitor their own learning. This is accomplished through the development of reflective cognitive monitoring and metacognitive skills (Jones, Palinscar, Ogle, & Carr, 1987). The goal is to prepare independent and metacognitively aware students. This teaching strategy makes explicit for students the structures of various text types used in academic settings and assists students in identifying various strategies for effectively comprehending the various genres. Although text structures and strategies for dissecting the particular structures are presented by the teacher, a key component of these lessons is the elicitation of students' knowledge about text types and their own strategies for making meaning before presenting them with more conventional academic strategies.

Examples of learning strategies include teaching various text structures (i.e., stories and reports) through frames and graphic organizers. *Frames* are sets of questions that help students understand a given topic. Readers monitor their understanding of a text by asking questions, making predictions, and testing their predictions as they read. Before reading, frames serve as an advance organizer to activate prior knowledge and facilitate understanding. Frames can also be utilized during the reading process by the reader to monitor self-learning. Finally, frames can be used after a reading lesson to summarize and integrate newly acquired information.

Graphic organizers are visual maps that represent text structures and organizational patterns used in texts and in student writing. Ideally, graphic organizers reflect both the content and text structure. Graphic organizers include semantic maps, chains, and concept hierarchies, and assist the student in visualizing the rhetorical structure of the text. Beau Jones and colleagues (1987) explain that frames and graphic organizers can be "powerful tools to help the student locate, select, sequence, integrate and restructure information — both from the perspective of understanding and from the perspective of producing information in written responses" (p. 38).

Although much of the research on strategic teaching focuses on English monolingual mainstream students, recent efforts to study linguistic minority students' use of these strategies show similar success. This literature shows that strategic teaching improved the students' reading comprehension, as well as their conscious use of effective learning strategies in their native language (Avelar La Salle, 1991; Chamot, 1983; Hernandez, 1991; O'Malley & Chamot, 1990; Reyes, 1987). Furthermore, these studies show that students, despite limited English proficiency, were able to transfer or apply their knowledge of specific learning strategies and text structure to English reading texts. For example, Jose Hernandez (1991) reports that sixth-grade limited English proficient students learned, in the native language (Spanish), to generate hypotheses, summarize, and make predictions about readings. He reports:

Students were able to demonstrate use of comprehension strategies even when they could not decode the English text aloud. When asked in Spanish about English texts the students were able to generate questions, summarize stories, and predict future events in Spanish. (p. 101)

Robin Avelar La Salle's (1991) study of third- and fourth-grade bilingual students shows that strategic teaching in the native language of three expository text structures commonly found in elementary social studies and science texts (topical net, matrix, and hierarchy) improved comprehension of these types of texts in both Spanish and English.

Such explicit and strategic teaching is most important in the upper elementary grades, where students are expected to focus on the development of more advanced English literacy skills. Beginning at about third grade, students face literacy demands distinct from those encountered in earlier grades. Jeanne Chall (1983) describes the change in literacy demands in terms of stages of readings. She explains that at a stage three of reading, students cease to "learn to read" and begin "reading to learn." Students in third and fourth grade are introduced to content area subjects such as social studies, science, and health. In addition, students are introduced to expository texts (reports). This change in texts, text structures, and in the functions of reading (reading for information) calls for teaching strategies that will prepare students to comprehend various expository texts (e.g., cause/effect, compare/contrast) used across the curriculum.

Strategic teaching holds great promise for preparing linguistic minority students to face the new literacy challenges in the upper grades. As discussed before, the primary goal of strategic instruction is to foster learner independence. This goal in and of itself is laudable. However, the characteristics of strategic instruction that I find most promising grow out of the premise that teachers and students must interact and negotiate meaning as equals in order to reach a goal.

Teachers, by permitting learners to speak from their own vantage points, create learning contexts in which students are able to empower themselves throughout the strategic learning process. Before teachers attempt to instruct students in new content or learning strategies, efforts are made by the teacher to access student prior knowledge so as to link it with new information. In allowing students to present and discuss their prior knowledge and experiences, the teacher legitimizes and treats as valuable student language and cultural experiences usually ignored in classrooms. If students are encouraged to speak on what they know best, then they are, in a sense, treated as experts — experts who are expected to refine their knowledge bases with the additional new content and strategy information presented by the teacher.

Teachers play a significant role in creating learning contexts in which students are able to empower themselves. Teachers act as cultural mentors of sorts when they introduce students not only to the culture of the classroom, but to particular subjects and discourse styles as well. In the process, teachers assist the students in appropriating the skills (in an additive fashion) for themselves so as to enable them to behave as "insiders" in the particular subject or discipline. Jim Gee (1989) reminds us that the social nature of teaching and learning must involve apprenticeship into the subject's or discipline's discourse in order for students to do well in school. This apprenticeship includes acquisition of particular content matter, ways of organizing content, and ways of using language (oral and written). Gee adds that these discourses are not mastered solely through teacher-centered and directed instruction, but also by "apprenticeship into social practices through scaffolded and supported interaction with people who have already mastered the discourse" (p. 7). The apprenticeship notion can be immensely useful with subordinated students if it facilitates the acceptance and valorization of students' prior knowledge through a mentoring process.

Models of instruction, such as strategic teaching, can promote such an apprenticeship. In the process of apprenticing linguistic minority students, teachers must interact in meaningful ways with them. This human interaction not only assists students in acquiring new knowledge and skills, but it also often familiarizes individuals from different SES and racial/ethnic groups, and creates mutual respect instead of the antagonism that so frequently occurs between teachers and their students from subordinated groups. In this learning environment, teachers and students learn from each other. The strategies serve, then, not to "fix" the student, but to equalize power relations and to humanize the teacher-student relationship. Ideally, teachers are forced to challenge implicitly or explicitly held deficit attitudes and beliefs about their students and the cultural groups to which they belong.

Beyond Teaching Strategies: Towards a Humanizing Pedagogy

When I recall a special education teacher's experience related in a bilingualism and literacy course that I taught, I am reminded of the humanizing effects of teaching strategies that, similar to culturally responsive instruction and strategic teaching, allow teachers to listen, learn from, and mentor their students. This teacher, for most of her career, had been required to assess her students through a variety of closed-ended instruments, and then to remediate their diagnosed "weaknesses" with discrete skills instruction. The assessment instruments provided little information to explain why the student answered a question either correctly or incorrectly, and they often confirmed perceived student academic, linguistic, and cognitive weaknesses. This fragmented discrete skills approach to instruction restricts the teacher's access to existing student knowledge and experiences not specifically elicited by the academic tasks. Needless to say, this teacher knew very little about her students other than her deficit descriptions of them.

As part of the requirements for my course, she was asked to focus on one Spanish-speaking, limited English proficient special education student over the semester. She observed the student in a number of formal and informal contexts, and she engaged him in a number of open-ended tasks. These tasks included allowing him to write entire texts, such as stories and poems (despite diagnosed limited English proficiency), and to engage in "think-alouds" during reading.[9] Through these open-ended activities, the teacher learned about her student's English writing ability (both strengths and weaknesses), his life experiences and world views, and his meaning-making strategies for reading. Consequently, the teacher constructed an instructional plan much better suited to her student's academic needs and interests. And even more important, she underwent a humanizing process that allowed her to recognize the varied and valuable life experiences and knowledge her student brought into the classroom.

This teacher was admirably candid when she shared her initial negative and stereotypic views of the student and her radical transformation. Despite this teacher's mastery of content area, her lack of political clarity blinded her to the oppressive and dehumanizing nature of instruction offered to linguistic minority students. Initially, she had formed an erroneous notion of her student's personality, worldview, academic ability, motivation, and academic potential on the basis of his Puerto Rican ethnicity, low SES background, limited English proficiency, and moderately learning-disabled label. Because of the restricted and closed nature of earlier assessment and instruction, the teacher had never received information about her student that challenged her negative perceptions. Listening to her student and reading his poetry and stories, she discovered his loving and sunny personality, learned his personal history, and identified academic strengths and weaknesses. In the process, she discovered and challenged her deficit orientation. The following excerpt from this student's writing exemplifies the power of the student voice for humanizing teachers:

My Father

> I love my father very much. I will never forget what my father has done for me and my brothers and sisters. When we first came from Puerto Rico we didn't have food to eat and we were very poor. My father had to work three jobs to put food and milk on the table. Those were hard times and my father worked so hard that we hardly saw him. But even when I didn't see him, I always knew he loved me very much. I will always be grateful to my father. We are not so poor now and so he works only one job. But I will never forget what my father did for me. I will also work to help my father have a better life when I grow up. I love my father very much.

The process of learning about her student's rich and multifaceted background enabled this teacher to move beyond the rigid methodology that had required her to distance herself from the student and to confirm the deficit model to which she unconsciously adhered. In this case, the meaningful teacher-student interaction served to equalize the teacher-student power relations and to humanize instruction by expanding the horizons through which the student demonstrated human qualities, dreams, desires, and capacities that closed-ended tests and instruction never captured.

I believe that the specific teaching methods implemented by the teacher, in and of themselves, were not the significant factors. The actual strengths of methods depend, first and foremost, on the degree to which they embrace a humanizing pedagogy that values the students' background knowledge, culture, and life experiences, and creates learning contexts where power is shared by students and teachers. Teaching methods are a means to an end — humanizing education to promote academic success for students historically underserved by the schools. A teaching strategy is a vehicle to a greater goal. A number of vehicles exist that may or may not lead to a humanizing pedagogy, depending on the sociocultural reality in which teachers and students operate.

The critical issue is the degree to which we hold the moral conviction that we must humanize the educational experience of students from subordinated populations by eliminating the hostility that often confronts these students. This process would require that we cease to be overly dependent on methods as technical instruments and adopt a pedagogy that seeks to forge a cultural democracy where all students are treated with respect and dignity. A true cultural democracy forces teachers to recognize that students' lack of familiarity with the dominant values of the curriculum "does not mean . . . that the lack of these experiences develop in these children a different 'nature' that determines their absolute incompetence" (Freire, 1993, p. 17).

Unless educational methods are situated in the students' cultural experiences, students will continue to show difficulty in mastering content area that is not only alien to their reality, but is often antagonistic toward their culture and lived experiences. Further, not only will these methods continue to fail students, particularly those from subordinated groups, but they will never lead to the creation of schools as true cultural democratic sites. For this reason, it is imperative that teachers problematize the prevalent notion of "magical" methods and incorporate what Macedo (1993) calls an anti-methods pedagogy, a process through which teachers 1) critically deconstruct the ideology that informs the methods fetish prevalent in education, 2) understand the intimate relationships between methods and the theoretical underpinnings that inform these methods, and 3) evaluate the pedagogical consequences of blindly and uncritically replicating methods without regard to students' subordinate status in terms of cultural, class, gender, and linguistic difference. In short, we need

> an anti-methods pedagogy that would reject the mechanization of intellectualism . . . [and] challenge teachers to work toward reappropriation of endangered dignity and toward reclaiming our humanity. The anti-methods pedagogy adheres to the eloquence of Antonio Machado's poem, "Caminante, no hay camino, se hace camino al andar." (Traveler, there are no roads. The road is created as we walk it [together])." (Macedo, 1993, p. 8)

Notes

1. The term "technical" refers to the positivist tradition in education that presents teaching as a precise and scientific undertaking and teachers as technicians responsible for carrying out (preselected) instructional programs and strategies.
2. "Subordinated" refers to cultural groups that are politically, socially, and economically subordinate in the greater society. While individual members of these groups may not consider themselves subordinate in any manner to the White "mainstream," they nevertheless are members of a greater collective that historically has been perceived and treated as subordinate and inferior by the dominant society. Thus it is not entirely accurate to describe these students as "minority" students, since the term connotes numerical minority rather than the general low status (economic, political, and social) these groups have held and that I think is important to recognize when discussing their historical academic underachievement.
3. "Chicana" refers to a woman of Mexican ancestry who was born and/or reared in the United States.
4. "Mainstream" refers to the U.S. macroculture that has its roots in Western European traditions. More specifically, the major influence on the United States, particularly on its institutions, has been the culture and traditions of White, Anglo-Saxon Protestants (WASP) (Golnick & Chinn, 1986). Although the mainstream group is no longer composed solely of WASPs, members of the middle class have adopted traditionally WASP bodies of knowledge, language use, values, norms, and beliefs.
5. "Political clarity" refers to the process by which individuals achieve a deepening awareness of the sociopolitical and economic realities that shape their lives and their capacity to recreate them. In addition, it refers to the process by which individuals come to better understand possible linkages between macro-level political, economic, and social variables and subordinated groups' academic performance at the micro-level classroom. Thus, it invariably requires linkages between sociocultural structures and schooling.
6. Elizabeth Cohen (1986) explains that in the society at large there are status distinctions made on the basis of social class, ethnic group, and gender. These status distinctions are often reproduced at the classroom level, unless teachers make conscious efforts to prevent this reproduction.
7. For detailed discussions regarding various deficit views of subordinated students over time, see Flores, Cousin, and Diaz, 1991; also see Sue and Padilla, 1986.
8. "Cultural capital" refers to Pierre Bourdieu's concept that certain forms of cultural knowledge are the equivalent of symbolic wealth in that these forms of "high" culture are socially designated as worthy of being sought and possessed. These cultural (and linguistic) knowledge bases and skills are socially inherited and are believed to facilitate academic achievement. See Lamont and Lareau, 1988, for a more in-depth discussion regarding the multiple meanings of cultural capital in the literature.
9. "Think-alouds" refers to an informal assessment procedure where readers verbalize all their thoughts during reading and writing tasks. See J. A. Langer, 1986, for a more in-depth discussion of think-aloud procedures.

References

Anyon, J. (1988). Social class and the hidden curriculum of work. In J. R. Gress (Ed.), *Curriculum: An introduction to the field* (pp. 366–389). Berkeley, CA: McCutchan.

Au, K. H. (1979). Using the experience text relationship method with minority children. *The Reading Teacher, 32,* 677–679.

Au, K. H. (1980). Participant structures in a reading lesson with Hawaiian children: Analysis of a culturally appropriate instructional event. *Anthropology and Educational Quarterly, 11,* 91–115.

Au, K. H., & Mason, J. M. (1983). Cultural congruence in classroom participation structures: Achieving a balance of rights. *Discourse Processes, 6,* 145–168.

Avelar La Salle, R. (1991). *The effect of metacognitive instruction on the transfer of expository comprehension skills: The interlingual and cross-lingual cases.* Unpublished doctoral dissertation, Stanford University.

Bloom, G. M. (1991). *The effects of speech style and skin color on bilingual teaching candidates' and bilingual teachers' attitudes toward Mexican American pupils.* Unpublished doctoral dissertation, Stanford University.

Boykin, A. W. (1983). The academic performance of Afro-American children. In J. T. Spence (Ed.), *Achievement and achievement motives: Psychological and sociological approaches* (pp. 322–369). San Francisco: W. H. Freeman.

Carter, T. P., & Chatfield, M. L. (1986) Effective bilingual schools: Implications for policy and practice. *American Journal of Education, 95,* 200–232.

Cazden, C. (1988). *Classroom discourse: The language of teaching and learning.* Portsmouth, NH: Heinemann.

Chall, J. (1983). *Stages of reading development.* New York: McGraw-Hill.

Chamot, A. U. (1983). How to plan to transfer curriculum from bilingual to mainstream instruction. *Focus, 12.* (A newsletter aviailable from The George Washington University National Clearinghouse for Bilingual Education, 1118 22nd St. NW, Washington, DC 20037)

Cohen, E. G. (1986). *Designing groupwork: Strategies for the heterogeneous classroom.* New York: Teachers College Press.

Cummins, J. (1989). *Empowering minority students.* Sacramento: California Association of Bilingual Education.

Delpit, L. (1986). Skills and other dilemmas of a progressive black educator. *Harvard Educational Review, 56,* 379–385.

Delpit, L. (1988). The silenced dialogue: Power and pedagogy in educating other people's children. *Harvard Educational Review, 58,* 280-298.

Diaz, S., Moll, L. C., & Mehan, H. (1986). Sociocultural resources in instruction: A context-specific approach. In *Beyond language: Social and cultural factors in schooling language minority students* (pp. 187–230). Los Angeles: California State University, Evaluation, Dissemination and Assessment Center.

Edelsky, C., Altwerger, B., & Flores, B. (1991). *Whole language: What's the difference?* Portsmouth, NH: Heinemann.

Erickson, F., & Mohatt, G. (1982). Cultural organization of participation structures in two classrooms of Indian students. In G. Spindler (Ed.), *Doing the ethnography of schooling: Educational anthropology in action* (pp. 133–174). New York: Holt, Rinehart and Winston.

Flores, B. M. (1982). *Language interference or influence: Toward a theory for Hispanic bilingualism.* Unpublished doctoral dissertation, University of Arizona at Tucson.

Flores, B. M. (1993, April). *Interrogating the genesis of the deficit view of Latino children in the educational literature during the 20th century.* Paper presented at the American Educational Research Association Conference, Atlanta.

Flores, B., Cousin, P. T., & Diaz, E. (1991). Critiquing and transforming the deficit myths about learning, language and culture. *Language Arts, 68,* 369-379.

Freire, P. (1985). *The politics of education: Culture, power and liberation.* South Hadley, MA: Bergin & Garvey.

Freire, P. (1987). Letter to North-American teachers. In I. Shor (Ed.), *Freire for the classroom* (pp. 211–214). Portsmouth, NJ: Boynton/Cook.

Freire, P. (1993). *A pedagogy of the city.* New York: Continuum Press.

Freire, P., & Macedo, D. (1987). *Literacy: Reading the word and the world.* South Hadley, MA: Bergin & Garvey.

Gee, J. P. (1989). Literacy, discourse, and linguistics: Introduction. *Journal of Education, 171,* 5–17.

Gibson, M. A., & Ogbu, J. U. (1991). *Minority status and schooling: A comparative study of immigrant and involuntary minorities.* New York: Garland.

Giroux, H. (1985). Introduction. In P. Freire, *The politics of education: Culture, power and liberation* (pp. xi-xxv). South Hadley, MA.: Bergin & Garvey.

Giroux, H. (1992). *Border crossing: Cultural workers and the politics of education.* New York: Routledge.

Giroux, H., & McLaren, P. (1986). Teacher education and the politics of engagement: The case for democratic schooling. *Harvard Educational Review, 56,* 213–238.

Golnick, D. M., & Chinn, P. C. (1986). *Multicultural education in a pluralistic society.* Columbus, OH: Merrill.

Heath, S. B. (1983). *Ways with words.* New York: Cambridge University Press.

Hernandez, J. S. (1991). Assisted performance in reading comprehension strategies with non-English proficient students. *Journal of Educational Issues of Language Minority Students, 8,* 91–112.

Jones, B. F., Palinscar, A. S., Ogle, D. S., & Carr, E. G. (1987). *Strategic teaching and learning: Cognitive instruction in the content areas.* Alexandria, VA: Association for Supervision and Curriculum Development.

Knapp, M. S., & Shields, P. M. (1990). *Better schooling for the children of poverty: Alternatives to conventional wisdom: Vol. 2. Commissioned papers and literature review.* Washington, DC: U.S. Department of Education.

Lamont, M., & Lareau, A. (1988). Cultural capital-allusions, gaps and glissandos in recent theoretical developments. *Sociological Theory, 6,* 153–168.

Langer, J. A. (1986). *Children reading and writing: Structures and strategies.* Norwood, New Jersey: Ablex.

Lareau, A. (1990). *Home advantage: Social class and parental intervention in elementary education.* New York: Falmer Press.

Lucas, T., Henze, R., & Donato, R. (1990). Promoting the success of Latino language-minority students: An exploratory study of six high schools. *Harvard Educational Review, 60,* 315–340.

Macedo, D. (1994). Preface. In P. McLaren & C. Lankshear (Eds.), *Conscientization and resistance* (pp. 1–8). New York: Routledge.

McDermott, R. P. (1977). Social relations as contexts for learning in school. *Harvard Educational Review, 47,* 198–213.

McLeod, B. (Ed.). (in press). *Cultural diversity and second language learning.* Albany: State University of New York Press.

Means, B., & Knapp, M. S. (1991). *Teaching advanced skills to educationally disadvantaged students.* Washington, DC: U.S. Department of Education.

Mehan, H. (1992). Understanding inequality in schools: The contribution of interpretive studies. *Sociology of Education, 65*(1), 1-20.

Menchaca, M., & Valencia, R. (1990). Anglo-Saxon ideologies in the 1920s–1930s: Their impact on the segregation of Mexican students in California. *Anthropology and Education Quarterly, 21,* 222–245.

Moll, L. C. (1986). Writing as communication: Creating learning environments for students. *Theory Into Practice, 25,* 102–110.

Oaks, J. (1986). Tracking, inequality, and the rhetoric of school reform: Why schools don't change. *Journal of Education, 168,* 61–80.

Ogbu, J. (1987). Variability in minority responses to schooling: Nonimmigrants vs. immigrants. In G. Spindler & L. Spindler (Eds.), *Interpretive ethnography of education* (pp. 255–280). Hillsdale, NJ: Lawrence Erlbaum Associates.

O'Malley, J., & Chamot, A. U. (1990). *Learning strategies in second language acquisition.* New York: Cambridge University Press.

Palinscar, A. S., & Brown, A. L. (1984). Reciprocal teaching of comprehension fostering and comprehension-monitoring activities. *Cognition and Instruction, 1*(23), 117–175.

Pérez, B., & Torres-Guzmán, M. E. (1992). *Learning in two worlds: An integrated Spanish/English biliteracy approach.* New York: Longman.

Philips, S. U. (1972). Participant structures and communication competence: Warm Springs children in community and classroom. In C. B. Cazden, V. P. John, & D. Hymes (Eds.), *Functions of language in the classroom* (pp. 370–394). New York: Teachers College Press.

Reyes, M. de la Luz. (1987). Comprehension of content area passages: A study of Spanish/English readers in the third and fourth grade. In S. R. Goldman & H. T. Trueba (Eds.), *Becoming literate in English as a second language* (pp. 107–126). Norwood, NJ: Ablex.

Reyes, M. de la Luz. (1991). A process approach to literacy during dialogue journals and literature logs with second language learners. *Research in the Teaching of English, 25,* 291–313.

Reyes, M. de la Luz. (1992). Challenging venerable assumptions: Literacy instruction for linguistically different students. *Harvard Educational Review, 62,* 427–446.

Sue, S., & Padilla, A. (1986). Ethnic minority issues in the U.S.: Challenges for the educational system. In *Beyond language: Social and cultural factors in schooling language minority students* (pp. 35–72). Los Angeles: California State University, Evaluation, Dissemination and Assessment Center.

Tikunoff, W. (1985). *Applying significant bilingual instructional features in the classroom.* Rosslyn, VA: National Clearinghouse for Bilingual Education.

Tinajero, J. V., & Ada, A. F. (1993). *The power of two languages: Literacy and biliteracy for Spanish-speaking students.* New York: Macmillan/McGraw-Hill.

Trueba, H. T. (1989). Sociocultural integration of minorities and minority school achievement. In *Raising silent voices: Educating the linguistic minorities for the 21st century* (pp. 1–27). New York: Newbury House.

U. S. Commission on Civil Rights. (1973). *Teachers and students: Report V. Mexican-American study: Differences in teacher interaction with Mexican-American and Anglo students.* Washington, DC: Government Printing Office.

Valencia, R. (1986, November 25). *Minority academic underachievement: Conceptual and theoretical considerations for understanding the achievement problems of Chicano students.* Paper presented to the Chicano Faculty Seminar, Stanford University.

Valencia, R. (1991). *Chicano school failure and success: Research and policy agendas for the 1990s.* New York: Falmer Press.

Villegas, A. M. (1988). School failure and cultural mismatch: Another view. *Urban Review, 20,* 253–265.

Villegas, A. M. (1991). *Culturally responsive pedagogy for the 1990s and beyond.* Paper prepared for the Educational Testing Service, Princeton, NJ.

Vogt, L. A., Jordan, C., & Tharp, R. G. (1987). Explaining school failure, producing school success: Two cases. *Anthropology & Education Quarterly, 18,* 276–286.

Walker, C. L. (1987). Hispanic achievement: Old views and new perspectives. In H. T. Trueba (Ed.), *Success or failure: Learning and the language minority student* (pp. 15–32). New York: Newbury House.

Webb, L. C. (1987). *Raising achievement among minority students.* Arlington, VA: American Associates of School Administrators.

Winfield, L. F. (1986). Teachers beliefs toward academically at risk students in inner urban schools. *Urban Review, 18,* 253–267.

Zamel, V. (1982). Writing: The process of discovering meaning. *TESOL Quarterly, 16,* 195–209.

Violence, Nonviolence, and the Lessons of History: Project HIP-HOP Journeys South

NANCY UHLAR MURRAY
MARCO GARRIDO

> History, despite its wrenching pain,
> Cannot be unlived, but if faced
> With courage, need not be lived again.
>
> — Maya Angelou, *On the Pulse of Morning*[1]

In July 1994, fourteen students from the Boston area traveled with five educators to the South to visit key sites of the civil rights movement of the 1950s and 1960s, and to learn about the power of nonviolence from people who were often teenagers themselves when they risked their lives and filled the jails on their quest for civil rights.

The students had been chosen to take part in the second summer tour of Project HIP-HOP (Highways into the Past: History, Organizing and Power), a "rolling classroom" devised by the Bill of Rights Education Project, which I direct, and the Massachusetts Student Alliance Against Racism and Violence, directed by Pam Ellis. Project HIP-HOP grew out of a "Youth Against Racism" weekend retreat that the Bill of Rights Education Project held in October 1992 for forty-five high school students from twenty-two schools, half urban, and half suburban and rural.[2] The retreat had been requested by students who were searching for ways to make their voices heard in the aftermath of the acquittal of the police officers who beat Rodney King. It was enormously encouraging in what it revealed about young people's commitment to justice and their willingness to tackle social problems and to listen to each other.

During that weekend retreat, the staff discovered that they shared an admiration for the philosophy and practice of Myles Horton's Highlander Folk School in eastern Tennessee.[3] For sixty years, people of different races had been gathering at the Highlander to share and draw authority from their own experiences and to find ways to participate together in the creation of a more democratic society. Rosa Parks, while executive secretary of the NAACP in Montgomery, Alabama, was sent to a Highlander workshop by the Alabama NAACP president. Shortly thereafter she made the individual and historic decision not to move from her seat on a Montgomery bus. She later spoke of the strength that first Highlander workshop had given her "to persevere in my work for freedom, not just for blacks, but for all oppressed people."[4]

The Highlander has opened its doors to a range of movement activists, including Dr. Martin Luther King Jr., who was later pictured on Southern billboards attending a "Communist training school."[5] It also has served as the organizing base for the Citizenship Schools that Septima Clark established in several Southern states to train people to read so they could register to vote. Drawing further inspiration from *Eyes on the Prize*, and from the educational vision of movement veteran and theology professor Vincent Harding, we resolved to visit the Highlander as part of an educational tour of the South during the summer of 1993.[6] Seven high school students, including several who participated in the planning process, and four educators participated in this first Project HIP-HOP tour.

Expanding the Dialogue about Violence and Racism

In his lyrical book, *Hope and History: Why We Must Share the Story of the Movement*, Vincent Harding asks what the movement for freedom in the 1950s and 1960s means now "for the gun-filled streets of Dorchester, of Lawndale, of L.A.?"[7]

> Something tells us that one of the deep wounds of the life of the streets . . . is that young people have been separated from both their past and their future, leaving a vast and aching void, often to be filled with nothing more than the most destructive values of society. *Eyes on the Prize* opens a way for such young people to re-enter the humanizing flow of history, to consider the possibility that there is purpose and meaning for their lives far beyond the terror and temptations of their immediate situation.[8]

Students, he contends, can be put in touch with the best in themselves by learning about the lives of those who have created "a powerful heritage, one filled with questions for reflection, discussion, and action. It is a heritage each new generation needs to know, perhaps to claim as a source of power, as a path toward the discovery of its own largest possibilities."[9]

However, it often takes more than showing *Eyes on the Prize* to have the lessons of the series come alive in the classroom. Many young people today, overwhelmed by a sense of being powerless and futureless, may react initially to what Harding calls America's "pro-democracy movement" with anger, cynicism, and even desperation, rather than hope.[10] In schools where the institution of slavery and the resistance to it is "covered" in a lesson or two, and the civil rights movement makes an appearance mainly around the time of Martin Luther King Jr.'s birthday, it is hardly surprising that students feel either incredulous or lied to when they encounter the all-pervasive nature of racism in the United States in the 1950s and 1960s. Many students become enraged when they find out about the level of officially sanctioned violence that sustained an American apartheid. To those adolescents honing their survival skills in today's urban war zones, the techniques of nonviolent civil disobedience depicted in *Eyes on the Prize* seem all but incomprehensible. These young people are often less touched by the movement's triumphs than by a sense of its unfinished business. At a summer institute for teachers on the theme of racism and how to fight it, organized by the Bill of Rights Education Project in August 1993, participants shared with Harding their concerns about the rage that was "a constant undercurrent" when they showed segments of *Eyes on the Prize* to their students.[11] A few teachers said they feared that the series could lead directly to violence, since some of their African American students talked bitterly about the need for "revenge" after viewing one of the episodes.

Young people of color suspect they are not getting the real story in schools, and are well aware that past injustices have not entirely been laid to rest. After a conference on violence held by the Bill of Rights Education Project for 350 students on April 5, 1994, the *Boston Globe* reporter who was present at the event wrote that no one could "stop the teenagers from returning to a bitter, haunting matter the youths say adults try to avoid: the role institutional racism plays in the escalating violence among young people."[12]

This "haunting matter" has been a constant refrain in the dozen conferences and several smaller workshops and retreats the Bill of Rights Education Project has held for students over the past six years. No matter what the theme — be it censorship or teen curfews, "stop and search" policing or dress codes in schools — students inevitably steer the discussion to the issues of racism, intolerance, and violence. African American and Latino students invariably relate these problems to a lack of "respect." They express a deep longing to be treated justly, and to know they count for something in school and in society. Students have frequently said how much they appreciate the opportunity offered by our forums to talk openly about these issues — a chance they rarely get in their daily lives.[13]

Teachers have generally lacked the support, the confidence, the resources, or the incentive to discuss "institutional racism" — a phrase that must be as rare in the classroom as in the *Boston Globe*.[14] School authorities for the most part have preferred the "quick fix" of ready-made violence prevention programs to the long-haul effort of listening to their students on a day-to-day basis, and embarking with them on an exploration of the root causes of the violence engulfing so many young lives. In a nation founded on the extermination and dispossession of the native inhabitants and the brutal enslavement of African peoples, it is remarkable that "violence" is so often talked about today as if it were unique to this generation of urban youth, a product of their defective families and guns-and-drugs culture, and virtually unknown in earlier eras.[15]

This largely ahistorical outlook serves neither students nor the country and its future. Schools seem fearful of controversy, regardless of its educational potential. Young people exposed only to the sanitized history offered by textbooks have little understanding of why things are the way they are. They are seldom exposed to the sort of questions that would help them make sense of the world around them and that could be the subjects of stimulating educational debates.

Did the civil rights movement make the playing field level in racial terms? Where has our society been heading since the Kerner Commission more than a quarter century ago condemned ghetto poverty as the root cause of the burning of the cities?[16] Are growing economic inequalities reversible, or simply part of the natural order? What did Martin Luther King Jr. mean when he reflected during a November 1966 staff retreat on the gains of the civil rights movement, stating: "The changes that came about during this period were at best surface changes; they were not really substantive changes. . . . The roots of racism are very deep in America; our society is still structured on the basis of racism"?[17] What, if any, is the historical basis for his statement? Are there still "substantive changes" to be made before we can say that the battle against racism has been won?

Those who feel that questions like these have no place in the classroom because they could inflame wounds and deepen divisions might agree with members of the Mississippi state textbook committee who rejected a new textbook in 1974 out of fear that it would "cause bad feeling between black and white students."[18] But as Cornel West argues in his book *Race Matters,* "our truncated public discussions of race suppress the best of who and what we are as a people because they fail to confront the complexity of the issue in a candid and critical manner."[19] Tackling these issues head-on in schools and ending the silence or evasiveness that has so often surrounded the issue of race can be an effective means of bringing back into the learning process young people who are currently convinced that school has nothing worthwhile to teach them.[20]

We can only know the best of who we are and what we are capable of as a people if we look at the whole picture. This means examining our society's flaws and tracing their roots back into history. Historian John Hope Franklin has written eloquently of the importance of facing up to history in his book, *The Color Line: Legacy for the Twenty-First Century:*

> Perhaps the very first thing we need to do as a nation and as individual members of society is to confront our past, and see it for what it is. It is a past that is filled with some of the ugliest possible examples of racial brutality and degradation in human history. We need to recognize it for what it was and is and not explain it away, excuse it, or justify it. Having done that, we should then make a good-faith effort to turn our history around so that we can see it in

front of us, so that we can avoid doing what we have done for so long. . . . Then, we need to do everything possible to emphasize the positive qualities that all of us have, qualities which we have never utilized to the fullest, but which we must utilize if we are to solve the problem of the color line in the twenty-first century.[21]

Turning Our History Around

Many young people today, who have little grasp of where they have come from, where we as a nation have been, and what we have been able to achieve, appear bereft of a vision for the future of our country. Unlike the thousands of children and young adults who, in the 1960s, marched and sat in at lunch counters and spearheaded drives for voter registration, large numbers of students today have little notion of how they can participate in the creation of a United States of America that at last lives up to its democratic promise — or, indeed, of why they should bother.

Vincent Harding believes that the civil rights movement — once the catalyst for the whole "rights revolution" galvanizing women, gays and lesbians, the disabled, and other groups to demand full participation in the body politic — retains its capacity to energize a generation:

> I have seen students of every kind literally moved to tears and to new questions, opened to excitement and new personal resolves, when they have been creatively exposed to this dramatic story of human beings risking all to renew and transform their lives and their communities. Thus the exciting struggle for democracy has come alive for them. They have been able to imagine what it was like not long ago when American citizens, often led by young people, took their rights and responsibilities so seriously that they, like the white Founders of 1776, were prepared to risk their lives, their fortunes, and their sacred honor to create a more just, a more democratic, nation. These were the new founders of the emerging multiracial American nation for the twenty-first century, and they may help our students understand the meaning of the continuing creation of American democracy.[22]

The Bill of Rights Education Project embarked on Project HIP-HOP in anticipation that young people would be opened to the excitement and new personal resolves described by Harding. They would then be in a position to participate in a process that could eventually, in John Hope Franklin's words, begin to "turn our history around." Our 1993 pilot tour generated considerable interest. In the South we were frequently trailed by TV cameras. Producers of programs based in southern African American communities hoped that interviews with young northerners who had come so far to talk with movement veterans would awaken their own youth to a history almost entirely ignored in their schools.[23] We also had enthusiastic audiences in Massachusetts, where participants took slide shows into classrooms and community centers and addressed teachers at workshops and at our 1993 summer institute.

The 1993 tour has certainly had a positive impact on the lives of the participants. Marc Germain, a Randolph, Massachusetts, high school student, said in an interview shortly after his return, "It made me realize that young people can empower themselves to do anything. It gave me hope for the future."[24] Kim Howard, who went on the HIP-HOP trip after completing her final year at Boston Latin School, told the *Boston Globe*, "The trip couldn't have come at a better time for me. I'm about to go off to college, and there is no way I am not going to work my hardest, do my best, after seeing what people went through so I could be where I am today."[25] One fifteen-year-old HIP-HOP participant resolved to break away from his gang, while another, who had always regarded herself as a "non-joiner," subsequently became thoroughly involved in community service activities. Her mother described the trip's impact on her daughter:

> The Project HIP-HOP teens learned lessons that no history book can teach. They came to understand that ordinary people in ordinary places have the power to transform society. For my child, the Project HIP-HOP experience was not simply an intellectual revelation. She has become an activist in her school community on issues relating to racism, sexism and homophobia. Before Project HIP-HOP, this simply would not have been possible.[26]

Part of Project HIP-HOP's power to transform lies in its physical and emotional intensity, attributes it shares with certain Outward Bound programs.[27] The van journeys are long and hard, meals are unpredictable, and sleeping arrangements, often rugged, are sometimes an adventure in themselves. We camped in tents and slept on the floors of homes and community centers. We were permitted to spend the night inside the Lorraine Motel, now the National Civil Rights Museum in Memphis, and we slept in college dormitories and trailers. Some of our students had never been out of New England. Many had never camped before or seen a farm. Most had rarely strayed from an interstate highway. Whether it was going down a coal mine in southern West Virginia, or spending time among the descendants of the original African American inhabitants on an island off the coast of Georgia, students and adults alike were presented every day with new situations, and their horizons were constantly expanded.

Student participants in Project HIP-HOP's pilot year helped interview and select the young people for the 1994 trip. The applicants had already submitted answers in written form or on audiotape to questions such as: What would you like to be doing in ten years' time? How would you describe racism today? What are the similarities and differences between today's racism and that of the 1950s and 1960s? They were also asked to identify the individual(s) whom they admire in public life today, and explain why.

We selected some students who had already seen Henry Hampton's award-winning *Eyes on the Prize* series about the civil rights movement and wanted to learn more, and chose others who were already involved in anti-racism work or showed promise as student organizers. But we were also on the lookout for other forms of motivation. We interviewed one young woman of working-class background who intends to be the first person in her family to graduate from high school. She had read about Project HIP-HOP in a newspaper article and found her way to us without the encouragement of a teacher or other adult. Possessing a strong sense that the world was not the way it should be, and the desire to understand why her family was, as she put it, "so racist," she was among those selected for the 1994 tour. We also decided to offer places to young men who had been immersed in the life of the streets, and were in the process of turning their lives around.

As co-organizers of the program, Pam Ellis and I were seeking to bring together an ethnically diverse group of young people of widely varying backgrounds and experiences who would learn from each other during the grueling five thousand mile trip. All of the students were aged fifteen to seventeen and from the greater Boston area. They were of African American, European American, Latino, Filipino, Haitian, Indian, and Native American heritage, and represented a broad spectrum in economic class. Some of the participants lived in public housing projects; two had no fixed address. Most attended public schools, two went to private schools, one was in the METCO program, and two had dropped out of high school.[28] Four participants were peer leaders in anti-gang violence prevention programs, and one was the student head of her school's conflict resolution program.

Our aim was to connect these students with a history of social transformation brought about not long ago by young people; to bring them into contact with students in the South who are grappling today with issues of racism, violence, and stunted aspirations; and to provide them with the opportunity and skills to reach out to their peers and to share what they learn on the trip in schools and community centers around Boston and the Commonwealth during the 1994–1995 academic year.

Discussion during our seventeen days on the road in July 1994 was framed by the tension between the rhetoric and reality of democracy in the United States. We began our explorations at Philadelphia's Independence Hall, where we viewed the Liberty Bell, and then met with Ramona Africa, the only adult member of the MOVE commune to survive when the Philadelphia police, in a stunning example of state-sponsored violence, dropped a bomb from a helicopter on the commune's house in May 1985.[29] The following day we traveled to Harper's Ferry, where, a year after drawing up plans for a biracial republic and a new Constitution, John Brown resorted to violence to strike what he hoped would be a revolutionary blow against the slave system.

There was no such redemptive purpose behind the violence we confronted as we journeyed into the history of our own century; for example, in the museum built on the site of Martin Luther King Jr.'s assassination in Memphis; or in another Philadelphia, this one in Mississippi, where three civil rights workers were abducted and murdered thirty years ago. Near the site of the memorial erected in their honor, we met under an old oak tree with ninety-eight-year-old Caesar Moore, born in the year of *Plessy v. Ferguson,* who talked to us about his life and about ongoing Klan activity in the area.[30] He challenged us always to be vigorous in the fight against racism. In the Mississippi Delta town of Mound Bayou, founded by African Americans in 1887, we were touched by the spirit of the young people who presented a pageant for us about the creation of their town by former slaves seeking the promise of freedom. We learned about the price young people paid for freedom at the Civil Rights Institute in Birmingham, Alabama, which is adjacent to the Sixteenth Street Baptist Church, where four young girls died in a bombing, and we visited the Kelly Ingram Park, where children were attacked by "Bull" Connor's dogs and fire hoses in 1963 and imprisoned by the thousands.[31] We heard about native people's struggles in Pembroke County, North Carolina, where Lumbees, a Native American tribe that constituted a majority of the population, took it upon themselves to chase away the Ku Klux Klan in the 1950s and 1960s. We literally put ourselves in the footsteps of the demonstrators who crossed the Edmund Pettus Bridge in Selma, Alabama, in March 1965 and were viciously beaten as they tried to march to the state capital of Montgomery to demand the right to vote.

As we learned more about the role that racism has played in our history and continues to play today, the students kept up a dialogue with each other about their own encounters with racism and violence. In the words of *New York Times* journalist Sara Rimer, who accompanied the group for three days, Project HIP-HOP "is a journey not only into the past, but also through their own lives."[32]

The more we talked with young people in the South about the civil rights movement's unfinished business and the problems they are confronting today, the more our group began to find connections between their own situation in Massachusetts and settings as different as rural Mississippi and New Orleans' oldest public housing project, where teenagers working at the Kuji Center met with us after staging a sit-in at the city hall to protest the cutting of funds for their work against violence and teen pregnancy.[33]

The notion of seeking social and political change through nonviolent means did not strike an immediate chord with all Project HIP-HOP participants. At the Highlander Center in eastern Tennessee, we met with students from around the South to talk about violence in communities, discussing, for example, who benefits and who loses by violent actions. We also took part in a workshop on the techniques of nonviolence. Many in our group found it difficult to understand how people could sit passively at lunch counters and endure insults and physical attacks. But as the trip continued, the message driven home by movement veterans was that under the circumstances that prevailed in the 1950s and 1960s, nonviolence was not so much a choice as a necessity. White supremacists, after all, had superior fire power, and if protestors had retaliated in self-defense, they would have attracted neither the mass support nor the national sympathy essential to overcome Jim Crow.[34] And as the members of our group grew closer to each other, we personally glimpsed the kind of unity and shared aspirations that made nonviolent protest possible. Musing about the ethnic and economic barriers that generally separate people today, one young woman commented that nonviolence was not outdated, and could still be an effective tool if we could just get people to work for a common end and respect each other.

But what common end could there be under today's complex conditions, given the absence of a single target as compelling as Jim Crow segregation? This is a question the HIP-HOP youth, now that they have begun to take the measure of their country's problems, will grapple with during our future meetings and in their chosen fields of social activism. We know it will not be easy to nurture their new consciousness under the conditions some of them endure, including all the tensions of inner-city street life and homelessness. But they seem determined to continue the dialogue already begun, and to make sure it includes many different voices. In the words of fifteen-year-old Arnold Chamanlal from Boston, Massachusetts, a sophomore at Jeremiah E. Burke High School, "This trip made a lot of people come together. We were all different races, but on this trip we were one. It worked."[35]

Arnold, a former gang member who now works with the Boston Violence Prevention Program, was the poet of our group. Here is how he sees the challenge facing his generation:

> Right now I'm looking at two strange hands
> Could be a woman could be a man's
> Everybody has something deep in their soul
> Their own little story to be told.
> Stories about their life and their past
> Will come out at last
> One man fighting for freedom
> Is better than a king's whole kingdom.
> We fight for what's right
> To put our children's future in sight
> The hands fight to be free
> One day we all shall see
> That hate is destroying the world.
> If that happens there will be no more stories to be told.
> We must come together and do what's good not what's bad
> And our parents will be glad.
> My father will say I'm truly his son
> I did what's right not what's wrong
> And for that I will be a man, my soul will be strong.
> And with the blood in my veins
> I will defend my home not go insane.
> For my hands are strong
> and I promise I'll do what's right
> And not what's wrong.

Copyright © 1995 by Arnold Chamanlal. Used with permission.

The Next Steps

By the end of February 1995, the students of Project HIP-HOP 1994 had shown slides of their trip and made presentations in classes and assemblies to over two thousand suburban and urban high school students, at universities, and to afterschool groups in Boston. They gave the address at the City of Quincy (Massachusetts) Martin Luther King Jr. Day Breakfast on January 16, 1995, and they have a full schedule of commitments throughout the spring, including speaking at the American Civil Liberties Union Biennial Conference and the National Coalition of Education Activists Conference.

Their message is essentially one of hope, of new possibilities. When asked what the trip meant to her personally, a student who was born in Puerto Rico told young people in a largely Latino neighborhood that she used to feel as if she didn't belong in the United States. Now she feels as if the movement was speaking for her, too, and that U.S. history is her history. Another student said that before the trip he never thought he would like or trust a White person, but now the White students from Project HIP-HOP are his close friends, and he realizes how wrong it is to think in simple racial terms. A fifteen-year-old from Boston, who became involved in a voter registration drive before an election, tells her high school and college audiences that people in the movement paid too heavy a price for them to say they can't be bothered registering for the polls. A former member of a Latino gang is spreading the message that Latinos and African Americans, turf rivals in Roxbury, Massachusetts, have far too much in common to be fighting each other.

As they reflect on their experiences, speak publicly, and carry out research for our *Racism, Rights and History* curriculum on the role of young people in the movement, the youth of Project HIP-HOP are continuing to grow in ways that are exciting to witness. Our challenge is to find ways to sustain the excitement and spirit engendered by the trip, and to enable HIP-HOP participants to convey what they learned to their peers in a way that will begin the process of turning our history around.

The evaluations we have received about the impact of Project HIP-HOP presentations indicate that the program can be a powerful motivation to both learning and social involvement. It is perhaps not surprising that Project HIP-HOP has struck a real chord in Boston schools, where the majority of students are African American and Latino. We are now discovering the important role that the program can play in surburban settings, including those where there are very few students of color.

After speaking to classes at a school outside Boston where there had recently been open conflicts between the resident students and students in the METCO program, we have been invited to be part of a school-wide assembly that organizers hope will lead to frank exchanges about inter-racial problems in the school. Beginning this dialogue with a student-led look at this nation's record of positive social change and the "unfinished business" of the movement seems to be a way of getting a discussion going that might otherwise never move beyond the threshold of personal prejudices and painful feelings.

As exciting as many of Project Hip-Hop's school visits have been, we still are aware of how much more needs to be done if the program is to realize its transforming potential. We recognize the need to prepare future HIP-HOP participants more fully for the history they encounter on trips, so that they better understand the significance of what they are hearing and seeing, and are in a position to ask searching questions. We would also like them to have the opportunity for more sustained dialogue with their peers.

These problems could be overcome if we succeed in arranging for Project HIP-HOP to be considered a form of community service, with student participants getting academic credit for the work they do with other schools. We are also laying the groundwork for participants to serve as student teachers who would facilitate a sequence of lessons in particular schools. Eventually, we would like them to be able to teach those parts of our forthcoming curriculum relating to the movement and to the role of young people as agents of social change, which two Project HIP-HOP students are currently helping to create.

Project HIP-HOP needs a consistent source of funding if it is to succeed in putting young people in touch with what Vincent Harding calls the "powerful heritage" of the movement, and to motivate them to work to develop a nation that at last lives up to the promise of its rhetoric and founding ideals. Assuming the resources are available, I am encouraged to imagine a future in which representatives from each year's HIP-HOP tour come together in annual or biennial meetings. These energizing reunions would enable participants to draw strength from each other and give us the opportunity to observe, over a period of several years, what a critical mass of young people who share a common set of potentially transforming experiences can achieve.

We want to continue to build an understanding of the way racism has operated across time and across cultures. We believe the best way to do this is to put students in touch with people who have worked to transform U.S. society. We plan to continue to bring young people together with movement veterans, including those who live locally, and others who have stories to tell about their struggles to make "liberty and justice for all" more than a pious hope. We may in fact find it is not essential to travel five thousand miles to experience what one 1994 HIP-HOP participant described as "the type of 'hands-on' and 'ears-on' learning" that "surpasses anything read in a history book."

Nevertheless, the journey through the South, which is also a journey into history, into our inner beings, and through our own lives, has a very special power. One of the most inspiring dimensions of Project HIP-HOP was that wherever we went we found people who had played a role in the movement, many as teenagers or even younger. We met people on the streets of Mound Bayou, Mississippi, who had marched and sung with Fannie Lou Hamer.[36] We were welcomed into homes and slept on floors. This gave history an immediacy that allowed our young people to feel part of things, and made it seem that the torch was being passed.

Before we turned northward again, we paused at the Civil Rights Memorial in Montgomery, Alabama, to remember the movement's triumphs and those who had died in the struggle. As we leaned our heads against a wall streaming with water, Philippines-born Marco Garrido, now a senior at Boston College High School, summed up the moment for us: "I feel we have just been baptized by the waters of freedom."

Project HIP-HOP Lifts the Spirit and Teaches Lessons

The second part of this article was written by Marco Garrido. His reflections on the tour are based on his journal. Photographs by James Blackwell.

There is a place in the Lorraine Motel, now the National Civil Rights Museum, that has more than its usual share of ghosts. Not far from where we slept, the left side of the second floor pinches off into an enclosure. A balcony juts out. Martin Luther King Jr., looking out, was shot here. The bullet blew his necktie to pieces and left a bloodstain on the concrete. Just before the balcony, the rooms King had used are on display. The beds are unmade, the breakfast half-eaten, and the coffee seems stale from waiting. A slow lament, sung by Gospel singer Mahalia Jackson, wafts around us. And we stare, noses up to the thin glass divider, out at the still blood-stained balcony.

The Civil Rights Monument in Montgomery, Alabama, has a quiet elegance. The names are carved in the deep, dark granite. The smooth stone slab is circular, and the names are beneath the surface, under a stream of water. The names of the heroes, the martyrs, the leaders, the people, the victims. An upright slab stands adjoining, and beneath a curtain of water the stone's inscription reads, "Until Justice Rolls Down Like Waters and Righteousness Like a Mighty Stream." We wet our fingers, tracing the names in the granite, and we wet our heads as the Alabama sun beats down, letting the flowing water cool us.

The Highlander Center nestled in the misty Tennessee hills — a place where social activists come to listen, learn, regroup, feel empowered — hosts us as it once did Martin Luther King Jr. and Rosa Parks. We are gathered together, each hand clasped by another; and we sing "We Shall Overcome," and our voices lift our spirits. There is a warm intimacy radiating from the hardwood floor, the subdued light reflected in each of our faces, half shadowed, and in the air pregnant with ideas.

In Mound Bayou, Mississippi, at the Founder's Day Pageant, the children, rich in spirit, very aware of their African heritage, take on the guise of the

Luis Rodriguez and Sarah Wedge look at late-nineteenth-century KKK gear at the National Civil Rights Museum, located in the Lorraine Motel, Memphis, Tennessee. Photo by James Blackwell.

ghosts of the town founders. The small dark face bobbed a bit. His eyes swept the pews. We, his audience, sat expectant. Then he began. It turned out he was a ghost. Isaiah Montgomery, he said his name was. In 1887, he and his cousin settled this African American-owned town, Mound Bayou. After Isaiah, the other townspeople spoke to us, recounted their history in sweet voices. All were over a hundred years old. Folk of iron determination, they built Mound Bayou shortly after the Civil War. They knew that obstacles lay ahead. But as a community they would overcome. And the ghosts quite clearly expressed to us, through the words of Maya Angelou, Langston Hughes, and N'Kosi Sikelela Africa, a tireless and exuberant spirit.

I can feel the mercilessness of the Selma sun as we walk across the Edmund Pettus Bridge, where only a few decades before civil rights activists were viciously beaten, pummelled by water, sticks, fists, as they tried to march where we now march.

I still see the crack on the back of the Bell of Liberty.

The experiences are vivid, branded into my memory. Project HIP-HOP has furnished us, an interracial group of Boston area students, with intense experiences that continue to enrich us. Our meetings aptly began in Philadelphia, where the hallowed specters of the Founding Fathers, who tried to hammer out a constitution securing liberty, skirted about Independence Hall. Across from the Hall, the Liberty Bell is silent. In the days that followed, as the accent thickened, Boston became a shrinking speck in the rear-view window. Here was a different environment, one ripe with lessons. We had only to open our ears to the voices of the activist, the farmer, the drugstore clerk, the little boy, the corpse, the poetry of the fields, hills, and highway.

The lessons were garnered like pearls for us who were combing the shore.

A Walk Through St. Thomas

The youths of Kujichagulia marched into the Kuji Center. Kujichagulia, "self-determination" in Ki-Swahili, is a youth project based near St. Thomas, one of the oldest federal housing projects in the country, which is located in New Orleans, Louisiana. The youths had marched on the New Orleans City Hall, demanding further funding for youth summer employment programs. We, the HIP-HOPers, watched them stream in. Triumphant smiles bedecked each face.

The youths spoke in iron tones about their protest: "The political system needs a push now and again. So we push." Kujichagulia celebrated in a joyful uproar. The dancers danced traditional African dances furiously, the rappers rapped the raps of St. Thomas with spirit, and the rest of us talked about life. "So what y'all doin' in Bawhston?" they asked. "Well, tell us what you're doing here," we countered. We, the HIP-HOPers, and they, the youth of Kujichagulia, gathered in a circle. What was life like anyway? Some in our group and all in theirs spoke in angry, sad, determined, tones of similar things: money, drugs, gangs, and guns. I listened and tried to understand the lives they spoke of.

Ninety-eight-year-old Caesar Moore in Philadelphia, Mississippi, near the site where three civil rights workers were murdered in 1964. Photo by James Blackwell.

Heedful of the warnings of the Kuji Center youth, I paced on the pavement and looked down at St. Thomas. A block from where I wavered lay the housing project, supposedly infested with drugs, gangs, and guns. To go or not to go. Curiosity compelled me. I went.

As I walked down, I fastened a red bandanna about my head. I slipped on shades and unstrapped my watch, pocketing it. This isn't enough, I thought. I surveyed my clothes: my tan, khaki shorts, grass-green New Orleans "We be jazzin'" tourist t-shirt, my clean white socks snug in black Nike shoes. It wasn't enough.

> Heart rages in a palpitating frenzy
> Senses on end like a frightened cat
> Every engine hum whips my head back.
> It is mere silliness, yes?
> These phantom images thumbing their noses at me.
> Or stupidity?
> The headlines lay before me.

A church stood beside St. Thomas. Its steeples stretched high, and saints looked down kindly from elegantly carved niches. This seems out of place, I thought. On the towering doors, ladders leaned. Men stood upon them and installed heavy iron rings. I found myself wondering, was this church full on Sundays?

The boundary was clearly marked. A "No Trespassing" sign stared sternly down from the side of one building. I paused. Here was a chance to turn back. The sign certainly couldn't be disobeyed. Such a rationalization was so transparent that I knew if I didn't continue on, this instance of weakness would linger uncomfortably in my memory. I was also goaded on by pride: I am fearless, adventurous, open to experience. Oh, yes I am. Such an assertion, based on petty experiences, needed to be challenged. If I retreated, my perception of myself would be exposed for the smoke that it was. I knew I had to continue.

I entered St. Thomas. There was a geometry in the arrangement: similar houses stood on square plots; each plot was evenly spaced from the other, and the rows of plots stretched on. Yet a prickly vibrance defied the gray geometry. Life was lived in this place. The houses had red roofs. Green iron railings snaked from a tan wood porch to a balcony overhang. On the balcony lay a mess of discarded furniture; chairs were set for observation and coffee, and little legs hung down. The kids grasped the green bars with little hands, stuck little faces between their hands, and looked at me with big eyes. On a porch, grandmothers rocked in rocking chairs, a periodic creak weaving into the comfortable hum of life. Tired middle-aged women sat on the steps, their heads heavy in their hands. And by their bare feet, little kids played: cards, pattycake, jacks, tag, hide-and-seek.

As I walked on, those on their porches eyed me warily. I felt sorely out of place. I held my head high. My cheeks pricked with humiliated discomfort. Their eyes stung. An elderly woman rose from her rocking chair, leaned on the porch railing, and timidly asked: "Excuse me, sir. Are you looking for someone?" I, not looking at her, mumbled "Just looking" and walked on. I heard the footsteps of her eyes behind me.

The puddles on the pavement telegraphed the swish of footsteps. Deep in my belly's pit, a big man with a megaphone yelled at me: turn back, turn around, turn away! My senses pricked up. There was significance in everything: a tree's limbs gnarled upward towards the sky; the slap of the jump-rope tapped the time; a Black youth walked past me. As he approached, a climax built. When he lined up with me, he gelled with a media image. And when he passed, relief.

There I stood, awash in pretense. I, who had thought myself free of racist stereotypes, succumbed to paranoia each time a Black youth passed. The big man with the megaphone drowned out the tiny voice of sense. Here, in St. Thomas, I was jelly.

In indignation, I walked on.

On that day, I learned this: it takes time to develop a strong and free mind. That small voice of reason needs to be consciously nurtured, so it cannot be so easily obliterated by the man with the megaphone. It'll take plenty of time, and plenty of practice. And so, I walked on.

A street scene in Jackson, Mississippi. Photo by James Blackwell.

Some Things Thought About

My lack of direct experience with urban life puts me in somewhat of an observer position. There were a few people on the HIP-HOP tour who lived in an inner city deformed by gang life, drug-trading, guns. The time spent travelling in the vans was long, and the conversations rich. The journey, looked at from a different angle, can be said to have taken place entirely within the vans, within the community, within the individual, and in the sharing of ourselves.

I have been amply exposed to the representations set forth by the media and, as I jarringly learned walking through St. Thomas, representation and reality are often at odds. These images have a sinister way of weaving into the subconscious, and then surfacing when in an environment that has been represented before it has been experienced. Some may profess to enlightenment, but when thrust into a situation challenging this claim, instinct founded on stereotypes, prejudices, often upstages rationality. What then is there to do? Experience everything? (I wish, but not likely.) Profound thought? (A pipe dream.) More likely it is a mix of both: experience, reflection on experience and reflection on ideas, and the experience of others. Then something of a collective experience is gathered, the essence of human wisdom. And so I set to learn.

And as I learned, I had to remind myself that what was being shared with me was real, was lived. I had been so inundated by media images of what life was supposed to be. But life, it seemed, was more elusive than that. My friends spoke of street fights, car break-ins, respect, honor, a drive to rise beyond circumstances, dreams, how to hold a gun to minimize backlash, bullet-wounds, beauty, gang stand-offs, raunchy jokes, perseverance, and love. No, the sense of what I possessed, and what I had taken for granted, did not wash over me as a wave does; instead, I admired these friends, for they seemed to be in the midst of life, a life I had heard about but which for me always seemed to be elsewhere.

It did strike me that my life seemed to progress upon a structure, upward like a leaning ladder: grade school, high school, college, and then . . . life? But with my friends, the "and then . . ." came sooner and the ellipses stretched on, punctuated by a very definite question mark. Should I drop out of high school, sell drugs and strip cars — I need the money, and besides, how will algebra help me get respect, be hip, be feared, be loved? And I'm tired of dodging the kids who have it in for me, uncertain whether I'll limp home, hand over my puffed eye; I need a gun, but only for protection.

I have reflected upon the sense of thick uncertainty, where individual efforts and actions are not judged by some absolute, for everything now seems relative — where killing's fine if you believe you're justified; where nihilism seems to be the life philosophy; where conscience, with a sweeping gesture, may now be proclaimed dead; where, as Kurt Cobain screamed it, "all in all is all we are."[37] But then I think about how wrong I am when my thoughts run like that. The inner city may be seen in such a bleak light, but then the observer will not have seen it all. As I listened to my friends, I also learned about love, tolerance, responsibility, innocence, wonder, kindness, magnanimity . . . humanity. I respect these friends unreservedly, and what I admire them for most is their lovely humanity.

Where the Movement Left Off

I remember clearly one morning at an Alabama campsite when, while leaning upon a buzzing washing machine, a middle-aged White woman said, her index finger rising to us, "I pity young people today. They are taught by history to hate." She continued, evidently backed by a feeling of self-righteousness, to say that the movement had unnecessarily angered Black people, stirring them to rail against phantom injustices. Earlier in the morning she had encountered a staff member on our trip, and when told that we comprised a civil rights history tour, she reportedly countered: "Now let me tell you about civil rights." And she did. She said that the movement bred hate; that during pre-movement days, Blacks were content enough. As she spoke to us, she smilingly described her childhood as one filled with a community of Black people with large smiles, people who were happy and untroublesome. And she did not let us leave without calling after us, "Remember what I have said. Remember how it was."

Project HIP-HOP participants. Bottom row (l-r): Nancy Murray, Tanya Daniels, Veronica Valentine, Todd Fry; row 2: Quetzal Mount, James Blackwell, Sarah Wedge, Pam Ellis, Anibal Zayas, Vaughn Simkins; row 3, on bar: Astride Joseph, Marco Garrido, Brenda Velez, Luis Rodriguez, Melody Baker; back row: Mario Taylor, Antoinette Johnson, Marian Hammond, Arnold Chamantal.

FACING RACISM IN EDUCATION

And the words continue to resonate. The purpose of our tour crystallized: remember how it was.

The word "history" relegates what is read in a classroom textbook — no matter how recently it may have occurred — into the cobwebs and dust with the white armless statue. But to actually see history still happening, to see and feel and almost taste without the pages and the classroom walls and windows, then life is breathed into history, and history is no longer history but life.

And life is harder to ignore. I never fully realized the immense significance of the civil rights movement until I could no longer ignore the untied strings where the movement trailed off: the Memphis NAACP youth chapter members speaking to us in the Lorraine Motel alluded quite casually to the schools they attended which remained segregated in practice after the legal barriers had been dismantled, while civil rights veteran Hollis Watkins of the grassroots organization Southern Echo spoke in impassioned tones about the resistance of the "good ole boys" network to any disruption of the status quo, that is, white rule. U.S. Representative Cynthia McKinney of Georgia graciously accommodated us in her Capitol Hill office, despite being in the midst of a redistricting battle begun by her opponent for the seat who, only upon losing, decided that the district boundaries were drawn unfairly. He would rather have it re-drawn in a way that would all but prevent further Black political victories. There is a palpable sense of tension in the stares sometimes received, the ubiquity of the Confederate flag, the pride with which "Dixie" is sung. Injustice and harsh inequality are no myths; if you will dismiss the complaints of the oppressed, look instead at the difference in the quality of things: schools, shelter, streets, life. In the drab city projects, the face within will most likely be Black. The South is not so far from Boston, after all.

A visit in Greenville, Mississippi, with Boston-born Owen Brooks, a movement veteran and continuing activist, made the connection between poverty in the North and South. He surprised us one late Mississippi night when he proclaimed, "The movement has failed!" Slouched bodies, exhausted from a full day, sat up; eyes questioned his face and the seriousness with which he made the statement. The thrust of the movement, he explained, was misdirected; the focus should have been on the economic disparities underlying the intolerance, inequality, injustice. An economic upheaval of such a scale went far beyond the often serene vignettes of Black and White hands clasped in friendship during the civil rights era, but would instead imply a change of revolutionary proportions. The past, with all the human failings and injustices that we might flatter ourselves as a society to have put behind us, still lives. The past is mostly alive, according to Peter Applebome, writing in a special *New York Times* series on the South, "because, for all the sacrifice and triumph of the civil rights era, nothing touched the economic structure that continued to give whites control of the land, the jobs, and the capital, as well as the tax system that revolves around them."[38]

The South and the North are deeply scarred, and although the movement has incompletely stitched the wound, it has not failed, but goes on. The challenge is put to us, the "post"-movement generation that must still contend with all the ugliness that the 1960s activists struggled against. Our challenge, then, is to rise beyond remembering how it was, and to look forward and prepare for how it should be. We must continue the struggle.

And the movement does continue, with an exuberant and tireless spirit. The cool air of the Lorraine Motel is refreshing, providing respite from the searing Memphis sun. Upon entering the National Civil Rights Museum, a gigantic metal mountain stands imposingly before me, yet curves with surprising fluidity. Carved along the mountainside are people bent under immense loads: mothers carrying children, children with parents in their arms, men dragging themselves, women plodding onward — all headed to the top of the mountain, but none has yet reached the summit. But despite their burden, the steepness of the incline and the treachery of the jagged peaks, they march on, with an exuberant and tireless spirit. The robust life that energized the movement is palpable; it refreshes like cool water on tired hair on a hot day. And it energizes us — our spirit, once moved, remembers. And we will go on.

Later Reflections: A Personal Movement

My family emigrated from the Philippines when I was nine. The next few years were awkward. I was old enough to be impacted by the old country, but still too young to be secure in an identity. I wanted to fit in. The sting of racism was of course not a foreign barb to me: I, a Filipino, in a mostly White elementary school. That time, in my insecurity, was painful. I felt the pain of exclusion. At that tender age I learned what injustice was, what it was to be a "non-White" in a White society.

By injustice I mean a weight of oppression. Words oppress. Eyes oppress. History oppresses. What I see — the way people act, the media — is oppressive. I felt discounted because I wasn't White. Everyone was White but me. In the classroom, the teachers were White, we learned U.S. (= White) history, the issues were White, the White students discussed White concerns, the walls were white, my pencil wrote white words. Everything was White but me. The beautiful White people sold white goods, the President was White, the Pope was White, God was White.

The African Americans, the Native Americans, the Latinos, the Asians, we weren't White. We were not part of this White society. Yes, I'd seen the faces, the non-White faces, the faces of those who didn't act White, and I'd see them as outsiders, people who like me didn't fit in because we had the misfortune of being born non-White.

In my exclusion, I felt less human than a White person. White to me was more than skin color. It represented those in power. This society was theirs. I, in my fragile youth, felt inundated by White images. As I grew up, my models were White. I had no Asian role models. My Asian identity for the time was buried. I was, but for that pained voice in the back of my head, White.

I felt the drill of the eleven-year-old eyes of my classmates when issues of race were broached in class. I was uncomfortable. My non-Whiteness, it seemed, was on stage. The fact that people who were not White had to fight to secure rights was testimony to their oppression, to my oppression, to injustice. In my state of "racelessness," this was an all too painful reminder. So, I buried the subject.

I needed time to sort things out: who I was, why race tinted how others saw me, why race seemed part of the inner-city violence, what race really was and why it mattered so much. I still wasn't ready to deal with the movement, its implications, the unfinished business left (for me?). In one fundamental way, my tortured self-reflection did deal with the same issue the movement dealt with: injustice. It wasn't I who was flawed. No. Something else was wrong, and it affected more than simply me.

Then, last summer I had the opportunity to share a van with people of different backgrounds and colors. By the end of seventeen days we would be bound together by an intense experience. Our journey to the heart of the civil rights movement would tie us together as a community. Each of us had a story to tell, and all listened. We learned from one another. Our lives, we found, were lived in many ways. But by our youth we shared a common future, and the shadow of the movement's unfinished business hung over us all. Together we would have to take steps forward to finish what had been begun.

Project HIP-HOP focused what I had been wrestling with into more fluid thoughts. It was a celebration of the movement. The movement had, by the trip's end, come to be symbolically significant to me. I felt the spirit that drove the oppressed into action. Oppressed people who had fought, despite the odds, against injustice. I know how injustice can overwhelm you, and strip you of any sense of efficacy. I could relate to the inertia that kept the oppressed powerless, and the oppressors in power. But with the movement, I had hope. Rosa Park's toughness, Dr. King's vision, the faith each activist (many of them young) had that their fight would lead to justice — all this gave me strength.

HIP-HOP was also a celebration of diversity. Pick a van and you'd find Black, Latino, Indian, Filipino, Native American, European American. And no oppressors — no one who, because of race, acted in a superior way. Our HIP-HOP group was a model community. I felt at ease with each HIP-HOPer. Being in such an environment, where we of all races communed on a human to human basis, gave me strength in my own identity. I didn't feel as I did in my younger grade school days, that I'd be better off being White. No, in our HIP-HOP community, I was proud to be a Filipino. I saw in our group's chemistry the strength in being not only White, but African American, Latino, Indian, Filipino, Native American.

Talks with my fellow HIP-HOPers, be they from the city or suburbs, ex-gang members or high schoolers, made one thing clear: they have felt the same injustice I have experienced, this feeling of oppression. Some are, of course, weighed down more than I, but it's the same kind of weight. This racism is institutional. Society sustains it. It gnaws at us as youths, as non-Whites. It's at the root of the slurs hurled by the kid: nigger, gook, chink, flip. It sustains those who believe that Blacks are lazy, Asians are good at math. It frequently leads to violence.

My own experience tells me that racism isn't simply a remnant of the Old South. It flourishes up here, an off-shoot of societal injustice. While down south you may see Confederate flags, stereotypical and demeaning Black caricatures, up north racism is as intense, but not as blatant. I've been told that African Americans don't want to work, that they whine about phantom injustice, and that society unjustly favors them — all this prefaced with, "I'm not racist but . . ." "Why do Black people have to act the way they do?" a kid asked me, "Why can't they just act normal?" In other words, White.

Through HIP-HOP, I have felt the spirit that fueled the movement. Our HIP-HOP model community has given me hope that such an environment can exist. One without the oppressive weight of injustice. One where diversity is celebrated. Through this experience, I have grown. HIP-HOP has stirred me to social consciousness. Yes, I saw the good the movement had done, the untiring vigor of its activists, but I have also seen and heard and felt the injustice the movement sought to end. This injustice, which before had overwhelmed me, now angers me. Stronger, I accept my responsibility to continue what the movement began, to finish the unfinished business.

Notes

1. Maya Angelou delivered the poem *On the Pulse of Morning* (copyright © 1993) at the inauguration ceremony of President Clinton. *The Complete Collected Poems of Maya Angelou* (New York: Random House, 1994), p. 272.
2. The Bill of Rights Education Project was founded in November 1987 by the Massachusetts Civil Liberties Union Foundation, in cooperation with the Massachusetts Department of Education and the Massachusetts Bar Association. Through its conferences, institutes, workshops, and curricula, the Project encourages teachers and middle school and high school students to think critically about the difficult issues being debated in society and the courts, seeing this as essential to the future well-being of democracy. The Project, which recognizes that racism has been the prime force in undermining constitutional liberties and protections throughout our nation's history and into the present, has placed a particular emphasis on anti-racism education. Providing an opportunity for students to talk with each other across racial lines has become an important part of our anti-racism work.
3. Staff members at the retreat included Pam Ellis, director of the Massachusetts Student Alliance Against Racism and Violence, which is based at the office of the District Attorney for Norfolk County, Massachusetts; William Batson, who at the time was executive director of the Boston-based Teens as Community Resources; and me. Project HIP-HOP owes its name and much of its early impetus to Batson.
4. Myles Horton, *The Long Haul: An Autobiography* (New York: Doubleday/Anchor Books, 1990), pp. 149, 150.
5. See Horton, *The Long Haul,* p. 121, for a picture of the billboard that features King attending the Highlander's twenty-fifth anniversary celebration in 1957.
6. The series *Eyes on the Prize,* which was produced by Boston-based Blackside, Inc., and first broadcast in 1987, is the most comprehensive television documentary on the civil rights movement ever produced. It is the winner of six Emmys and numerous

other awards. *Eyes on the Prize, Part I* (America's Civil Rights Years – 1954 to 1965) uses historical film and present-day interviews to bring to life the grassroots struggle for racial equality. *Eyes on the Prize, Part II* (America at the Racial Crossroads – 1964 to 1985) depicts the changing face of the struggle for civil rights and economic equality, beginning with the emergence of the movement for Black Power. It is available from PBS Video by calling (800) 344-3337.

7. Vincent Harding, *Hope and History: Why We Must Share the Story of the Movement* (Maryknoll, NY: Orbis Books, 1991), p. 193.
8. Harding, *Hope and History,* p. 198.
9. Harding, *Hope and History,* p. 71.
10. In his introduction to *Hope and History,* Vincent Harding describes his reaction to seeing "We Shall Overcome" inscribed on banners in Beijing's Tiananmen Square at the peak of China's "pro-democracy movement," and hearing it sung by thousands of citizens who marched for democracy in Leipzig, then East Germany, and elsewhere in Eastern Europe. He writes that "when we look back now from the vantage point of Beijing and Prague, from Berlin and Soweto, we realize that the post-World War II African American freedom movement was our own seminal contribution to the massive pro-democracy struggles that have set the globe spinning in these times.... When seen as far more than a contest for legal rights, when understood as a Black-led, multiracial quest for democracy in America, for the healing of the nation, for the freeing of all our spirits, then the story belongs to every one of us in this country — just as the students in Tiananmen Square and the marchers, organizers, and martyrs in Eastern Europe and South Africa realized it belongs to them" (pp. 6–7).
11. Racism, Rights & History: A Summer Institute for Teachers was the third summer institute the Bill of Rights Education Project held for middle school and high school teachers specifically on the theme of racism. Vincent Harding, Jan Carew, and Ron Chisom of the New Orleans-based People's History for Survival and Beyond were among the staff members. Pam Ellis and I used the occasion of this institute to introduce teachers to our work in progress, *Racism, Rights and History: A Curriculum for High School Students.* At the institute, the teachers generally agreed that it was critical to teach about racism in a way that opens up new possibilities for social transformation. That meant digging deep: "Surface stuff will not do any more," one teacher commented. This was an urgent national priority. "What happens," another mused, "if there is no alternative to rage?"
12. Jordana Hart, writing about "Guns, Drugs, Rap & Rights: A Student Forum on Violence and Social Change" in "Some Say Violence is Skin Deep," *Boston Globe,* April 6, 1994, p. 17.
13. The efforts of the Bill of Rights Education Project to span the gulf dividing students from predominantly White and predominantly Black schools began with a conference for four hundred high school students on March 26, 1990, called Rap about Racism. Follow-up essays, which teachers asked participating students to write, showed considerable confusion about what racism is, or if it even still exists. Many students from largely White schools, some in decayed industrial towns, had felt intimidated by Black students at the conference: they claimed they were "hostile," that they "held a grudge," that they were to blame for an increase in racism since they were now more racist than Whites, and so on. After reading the essays, I visited several schools to talk directly to the students who wrote them. I was surprised at how many students knew the term "reverse discrimination" and seemed to have internalized the view that now the playing field was level, and if "minorities" do not get ahead, they have only themselves to blame. Other White students were more open. One said that "racism is something that just can't be ignored any longer." Another wrote, "What I think we as the White population should do is listen to Black people's experiences and try to get a sense of what's going on. Once we can understand this, we can start to work on it."

14. Schools seem a little more at ease dealing with "prejudice reduction" and the "celebration of differences" than with an examination of the racism embedded in our history. Racism (when it appears at all) is generally used interchangeably with bigotry and prejudice, and is interpreted solely in terms of personal beliefs and attitudes, to be confronted on a purely personal (and not institutional) level. Fighting racism then becomes a personal matter of changing attitudes and feelings — of learning how to get along with someone who may be different from you. Although this may be useful as far as it goes, it does not in fact take us very far. If students believe that this is where the entire struggle against racism lies — in the individual psyche — they may never go on to learn about the way "race" has been manipulated to shape our social, legal, and economic institutions, and is still being manipulated to preserve existing power structures and the status quo. When students realize that there is nothing fixed about racial categories, that categories like "Black" and "White" are social constructions, not biological essences, the students open up to other questions: Where did these categories come from? Whose interests did they serve? What role do they play in society today?
15. I recently had the experience of visiting a school on the perimeter of Boston for an in-service training session with teachers to discuss how the social studies curriculum could be changed to make it more "inclusive." On arrival, I was struck to find all the doors locked. To gain entry, I had to stand in front of a surveillance camera and announce my name and purpose into a microphone. It turned out this kind of security was a preventive measure taken because of the proximity of a largely "minority" part of Boston: there had been no episode precipitating it. In the course of discussion with the teachers, I mentioned the need to go beyond "band-aid" solutions to violence in schools, and to try to engage students in a far-reaching dialogue about violence, which would include a search for the roots of violence in our nation's history. I was immediately cut short by a teacher who insisted that before the last decade or so, violence was practically unknown in this country. He maintained this position, in which he was supported by several other teachers, when I tried to suggest that there was indeed something inherently violent about the process of dispossessing native peoples, upholding the institution of slavery, using the terror of lynch law to regain and retain the upper hand after a Civil War that set a new world record for known casualties, and so on. In his mind, this simply did not count as "violence." Seldom had I so strongly felt the power of Norman Rockwell's images — and those of the everyday media!
16. The National Advisory Commission on Civil Disorders, chaired by Governor Otto Kerner of Illinois, released its report in 1968 on the causes of the riots that swept U.S. cities in the mid-1960s. The Kerner Commission warned that the nation was becoming permanently divided into two societies: "one, largely Negro and poor, located in the central cities; the other, predominantly white and affluent, located in the suburbs" (p. 22). The report also stated: "What white Americans have never fully understood — but what the Negro can never forget — is that white society is deeply implicated in the ghetto. White institutions created it, white institutions maintain it, and white society condones it." From U.S. Advisory Commission on Civil Disorders, The Kerner Report (New York: Pantheon Books, 1988).
17. Quoted in David J. Garrow, *Bearing the Cross: Martin Luther King and the Southern Christian Leadership Conference* (New York: Vintage Books, 1986), p. 537.
18. Adam Nossiter, *Of Long Memory: Mississippi and the Murder of Medgar Evers* (Reading, MA: Addison-Wesley, 1994), p. 15.
19. Cornel West, *Race Matters* (Boston: Beacon Press, 1993), p. 2.
20. Several teachers who are using parts of our *Racism, Rights and History* curriculum with students deemed hard to reach report a new level of excitement and interest in their high school classes and in their work with G.E.D. students.

21. John Hope Franklin, *The Color Line: Legacy for the Twenty-First Century* (Columbia: University of Missouri Press, 1993), pp. 74–75.
22. Harding, *Hope and History*, p. 32.
23. Movement veterans told us of their regrets at not having "passed the torch" to the next generation. In *Of Long Memory*, Adam Nossiter writes of the way the movement is ignored in schools in Mississippi: "My own contemporaries in Mississippi, people born around 1960, often seemed shocked to learn of events that had been on the front pages of national newspapers thirty years before. They were dimly aware, from listening to their parents on the subject, that there had been unpleasantness during the 1960s. But the sheer ugliness of the white backlash eluded them" (pp. 14–16). He cites a 1975 revision of the standard textbook by John K. Bettersworthy, *Your Mississippi*, which ignores White violence and passes over the movement of the 1950s and 1960s with these words: "Gradually Mississippians, black and white, found that they could get along together — as they always had."(*Of Long Memory*, pp. 14–16). He then goes on to describe the feelings expressed at a Black History class at the University of Southern Mississippi when African Americans hear what life had been like under Jim Crow. The Black students and the few White students who took the class were, its teacher claimed, "hungry" for the information.
24. Marc Germain in Carol Gerwin, "Visiting the Past: Rights Workers' Graves Bring Reality," *Patriot Ledger*, July 31/August 1, 1993, p. 10.
25. Kim Howard in Constance E. Putnam, "Roots of Civil Rights Movement Open Their Eyes," *Boston Globe*, July 25, 1993, p. 35.
26. Letter of support from Geraldine Hines, March 24, 1994.
27. Outward Bound is an adventure-based program aimed at self-discovery and leadership training through challenging physical activities. It has regional offices around the United States and a national office in Greenwich, Connecticut.
28. The state-funded METCO program (Metropolitan Council for Educational Opportunity) was founded in Massachusetts in the late 1960s to enable "minority" students from Boston's deteriorating city schools to attend elementary and secondary schools in suburban districts. School districts from Massachusetts' North Shore to the Foxboro area west of Boston have adopted the program as a way of introducing diversity into their own student body. Approximately eight hundred students are currently involved in the METCO program, which has a waiting list of ten thousand.
29. MOVE, which was formed in 1972, is an organization of radical utopians, mostly African American, who follow the teachings of John Africa. Denouncing the U.S. political and economic system for poisoning air, land, and water and destroying life on the planet, they were in turn denounced for many of their allegedly unsanitary "back to nature" practices. Thirteen of the up to 150 MOVE members were inside the house at 6221 Osage Avenue in Philadelphia when it was bombed with C-4 explosives provided by the FBI on May 13, 1985. The resulting firestorm killed six adults and five children and gutted sixty-one row houses, leaving 250 people homeless. Our three-hour conversation with Ramona Africa at the offices of the American Friends Service Committee opened students to the importance of critical thinking, questioning sources, and weighing evidence from all sides, and enlarged our ongoing discussion of the nature and uses of violence. It also provoked a dialogue about the limits of dissent and repression in a country born in revolution — another subject rarely explored in schools.
30. On May 18, 1896, the Supreme Court ruled in *Plessy v. Ferguson* (163 U.S. 537 [1896]) that a Louisiana law mandating "equal but separate accommodations for the white and colored races" on passenger trains was constitutional. The lone dissenter was a former slaveholder, Justice John Marshall Harlan of Kentucky. He wrote: "In my opinion, the judgement this day rendered will, in time, prove to be quite as pernicious as the decision made by this tribunal in the Dred Scott case.... The destinies of the two

races, in this country, are indissolubly linked together, and the interests of both require that the common government of all shall not permit the seeds of race hate to be planted under the sanction of law." Quoted in Norman Dorsen, Paul Bender, Burt Neuborne, and Sylvia Law, *Political and Civil Rights in the United States*, Vol. II (Boston: Little, Brown, 1979), p. 53.

31. Eugene "Bull" Connor was the police commissioner of Birmingham who became infamous nationally for the brutal methods he used against demonstrations protesting segregation.
32. Sara Rimer, "Trip To History for Boston Teenagers: To the South of the Civil Rights Fight," *New York Times*, July 29, 1994, p. A10.
33. The Kuji Center was organized by the dozen diverse neighborhood groups of the St. Thomas/Irish Channel Consortium in New Orleans in 1990. The Center aims to reduce teen pregnancy by offering young people, ages eleven to eighteen, a holistic program of career development, education, recreation, culture, and classes on family life and sexuality.
34. "Jim Crow" refers to the laws and ordinances passed in the closing decades of the nineteenth century throughout the South that mandated racial segregation in public facilities and deprived African Americans of the right to vote. The U.S. Supreme Court had opened the door to Jim Crow segregation when it ruled in *The Slaughterhouse Cases* (1871) that the Fourteenth Amendment did not place the rights of citizens under federal protection. The Court denied that the national government could interfere with a state's "right" to fail to protect the civil rights of its citizens. If a state chose not to extend the Fourteenth Amendment's "equal protection" and "due process" clauses to all its citizens, that was its business.
35. Excerpt from the evaluation of the tour submitted by Arnold Chamanlal in August 1994.
36. Fannie Lou Hamer, born and buried in Ruleville, Mississippi, was the youngest of twenty children. She worked in the cotton fields with her sharecropper parents from the age of six. Forty years later she attended a SNCC meeting and learned that she had the right to vote. Trying to exercise that right got her imprisoned and viciously beaten. Her courage, powerful singing, and the eloquence of her nationally televised testimony before the Democratic Party Credential Committee that was considering whether the all-White delegation from Mississippi should be replaced by delegates from the multiracial Mississippi Freedom Democratic Party at the 1964 Party Convention in Atlantic City made her an inspiring symbol of the civil rights movement.
37. Kurt Cobain was the lead singer of an alternative music group called Nirvana. This quote is from the song, "All Apologies," on the album *In Utero*.
38. Peter Applebome, "In Selma, Everything and Nothing Changed," *New York Times*, August 2, 1994, p. B6.

Blind Vision: Unlearning Racism in Teacher Education

MARILYN COCHRAN-SMITH

Literary theorist Barbara Hardy (1978) once asserted that narrative ought not be regarded as an "aesthetic invention used by artists to control, manipulate, and order experience, but as a primary act of mind transferred to art from life" (p. 12). Elaborating on the primacy of narrative in both our interior and exterior lives, Hardy suggests that

> storytelling plays a major role in our sleeping and waking lives. We dream in narrative, daydream in narrative, remember, anticipate, hope, despair, believe, doubt, plan, revise, criticize, construct, gossip, learn, hate and love by narrative. (p. 13)

From this perspective, narrative can be regarded as locally illuminating, a central way we organize and understand experience (Mishler, 1986; VanManen, 1990). It is also a primary way we construct our multiple identities as human beings for whom race, gender, class, culture, ethnicity, language, ability, sexual orientation, role, and position make a profound difference in the nature and interpretation of experience (Tatum, 1997; Thompson & Tyagi, 1996).

In this article, I explore and write about *un*learning racism in teaching and teacher education. I do not begin in the scholarly tradition of crisply framing an educational problem by connecting it to current policy and practice and/or to the relevant research literature. Instead, I begin with a lengthy narrative based on my experiences as a teacher educator at a moment in time when issues of race and racism were brought into unexpectedly sharp relief. I do so with the assumption that narrative is not only locally illuminating, as Hardy's work suggests, but also that it has the capacity to contain and entertain within it contradictions, nuances, tensions, and complexities that traditional academic discourse with its expository stance and more distanced impersonal voice cannot (Fine, 1994; Gitlin, 1994; Metzger, 1986).

The idea that racism is something that all of us have inevitably learned simply by living in a racist society is profoundly provocative (King, Hollins, & Hayman, 1997; McIntosh, 1989; Tatum, 1992, 1994). For many of us, it challenges not only our most precious democratic ideals about equitable access to opportunity, but also our most persistent beliefs in the possibilities of school and social change through enlightened human agency (Apple, 1996; Giroux, 1988; Leistyna, Woodrum, & Sherblom, 1996; Noffke, 1997). Perhaps even more provocative is the position that part of our responsibility as teachers and teacher educators is to struggle along with others in order to *un*learn racism (Britzman, 1991; Cochran-Smith, 1995a; Sleeter, 1992), or to interrogate the racist assumptions that may be deeply embedded in our own courses and curricula, to own our own complicity in maintaining existing systems of privilege and oppression, and to grapple with our own failures to produce the kinds of changes we advocate. Attempting to make the unending process of *un*learning racism explicit and public is challenging and somewhat risky. Easily susceptible to misinterpretation and misrepresentation, going public involves complex nuances of interpretation, multiple layers of contradiction, competing perspectives, and personal exposure (Cochran-Smith, 1995b; Cole & Knowles, 1998; Rosenberg, 1997). I go public with the stories in this article not because they offer explicit directions for unlearning racism, but because they pointedly suggest some of the most complex questions we need to wrestle with in teacher education: In our everyday lives as teachers and teacher educators, how are we complicit — intentionally or otherwise — in maintaining the cycles of oppression (Lawrence & Tatum, 1997) that operate daily in our courses, our universities, our schools, and our society? Under what conditions is it possible to examine, expand, and alter long-standing (and often implicit) assumptions, attitudes, beliefs, and practices about schools, teaching, students, and communities? What roles do collaboration, inquiry, self-examination, and story play in learning of this kind? As teacher educators, what should we say about race and racism, what should we have our students read and write? What should we tell them about who can teach whom, who can speak for whom, and who has the right to speak at all about racism and teaching?

Blind Vision: A Story from a Teacher Educator

A White European American woman, I taught for many years at the University of Pennsylvania, a large research university in urban Philadelphia whose population was predominantly White, but whose next-door neighbors in west Philadelphia were schools and communities populated by African Americans and Asian immigrants. Seventy-five to 80 percent of the students I taught were White European Americans, but they worked as student teachers primarily in the public schools of Philadelphia where the population was often mostly African American or — in parts of north and northeast Philadelphia — mostly Latino. In those schools that appeared on the surface to be more ideally integrated, the racial tension was sometimes intense, with individual groups insulated from or even hostile toward one another.

The teacher education program I directed had for years included in the curriculum an examination of race, class, and culture and the ways these structure both the U.S. educational system and the experiences of individuals in that system.[1] For years my students read Comer (1989), Delpit (1986, 1988), Giroux (1984), Heath (1982 a, 1982b), Ogbu (1978), as well as Asante (1991), McIntosh (1989), Moll, Amanti, Neff, and Gonzalez (1992), Rose (1989), Sleeter and Grant (1987), Tatum (1992), and others who explore issues of race, class, culture, and language from critical and other perspectives. I thought that the commitment of my program to urban student-teaching placements and to devoting a significant portion of the curriculum to issues of race and racism gave me a certain right to speak about these issues as a teacher educator. I thought this with some degree of confidence until an event occurred that was to change forever the way I thought about racism and teacher education. This event was to influence the work I did with colleagues in the Penn program over the next six years, as well as the work in which I am presently engaged as a teacher educator at Boston College, where I collaborate with other teacher educators, teachers, and student teachers in the Boston area.

The event that is described in the following narrative occurred at the end of a two-hour student teaching seminar that was held biweekly for the thirty-some students in the Penn program at the time.[2]

* * * * *

We had come to the end of a powerful presentation about the speaker's personal experiences with racism, both as a young Native boy in an all-White class and later as the single minority teacher in a small rural school. The presentation had visibly moved many of us. The guest speaker — a Native American who worked in a teacher education program at another university — asked my student teachers about their program at Penn. I had no qualms. Our program was well known and well received. Students often raved about it to visitors from outside. Knowing and sharing the commitment of my program to exploring issues of race, my guest asked in the last few minutes of our two-hour seminar, "And what does this program do to help you examine questions about race and racism in teaching and schooling?" Without hesitation, one student teacher, a Puerto Rican woman, raised her hand and said with passion and an anger that bordered on rage, "Nothing! This program does *nothing* to address issues of race!" After a few seconds of silence that felt to me like hours, two other students — one African American and one Black South African — agreed with her, adding their frustration and criticism to the first comment and indicating that we read nothing and said nothing that addressed these questions. I was stunned. With another class waiting to enter the room, students — and I — quickly exited the room.

My first responses to this event included every personally defensive strategy I could muster. In the same way that my students sometimes did, I identified and equated myself with "the program." And in certain important ways, I suppose I *was* the program in that I had been the major architect of its social and organizational structures, and I was ultimately responsible for its decisions. I relived the final moments of the seminar, turning the same thoughts over and over in my head: How could she say that? How could others agree? After all, the compelling presentation we had all just heard was in and of itself evidence that we addressed issues of race in our program. And besides, just a few days earlier, she and a group of five other women students had presented a paper at a teacher research conference at Penn. They had chosen to be part of an inquiry group that was to write a paper about race and their student-teaching experiences because I had invited them to, I had suggested the topic. They had used the data of their writing and teacher research projects from my class to examine the impact of race and racism on their student-teaching experiences. How could she say that?

I counted up the ongoing efforts I had made to increase the diversity in our supervisory staff and in our pool of cooperating teachers. I had insisted that we send student teachers to schools where the population was nearly 100 percent African American and Latino, schools that some colleagues cautioned me were too tough for student teachers, that some student teachers complained were too dangerous, and one had once threatened to sue me if I made her go there even for a brief field visit. I talked about issues of race openly and, I thought, authentically in my classes — all of them, no matter what the course title or the topic. I thought about the individual and personal efforts I had made on behalf of some of those students — helping them get scholarships, intervening with cooperating teachers or supervisors, working for hours with them on papers, lending books and articles. I constructed a long and convincing mental argument that I was one of the people on the right side of this issue. Nobody can do everything, and I was sure that I already paid more attention to questions of racism and teaching than did many teacher educators. How could she say that? I was stunned by what had happened, and deeply hurt — surprised as much as angry.

During the first few days after that seminar session, many students — most of them White — stopped by my office to tell me that they thought we were indeed doing a great deal to address issues of race and racism in the program, but they had clearly heard the outrage and dissatisfaction of their fellow students and they wanted to learn more, to figure out what we should do differently. Some students — both White students and students of color — stopped by or wrote notes saying that they thought we were currently doing exactly what we should be doing to address issues of race in the program. And a few students — all White — stopped by to say that all we ever talked about in the program and in my classes was race and racism and what they really wanted to know was when we were going to learn how to teach reading.

I knew that the next meeting of the seminar group would be a turning point for me and for the program. I struggled with what to say, how to proceed, what kind of stance I needed to take and would be able to take. I knew that I needed to open (not foreclose) the discussion, to acknowledge the frustration and anger (even the rage) that had been expressed, and, above all, I knew that I needed not to be defensive. I felt very heavy — it was clear to me that I was about to teach my student teachers one of the most important lessons I would ever teach them. I was about to teach them how a White teacher, who — notwithstanding the rhetoric in my classes about collaboration, shared learning, and co-construction of knowledge — had a great deal of power over their futures in the program and in the job market, how that White teacher, who fancied herself pretty liberal and enlightened, responded when confronted directly and angrily about some of the issues of race that were right in front of her in her own teaching and her own work as a teacher educator.

The very different responses of my students and my own shock and hurt at some of those responses pointed out to me on a visceral level the truth that many of the articles we were reading in class argued on a more intellectual level: how we are positioned in terms of race and power vis-à-vis others has a great deal to do with how we see, what we see or want to see, and what we are able not to see. I thought of Clifford Geertz's discussion of the difficulties involved in representing insider knowledge and meaning perspectives. He suggests that, ultimately, anthropologists cannot really represent "local knowledge" — what native inhabitants see — but only what they see through; that is, their interpretive perspectives on their own experiences. This situation laid bare the enormous differences between what I — and people differently situated from me — saw and saw through as we constructed our lives as teachers and students.

I didn't decide until right before the seminar exactly what I would say. I had thought of little else during the week. I felt exposed, failed, trapped, and completely inadequate to the task. In the end, I commented briefly then opened up the two hours for students to say whatever they wished. I tried to sort out and say back as clearly as I could both what I had heard people say at the seminar and the quite disparate responses I had heard in the ensuing week. It was clear from these, I said, that nobody speaks for anybody or everybody else. As I spoke, I tried not to gloss over the scathing critique or make the discrepancies appear to be less discrepant than they were. Especially for many of the students of color in the program, I said that I had clearly heard that there was a feeling of isolation, of being silenced, a feeling that we had not dealt with issues of race and racism in a "real" way — briefly perhaps, but in ways that were too intellectualized and theoretical rather than personal and honest. Notwithstanding the view expressed by some students that all we ever talked about was race, I reported a strong consensus that an important conversation had been opened up and needed to continue, although I also noted that it was clear some conversations about race and racism, maybe the most important ones, could not be led by me, a White teacher.

I concluded by saying that despite my deep commitments to an antiracist curriculum for all students, whether children or adults, and despite my intentions to promote constructive discourse about the issues in teacher education, I realized I didn't "get it" some (or much) of the time. This seemed to be one of those times. I admitted that these things were hard, uncomfortable, and sometimes even devastating to hear, but we needed to hear, to listen hard, and to stay with it.

What I remember most vividly about that seminar are the tension and the long silence that followed my comments and my open invitation to others to speak. My seminar co-leader (and friend) told me later that she was sure we all sat in silence for at least twenty minutes (my watch indicated that about three minutes had passed). The same woman who had responded so angrily the week before spoke first, thanking us for hearing and for providing time for people to name the issues. Others followed. All of the women of color in the program spoke, most of them many times. A small portion of the White students participated actively. Students critiqued their inner-city school placements, describing the inability or unwillingness of some of the experienced teachers at their schools to talk about issues of race and racism, to be mentors to them about these issues. They said we needed more cooperating teachers and more student teachers of color. They spoke of middle-class, mostly White teachers treating poor children, mostly children of color, in ways that were abrupt and disrespectful at best, reprehensible and racist at worst. Some spoke passionately about the disparities they had observed between their home schools and the schools they had cross-visited — disparities in resources and facilities, but even more in the fundamental ways teachers treated children in poor urban schools on the one hand, and in middle-class urban or suburban schools on the other. They complained that our Penn faculty and administrators were all White, naming and counting up each of us and assuming I had the power and authority, but not the will, to change things. They said that the lack of faculty of color and the small number of students of color in the program gave little validation to the issues they wished to raise as women and prospective teachers of color. Many of them were angry, bitter. They spoke with a certain sense of unity as if their scattered, restrained voices had been conjoined, unleashed.

The coleader and I avoided eye contact with one another, our faces serious and intense but carefully trying not to signal approval or disapproval, agreement or disagreement. Many White students were silent, some almost ashen. Some seemed afraid to speak. One said people were at different levels with issues of race and racism, implying that others in the room might not understand but that she herself was beyond that. Another commented that she too had experienced racism, especially because her boyfriend was African American. One said that when she looked around her student-teaching classroom, she saw only children, not color. Another complained that she didn't see why somebody couldn't just tell her what she didn't get so she could just get it and get on with teaching. I cringed inside at some of these comments, while several of the women of color rolled their eyes, whispered among themselves. One who was older than most of the students in the program eventually stopped making any attempt to hide her hostility and exasperation. She was openly disdainful in her side comments. Finally, a young White woman, with clear eyes and steady voice, turned to the older woman and said she was willing to hear any criticism, any truth about herself, but she wanted it said in front of her, to her face. The only man of color in the program, who sat apart from the other students, said all he wanted to do was to be an effective teacher. He did not want to be seen as a Black male teacher and a role model for Black children, but as a good teacher. Others immediately challenged him on the impossibility and irresponsibility of that stance.

For nearly two hours, the tension in the room was palpable, raw. As leaders we said little, partly because we had little idea what to say, partly because we had agreed to open up the time to the students. We nodded, listened, took notes. Toward the end, we asked for suggestions — how the group wanted to spend the two or three seminar sessions remaining in the year that had any flexibility in terms of topic, schedule, or speakers. We asked for recommendations. There were many suggestions but only a few that we could actually do something about in the six weeks or so that remained before the students graduated, given the already full schedule and the final press of certification and graduation details. (Many of the suggestions that we took up in the following year are described in the remainder of this article. For the current year, we opened up discussion time and included student teachers in planning and evaluation groups.)

Two students wrote me letters shortly after this seminar. One was appreciative, one was disgusted. Both, I believe, were heartfelt. A White woman wrote: "When you began to speak at the last seminar, I held my breath. The atmosphere in the room was so loaded, so brooding. It felt very unsafe. What would you say? What could you say? It would have been so very easy at this point to retreat into academe — to play The Professor, The Program Director, and not respond or address the fact that there were painful unresolved issues to be acknowledged, if not confronted. . . . Instead you responded honestly and openly, telling us how you were thinking about things, how you felt and the dilemmas you encountered as you too struggled to 'get it.' . . . Your words were carefully considered . . . and seemed spoken not without some cost to you." In contrast, a White man wrote:

> After this evening's seminar, I thought I would drop you this note to let you know how I react to the issues that were (and were not) confronted. . . . To be honest, I feel that the critical issues of race and racism have been made apparent and important in my studies . . . since I began [the program]. That they should have been made the fulcrum point of the curriculum and each course is problematic. I would say no; others (more vehemently) would insist on it. . . . I really have no idea how to most effectively proceed. I do know one thing.

I am committed to bringing issues of race into my classroom, wherever I may teach. However, being nonconfrontational by nature, and with sincere respect for the opinions of my fellow students, I will probably not attend another session about this. Frankly, I, my students, and my career in education will benefit a lot more by staying at home and spending a few hours trying to integrate multicultural issues into my lesson plans than they will by talking one more time about race.

* * * * *

It would be an understatement to say that these events were galvanizing as well as destabilizing for me, for the people I worked closely with, and for the students who graduated just six weeks later. Everything was called into question — what we thought we were about as a program, who we were as a community, what learning opportunities were available in our curriculum, whose interests were served, whose needs were met, and whose were not. But it would be inaccurate to say that these events *caused* changes in the program over the next six years or that we proceeded from this point in a linear way, learning from our "mistakes" and then correcting them. Although the story of "so then what happened?" is of course chronological in one sense, it is decidedly *not* a story of year-by-year, closer and closer approximations of "the right way" to open and sustain a discourse about race and racism in teacher education programs aimed at preparing both students of color and White students to be teachers in both urban and other schools. Rather, the story is an evolving, recursive, and current one about what it means to grapple with the issues of racism and teaching in deeper and more uncertain ways.

It is also important to say, I think, that the above account of what happened is a fiction, not reality or truth, but my interpretation of my own and other people's experience in a way that makes sense to me and speaks for me. Although part of my intention in telling this story is to uncover my failure and unravel my complicity in maintaining the existing system of privilege and oppression, it is impossible for me to do so without sympathy for my own predicament. My experience as a first-generation-to-college, working-class girl who pushed into a middle-class, highly educated male profession has helped give me some vision about the personal and institutional impact of class and gender differences on work, status, and ways of knowing. But my lifelong membership in the privileged racial group has helped keep me blind about much of the impact of race. In fact, I have come to think of the story related above as a story of "blind vision" — a White female teacher educator with a vision about the importance of making issues of race and diversity explicit parts of the preservice curriculum and, in the process, grappling (sometimes blindly) with the tension, contradiction, difficulty, pain, and failure inherent in unlearning racism.

Of course, it is what we do after we tell stories like this one that matters most, or, more correctly, it is what we do afterwards that makes these stories matter at all. In the remainder of this article, I examine what I tried to do as a teacher educator and what we tried to do in our teacher education community after this story was told. We wanted to do nothing short of total transformation, nothing short of inventing a curriculum that was once and for all free of racism. What we *did* do over time was much more modest. Over time we struggled to unlearn racism by learning to read teacher education as racial text,[3] a process that involved analyzing and altering the learning opportunities available in our program along the lines of their implicit and explicit messages about race, racism, and teaching, as well as — and as important as — acknowledging to each other and to our students that this process would never be finished, would never be "once and for all." In the pages that follow, I analyze and illustrate this process, drawing on the following experiences and data sources: the evolution of three courses I regularly taught during the years that followed these events; the changes we made over time in the intellectual, social, and organizational contexts of the program; and the persistent doubts, questions, and failures we experienced as recorded in notes, reflections, conversations, and other correspondence.[4] In the final section of the article, I consider lessons learned and unlearned. I address the implications of reading teacher education as racial text for my own continuing efforts as a teacher educator now working with student teachers and teacher educators in a different urban context (Cochran-Smith et al., 1999; Cochran-Smith & Lytle, 1998).

Reading Teacher Education as Racial Text

Reading teacher education as racial text is an analytical approach that draws from three interrelated and somewhat overlapping ideas. First is the idea that teaching and teacher education — in terms of both curriculum and pedagogy — can be regarded and read as "text." Second is the idea that preservice teacher education has both an explicit text (a sequence of required courses and fieldwork experiences, as well as the public documents that advertise or represent the goals of a given program) and a subtext (implicit messages, subtle aspects of formal and informal program arrangements, and the underlying perspectives conveyed in discourse, materials, and consistency/inconsistency between ideals and realities). Third is the notion that any curriculum, teacher education or otherwise, can and — given the racialized society in which we live — ought to be read not simply as text but as racial text.

Teaching as Text

A number of recent writers have advanced the idea that the work of teaching can be regarded as "text" that can — like any other text — be read, reread, analyzed, critiqued, revised, and made public by the teacher and his or her local community. This assumes that teaching, like all human experience, is constructed primarily out of the social and language interactions of participants. To make teaching into readable "text," it is necessary to establish space between teachers and their everyday work in order to find what McDonald (1992) calls "apartness." He suggests:

> This is the gist of reading teaching, its minimal core: to step outside the room, figuratively speaking, and to search for perspective on the events inside. It is simple work on its face, private and comparatively safe, the consequence perhaps of deliberately noticing one's own practice in the eyes of a student teacher, of undertaking some classroom research, even — as in my case — of keeping a simple journal and doing a little theoretical browsing. By such means, teachers may spot the uncertainty in their own practice. They may spot it, as I did, in unexpected tangles of conflicting values, in stubborn ambivalence, in a surprising prevalence of half-steps. (p. 11)

McDonald suggests that reading teaching collaboratively is difficult and complex, requiring group members to set aside the pretensions and fears born of isolation, but also allowing, eventually, for the discovery of voice and a certain sense of unity.

Along related but different lines, I have been suggesting in work with Susan Lytle (Cochran-Smith & Lytle, 1992, 1993, 1999) that communities of teachers use multiple forms of inquiry to help make visible and accessible everyday events and practices and the ways they are differently understood by different stakeholders in the educational process. Oral and written inquiry that is systematic and intentional, we have argued, "transforms what is ordinarily regarded as 'just teaching' . . . into multi-layered portraits of school life" (Cochran-Smith & Lytle, 1992, p. 310). These portraits and the ways teachers shape and interpret them draw on, but also make problematic, the knowledge about teaching and learning that has been generated by others. At the same time, they help to build bodies of evidence, provide analytic frameworks, and suggest cross-references for comparison. Part of the point in McDonald's work, and in ours, is that "reading teaching as text" means representing teaching through oral and written language as well as other means of documentation that can be revisited, "REsearched" — to use Ann Berthoff's language (Berthoff, 1987) — connected to other "texts" of teaching, and made accessible and public beyond the immediate local context. Using the metaphor "teaching as text" makes it possible to see that connecting the various texts of teaching in the context of local inquiry communities (Cochran-Smith & Lytle, 1999) can be understood as a kind of social and collective construction of intertextuality or dialogue among texts. This leads to the second aspect of conceptualizing teacher education as text — examining not only what is explicit (the major text), but also what is not easily visible or openly public (the subtext).

Texts and Subtexts in Teacher Education

As text, teacher education is dynamic and complex — much more than a sequence of courses, a set of fieldwork experiences, or the readings and written assignments that are required for certification or credentialing purposes. Although these are part of what it means to take teacher education as text, they are not all of it. This also means examining its subtexts, hidden texts, and intertexts — reading between the lines as well as reading under, behind, through, and beyond them. This includes scrutinizing what is absent from the main texts and what themes are central to them, what happens to the formal texts, how differently positioned people read and write these texts differently, what they do and do not do with them, and what happens that is not planned or public. Ginsburg and Clift's (1990) concept of the hidden curriculum in teacher education is illuminating here, as is Rosenberg's (1997) discussion of the underground discourses of teacher education. Both of these call attention to the missing, obscured, or subverted texts — what is left out, implied, veiled, or subtly signaled as the norm by virtue of being unmarked or marked with modifying language. Ginsburg and Clift suggest that

> [the] sources of hidden curricular messages include the institutional and broader social contexts in which teacher education operates and the structure and processes of the teacher education program, including pedagogical techniques and texts and materials within the program. Messages are also sent by the . . . interpersonal relationships that exist between the numerous groups who might be considered to be educators of teachers. (p. 451)

Along more specific lines, Rosenberg (1997) describes the underground discourse about race in a small teacher education program in a rural area of New England. Rosenberg refers to "the presence of an absence," or the figurative presence of racism even in the actual absence of people of color at an overwhelmingly White institution. Rosenberg's characterization of an underground discourse about race connects to the third idea I have drawn upon in this discussion: the necessity of reading teacher education not just as complicated and dynamic text, but as racial text.

Teacher Education as Racial Text

Castenell and Pinar (1993) argue that curriculum can and ought to be regarded as racial text. Their introduction to a collection of essays by that name, *Understanding Curriculum as Racial Text*, develops this argument by locating current curriculum issues within the context of public debates about the canon and about the racial issues that are embedded within curriculum controversies. To understand curriculum as racial text, they suggest, is to understand that

> all Americans are racialized beings; knowledge of who we have been, who we are, and who we will become is a story or text we construct. In this sense curriculum — our construction and reconstruction of this knowledge for dissemination to the young — is racial text. (p. 8)

In forwarding this view of curriculum, Castenell and Pinar imply that it is critical to analyze any curriculum to see what kind of message or story about race and racism is being told, what assumptions are being made, what identity perspectives and points of view are implicit, and what is valued or devalued. They acknowledge, of course, that curriculum is not only racial text, but is also a text that is political, aesthetic, and gendered. They argue, however, that it is, "to a degree that European Americans have been unlikely to acknowledge, racial text" (p. 4). In conceptualizing curriculum as racial text, then, they link knowledge and identity, focusing particularly on issues of representation and difference. They argue that, although it is true that "We are what we know. We are, however, also what we do not know" (p. 4).

Taken together, the three ideas just outlined — that all teaching (including teacher education) can be regarded as text, that teacher education has both public and implicit or hidden texts, and that the text of teacher education is (in large part) racial text — lay the groundwork for the two sections that follow. In these sections I suggest that my colleagues and I — as participants in one teacher education community — struggled to unlearn racism by learning to read teacher education as racial text. In the first section I discuss both the possibilities and the pitfalls of making race and racism central to the curriculum by using "up close and personal" narratives, as well as distanced and more intellectualized theories and accounts. Next I show that it is necessary to "read between the lines," or to scrutinize closely the implicit messages about perspective, identity, and difference in a curriculum even after race and racism have been made central. Finally I turn to more general issues in teacher education offering brief lessons learned and unlearned when teacher education is regarded as racial text and when narrative is used to interrogate race and racism.

Getting Personal: Using Stories about Race and Racism in the Curriculum

For the teacher education community referred to in the opening narrative of this article, reading teacher education as racial text came to mean making issues of diversity (particularly of race and racism) central and integral, rather than marginal and piecemeal, to what we as student teachers, cooperating teachers, and teacher educators read, wrote, and talked about. Consciously deciding to privilege these issues meant rewriting course syllabi and program materials, reinventing the ways we evaluated student teachers, changing the composition of faculty and staff, drawing on the expertise and experience of people beyond ourselves, and altering the content of teacher research groups, student seminars, and whole-community sessions. For example, in response to the events described above, we worked the following year with a group of outside consultants to plan and participate in a series of "cultural diversity workshops" jointly attended by students, cooperating teachers, supervisors, and program directors. In the next year, we focused monthly seminars for the same groups on race and culture through the medium of story, led by Charlotte Blake Alston, a nationally known African American storyteller and staff-development leader. In the years to follow, we participated in sessions on Afrocentric curriculum led by Molefi Asante; on Black family socialization patterns and school culture led by Michele Foster; on multicultural teaching and

Asian American issues in urban schools led by Deborah Wei; on constructing curriculum based on Hispanic children's literature, particularly using books with Puerto Rican themes and characters, led by Sonia Nieto; and on learning to talk about racial identity and racism led by Beverly Tatum. In addition, we offered sessions on using children's cultural and linguistic resources in the classroom and on constructing antiracist pedagogy led by our program's most experienced cooperating teachers — both teachers of color and White teachers — from urban and suburban, public and private, poor and privileged schools in the Philadelphia area.

Telling Stories

A central part of these activities was "getting personal" about race and racism — putting more emphasis on reading, writing, and sharing personal experiences of racism and digging at the roots of our own attitudes at the same time that we continued to read the more intellectualized, and thus somewhat safer, discourse of the academy. This meant making individual insider accounts (even though not as well known as the writing of the academy) a larger part of the required reading. Along with the usual reading of Comer, Delpit, Ogbu, Heath, and Tatum we began to read more of Parham, Foreman, Eastman, Cohen, and Creighton — all of whom were student teachers, cooperating teachers, and supervisors in our program.[5]

All of us in the community wrote and read personal accounts about race and class that were published in-house in an annual collection we called, "A Sense of Who We Are." These were used as the starting point for many class discussions, school-site meetings, and monthly seminars. For example, Daryl Foreman, an experienced cooperating teacher, wrote about her experiences as a child whose mother took her north to Pennsylvania for a summer visit. She wrote about the sights and scenes of 1960s Harrisburg and then turned to one unforgettable experience:

> It had been four days since my mother left Harrisburg. . . . She left us in the warm and capable hands of my aunt. We'd been behaving as tourists. But now, my younger sister and I had to accompany my aunt to work. For years, she'd been employed by a well-to-do White family whom I'd never met. . . .
>
> At four o'clock, I was starving and my aunt informed me that it was "normal" for us to eat in the kitchen while [the family] dined elsewhere.
>
> Before dinner, the woman of the house entered the kitchen offering to set the tables — one in the kitchen and the other in the dining room. She grabbed two sets of dishes from the cupboard. She delivered a pretty set of yellow plastic plates to the kitchen dining area and a set of blue china to the dining room. After dinner she came back and thanked my aunt for the delicious meal, then prepared to feed the dog. She walked toward the cupboard and opened it. Her eyes and hands traveled past the pretty set of plastic dishes and landed on the blue china plates. After she pulled a blue china plate from the cupboard, she filled it with moist dog food and placed it on the floor. He ran for the plate. I shrieked! . . .

To this day, I'm not sure if I shrieked at the shock of [people] sharing dinnerware with a dog or because the dog got a piece of blue china while I ate from yellow plastic.

David Creighton, a student teacher, wrote about working in an Italian restaurant in South Philadelphia in the 1990s:

"Yo, Dave, what *are* you anyway?" said Tony Meoli, a waiter in LaTrattoria in South Philadelphia.
"Whaddaya mean?" I, the new busboy, said.
"Like, uh, what's your nationality? You know, where are you from? I mean, you're obviously not Italian."
"Oh. Well, I'm Russian with some German mixed in," I said.
"Well, just as long as you're not Jewish," said Tony. "We don't like Jews around here."
"Actually, I am Jewish," I said.
"Oh, sorry, I was just kiddin' you know."
"Don't worry about it," I said . . .

Creighton went on to describe the culture of South Philadelphia, pointing out the racial and ethnic insulation and the considerable hostility between and among various groups. Then he continued:

I had only worked there about four months when at the end of my Sunday night shift I was told with no warning, "We won't be needing you anymore."
"What?" I said. I felt I had done a good job. No one ever complained about my work. I was always on time, and I was developing a good rapport with the waiters who often commended me on my efforts. Also, I really needed the money. "Why?" I said.
"I don't know," said the bartender.
"You know, Dave, Hitler had the right idea for you people, with the gas chambers and all," said Joe Piselli only half jokingly. "One day I'm gonna gas you down there in the kitchen."
"You know, Joe, Hitler wasn't all that crazy about Catholics either. You woulda been next," I said.
"Yeah, well at least I ain't no Jew," he said.
"Thank God," I said.

Reading and writing first-person accounts like these as starting points for interrogating unexamined assumptions and practices can evoke a shared vulnerability that helps a group of loosely connected individuals gel into a community committed to dealing with issues of race more openly. Accounts like these can move a preservice curriculum beyond the level of celebrating diversity, enhancing human relations, or incorporating ethnic studies into the curriculum, positions that are rightly criticized for their focus on ethnicity as individual choice and their limited goal of attitudinal change (McCarthy, 1990, 1993; Nieto, 1999; Sleeter & Grant, 1987) rather than analysis of systemic and institutional structures and practices that perpetuate racism and oppression. As I pointed out above, narratives also have the capacity to contain many of the contradictions, nuances, and complexities that are necessary for understanding the roots and twists of racism and the many ways these interact with the social life of schools and classrooms. But the considerable power of accounts that "get personal" about race is also their pitfall. They can use some people's pain in the service of others' understanding, as I suggest below, and they can also imply that we all share similar experiences with racism, experiences that beneath the surface of their details and contexts are the same. Over the years, I have come to realize that this lesson in unlearning racism, which is an especially difficult one to hold onto, helps to explain some of the depth of anger expressed by the student teachers in the story with which this article began.

Stories about Whom? Stories for Whom?

Several of the students of color in the blind vision story related above claimed we had done nothing in the program to help students understand issues of race, that we did not talk about it in "real" ways. Factually, this was not the case. We had read a large number of articles by both White scholars and scholars of color, and we had shared some personal incidents in class and had intellectualized discussions. It is clear to me now, though, that these discussions were framed primarily for the benefit of White students who were invited to learn more about racism through stories of other people's oppression. The stories were not sufficiently linked to larger issues or framed in ways that pushed everybody to learn not *regardless of* but *with full regard for* differences in race, culture, and ethnicity.

I should have learned this lesson a long time ago. I had known it in certain ways even at the time of the incident described in my narrative — my detailed notes indicate that it was one of the points I tried to make to the students after the incident occurred. But for me, as a White teacher educator, it is a lesson that needs to be learned over and over again. Although I thought I had learned this lesson then, I learned it again several years later from Tuesday Vanstory, an African American woman who was a supervisor in the program that year but had been a student in the program years before. We had had a difficult discussion about race in our supervisors' inquiry group where we had considered ways to respond to a particularly troubling journal entry written by a White student teacher. In it she had complained about the students of color in the program sometimes separating themselves from the others, sitting together on the perimeter of the classroom and/or not participating in certain discussions. The journal writer used the phrase "reverse discrimination" and questioned how we could ever move forward if everybody would not even talk to each other. Several White members of the supervisors' group voiced somewhat similar concerns. They were genuinely distressed, wanting open conversations and resentful of the figurative as well as literal separation along racial lines of some members from the larger group when certain topics arose.

Vanstory had sat silent for a long time during this discussion, then finally burst out and demanded, "But *who* are those discussions *for? Who* do they really serve?" There was silence for a while and then confusion. She wrote to me that same day about the discussion:

> I must say that I was very upset after today's supervisors' meeting. There's nothing like a discussion on race, class, and culture to get my blood boiling, especially when I am one of a few who is in the "minority." Believe me, it is not at all comfortable. I really wanted to say nothing. I didn't want to blow my cool. I wanted to remain silent, tranquil. Instead I spouted off in what felt like a very emotional and, at times, a nonsensical response. . . .
>
> I ran across a sociological term a few years ago: "master status." It is the thing you can never get away from, the label that others give you that they won't ever release and they won't let you forget. Can you imagine the constant confrontation of the issue of race permeating every day of your life for one reason or another? (Over representation or under representation of people who look like you do in whatever arena, the blatant inequities in quality of life for the masses — educational opportunities, housing, ability to pass down wealth or privilege, the stinging humiliations that come from the mouths or pens of others who may or may not be well-intentioned, IQ scores being thrown in your face, etc.). It is reality for us. It is not a discussion, not a theory. It is flesh and blood. . . .
>
> And to come to school and have to play "educator" to the others who want to discuss race or understand, or release some guilt, or even in a very few cases, people who want to see a real change . . . It gets tired . . .
>
> Marilyn, I think that you are very brave and genuine to ask the tough questions that you ask yourself and your White students. But the truth is, your perspective, your reality does not necessarily reflect ours.

In *Teaching to Transgress* (1994), bell hooks makes a point remarkably similar to Vanstory's. Although hooks is discussing White feminist writers rather than teachers or teacher educators as Vanstory was, her comments contribute to a larger argument about the necessity of rethinking pedagogy in the current age of multiculturalism:

> Now Black women are placed in the position of serving White female desire to know more about race and racism, to "master" the subject. Drawing on the work of Black women, work that they once dismissed as irrelevant, they now reproduce the servant-served paradigms in their scholarship. Armed with new knowledge of race, their willingness to say that their work is coming from a White perspective (usually without explaining what that means), they forget that the very focus on racism emerged from the concrete political effort to forge meaningful ties between women of different race and class groups. This struggle is often completely ignored. (pp. 103–104)

I am convinced that reading and writing accounts about race and racism that get personal, as well as reading more intellectualized arguments about these issues, is vital to preservice teacher education. As I have tried to suggest, however, reading teacher education as racial text reveals that this is also a complex activity that is fraught with problems. Compelling personal stories often evoke a strong sense of empathy for others (Rosenberg, 1997), a false sense that all of us have experienced hurt and frustration varying in degree but not in kind, that all of us underneath have the same issues, that all of us can understand racism as personal struggle, as individual instance of cruelty, discrete moment of shame, outrage, or fear. In addition to using some people's experience in the service of others' education, then, personal narratives can also obscure more direct confrontation of the ways that individual instances of prejudice are *not* all the same — that some are deeply embedded in and entangled with institutional and historical systems of racism based on power and privilege, and some are not. Reading teacher education as racial text means trying to make issues of racism central, not marginal, and close and personal, not distant and academic. But it also means helping all of the readers and writers of such stories understand that schools and other organizational contexts are always sites for institutional and collective struggles of power and oppression (Villegas, 1991), not neutral backdrops for individual achievement and failure (McCarthy, 1993). And it means being very careful about what is said after stories are told and considering carefully whose stories are used in whose interest.

The foregoing discussion is not meant to suggest that racism was or should be the only topic in the teacher education curriculum or that everything else is secondary. I am not suggesting here that student teachers and their more experienced mentors should talk only about racism or that if we learn to talk about race and racism constructively, we do not need to learn anything else in the teacher education curriculum. It is a problem, for example, if there is no time in courses on language and literacy in the elementary school to explore and critique process writing, basal reading programs, whole language, phonics instruction, and standardized and nonstandardized means of assessing verbal aptitude and achievement. But issues of language, race, and cultural diversity are implicated in and by all of these topics, as I discuss in the next section of this article, and it is a fallacy to assume that there is a forced and mutually exclusive choice in preservice education — emphasizing *either* pedagogical and subject matter knowledge *or* knowledge about culture, racism, and schools as reflections of societal conflicts and sites for power struggle.

Reading Between the Lines: Perspectives, Identity, and Difference

Understanding curriculum as racial text requires thorough scrutiny of implicit perspectives about race and careful attention to issues of identity and difference (Castenell & Pinar, 1993). In teacher education this means not looking simply at a synopsis of the "plot" of a preservice program (to carry the text metaphor further). It also means examining the roles of starring and supporting characters and analyzing the plot line by line, as well as between the lines, for underlying themes and for the twists and turns of the stories told or implied about race, racism, and teaching.

Following the events recounted in the "blind vision" story, our teacher education community attempted not only to make issues of race up close and personal, but also to "read between the lines" of the curriculum. As director of the program and instructor of core courses on language, learning, and literacy, I had earlier examined class discussions that explicitly dealt with racism and teaching, as well as the essays and projects my students completed (see Cochran-Smith, 1995a, 1995b). In these analyses, I had tried to understand how student teachers constructed issues related to race and racism and how they linked these to their roles as prospective teachers. I had also looked at how I constructed the issues and how I linked them to my role as teacher educator and mentor. But at this point, as part of our group's larger, more intensive efforts, I wanted to look further — between and underneath the explicit lines that narrated my courses. I wanted to get at the implicit, more subtle perspectives by scrutinizing what was included and omitted from readings and discussions, how issues were sequenced and juxtaposed with one another, which messages were consistent and fundamental, and — inevitably — which were not. To do so, I used as data the evolution of course syllabi, assignments, and activities, as well as students' responses, class discussions, and my own detailed notes and reflections on three required courses I taught (a two-course sequence on reading and language arts in the elementary school and a course on children's literature). All three were designed to explore the relationships of literacy, learning, and culture and their implications for the teaching of reading, writing, literature, and oral language development.

What I found was in one sense exactly what I expected to find. Over the years we had increased the amount of time and attention we gave to questions of culture, race, and racism. In fact, these issues had become a central theme of my courses and of the program in general. But what I found when I read between and under the lines of the curriculum as racial text was a contradiction. On the one hand, the first part of the course presented heavy critique of the inequities embedded in the status quo and of the ways these were perpetuated by the current arrangements of schooling. On the other hand, the latter part of the course privileged pedagogical perspectives drawn from theories and practices developed primarily by White teachers and scholars of child development, language learning, and progressive education. There was as well an underlying White European American construction of self-identity and other, of "we" and "they."

White Theory, White Practice

My courses were intended to help students think through the relationships of theory and practice, learn how to learn from children, and construct principled perspectives about teaching and assessing language and literacy learning. Two themes ran throughout that were not about literacy and literature per se but were intended to be fundamental to these courses and to the entire program: 1) understanding teaching as an intellectual and political activity and the teacher as active constructor (not simply receiver) of meaning, knowledge, and curriculum; and 2) developing critical perspectives about the relationships of race, class, culture, and schooling.

A between-the-lines analysis revealed a sharp contrast in the subtle messages my courses projected about these two themes. The notion of teacher as a constructor of meaning and active decisionmaker was consistent. Readings and class discussions conceptualized the teacher as knowledge generator, as well as critical consumer of others' knowledge, as active constructor of interpretive frameworks as well as poser and ponderer of questions, and as agent for school and social change within local communities and larger social movements. Student teachers were required to construct (rather than simply implement) literature and literacy curriculum, critique teachers' manuals and reading textbooks according to their assumptions about teacher and student agency, and function as researchers by treating their ongoing work with children as sites for inquiry about language learning access and opportunity. Research and writing by experienced teachers from the local and larger inquiry communities were part of the required reading for every topic on the syllabi.

In addition, the knowledge and interpretive frameworks generated by teachers were regarded as part of the knowledge base for language and literacy teaching. They were *not* mentioned only when the topic was teacher research itself or when the point was to provide examples of classroom practice or of the application of others' ideas. Guest speakers included teachers as often as university-based experts. Teachers' ways of analyzing and interpreting data, creating theories, assessing children's progress, and constructing and critiquing practice (Lytle & Cochran-Smith, 1992) were foregrounded and valued as much as those generated by researchers based outside classrooms and schools. In addition, in multiple assignments in my courses, students were required to alter and analyze conventional curriculum and pedagogy based on systematic data collection about teaching and learning. They were prompted to challenge conventional labeling and grouping practices, and they were invited to be part of teacher-initiated alternative professional development groups struggling to "teach against the grain" (Cochran-Smith, 1991). Reading between and under the lines exposed little discrepancy, with regard to teachers' roles as knowledge generators and change agents, between the texts and subtexts of the curriculum.

By contrast, the same kind of close reading with regard to critical perspectives on race and racism led to different and more troubling insights. In my two-semester language and literacy course, a major segment early in the syllabus had to do with race, class, and culture. For this segment students read selections by the well-known scholars mentioned earlier, as well as personal narratives written by members of the local and larger teacher education communities. Spread over three to four weeks, this portion of the course emphasized the following: both schooling systems and individuals' school experiences are deeply embedded within social, cultural, and historical contexts, including institutional and historical racism; European perspectives are not universal standards of the evolution of higher order thought, but culturally and historically constructed habits of mind; and the standard "neutral" U.S. school and its curriculum have been generated out of, and help to sustain, unearned advantages and disadvantages for particular groups of students based on race, class, culture, gender, linguistic background, and ability/disability. Described in detail elsewhere (Cochran-Smith, 1995b), this part of the course gave students the opportunity to "rewrite their autobiographies" or reinterpret some of their own life stories and experiences based on new insights about power, privilege, and oppression. This part of the course also prompted students to "construct uncertainty" — that is, to pose and investigate questions of curriculum and instructional strategies informed by their experiences as raced, classed, and gendered beings and contingent upon the varying school contexts and student populations with whom they worked.

The remainder of the course was organized around major topics in elementary school language and literacy: controversies about learning to read and write (including child language acquisition, whole language as a theory of practice, basal reading approaches, reading groups, and phonics instruction); teaching reading and writing in elementary classrooms (including emergent literacy and extending literacy through reading aloud, language experience, literature study, process writing, journals, and other activities and strategies); and interpretation and use of assessments in language and literacy (including standardized tests and alternative assessments such as portfolios, informal reading inventories, and holistic assessments). For each topic, underlying assumptions about the nature of language, children as learners, teaching and learning as constructive processes, and classrooms/schools as social and cultural contexts were identified and critiqued.

The pedagogy that was advocated was more or less "progressive," "whole language," "developmental," and "meaning-centered," with emphasis on children as readers and writers of authentic texts and the classroom as a social context within which children and teachers together construct knowledge. There was a distinct bias against skills-centered approaches that taught reading and writing in isolated bits and pieces using texts and exercises constructed specifically for that purpose. Instead it was emphasized that language skills emerged from authentic language use and from instruction within the context of language use.

Reading between the lines forced other realizations. The pedagogy I advocated was drawn from theories and practices developed primarily by White teachers and scholars. The prominent names on this part of the syllabus were revealing — Dewey (1916), Britton (1987), Berthoff (1987), Graves (1983), Calkins (1991, 1994), Edelsky, Altwerger, and Flores (1991), Dyson (1987), Paley (1979), Rosenblatt (1976), and Goodman (1988), as well as teachers and teacher groups at the North Dakota Study Group (Strieb, 1985), the Prospect School (Carini, 1986), the National Writing Project (Pincus, 1993; Waff, 1994), the Breadloaf School of English (Goswami & Stillman, 1987), the Philadelphia Teachers Learning Cooperative (1984), and other local teacher and practitioner groups.[6] Absent from these segments of the syllabus and from our discussions were contrasting cultural perspectives on child language and learning and child socialization. Also absent were rich accounts of successful pedagogies, particularly with poor children and children of color, that were not necessarily "progressive" or "whole language" oriented.

Notwithstanding the fact that students read Lisa Delpit, Shirley Brice Heath, and others earlier in the course, it became clear to me by reading between the lines that there was a powerful contradictory subtext in the course about pedagogy for language and literacy. The subtle message was that pedagogy developed primarily from research and writing by and about White mainstream persons was the pedagogy that was best for everybody — Dewey's argument, more or less, that what the "wisest and best" parent wants for his or her child is what we should want for all children, or what we should want for "other people's children" (Delpit, 1988, 1995; Kozol, 1991). This subtle message implied that "progressive" language pedagogy was culture neutral, although just weeks earlier the course had emphasized that all aspects of schooling were socially and culturally constructed and needed to be understood within particular historical and cultural contexts. Because progressive language pedagogy was unmarked as cultural theory, culturally embedded practice, and/or cultural perspective, however, the subtle message was that it was an a-cultural position about how best to teach language and literacy that applied across contexts, historical moments, and school populations.

Part of what this meant was that my courses offered student teachers no theoretical framework for understanding the successful teachers they observed in their fieldwork schools who used traditional, skills-based reading and writing pedagogies with their students, particularly in urban schools where there were large numbers of poor children and children of color. Although my courses explicitly emphasized the importance of teachers' knowledge, there was a contradictory and perhaps more powerful implicit message: the knowledge of some teachers was more valuable than others, the knowledge of teachers who worked (successfully) from a more or less skills-based, direct-instruction perspective was perhaps not so important, and the pedagogy of these teachers was somewhat misguided and out of date. Reading between the lines of my students' discussions and writings revealed that they were confused about what to make of the successes they observed in urban classrooms when the pedagogy we read about and valued in class was not apparent. On the other hand, my student teachers knew precisely what to make of the unsuccessful teachers they observed in those same contexts. My students had a powerful framework for critique and could easily conclude that many urban teachers were unsuccessful because they were too traditional, too focused on skills, not progressive enough.

What was missing from the sections of my courses that dealt specifically with reading and language pedagogy were theories of practice developed by and about people of color, as well as rich and detailed analyses of successful teachers of urban children, particularly poor children of color, who used a variety of pedagogies including, but not necessarily limited to, those pedagogies that could be called "progressive." Gloria Ladson-Billings's work (1994, 1995) had just been published at the time I was struggling to read deeply between the lines of my courses and our larger curriculum. Hers and related analyses of culturally appropriate, culturally relevant, and/or culturally sensitive pedagogies (Au & Kawakami, 1994; Ballenger, 1992; Foster, 1993, 1994; Hollins, King, & Hayman, 1994; Irvine, 1990; Irvine & York, 1995; King, 1994) were extremely useful in my efforts to rethink the ways I taught my courses and structured the program. In fact, Ladson-Billings's book, *The Dreamkeepers: Successful Teachers of African American Children* (1994), speaks directly to the issue of skills- and whole language–based approaches to language instruction by contrasting two very different but highly successful teachers of reading to African American children. One of these taught from a (more or less) whole language perspective, focusing on student-teacher interactions, skills in the context of meaning, and use of literature and other authentic texts, while the other taught from a (more or less) traditional skills perspective, focusing on direct instruction, phonics and word identification skills, and basal texts written for the explicit purpose of instruction. Ladson-Billings points out what is wrong with framing the debate about how to teach African American children in terms of whole language versus a purely skill-based approach:

> In some ways their differences represent the larger debate about literacy teaching, that of whole-language versus basal-text techniques. However, beneath the surface, at the personal ideological level, the differences between these instructional strategies lose meaning. Both teachers want their students to become literate. Both believe that their students are capable of high levels of literacy. (p. 116)

Ladson-Billings's commentary lifts the debates about literacy instruction out of the realm of language theory and practice *only* and into the realm of ideology and politics as well — that is, into the realm of teachers' commitments to communities, to parents, and to activism.[7] Her analysis of successful and culturally relevant pedagogy for African American children repeatedly emphasizes teachers' ties to the school community, teachers' belief in the learning ability of all children (not just an exceptional few who, through education, can make their way "out" of the lives common to their parents and community members), and teachers' strategies for establishing personal connections with students and helping them connect new knowledge to previous experiences and ideas.

When I revised my language and reading courses, Ladson-Billings's *The Dreamkeepers* was one of the central texts, and I included in discussions about reading/writing pedagogy many other readings about culturally relevant language pedagogy (e.g., Au & Kawakami, 1994; Ballenger, 1992; Foster, 1993). In addition to readings about language and literacy theory, debates about pedagogy, and so on, new additions were intended in part to alter the curriculum as racial text. Particularly, they were intended to provide frameworks for understanding successful and unsuccessful teaching of poor and privileged White children and children of color — frameworks that were not dichotomous and that included but were more complex than whole language versus basals. These were also intended to prompt more attention to issues of community, as well as richer and more diverse perspectives on pedagogy, skills, and explicit versus implicit instruction (Delpit, 1988). I also wanted to diminish the implicit subtext of criticism of teachers who worked successfully, particularly with children of color, using methods other than those that might be termed "progressive" or "whole." Including these new readings also made the course more complicated and made its underlying conception of teaching as an uncertain activity (Dudley-Marling, 1997; McDonald, 1992) even more pronounced than it had been. Always eschewing the possibility of "best practices" that cut across the contexts and conditions of local settings, I had for years told students that the answer to most questions about "the best" ways to teach something was "it depends" (Cochran-Smith, 1995b). Having uncovered unintended contradictions in the lessons I taught my students made me realize that pedagogical decisions "depend" on an even wider, richer, and more nuanced array of variables and conditions than I had implied.[8]

Identity and Difference: We and They

Understanding the racial narrative that underlies a curriculum is a process that requires intense self-critical reflection and analysis, as Castenell and Pinar (1993) have made clear:

> Debates over what we teach the young are also — in addition to being debates over what knowledge is of most worth — debates over who we perceive ourselves to be, and how we will represent that identity, including what remains as "left over," as "difference." (p. 2)

Reading between the lines of my own courses and of the larger teacher education curriculum revealed a White European American construction of self-identity and "other." "We," I came to realize, often referred not to "we who are committed to teaching elementary school differently and improving the life chances of all children," but to "we White people (especially we White women) who are trying to learn how to teach people who are different from us." On the one hand, it could be argued that this perspective is exactly what is needed, given the demographic disparities, now well documented (National Education Goals Panel, 1997; Quality Education for Minorities Project, 1990), between the racial composition of the group entering the nation's teaching force (more than 90% White European American) and the nation's schoolchildren (increasingly a wide array of racial, cultural, and language groups). In elementary education, in addition to being White and European American, the group entering the teaching force is also overwhelmingly female. In a certain sense, then, one could make a persuasive case that a White European American and female construction of self and other is just what the preservice teacher education curriculum ought to have. On the other hand, the program I directed had 20–25 percent students of color and 15–20 percent male students. A curriculum for "White girls" was surely not the answer. Rather, we were committed to constructing a curriculum that helped all student teachers — with full acknowledgement of differences in race, culture, and gender — interrogate their experiences, understand schools and schooling as sites for struggles over power, and become prepared to teach in an increasingly multiracial and multicultural society. To do so, we had to revise the story the curriculum told about identity and rewrite the characters who were central in that story, particularly who "we and they," "self and other," "regular and left over" were.

One incident from my course on literature for children, which I have taught in various iterations for more than twenty years, provides an example of the ways I tried consciously to alter the assumed definition of self and other, we and they, in my courses. What I wanted to do was to construct discussions where "we and they" shifted *away from* "we White people who are trying to learn to teach those other people — those people of color" *and toward* "we educators who are trying to be sensitive to, and learn to teach, all students — both those who are different from us and those who are like us in race, class, and culture." I began to use Lynne Reid Banks's *The Indian in the Cupboard* (1981) as one of the six or eight novels my students read in common for the literature course.[9] My course had for years included many children's books that were highly regarded for their portrayals of the perspectives of African American, Asian, and Hispanic family and childhood experiences (Harris, 1993), and the course had for years focused on the politics of children's literature (Taxel, 1993). The point of adding *The Indian in the Cupboard* was *not* to add "the Native American experience" to the list of cultures represented in the course. Rather, the point was to create an opportunity to prompt an altered conception of self and other, an altered sense of who "we" were as teachers.

Published in 1981, when the *New York Times* called it "the best novel of the year," *The Indian in the Cupboard* continues to be highly acclaimed and widely used as a whole-class text in upper elementary and middle schools, and its popularity has increased since it was made into a Disney motion picture. A fantasy about Omri, a British boy who receives as a present a collector's cupboard, the book revolves around a plastic Indian figure who comes to life (but remains three inches high) when the boy casually places him inside the cupboard and closes the door. A toy cowboy and soldier eventually come to life too and interact with the Indian and the boy. The book is charming in many ways, well written and pivoting on premises that are extremely appealing to children — being bigger than adults, having toys come to life, and keeping a powerful secret. But in addition to positive reviews about the popularity of the book and the high quality of its writing, the book has also been criticized as racist, perpetuating stereotypes about Native Americans at the same time that it charms and appeals. The first year I used the book, all of my students were prospective teachers, many of whom were just completing a year of student teaching in urban schools where the population was primarily African American, Asian, and/or Puerto Rican. I asked the class to read the novel and jot down their responses and then read the critical commentary I had assigned.

In an excoriating critique of images of Native Americans in children's books, MacCann (1993) argues that the vast majority of children's books with Native American characters or themes are written from a non-Native perspective. With few exceptions, they portray Native American cultures as futile and obsolete and turn on the "persistent generalization" that American society has been "shaped by the pull of a vacant continent drawing population westward" and available to any enterprising European (p. 139). About *The Indian in the Cupboard* specifically, MacCann writes:

> Even in the fantasy genre the displacement of American Indian societies can be an underlying theme, as in *The Indian in the Cupboard* [Banks, 1981] and its sequel *The Return of the Indian* [Banks, 1986]. These narratives are set in modern times . . . but the cultural content is rooted in the image of the Indian as presented in Hollywood westerns and dime novels. Little Bear is a plastic toy Indian who comes to life in the boy's magical cupboard, but remains just three inches in height. He grunts and snarls his way through the story, attacking the child, Omri, with a hunting knife, and later attacking a traditional enemy, a three-inch cowboy. At every turn of plot, Little Bear is either violent or childishly petulant until he finally tramples upon his ceremonial headdress as a sign of remorse. The historical culpability of the cowboy and others who invaded [Native American] territory is ignored. Native Americans are seen as the primary perpetrators of havoc, even as they defend their own borders. (p. 145)

In *Through Indian Eyes* (Slapin & Seale, 1992), a collection of articles written primarily by Native Americans, the review of *The Indian in the Cupboard* and its sequel is also wholly negative. It concludes:

> My heart aches for the Native child unfortunate enough to stumble across, and read, these books. How could she, reading this, fail to be damaged? How could a White child fail to believe that he is far superior to the bloodthirsty, sub-human monsters portrayed here? (p. 122)

My students read these critiques after they had read and responded to the novel and came to class prepared to discuss both.

Most of my students reported that they were completely engrossed in the unfolding story, and some were shocked by the negative critiques and even embarrassed that they had not noticed the racist overtones (and undertones) until after they finished the book. Many were uncertain about what to think. The discussion was intense and animated:[10]

The book is full of stereotypes. If a book has stereotypes, does that mean you just shouldn't use it in your classroom?

There are lots of stereotypes about Indians, but there are also stereotypes about cowboys and soldiers — doesn't this make the book sort of balanced?

The very idea of an American Indian adult as the possession (and a miniature possession at that) of a White English child is totally offensive and off-putting — does it really matter what else the book does or doesn't do?

Since the boy's wrong assumptions about Indians are for the most part pointed out and corrected by the narrator as the story goes along, doesn't it actually sort of "teach" some correct facts?

In the final analysis, isn't what really matters how engaging the story is for kids and what the quality of the writing is?

How can we evaluate the realism of the characters in a story that is obviously fantasy rather than history or biography?

Since none of us had any Native American children in the classes we student taught this year, does that make the issue of potentially hurting a Native child reader irrelevant?

Students were divided about what they thought of the book. Many saw it as more or less harmless, assuming that those who considered the book racist were self-interested extremists, interested only in what was "politically correct," or manufacturing problems where there were none. Others strongly disagreed, assessing the book as promoting shallow stereotypes with little redeeming social value. At some point in this very intense discussion, I inserted, "What if it were *The* Jew *in the Cupboard* or *The* Black *in the Cupboard?* Would that be all right?" For a few minutes there was dead silence. The looks on the faces of my students, many of whom were Jewish, African American, or Hispanic, indicated that it would decidedly *not* be all right to have a children's book with those titles or those story lines. Why then, I asked, was it all right for elementary and middle school teachers each year to teach to the whole class a children's book that had an Indian in the cupboard?

This was a turning point in the course, one that prompted some of the best discussion of the semester. Several students, African American and Hispanic, talked about how this opened their eyes to racism in a different way. They admitted that they had never worried too much about "Redskins" and tomahawks as symbols for sports teams, or grotesque caricatures and cigar-store Indians as icons for margarine, sports utility vehicles, and blue jeans. The discussion about race and racism changed that day. For a while everybody seemed to have new questions, and nobody seemed as sure as they had been about the answers. I believe this was because in this discussion there was a different underlying construction of identity and difference, an altered perspective on what was assumed to be the standard from which we defined "regular and different," "self and other." When "other" was Native American and "self" everyone else in the room, there were new opportunities for students to interrogate their assumptions, new opportunities to struggle with the issue of what it means to teach those who are different from and the same as our multiple selves.

Telling the story of what happened when I added *The Indian in the Cupboard* to my course is in no way intended to suggest that all we have to do in teacher education is figure out who is "not in the room" and then construct that person as the "other," that all we have to do is be certain to include in the curriculum fictional or research literature about racial or cultural groups that are not actually represented in a given teacher education program. That is not at all the point here. Nor is the point to claim that this kind of "inclusion" would be desirable or even possible. The point I do wish to make is that it is critically important to scrutinize the often very subtle messages about identity and difference that float between the lines of the curriculum and consciously work to construct opportunities in which all the members of the community are able to interrogate their constructions of self and other. As I have argued already, however, these opportunities must always be connected to larger understandings of the histories of oppression and privilege and must always be couched in understandings of institutional and organizational racism.

Conclusion: Lessons Learned and Unlearned

What are the lessons learned here about unlearning racism? One has to do with the power of narrative *in* teacher education and, as importantly, the power of teacher education *as* narrative. As I have tried to show throughout this article, both the personal and the fictional stories about race and racism that we invite participants to read and write can break down the barriers of distanced, academic discourse and make possible revelations about participants' positions, identity, and standpoint. Stories can serve as touchstones for shared experience and commitment. As one primary way we understand and construct our professional lives and our multiple identities, stories can help us scrutinize our own work and theorize our own experience. But stories can also be extremely negative, particularly when the stories of some groups are used — unintentionally or not — in the service of others' desire to learn and/or when powerful emotions are unleashed and participants are then left to fend for themselves in the aftermath. Stories can be negative if they prompt a false sense of sameness and personal empathy that is unconnected to historical and institutional racism, to schools as sites for power struggles, or to ownership of the roles privilege and oppression play in everyday life. It may also be the case that there are some stories that individuals should not be coaxed to share in mixed racial groups and some that group leaders should not attempt to solicit. Finally, it must be understood that the narratives we use as tools and texts in the teacher education curriculum confound and are confounded by larger and more deeply embedded messages, messages that are revealed only when the curriculum is interrogated, or consciously read as racial text.

The second lesson is connected to the title of this article, which implies two contradictions: blind vision, a phrase that suggests simultaneous seeing and not seeing; and "*un*learning," a word that signifies both growth and the undoing or reversing of that growth. These contradictions are intentional, chosen not only to signal the enormous complexities inherent in the ways race and culture are implicated in teaching and teacher education, but also to caution that blindness is an inevitable aspect of trying to act on a vision about including racism in the teacher education curriculum, that failing is an inherent aspect of unlearning racism. I am completely convinced that "reading the curriculum as racial text," in the sense that I have described it in this article, is critical to a vision for preservice education. But I am also convinced that this is a slow and stumbling journey and that along the way difficulty, pain, self-exposure, and disappointment are inevitable. To teach lessons about race and racism in teacher education is to struggle to unlearn racism itself — to interrogate the assumptions that are deeply embedded in the curriculum, to own our own complicity in maintaining existing systems of privilege and oppression, and to grapple with our own failure.

Nikki Giovanni's "A Journey" (1983, p. 47) eloquently conjures up the image of blind vision that I wish to connect to the idea of unlearning racism. I conclude this article with her poem:

A JOURNEY*

It's a journey . . . that I propose . . . I am not the guide . . . nor technical assistant . . . I will be your fellow passenger . . .

Though the rail has been ridden . . . winter clouds cover . . . autumn's exuberant guilt . . . we must provide our own guideposts . . . I have heard . . . from previous visitors . . . the road washes out sometimes . . . and passengers are compelled . . . to continue groping . . . or turn back . . . I am not afraid . . .

I am not afraid of rough spots . . . or lonely times . . . I don't fear . . . the success of this endeavor . . . I promise you nothing . . . I accept your promise . . . of the same we are simply riding . . . a wave . . . that may carry or crash . . . It's a journey . . . and I want . . . to go . . .

---

* "A Journey" from *Those Who Ride the Night Winds* by Nikki Giovanni. Copyright © 1983 by Nikki Giovanni. Reprinted by permission of HarperCollins Publishers, Inc.

Notes

1. I have outlined the ways this program addressed issues of race, class, and culture in a number of articles, particularly an earlier *Harvard Educational Review* piece (Cochran-Smith, 1995b).
2. This narrative was constructed based on my own and a colleague's notes about the seminar sessions, my own written reflections shortly following the event, notes on conversations with students and with other teacher educators prior to and following the sessions, written communications from students, and other program documents that described the structure and context of the program. Excerpts from written communications and students' comments and papers are used with permission of the authors.
3. The idea of "reading teacher education as racial text" emerges from a number of sources, as described in the following section. The term itself draws from Castenell and Pinar's (1993) concept of "understanding curriculum as racial text," which is also the title of their edited collection of articles about identity and difference in education, particularly how these are represented in curriculum.
4. The analysis I offer here is based on multiple curriculum and teaching documents, as well as experiences captured in my own reflections over a six-year period at the University of Pennsylvania. These include syllabi and assignments for courses that I taught each year during that time period; program handbooks and advertising literature; my own and others' writing about the program (both formal papers and more personal reflections), detailed notes from meetings of student teachers, university-based supervisors, and whole-community meetings that included school-based cooperating teachers; letters and personal notes sent to me by program participants; two student group papers about racism and teaching that were written and presented in public forums during this time; and analytic descriptions of several key events and critical incidents that occurred.
5. These members of the teacher education community shared their personal accounts with the larger group by presenting orally, including their pieces in the course reading packet and in-house booklets, and facilitating small-group discussions.
6. These were some of the readings regularly used.
7. This is in no way intended to suggest that whole language proponents are unaware of the political and ideological aspects of language instruction, nor is it intended to suggest that they do not address issues of culture. Many whole language theorists locate their work and the debates about whole language perspectives squarely within a cultural and political context (Dudley-Marling, 1997; Edelsky, 1986, 1990; Edelsky, Altwerger, & Flores, 1991; Goodman, 1988; Shannon, 1988). Indeed, Carol Edelsky, arguably one of the best known and most articulate spokespersons and theorists for the whole language movement, gives explicit attention to the politics of pedagogy and to whole language as a theory of practice aimed at social justice and democracy (Edelsky, 1990; Edelsky et al., 1991). Edelsky's work on bilingual education is also explicitly connected to cultural contexts. The popular media debates about whole language and phonics, however, rarely frame these issues as cultural and political questions, and some of those who advocate whole language ignore cultural and political issues altogether and speak as if teaching from a whole language perspective were merely a matter of using certain materials and approaches to teaching.
8. The questions my students posed, the interpretations they constructed, and the pedagogies they developed when their readings and discussions included these new additions are part of a larger analysis I am currently completing.
9. I have used this example in a different way in a discussion about the politics of children's literature and the responsibility of teachers as agents for social change (see Cochran-Smith, 1999).

10. These excerpts represent a range of comments made by students in class discussions and/or in brief written responses to the book. This is not a direct transcription of the actual discussion that unfolded, but is rather a set of excerpts from written and oral comments.

References

Apple, M. (1996). *Cultural politics in education.* New York: Teachers College Press.

Asante, M. (1991). The Afro-centric idea in education. *Journal of Negro Education, 62,* 170–180.

Au, K., & Kawakami, A. (1994). Cultural congruence in instruction. In E. Hollins, J. King, & W. Hayman (Eds.), *Teaching diverse population: Formulating a knowledge base* (pp. 5–23). Albany: State University of New York Press.

Ballenger, C. (1992). Because you like us: The language of control. *Harvard Educational Review, 62,* 199–208.

Banks, L. (1981). *The Indian in the cupboard.* Garden City, NY: Doubleday.

Banks, L. (1986). *The return of the Indian.* Garden City, NY: Doubleday.

Berthoff, A. (1987). The teacher as researcher. In D. Goswami & P. R. Stillman (Eds.), *Reclaiming the classroom: Teacher research as an agency for change* (pp. 28–48). Upper Montclair, NJ: Boynton/Cook.

Britton, J. (1987). A quiet form of research. In D. Goswami & P. Stillman (Eds.), *Reclaiming the classroom: Teacher research as an agency for change* (pp. 13–19). Upper Montclair, NJ: Boynton/Cook.

Britzman, D. (1991). *Practice makes practice: A critical study of learning to teach.* Albany: State University of New York Press.

Calkins, L. (1991). *Living between the lines.* Portsmouth, NH: Heinemann.

Calkins, L. (1994). *The art of teaching writing.* Portsmouth, NH: Heinemann.

Carini, P. (1986). *Prospect's documentary process.* Bennington, VT: Prospect School Center.

Castenell, L., & Pinar, W. (Eds.). (1993). *Understanding curriculum as racial text: Representations of identity and difference in education.* Albany: State University of New York Press.

Cochran-Smith, M. (1991). Learning to teach against the grain. *Harvard Educational Review, 51,* 279–310.

Cochran-Smith, M. (1995a). Color blindness and basket making are not the answers: Confronting the dilemmas of race, culture, and language diversity in teacher education. *American Educational Research Journal, 32,* 493–522.

Cochran-Smith, M. (1995b). Uncertain allies: Understanding the boundaries of race and teaching. *Harvard Educational Review, 65,* 541–570.

Cochran-Smith, M. (1999). Learning to teach for social justice. In G. Griffin (Ed.), *98th yearbook of NSSE: Teacher education for a new century: Emerging perspectives, promising practices, and future possibilities.* Chicago: University of Chicago Press.

Cochran-Smith, M., Dimattia, P., Dudley-Marling, C., Freedman, S., Friedman, A., Jackson, J., Jackson, R., Loftus, F., Mooney, J., Neisler, O., Peck, A., Pelletier, C., Pine, G., Scanlon, D., & Zollers, N. (1999, April). *Seeking social justice: A teacher education faculty's self study, year III.* Paper presented at the Annual Meeting of the American Educational Research Association, Montreal.

Cochran-Smith, M., & Lytle, S. (1992). Communities for teacher research: Fringe or forefront. *American Journal of Education, 100,* 298–323.

Cochran-Smith, M., & Lytle, S. (1993). *Inside/outside: Teacher research and knowledge.* New York: Teachers College Press.

Cochran-Smith, M., & Lytle, S. (1998). Teacher research: The question that persists. *International Journal of Leadership in Education, 1*(1), 19–36.

Cochran-Smith, M., & Lytle, S. (1999). Relationships of knowledge and practice: Teacher learning in communities. In A. Iran-Nejad & C. D. Pearson (Eds.), *Review of research in education* (vol. 24, pp. 251–307). Washington, DC: American Educational Research Association.

Cole, A., & Knowles, J. (1998). The self-study of teacher education practices and the reform of teacher education. In M. L. Hamilton (Ed.), *Reconceptualizing teaching practice: Self-study in teacher education* (pp. 224–234). London: Falmer Press.

Comer, J. (1989). Racism and the education of young children. *Teachers College Record, 90*, 352–361.

Delpit, L. (1986). Skills and other dilemmas of a progressive Black educator. *Harvard Educational Review, 56*, 379–385.

Delpit, L. (1988). The silenced dialogue: Power and pedagogy in educating other people's children. *Harvard Educational Review, 58*, 280–298.

Delpit, L. (1995). *Other people's children: Cultural conflict in the classroom.* New York: New Press.

Dewey, J. (1916). *Democracy and education: An introduction to the philosophy of education.* New York: Free Press.

Dudley-Marling, C. (1997). *Living with uncertainty: The messy reality of classroom practice.* Portsmouth, NH: Heinemann.

Dyson, A. (1987). The value of "time off-task": Young children's spontaneous talk and deliberate text. *Harvard Educational Review, 57*, 396–420.

Edelsky, C. (1986). *Writing in a bilingual program.* Norwood, NJ: Ablex.

Edelsky, C. (1990). Whose agenda is this anyway? A response to McKenna, Robinson, and Miller. *Educational Researcher, 19* (8), 3–6.

Edelsky, C., Altwerger, B., & Flores, B. (1991). *Whole language: What's the difference?* Portsmouth, NH: Heinemann.

Fine, M. (Ed.). (1994). *Chartering urban school reform: Reflections on public high schools in the midst of change.* New York: Teachers College Press.

Foster, M. (1993). Educating for competence in community and culture: Exploring views of exemplary African-American teachers. *Urban Education, 27*, 370–394.

Foster, M. (1994). Effective Black teachers: A literature review. In E. Hollins, J. King, & W. Hayman (Eds.), *Teaching diverse populations: Formulating a knowledge base* (pp. 225–241). Albany: State University of New York Press.

Ginsberg, M., & Clift, R. (1990). The hidden curriculum of preservice teacher education. In R. W. Houston (Ed.), *Handbook of research on teacher education* (pp. 450–468). New York: MacWilliams.

Giovanni, N. (1983). A journey. In *Those who ride the night winds* (p. 47) New York: William Morrow.

Giroux, H. (1984). Rethinking the language of schooling. *Language Arts, 61*, 33–40.

Giroux, H. (1988). *Teachers as intellectuals: Toward a pedagogy of learning.* Westport, CT: Bergin & Garvey.

Gitlin, A. (Ed.). (1994). *Power and method: Political activism and educational research.* New York: Routledge.

Goodman, K. (1988). *Report card on basal readers.* New York: Richard C. Owen.

Goswami, P., & Stillman, P. (1987). *Reclaiming the classroom: Teacher research as an agency for change.* Upper Montclair, NJ: Boynton/Cook.

Graves, D. (1983). *Writing: Teachers and children at work.* Portsmouth, NH: Heinemann.

Hardy, B. (1978). Towards a poetics of fiction: An approach through narrative. In M. Meek & G. Barton (Eds.), *The cool web* (pp. 12–23). New York: Antheneum.

Harris, V. (Ed.). (1993). *Teaching multicultural literature in grades K-8.* Norwood, MA: Christopher-Gordon.

Heath, S. (1982a). Questioning at home and at school: A comparative study. In G. Spindler (Ed.), *Doing an ethnography of schooling* (pp. 103–131). New York: Holt, Rinehart & Winston.

Heath, S. (1982b). What no bedtime story means: Narrative skills at home and school. *Language in Society, 11*, 49–76.

Hollins, E., King, J., & Hayman, W. (Eds.). (1994). *Teaching diverse populations: Formulating a knowledge base*. Albany: State University of New York Press.

hooks, b. (1994). *Teaching to transgress: Education as the practice of freedom*. New York: Routledge.

Irvine, J. (1990). *Black students and school failure: Policies, practice and prescriptions*. New York: Greenwood Press.

Irvine, J., & York, D. (1995). Learning styles and culturally diverse students: A literature review. In J. A. Banks & C. A. M. Banks (Eds.), *Handbook of research on multicultural education*. (pp. 494–497). New York: Macmillan.

King, J. (1994). The purpose of schooling for African American children: Including cultural knowledge. In E. R. Hollins, J. E. King, & W. C. Hayman (Eds.), *Teaching diverse populations: Formulating a knowledge base* (pp. 25–56). Albany: State University of New York Press.

King, J., Hollins, E., & Hayman, W. (Eds.). (1997). *Preparing teachers for cultural diversity*. New York: Teachers College Press.

Kozol, J. (1991). *Savage inequalities: Children in America's schools*. New York: Crown.

Ladson-Billings, G. (1994). *The dreamkeepers: Successful teachers of African-American children*. San Francisco: Jossey Bass.

Ladson-Billings, G. (1995). Toward a theory of culturally relevant pedagogy. *American Educational Research Journal, 32*, 465–491.

Lawrence, S., & Tatum, B. (1997). Teachers in transition: The impact of antiracist professional development on classroom practice. *Teachers College Record, 99*, 162–178.

Leistyna, P., Woodrum, A., & Sherblom, S. A. (Eds.). (1996). *Breaking free: The transformative power of critical pedagogy*. Cambridge, MA: Harvard Educational Review.

Lytle, S., & Cochran-Smith, M. (1992). Teacher research as a way of knowing. *Harvard Educational Review, 62*, 447–474.

MacCann, D. (1993). Native Americans in books for the young. In V. Harris (Ed.), *Teaching multicultural literature in grades K-8* (pp. 137–170). Norwood, MA: Christopher-Gordon.

McCarthy, C. (1990). Multicultural education, minorities, identities, textbooks, and the challenge of curriculum reform. *Journal of Education, 172*, 118–129.

McCarthy, C. (1993). Multicultural approaches to racial inequality in the United States. In L. A. Castenell & W. F. Pinar (Eds.), *Understanding curriculum as racial text*, (pp. 245–246). Albany: State University of New York Press.

McDonald, J. (1992). *Teaching: Making sense of an uncertain craft*. New York: Teachers College Press.

McIntosh, P. (1989). White privilege: Unpacking the invisible knapsack. *Peace and Freedom, 49*(4), 10–12.

Metzger, D. (1986). Circles of stories. *Parabola, 4*(4), 1–4.

Mishler, E. (1986). *Research interviewing: Context and marriage*. Cambridge, MA: Harvard University Press.

Moll, L., Amanti, C., Neff, D., Gonzalez, N. (1992). Funds of knowledge for teaching: Using a qualitative approach to connect homes and classrooms. *Theory Into Practice, 31*, 32–41.

National Education Goals Panel. (1997). *National education goals report*. Washington, DC: Author.

Nieto, S. (1999). *The light in their eyes: Creating multicultural learning communities*. New York: Teachers College Press.

Noffke, S. (1997). Professional, personal, and political dimensions of action research. In M. Apple (Ed.), *Review of research in education* (pp. 305–343). Washington, DC: American Educational Research Association.

Ogbu, J. (1978). *Minority education and caste.* New York: Academic Press.

Paley, V. (1979). *White teacher.* Cambridge, MA: Harvard University Press.

Philadelphia Teachers Learning Cooperative. (1984). On becoming teacher experts: Buying time. *Language Arts, 6,* 731–735.

Pincus, M. (1993). Following the paper trail. In M. Cochran-Smith & S. Lytle, *Inside/outside: Teacher research and knowledge* (pp. 249–255). New York: Teachers College Press.

Quality Education for Minorities Project. (1990). *Education that works: An action plan for the education of minorities.* Cambridge, MA: Author.

Rodriguez, A. (1998). What is (should be) the researcher's role in terms of agency? A question for the 21st century. *Journal of Research in Science Teaching, 35,* 963–965.

Rose, M. (1989). *Lives on the boundary.* New York: Penguin.

Rosenberg, P. (1997). Underground discourses: Exploring Whiteness in teacher education. In M. Fine, L. Weis, L. Powell, & L. Wong (Eds.), *Off-white: readings on race and power in society* (pp. 79–86). New York: Routledge.

Rosenblatt, L. (1976). *Literature as exploration.* New York: Noble & Noble.

Shannon, P. (1988). *Merging literacy: Reading instruction in 20th century America.* South Hadley, MA: Bergin & Garvey.

Sleeter, C. (1992). Restructuring schools for multicultural education. *Journal of Teacher Education, 43,* 141–148.

Sleeter, C., & Grant, C. (1987). An analysis of multicultural education in the United States. *Harvard Educational Review, 57,* 421–444.

Slapin, B., & Seale, B. (1992). *Through Indian eyes: The native experience in books for children.* Philadelphia: New Society.

Strieb, L. (1985). *A (Philadelphia) teacher's journal.* Grand Forks: North Dakota Study Group Center for Teaching and Learning.

Tatum, B. (1992). Talking about race, learning about racism: The applications of racial identity development theory. *Harvard Educational Review, 62,* 1–24.

Tatum, B. (1994). Teaching White students about racism: The search for White allies and the restoration of hope. *Teachers College Record, 95,* 462–476.

Tatum, B. (1997). *"Why are all the Black kids sitting together in the cafeteria?" and other conversations about the development of racial identity.* New York: Basic Books.

Taxel, J. (1993) The politics of children's literature: Reflections on multiculturalism and Christopher Columbus. In V. Harris (Ed.), *Teaching multicultural literature in grades K-8* (pp. 1–36). Norwood, MA: Christopher-Gordon.

Thompson, B., & Tyagi, S. (Eds.). (1996). *Names we call home: Autobiography on racial identity.* New York: Routledge.

Van Manen, M. (1990). *Researching lived experience: Human science for an action sensitive pedagogy.* Albany: State University of New York Press.

Villegas, A. (1991). *Culturally responsive pedagogy for the 1990s and beyond.* Princeton, NJ: Educational Testing Service.

Waff, D. (1994). Romance in the classroom: Inviting discourse on gender and power. *The Voice, 3*(1), 7–14.

About the Contributors

—■—■—■—

Lilia I. Bartolomé is associate professor in the Applied Linguistics Graduate Program at the University of Massachusetts Boston. As a teacher educator, her research interests include the preparation of effective teachers of second-language learners. In particular, Bartolomé examines teachers' ideological orientations around their work with language-minority students, as well as classroom practices with this population. Her publications include "Critical Pedagogy and Teacher Education: Radicalizing Prospective Teachers" in *Teacher Education Quarterly* (2004), and *Dancing with Bigotry: The Poisoning of Culture* (with D. Macedo, 2000).

Marilyn Cochran-Smith is a professor of education and director of the Doctoral Program in Curriculum and Instruction at Boston College. She is also the current president of the American Educational Research Association. Her research and writing center around teacher education and teacher research, as well as issues of diversity in schools and universities. She is the author of *Walking the Road: Race, Diversity, and Social Justice in Teacher Education* (2004), and coauthor of "Sticks, Stones, and Ideology: The Discourse of Reform in Teacher Education" in *Educational Researcher* (with K. Fries, 2001).

Lisa D. Delpit is executive director of the Center for Urban Education and Innovation at Florida International University in Miami, where she is also an Eminent Scholar. She is interested in improving urban education, particularly for children of color, and in the perspectives and aspirations of teachers of color. Her publications include *The Skin That We Speak: Thoughts on Language and Culture in the Classroom* (coedited with J. Kilgour Dowdy, 2003) and *The Real Ebonics Debate* (coedited with T. Perry, 1998). She received a MacArthur Fellowship in 1990 and the Horace Mann Humanity Award in 2003.

Donna Deyhle is a professor in the Department of Education, Culture, and Society and the Ethnic Studies program at the University of Utah. She is interested in anthropology and education, American Indian education, and cultural and racial conflict and change. Her numerous articles have appeared in *Curriculum Inquiry, Theory Into Practice,* the *Journal of Educational Equity and Leadership,* and the *Journal of American Indian Education.* She received the 2002 George and Louise Spindler Award for Distinguished Career in Educational Anthropology from the American Anthropological Association.

Sandra Del Valle is associate counsel of the Puerto Rican Legal Defense and Education Fund, which is located in New York City. Her area of interest is language rights. Her publications include *Language Rights and the Law: Finding Our Voices* (2003) and "La Politica del Idioma en los Estados Unidos: Una Visión Histórica y la Necesidad de un Nuevo Paradigma" ("Language Policy in the United States: A Historical Vision and the Need for a New Paradigm") in *Revista de Ciencias Sociales* (1998).

Marco Garrido was a senior at Boston College High School in Dorchester, Massachusetts, when he wrote his piece. He has since received a B.A. in English Literature from Harvard University and an M.A. in International Peace Studies from the University of Notre Dame. He is currently the Philippines correspondent for *Asia Times* and will begin his doctoral studies in sociology at the University of Michigan in the fall of 2004.

Stacey J. Lee, a professor at the University of Wisconsin–Madison, is interested in ethnic identity and school achievement among Asian American students. Her published works include *Unraveling the Model Minority Stereotype: Listening to Asian American Youth* (1996).

Nancy Uhlar Murray has been the director of the ACLU of Massachusetts' Bill of Rights Education Project since its founding in 1987. In this role, she has encouraged teachers, students, and the general public to think critically about the difficult issues being debated in society and the courts, and to work for a future in which civil liberties and civil rights are safeguarded and enlarged. Her recent writing includes several articles about the post–9/11 crisis in civil liberties and civil rights, and a contribution to *Putting the Movement Back into Civil Rights Teaching* (2004). She is a member of the editorial committee of the periodical *Race and Class*.

Christian Neira is a corporate attorney at the law firm of Paul, Weiss, Rifkind, Wharton, and Garrison LLP in New York City, where he is a member of the Latin American practice group.

Bonny Norton is associate professor in the Department of Language and Literacy Education at the University of British Columbia. Her professional interests center on the social and political contexts of language learning, teaching, and assessment. She is the coeditor of *Critical Pedagogies and Language Learning* (with K. Toohey, 2004) and author of *Identity and Language Learning: Gender, Ethnicity, and Educational Change* (2000).

Irene Serna is currently a professor of education in the Department of Education and Child Development at Whittier College in Whittier, California. Her major research interests include college access, teacher preparation, and minority students.

Pippa Stein is an associate professor in the School of Literature and Language Studies at the University of Witwatersrand in Johannesburg, South Africa. Her primary research interests are multimodal communication, literacies, and social

ABOUT THE CONTRIBUTORS

semiotics. Her recent publications include chapters in *Critical Pedagogies and Language Learning* (edited by B. Norton and K. Tooney, 2004) and *Mutimodal Literacy* (edited by C. Jewitt and G. Kress, 2003).

Beverly Daniel Tatum is president of Spelman College in Atlanta. She is also a clinical psychologist and a former dean and acting president of Mount Holyoke College. Her areas of professional expertise include Black families in White America, racial identity in teens, and race in the classroom. A fifth anniversary edition of her book, *Why Are All the Black Kids Sitting Together in the Cafeteria? And Other Conversations about Race* was released in 2003. She is also the author of *Assimilation Blues: Black Families in a White Community* (1987).

Amy Stuart Wells is a professor of sociology and education at Teachers College, Columbia University. Her work focuses on issues of race and education, specifically educational policies such as school desegregation, school choice, charter schools, and tracking, and how they shape and constrain opportunities for students of color. She is the principal investigator of a study of adults who attended racially mixed high schools and the coauthor of a report from that study, "How Desegregation Changes Us: The Effects of Racially Mixed Schools on Students and Society" (with J. J. Holme, A. T. Revilla, and A. K. Atanda, 2004). They will be publishing a book from this study, *In Search of* Brown, in 2005.

Arlette Ingram Willis is a professor at the University of Illinois at Urbana Champaign. Her research and teaching interests include the examination of the sociohistorical foundations of literacy, teaching and learning in a multicultural/multiethnic society, and multicultural/multiethnic literature for grades 6–12. Her publications include *Multicultural Issues in Literacy Research and Practice* (coedited with G. E. Garcia, R. Barrera, V. J. Harris, and G. E. Garcia, 2002) and *Multiple and Intersecting Identities in Qualitative Research* (coedited with B. M. Merchant, 2000). She has also published articles in *Language Arts* and *Reading Research Quarterly*, among other journals.

About the Editors

Sonya L. Anderson has worked in the field of education since 1992, as a high school teacher and with the Ford Foundation, where she supported funding activities in a number of areas, including African Studies, girls' education in Africa, campus diversity, and service learning. Anderson is currently a doctoral candidate in Administration, Planning, and Social Policy at the Harvard Graduate School of Education. Her research examines the ways West African teachers incorporate their beliefs about gender equity into their teaching, and how such beliefs affect the way they interpret and respond to gender-equity policies in the course of their daily practice.

Polly F. Attwood taught high school social studies for twelve years before entering the doctoral program at the Harvard Graduate School of Education. Her work focuses on anti-racist multicultural education, multicultural curriculum, and multicultural teacher education. In her research, she examines the different ways teacher educators support and challenge beginning teachers to examine their multiple social locations as an integral part of the process of becoming multicultural/anti-oppressive classroom teachers.

Lionel C. Howard is a doctoral candidate in Human Development and Psychology at the Harvard Graduate School of Education. His research interests include gender identity development, academic achievement and motivation, and quantitative research methods. His research focuses in particular on the process through which African American boys construct a masculine identity, and the impact of this process on academic achievement.